Regulating Our Constitutional Rights

Regulating Our Constitutional Rights

Democratic Rule or Judicial Fiat?

William B. Glidden

LEXINGTON BOOKS
Lanham • Boulder • New York • London

Published by Lexington Books
An imprint of The Rowman & Littlefield Publishing Group, Inc.
4501 Forbes Boulevard, Suite 200, Lanham, Maryland 20706
www.rowman.com

86-90 Paul Street, London EC2A 4NE

British Library Cataloguing in Publication Information Available

Library of Congress Cataloging-in-Publication Data

Names: Glidden, William B., author. Title: Regulating our constitutional rights: democratic rule or judicial fiat? / William B. Glidden. Description: Lanham, Maryland : Lexington Books, [2023] | Includes bibliographical references and index. | Summary: "The author proposes and defends a constitutional amendment to require that laws of Congress be upheld unless the Supreme Court by unanimous vote decides that a particular law is unconstitutional. This will strengthen the people's right to be governed by majority rule, including in cases where rights are concerned" —Provided by publisher. Identifiers: LCCN 2023014449 (print) | LCCN 2023014450 (ebook) | ISBN 9781666936117 (cloth) | ISBN 9781666936124 (epub) Subjects: LCSH: Civil rights—United States. | United States. Constitution. 14th Amendment. | United States. Supreme Court. Classification: LCC JC599.U5 G533 2023 (print) | LCC JC599.U5 (ebook) | DDC 342.7302—dc23/eng/20230417 LC record available at https://lccn.loc.gov/2023014449LC ebook record available at https://lccn.loc.gov/2023014450

I dedicate this book with love and appreciation to my family, Laraine, Dan, Trina, and Maria

Contents

Introduction

Fulfilling a campaign promise, President Biden appointed a commission to consider the role and operation of the Supreme Court of the United States and to provide an analysis of the current arguments for and against reform of the Court. In its December 2021 report, the commission began its chapter on the role of the Court in our constitutional system with this summary, based on written statements it had received from dozens of experts in the legal academy and elsewhere:

> Many observers view the judiciary and especially the Supreme Court as vital to the preservation of individual rights, democracy, federalism, and other constitutional values. On this account, the Court serves as an important counterweight to majoritarian impulses, safeguards the Constitution, and helps ensure the rule of law. But others argue that the Supreme Court has exerted too much power in our system of constitutional governance by interfering with or taking control of matters that should be resolved by the elected branches and the political process. Under this view the Court has emerged as an obstacle to the realization of important social goals and undermined the ability of Congress and other political actors to protect rights.[1]

I join the ranks of the critics by favoring a constitutional amendment to recover the core original meaning of the Fourteenth Amendment and to require a unanimous vote of the Supreme Court before a federal law can be overturned as a constitutional violation. This book explains why such an amendment, designed to preserve the right of the American people to govern themselves through their elected representatives in Congress, would be a good idea.

Supporters of the status quo claimed to the Presidential Commission that the Court has been vital to the preservation of the constitutional values of democracy, federalism, and individual rights. Yet the historical record shows Congress, not the Court, has been the primary force to protect and nurture democracy. The Court's federalism decisions in two periods, 1870–1937 and since 1992, have promoted states' rights without any real support in the Constitution and have come at the expense of sound public policies. The

Court certainly has protected individual rights, overturning state laws which in its view infringed the freedoms of speech and religion, for example, and opposing discrimination against Black people, women, aliens, and gay men and lesbians. These cases are the basis for its reputation as a protector of individual rights against majoritarian oppression. However, it is also true that these praiseworthy cases reversed earlier holdings of the Court denying such protections, said nothing about the laws of Congress, and had reasonable public support when they were issued. Importantly, the Court has limited the ability of Congress to protect individual and minority rights. This overview sets the stage for many details to follow in the book, supporting the desirability of Court reform.

The Articles of Confederation failed as a form of government because the central government was too weak to develop and enforce policies for the nation. In drafting the Constitution to replace it, the framers fashioned compromises to strengthen the federal government while preserving the legitimate governance authorities of the states and being careful to leave secure the rights of the people. They divided and shared powers among the three federal branches and between the state and federal governments. The Constitution says in article VI that the members of Congress and the state legislatures and the executive and judicial officers of the United States and the states shall be bound by oath to support this Constitution, suggesting that all government departments in the states and nation have a duty to make sure their actions are constitutional. Article VI also says the Constitution and laws of the United States are the supreme law of the land, and the judges in every state shall be bound thereby, anything in the constitution or laws of any state to the contrary notwithstanding. This supremacy clause relies on judges in the states to ensure that the state legislative and executive branches obey the Constitution, but there is no comparable provision for federal judges to review the laws and executive actions of the nation for compliance with the Constitution. Each federal branch is left responsible to determine the meaning of the Constitution for its own activities, an approach which constitutional scholars have labeled "departmental interpretation."[2]

Moreover, the Constitution empowers Congress to control the jurisdiction of the lower federal courts (which it establishes) and the appellate jurisdiction of the Supreme Court. Article III, section two confers on the Supreme Court original jurisdiction in a few categories of cases, and confers appellate jurisdiction with such exceptions and regulations as the Congress shall make. Most of the Supreme Court's reviews of federal and state laws for compliance with the Constitution, as amended—including all the cases discussed in this book—have been exercises of appellate jurisdiction, subject to the exceptions and regulations authority of Congress. Michael Perry and Charles Black have observed that Congress could use its article III powers to preserve and protect majoritarian decision-making under the Constitution.[3] That it has not done this in any meaningful way has meant that in some respects our representative democracy, our republican form of government as the framers called it, has taken on the character of a judicial oligopoly.

James Madison presented to the First Congress a Bill of Rights he drafted based on amendments to the Constitution which had been proposed by the state ratification conventions. Madison believed the Bill would not change the Constitution, since the federal government had no delegated power to do things the Bill prohibited, but he wanted to alleviate the concerns of opponents of the Constitution. The Bill offers guarantees for states' rights and people's rights. The First Amendment freedoms of religion, speech, press, and assembly are assumed natural rights, placed off-limits to Congress and left within the control of the states. The remaining amendments provide substantive and procedural protections for people in their dealings with the federal government. The Fifth Amendment due process clause, for example, as originally understood, requires notice and a hearing on the facts when the federal government wants to deprive a person of life, liberty, or property. It was not intended to allow the courts to review the policies of statutes substantively, including statutes that regulate life, liberty, or property. In the antebellum era, the Supreme Court correctly held that the Bill of Rights does not apply to the states, and egregiously opined that Congress could not ban slavery in the territories because this would deprive slaveholders of their substantive property right under the Fifth Amendment.[4]

The Republican-dominated 1866 Congress undertook the momentous task of restoring the union after the Civil War, reforming the relationship between the states and the federal government, and providing better guarantees for the rights of the people. Their centerpiece legislation was the Fourteenth Amendment. Section one of the amendment says no state shall abridge the privileges or immunities of citizens of the United States nor deprive any person of life, liberty, or property without due process, nor deny to any person the equal protection of the laws, and section five empowers Congress to enforce these provisions by appropriate legislation. The amendment assumes the existence for all persons of life, liberty, and property rights, which cannot be deprived without due process. In addition, citizens have privileges and immunities, which cannot be abridged. Life, liberty, and property rights are natural rights possessed by everyone, while the privileges and immunities of citizens involve political rights, as established and regulated by the states. The core original meaning of the Fourteenth Amendment is this: the states must provide ("not deny") equal protection of the laws for all persons' life, liberty, and property rights, and Congress can enforce this duty of rights protection by appropriate legislation. The Republicans who enacted the amendment in 1866, secured its ratification two years later, and implemented it in some early laws explained the meaning this way: If a state improperly deprives people of life, liberty, or property rights by the enactment and enforcement of a law, the courts can intervene to overturn the law. The state's action generates a case or controversy which a court can adjudicate. Or Congress can enact legislation to correct the situation. If a state fails to protect people's rights against harms or discriminations by their fellow citizens through willful inaction, neglect, or lack of resources, this too amounts to a denial of equal protection. Although the courts can offer no relief, since there is no "state action" to review and overturn, Congress can step in to secure the rights by appropriate legislation.

The Supreme Court has delivered a meaning dramatically different from the original meaning just described: (1) Because the section one clauses address *state* abridgments, deprivations, and denials of rights, Congress under its section five authority cannot reach harmful or discriminatory conduct by private actors. Individual invasion of individual rights is not the subject-matter of the amendment. (*United States v. Harris*, and the *Civil Rights Cases*, both 1883). (2) The states have no duty to protect persons from harms inflicted upon them by others (*DeShaney v. Winnebago County Department of Social Services*, 1989). (3) Only the courts—not Congress—can decide what are people's rights under the Fourteenth Amendment and how they may be regulated (*City of Boerne v. Flores*, 1997).[5] The aggregate impact of the Supreme Court's decisions has been to effectively remove Congress from the Fourteenth Amendment.

Having protected states' rights in some early interpretations (1873–1896), the still conservative but now pro-business, laissez-faire Court in the "Lochner era" (1897–1937), so named after a liberty of contract case, *Lochner v. New York* (1905),[6] vigorously upheld economic liberty and property rights of persons and corporations, finding many substantive and procedural state due process violations. Then in what commentators have called the "New Deal settlement of 1937," and as a result of President Franklin Roosevelt's ability to replace seven justices who died or retired between 1937 and 1941, the Court changed its approach, deferring to federal and state regulations of the economy, requiring only fair process in the government's dealings with economic liberty or property, and limiting substantive judicial protection for people's "liberty" in the states to a few intimate personal rights, such as birth control and abortion (recently retracted), and to textually based guarantees in the Bill of Rights. Most modern commentators and the Court itself have been critical of the Lochner era's due process decisions that unreasonably interfered with government's ability to regulate business and labor relations, ameliorate some of the harsh socioeconomic effects of unrestrained capitalism, and to generally promote the public good.

For fifty years after the adoption of the Fourteenth Amendment, the Court consistently held that it does not apply the Bill of Rights to the states. Then in one of the praiseworthy opinions by the Lochner-era Court, *Gitlow v. New York* (1925)[7] ignored this precedent and assumed that the freedoms of speech and press, embodied in the First Amendment, should be extended to the states as aspects of due process "liberty." During the 1930s the Court applied all the First Amendment freedoms of religion, speech, press, and assembly and petition to the states, and ever since that time it has carefully scrutinized government actions involving these rights. Based upon the proposition that the First Amendment protects fundamentally important and fragile interests, the justices have strictly scrutinized state and local laws to avoid a slippery slope whereby the full enjoyment of these rights might be compromised. In my opinion, some of the decisions were clearly good ones, some clearly bad, and the majority were decisions in which reasonable people could disagree on the merits (the justices often disagreed among themselves, and a reader will undoubtedly disagree with some of my classifications in this book). During the 1960s the Court moved beyond the First Amendment to apply to the states most of the criminal law protections in the rest of the Bill of Rights. These decisions too were debated among the justices and were often controversial.

From the founding of the republic until the 1960s, the Supreme Court did not strike down a lot of federal laws as violations of the Bill of Rights. Then the liberal Warren Court (in the 1960s), the moderate Burger Court (1969–1986), and the conservative Rehnquist Court (1986–2005) and Roberts Court (2005 to the present) assumed a more active role in federal Bill of Rights cases, especially in support of the First Amendment free speech clause and the Fifth Amendment. The Court applied to Congress doctrines and precedents previously established in state cases. Although most of the thirty-five vetoes of Congress in free speech cases can be classified as reasonable-people-can-disagree decisions, on a range of acceptability I find myself more in agreement with Congress than with the Court. Free speech is a valuable constitutional right, but was it really necessary to conclude that Congress could not place restrictions on the photographic reproduction of US currency as a protective measure against counterfeiting; could not make it a crime to commercially produce and sell videos of animal cruelty; could not effectively regulate the broadcasting of "patently offensive" sex-related material on cable television; could not ban the "knowing" transmission of obscene or indecent messages to minors on the Internet; could not regulate or proscribe picketing and demonstrations on the grounds immediately surrounding the Capitol building or the Supreme Court building; could not outlaw the burning of the American flag; could not exempt "compounded" drugs from the Food and Drug Administration's standard approval requirements, on the condition that the providers of such drugs refrain from advertising or promoting their use; could not restrain casino gambling advertising in states where casino gambling is legal; could not tax the handlers of mushrooms in order to finance the promotion of mushroom sales; and could not penalize the disclosure of confidential communications illegally intercepted and recorded?[8] The list could go on, not only in free speech cases but in most of the other vetoes in Bill of Rights federal cases explored in this book.

During Reconstruction, the New Deal 1930s, and the Great Society 1960s, in bursts of progressive energy, Congress enacted laws to protect civil rights, to offer baseline economic security for the lower and middle classes, and to promote civil rights and economic welfare, in these respective periods. It is time for Congress to assert its long-dormant constitutional role under section five of the Fourteenth Amendment to define and implement private rights appropriately balanced with sound public policies. The book discusses some possible federal legislative improvements to the current state of our law in three important, controversial areas of rights policy: abortion, religious liberty, and free speech.

The December 2021 Report of the Presidential Commission on the Supreme Court discussed several reform options to change the role and operation of the judiciary: Set term limits for Supreme Court judges—eighteen years, for example—long enough to ensure their independence and short enough to keep them reasonably responsive to the outcomes of democratic elections. Increase the size of the Court. Strip the Supreme Court and other federal courts of jurisdiction to hear certain kinds of cases. Impose supermajority voting requirements on courts or otherwise require them to defer to legislative judgments about constitutionality. Authorize congressional overrides of judicial decisions striking down legislation. Some of these changes could be accomplished by a federal statute, and others would require a constitutional amendment. Some would tweak the system, and others would fundamentally alter the operation of our government under the Constitution. None of the reform options would accomplish a successful transfer of an appropriate amount of policy-making power from the Supreme Court to Congress. Since a few of the Court's overturns of federal law have been serious mistakes with permanent consequences, such as the rejections of a meaningful role for Congress under the Fourteenth Amendment, and most of the others have been Bill of Rights overturns debatable on the merits, the book concludes with a proposed constitutional amendment to clarify two points for Congress—it has the authority to independently interpret the Constitution, as amended, and it has Fourteenth Amendment power to protect people's rights against infringements by private actors or state actions—and to stipulate that no court can override a federal law unless the decision is affirmed by a unanimous vote of the Supreme Court. The unanimous vote proposal is based on the idea that the laws of Congress should be respected unless they clearly violate the Constitution.

NOTES

1. Presidential Commission on the Supreme Court of the United States, *Draft Final Report* (December 7, 2021), 152.

2. Walter F. Murphy, James E. Fleming, and Sotirios A. Barber, *American Constitutional Interpretation* (Westbury, NY: Foundation Press, 2nd ed., 1995), 262–65.

3. For Perry and Black, see Erwin Chemerinsky, *Federal Jurisdiction* (Philadelphia: Wolters Klewer, 8th ed., 2021), 215–16.

4. *Barron v. Mayor and City Council of Baltimore*, 32 U.S. 243 (1833) (Bill of Rights does not apply to the states); *Dred Scott v. Sandford*, 60 U.S. 393 (1857) (Congress cannot ban slavery in the territories).

5. *Harris*, 106 U.S. 629; *Civil Rights Cases*, 109 U.S. 3; *DeShaney*, 489 U.S. 189; and *City of Boerne*, 521 U.S. 507.

6. *Lochner*, 198 U.S. 45.

7. *Gitlow*, 268 U.S. 652.

8. *Regan v. Time, Inc.*, 468 U.S. 641 (1994) (counterfeiting prevention); *United States v. Stevens*, 559 U.S. 460 (2010) (videos of animal cruelty); *Denver Area Educational Telecommunications, Inc. v. FCC*, 518 U.S. 727 (1996) (sex-related material on cable TV); *Reno v. American Civil Liberties Union*, 521 U.S. 844 (1997) (obscene messages on the Internet); *Chief of Capitol Police v. Jeanette Rankin Brigade*. 342 F. Supp. 575 (D.D.C., 1972), affirmed 409 U.S. 972 (1972) (picketing on Capitol grounds); *United States v. Grace*, 461 U.S. 171 (1983) (demonstrating on Supreme Court grounds); *United States v. Eichman*, 496 U.S. 300 (1990) (flag burning); *Thompson v. Western States Medical Center*, 535 U.S. 357 (2002) (sale of specially compounded drugs); *United States v. United Foods, Inc.* 535 U.S. 405 (2001) (sale of mushrooms); and *Bartnicki v. Vopper*, 532 U.S. 514 (2001) (illegal interception and publication of private message).

Chapter 1

Should We Reform the Role and Operation of the Court?

The President's Commission appointed to review the role and operation of the Supreme Court reached no consensus on whether it should be reformed. Defenders of the status quo praised the Court for preserving the constitutional values of democracy, federalism, and individual rights. This chapter gives some background on these topics, and for reasons which are developed in the rest of the book, concludes that a constitutional amendment to transfer an appropriate amount of policy-making power from the Court to Congress in rights determinations would be a good idea.

With only one significant exception, from the founding of the republic (1788) until 1870 the Supreme Court in all important cases upheld federal statutes whenever they were challenged under the Constitution: *Hylton v. United States* (1796) (A tax on carriages is not a "direct tax," and therefore does not need to be apportioned among the states based upon population); *Stuart v. Laird* (1803) (Congress could abolish three circuit courts and deprive the judges appointed to them of their positions despite the good-behavior provision in article III, create six new circuit courts and staff them with different circuit court judges, and require justices of the Supreme Court to travel around the country and sit as judges in the new circuit courts); *Martin v. Hunter's Lessee* (1816) (Congress could empower the U.S. Supreme Court to review decisions of the states' highest courts); *McCulloch v. Maryland* (1819) (Congress has implied authority to charter a national bank, and the Court would tread upon legislative ground were it to inquire into whether the law was necessary); *Gibbons v. Ogden* (1824) (Navigation on water is part of commerce, and Congress can prescribe the rules by which commerce is governed among the states); *Prigg v. Pennsylvania* (1842) (Congress could pass the 1793 fugitive slave law implementing the slaveowner's right of recapture; when a right is conferred by the Constitution, Congress can provide a remedy); and the *License Tax Cases* (1867) (Congress's imposition of taxes and penalties for unlicensed dealing in lotteries and liquors is an expression of policy which the Court will not review on grounds of morality or expediency).[1]

This broad deference ceased after the Civil War. From 1870 to 1937 the Court curbed the powers of Congress, mostly in decisions that narrowly construed the article I commerce clause, poured substantive meaning into the Fifth Amendment's due process clause to protect the Court's view of peoples' and businesses' economic rights, and promoted states' rights under the federalism clause in the Tenth Amendment. The year 1870 can be marked as a turning point in the Court's jurisprudence because that is when the justices for the first time struck down an exercise of power delegated to Congress in article I, section eight of the Constitution, the authority to regulate commerce among the states. On the theory that Congress could not affect trade within the limits of any state under the commerce clause, *United States v. Dewitt* (1870) in a unanimous opinion held that a federal law which prohibits the sale of naphtha and illuminating oils if they are inflammable at a temperature of less than 110 degrees Fahrenheit is an impermissible police regulation, "except so far as . . . it operates without the limits of any State." The law could apply in the District of Columbia, where Congress has the exclusive right to legislate in all cases, and in the federal territories. Later interpretations held that the term "commerce" does not include manufacturing or the production of goods within a state, even though the goods might enter the stream of interstate commerce. Congress could not raise money by imposing an income tax on persons or property, nor ban the sale of alcohol to certain Native Americans who were wards of the state, nor impose limitations on child labor, nor establish a minimum wage for the benefit of female and child employees in the District of Columbia. At the end of this period, in nine cases decided in 1935 and 1936, the Court struck down provisions in federal statutes, mostly under article I, the Fifth Amendment due process clause, or the Tenth Amendment, curtailing the New Deal response to the Great Depression.[2]

Since the "New Deal settlement of 1937," when the Court decided to allow Congress (and the states within boundaries set by Congress) to regulate the economy without interference from the judiciary, the Bill of Rights and the Fourteenth Amendment have taken center stage in the Court's monitoring of federal and state statutes. *United States v. Carolene Products Co.* (1938) summarized the outlines of the new regime. The company in this case charged that the Filled Milk Act, which prohibited the interstate shipment of skimmed milk compounded with any fat or oil other than milk fat, exceeded the power of Congress to regulate commerce, violated the Fifth Amendment due process clause, or the Tenth Amendment. In upholding the law, the Court said that the power to regulate commerce among the states embraces the power "to prescribe the rules by which commerce is conducted," citing *Gibbons v. Ogden*

(1824), and accepted the legislative findings that the use of filled milk as a substitute for pure milk is injurious to health and facilitates fraud upon the public. Even in the absence of legislative findings, for regulations of ordinary commercial transactions, "the existence of facts supporting the legislative judgment is to be presumed" unless no rational basis exists for that judgment.

Then in its famous footnote four, the Court said it would abandon the presumption of constitutionality when legislation impinges on the specific prohibitions in the Bill of Rights, interferes with the operation of the ordinary political processes which could be expected to bring about the repeal of undesirable legislation, or appears to be influenced by prejudice against "discrete and insular minorities." While *Carolene Products* dealt with a federal law, and announced an intention to defer to Congress in commerce regulations, the footnote reserved an active role for the Court in reviews of statutes relating to personal liberties or equality under the law.[3]

The Court in *West Virginia State Board of Education v. Barnette* (1943) captured the new spirit well. It struck down a state law requiring public school students to pledge allegiance to the American flag at the start of each school day, agreeing with a Jehovah's Witnesses claim that the law violated the First Amendment freedoms of speech and religion. The Court said,

> The very purpose of the Bill of Rights was to withdraw certain subjects from the vicissitudes of political controversy, to place them beyond the reach of majorities and officials and to establish them as legal principles to be applied by the courts. One's right to life, liberty, and property, to free speech, a free press, freedom of worship and assembly, and other fundamental rights may not be submitted to vote; they depend on the outcome of no election. The Bill of Rights is beyond the reach of majorities, and its principles will be applied by the courts.[4]

This judicial hubris followed logically from the statement in *Carolene Products* (1938) that the Court would carefully scrutinize laws that impinge on the "specific prohibitions" in the Bill of Rights. The statement assumes that the Bill of Rights is so specific that violations could be easily detected and eradicated in the courts without interfering with legitimate majority rule. A few of the Bill's provisions are indeed clear and precise, such as the Third Amendment's mandate that in time of peace no soldier shall be quartered in any house without the owner's consent, but others are open-ended and vague. The First Amendment freedoms of speech and religion, and the due process clause in the Fifth Amendment, copied into the Fourteenth Amendment for application to the states, are neither precise nor self-defining, and judges have frequently assumed a decisive role under them to resolve public policy controversies.

JAMES MADISON'S INSIGHT ON JUDICIAL REVIEW

James Madison, who has been called the "Father of the Constitution" because of his influential role in its creation, worried that this might happen. At the convention of delegates which drafted the Constitution in 1787, he sponsored a council of revision plan whereby the executive and a convenient number of the national judiciary would be able to veto bills of Congress. Instead, the convention adopted an alternative procedure, giving the President alone the power to veto bills of Congress, subject to a legislative override. In a 1788 letter to a friend reviewing Thomas Jefferson's draft constitution for the Kentucky territory, Madison recommended the adoption of his council of revision concept, which had been rejected the previous year for the federal Constitution. Such a revisionary power "is meant to be a check to precipitate, to unjust, and to unconstitutional laws." This goal could be secured, "without disarming the Legislature of its requisite authority," by requiring that bills be sent to the executive and judiciary departments. If either department objects, two-thirds of both houses, and if both object, three-quarters of both houses, would be needed to enact the bill into law. If the legislature repasses the bill by the necessary margin, it becomes law and it "should not be allowed the Judges or the Executive to pronounce a law thus enacted unconstitutional and invalid." Constitutions need a procedure to resolve differences of interpretation about their meaning. "In the State Constitutions and indeed in the Federal one also," concluded Madison, "no provision is made for the case of a disagreement in expounding them; and as the Courts are generally the last in making their decision, it results to them, by refusing or not refusing to execute a law, to stamp it with its final character. This makes the Judiciary Department paramount to the Legislature, which was never intended, and can never be proper."[5]

Decades later, following President James Monroe's veto of an internal improvements bill for constitutional reasons, Madison wrote that this action reminded him "of the attempts in the Convention to vest in the Judiciary Department a qualified negative on Legislative *bills*. Such a Control, restricted to Constitutional points, besides giving greater stability and system to the rules of expounding the Instrument, would have precluded the question of a Judiciary annulment of Legislative *Acts*" (Madison's emphasis).[6] This comment indicates that he had sponsored the council of revision plan for two reasons, to improve the quality of legislative deliberation by providing executive and judicial inputs up front, and to make enacted laws uncontrollable by the courts.

These letters show that Madison believed Congress should be the ultimate decider of whether its work product complies with the Constitution, although admittedly with an executive and judicial filter on bills before they become law. He was concerned that because the courts generally act last in the lawmaking and law enforcement process, they could assume a legislative preeminence that is incompatible with republican government. He believed that his council of revision plan would have operated to prevent judicial overturns of enacted laws. Our nation's experience with the presidential veto confirms Madison's confidence on this point, namely, that the participation of supreme judiciary members along with the executive in the revisionary power over bills of Congress would prevent judicial overrides of statutes. Most Presidents have vetoed bills they deemed unwise or unconstitutional, but once laws are enacted, the executive branch enforces them. If the President believes that an existing statute is unconstitutional, his only recourse is to recommend that Congress change or repeal it. By common understanding and tradition, the executive cannot annul the law by refusing to enforce it.[7]

While the Supreme Court in the antebellum era almost never declared a law of Congress to be unconstitutional, its affirmations and explanations of why the federal laws it was enforcing in cases were constitutionally authorized gained currency for the idea that it is part of the Court's job to look at Congress's work product and make sure the judges agree it complies with the supreme law of the Constitution. Mark Tushnet has written that for many decades the nature of judicial review in the United States was "uncertain." Although *Marbury v. Madison* (1803) opined that the Supreme Court had the power to declare unconstitutional a statute enacted by Congress, the scope of the *Marbury* power, and its relation to the Constitution-interpreting roles of the other branches, remained contested. "At some point" in the nineteenth century the idea that all the branches of the government have the responsibility to review and interpret the Constitution weakened. "Judicial review changed from the means by which the courts expressed their view of the Constitution's meaning, in a system where other institutions expressed their own independent views, to a mechanism for lodging responsibility for constitutional interpretation in a single institution, the judiciary."[8] Madison's concern that the courts, as the last to speak in the lawmaking and law enforcement process, would be able to control constitutional interpretation, has proven to be a prescient insight.

DEMOCRACY

The opponents of Court reform have told the Presidential Commission on the Supreme Court that democracy is one of three specific constitutional values which the Court has had a vital role in preserving.[9] This is an odd value to cite on behalf of judicial review as practiced by a body of nine appointed, life-tenured justices, since democracy is based upon the principle of majority rule by the people through their elected and accountable representatives. Alexander Bickel in the 1960s famously described the Court as a deviant institution because it operates as a counter-majoritarian force in the American political system. He worried that besides being a check on the legislature and executive, judicial review may tend over time "to weaken the democratic process."[10]

Moreover, it has been primarily Congress, not the Supreme Court, which historically has promoted and nurtured democracy. For example, Congress has been responsible for a number of constitutional amendments to extend and protect the right to vote (which were ratified by the state legislatures). The Fifteenth Amendment (passed by Congress in 1868, and ratified by the states in 1870) says the right to vote shall not be denied or abridged on account of race or color. The Seventeenth Amendment (passed 1912, ratified 1913) provides for the direct election of United States senators (previously under the Constitution the state legislatures had chosen senators). The Nineteenth Amendment (passed 1919, ratified 1920) says that the right to vote shall not be denied or abridged on account of sex. The Twenty-fourth Amendment (passed 1962, ratified 1964) says the right to vote in federal elections shall not be denied or abridged by reason of failure to pay a poll tax or any other tax. Finally, the Twenty-sixth Amendment (passed and ratified in 1971) reduces the voting age to eighteen. Congress had first sought to make this change by statute, enacted during the Vietnam War on the theory that a citizen who is old enough to die for his or her country in military service should be old enough to vote. When the Supreme Court in *Oregon v. Mitchell* (1970) overturned this measure as a constitutional violation of states' rights to control state elections, Congress and the state legislatures promptly amended the Constitution.[11]

Although the Fifteenth Amendment prohibits racial discrimination in the right to vote, for decades the Jim Crow South used grandfather clauses, literacy tests, and various other devices to exclude Black voters at the polls. Black people risked harassment, intimidation, economic reprisals, and threats of physical violence when they tried to register to vote. In the early 1960s the murder of voting rights activists in Mississippi and the attack by state troopers on peaceful marchers in Selma, Alabama, gained national attention and helped to persuade Congress to pass the landmark 1965 Voting Rights Act. The law outlawed literacy tests, provided for the appointment of federal election examiners in named state and local jurisdictions with a history of racial discrimination, and in section five required these covered jurisdictions to obtain "preclearance" from officials in Washington, D.C., for any new voting practices and procedures. In the ensuing decades the preclearance provision proved to be an effective means of discouraging states from erecting new barriers to voting, stopping the most egregious policies from going forward, and providing communities and civil rights advocates with advanced notice of proposed changes that might suppress the vote. In 1975 Congress amended the law to require jurisdictions with significant numbers of voters with limited or no proficiency in English to provide voting materials in other languages and offer multilingual assistance at the polls. In 1982 Congress extended the Voting Rights Act for another twenty-five years, and required the states to make voting more accessible for the elderly and people with disabilities. Also, responding to historically low rates of voter registration, Congress in 1993 passed the National Voter Registration Act, requiring the states to allow citizens to register to vote when they obtained their driver's license or by simply mailing in an application form.[12]

Congress in 2006 by nearly unanimous vote renewed the Voting Rights Act for another twenty-five years. Then the Supreme Court in a five-to-four vote in *Shelby County, Alabama v. Holder* (2013) struck down the law's coverage of named state and local jurisdictions on the theory that the states should be treated as equals, and because in its view the preclearance provision was no longer needed. In the wake of *Shelby County*, according to the nonpartisan coalition Election Protection, twenty-three states adopted new voting restrictions between 2013 and 2018. *Brnovich v. Democratic National Committee* (2019) upheld Arizona laws that disenfranchised voters who voted in the wrong precinct and limited who could collect and deliver an absentee ballot to a polling place. *Rucho v. Common Cause* (2019) held that partisan gerrymandering in the states presents political questions beyond the reach of the federal courts. Given the current composition and approach of the Supreme Court, it is likely that any national initiative to support democratic reforms within the states will have to come from Congress.[13]

FEDERALISM

Federalism is a system of government whereby a national government and smaller political subdivisions occupy the same territory and have powers to govern (some of the powers are shared and some are exclusive to one level of government or another), and as is true for democracy, its preservation offers no persuasive reason to oppose reforming the role and operation of the Supreme Court. Three constitutional provisions have defined our federalism: article I of the Constitution prescribes the powers of Congress, the most important ones being the authorities to raise taxes and spend money, to regulate commerce among the states, and to raise and support military forces; the article VI supremacy clause says that the Constitution, laws and treaties of the United States are the "supreme Law of the Land," and that the judges in the states shall be bound thereby, anything in the laws or constitution of the state to the contrary notwithstanding; and the Tenth Amendment confirms that the powers not delegated to the United States by the Constitution, nor prohibited by it to the states, are reserved to the states or the people.[14]

In the early decades of the republic the Supreme Court upheld the supremacy of federal laws and federal judicial decisions vis-à-vis the states.[15] From 1870 to 1937 the Court actively protected states' rights in some narrow interpretations of the delegated powers of Congress (especially its power to regulate commerce) and broad interpretations of the reserved powers of the states in the Tenth Amendment.[16] Between 1937 and 1992 the Court largely abandoned line-drawing between the federal government and state government authorities, and ceded to Congress virtually unlimited discretion to regulate the economy and to allocate money with conditions attached. *United States v. Carolene Products Co.* (1938) declared the Court's change in focus from federalism concerns to the rights of individuals and minorities against government at any level.][17]

The Court since 1992, in three types of cases, has overturned federal laws and devolved power to the states in a jurisprudence that some commentators have labeled a "new federalism." First, Congress under its article I commerce clause authority cannot reach conduct within a state that does not substantially affect interstate economic activity. *United States v. Lopez* (1995) (federal law cannot create a gun-free zone inside or within 1,000 feet of a school building); *United States v. Morrison* (2000) (federal law cannot provide the victims of gender-motivated violence a right to sue for damages or other appropriate relief in court because this involves local criminal activity with no substantial effect on interstate commerce). Second, even though an article I delegation of power allows Congress to pursue a particular policy, Congress cannot "commandeer" state legislative or executive officials to enforce it. *New York v. United States* (1992) (the "core sovereignty" of the states embodied in the Tenth Amendment means that the Congress cannot use incentives to pressure a state legislature to comply with minimum federal standards in regulating the disposal of radioactive waste products within the state's borders); *Printz v. United States* (1997) (Congress cannot require, as an interim measure pending the establishment of a national program, that local law enforcement officials conduct background checks on prospective firearms purchasers to make sure they are not underage, a convicted felon, a substance abuser, or ineligible to own a firearm under state or local law). Third, article I laws cannot abrogate the states' sovereign immunity by granting a private cause of action against them in federal or state court. Even though a federal law is authorized by the Constitution, citizens harmed by the state's violation of the law cannot enforce their rights in court. *Seminole Tribe of Florida v. Florida* (1996) (Indian tribes cannot sue the state in federal court to enforce the state's obligation under the Indian Gaming Regulatory Act to negotiate gaming contracts in good faith); *Alden v. Maine* (1999) (employees cannot sue the state in state court to enforce their right to overtime pay under the Fair Labor Standards Act).[18]

In these two periods, 1870–1937 and since 1992, the Supreme Court's federalism decisions protecting states' rights often have come at the expense of good public policies and without any clear mandate from the relevant constitutional text. Nor were these interventions necessary. The checks and balances and the political incentives built into the federal government system operate to protect the ordinary mainstream interests of the states. Federal legislation must survive write-ups in committee, be supported by majorities in each house of Congress, and secure enactment with the President's blessing or by supermajority vote over his veto. Members of Congress and the President depend upon state elections to achieve and retain office, and we the people tend to be supportive of local government. Jesse Choper in his 1980 book explains in detail why the states do not need an additional checkmate from judges to defend their legitimate governance powers.[19]

PROTECTING RIGHTS

Both defenders and critics of the rights jurisprudence of the Supreme Court vis-à-vis Congress can draw upon theory to justify their respective positions. For example, defenders of an activist Court can argue: (1) One more screen to preserve private rights, independently from the political branches, cannot be a bad thing. (2) Constitutional rights which are specified in the text of the document deserve to be vigorously protected. (3) The majority cannot be trusted to honor minority rights. (4) Congress cannot be the judge of its own powers. Critics of an activist Court can counter each of these points: (1) The Court's interventions to preserve private rights can come at the expense of good public policies. (2) Prominent rights such as liberty and equality and the freedoms of speech, press, and religion are not self-defining concepts, and reasonable people regularly disagree about their scope and application. (3) If the majority will not honor minority rights, our representative democracy form of government must be replaced by . . . what? (4) Congress must judge its own powers as it considers legislation in order to ensure compliance with the Constitution. Congress has as much right to judge its own powers as the Court has to judge *its* own powers. This brief compilation of observations and counter-observations suggests that theory alone cannot tell us whether to pursue reform at the Court. We must look to history for guidance.

The Supreme Court has decided most of its rights cases under the first ten amendments to the Constitution, collectively called the Bill of Rights, which the First Congress drafted in 1789 and the state legislatures ratified over the next two years, and under the Fourteenth Amendment, which the post–Civil War Congress drafted in 1866 and the state legislatures ratified over the next two years.[20] Notice the role of Congress in establishing private rights. The Bill of Rights protect liberty and property rights of people and the governance powers of the states against oppression from the federal government. The Fourteenth Amendment applies to the states and shifts power back toward the federal government by placing limitations on the states. It says that no state shall abridge the privileges or immunities of citizens of the United States, nor deprive any person of life, liberty, or property without due process of law, nor deny to any person the equal protection of the law. Congress in drafting the amendment granted to itself the power to enforce the amendment by appropriate legislation.

The Court early rendered the Fourteenth Amendment's privileges or immunities clause irrelevant by holding that the rights of citizens remained almost exclusively under the control of the states, and beyond the reach of the federal government.[21] The Court has protected rights in two types of cases under the Fourteenth Amendment's due process of law clause. Since the 1890s, primarily, it has poured meaning into the "due process of law" concept by requiring that the states in their laws and actions comply with the Court's notion of what is procedurally fair or substantively just in the treatment of the liberty and property rights of persons and businesses. Also, starting with a 1925 case, it has used the due process clause as a vehicle to absorb and apply to the states most of the guarantees and limitations in the Bill of Rights.[22] The Court in the modern era has interpreted the equal protection of the laws clause to require that minorities and women be protected against state discriminations. Another way to phrase this is that protected group members have a right to equal treatment with others under the law.

Those who praise the Supreme Court's work as a stout defender of rights can point to landmark decisions under the Fourteenth Amendment. Some of these cases applied to the states the First Amendment freedoms of speech, press, or religion, and created vigorous defenses for these rights, under the due process clause. Others overturned state law discriminations against minorities or women under the equal protection clause. The Court's reputation as a defender of individual rights against majoritarian oppression rests upon such cases.

For First Amendment decisions see *Murdock v. Pennsylvania* (1943) (the First Amendment freedoms of speech, press, and religion "are in a preferred position," and must be applied accordingly, so the town's requirement that persons who solicit or deliver orders for goods, paintings, or merchandise of any kind must procure a license and pay a fee cannot be applied to Jehovah's Witnesses selling their religious literature); *New York Times Co. v. Sullivan*

(1964) (to sustain a public official's claim of defamation or libel against the press, the First Amendment requires the plaintiff official to show the defendant's "actual malice" by proof that the defendant either knew the statement was false or else was reckless in publishing the information without investigating its accuracy); and *Torasco v. Watkins* (1961) (state requirement that a person must declare his belief in God in order to become a notary public violates the freedom of belief and religion enshrined in the First Amendment).[23]

For antidiscrimination cases protecting the right to equal treatment under the law for Black people, women, legal aliens, and gay men and lesbians, see *Brown v. Board of Education* (1954) (racially segregated public schools violate the equal protection clause); *Loving v. Virginia* (1967) (state cannot ban interracial marriage); *Reed v. Reed* (1971) (the state cannot have a default rule which favors men over women as administrators of estates); *Graham v. Richardson* (1971) (state restrictions on welfare benefits for legal aliens but not for citizens violate the equal protection clause); *Lawrence v. Texas* (2003) (state cannot make homosexual sex between consenting adults a crime) and *Obergefeld v. Hodges* (2015) (the fundamental right to marry is guaranteed to same-sex couples by the due process and equal protection clauses).[24]

On the other hand, critics who want to reform the Court's role and operation might make four observations to place these praiseworthy rights-supporting cases into a proper context. First, they applied to state laws, not to laws of Congress. Other evidence will have to be considered in order to determine whether the Court's monitoring of Congress has been vital to the preservation of rights. Second, these cases, though admittedly commendable, overturned earlier precedents of the Court's own making. The Court consistently held until 1925 that the Bill of Rights does not apply to the states, and it legitimized state law discriminations against Black people, women, aliens, and gay men and lesbians. *Plessy v. Ferguson* (1896) (state can require passenger train cars to be racially segregated); *Pace v. Alabama* (1883) (state can make interracial marriage or fornication a crime); *Bradwell v. Illinois* (1873) (state can deny to women the right to practice law); *Terrace v. Thompson* (1923) (state can prohibit legal alien residents from owning farmland); and *Stanley v. Georgia* (1986) (state can make homosexual sex a crime).[25] Third, these initial cases on equal protection and their later reversals had public support when they were decided. Our society's attitudes concerning these groups changed over time, and the Court's opinions reflected the evolution.[26] Fourth, racial discrimination policies in the South and elsewhere persisted for a decade after *Brown* (1954), and effectively ended only with the enactment by Congress of such laws as the Civil Rights Act of 1964, the Voting Rights Act of 1965, and the Fair Housing Act of 1968. The greatest protection for rights comes when the Court and Congress are working together.[27]

In addition, critics who complain that the Court has "undermined the ability of Congress . . . to protect rights" can point to its evisceration of Congress's section five authority to enforce the Fourteenth Amendment. Two cases in 1883 held that since the amendment only deals with the actions of state governments, Congress cannot pass legislation to protect people against private actors' harmful or discriminatory conduct. *United States v. Harris* (1883) (federal law penalizing conspiracies of two or more people to interfere with state law enforcement efforts or to deprive individuals of their equal protection, privileges or immunities under law could not be enforced against a mob who killed four persons being held in custody by a deputy sheriff); *Civil Rights Cases* (1883) (overturns a federal law penalizing the owners of inns, theaters, or public conveyances who deny access to their accommodations on account of race or color because private acts of discrimination cannot be reached by the amendment).[28] These cases remain "good law" today.

When Congress enacted civil rights protections in the 1960s, after a long hiatus, it resorted to powers in the original Constitution to regulate commerce and spend money with conditions as a means of avoiding the state action doctrine of the Fourteenth Amendment. This reliance on economics diminished the human rights luster of the statutes and made some of them appear to be "stretches" of constitutional authority. More recently, the Court has insisted that Congress has no authority under the Fourteenth Amendment to exercise control over the policies and actions of the state governments either. It can only enforce judicially determined rights. See *City of Boerne v. Flores* (1997) (the section five enforcement power is "corrective or remedial, not definitional," and it would undermine the separation of powers between the legislature and the judiciary for Congress to independently effect a substantive change in constitutional rights protection).[29]

YES, WE SHOULD REFORM THE ROLE AND OPERATION OF THE COURT

This book explores the history of constitutional law interactions among the Supreme Court, Congress, and the states in their dealings with life, liberty, and property rights. The constitutional setting described in chapter 2, and original meanings of the Bill of Rights and the Fourteenth Amendment, established in chapters 3 and 4, lay the foundation for evaluating the Court's decisions on private rights and public policy options in chapters 5 through 9. Some of the Court's interpretations were clearly good, some clearly bad, and a substantial majority were cases where reasonable people could disagree on the merits.

Most of the clearly good overrides of law related to the states, and most of these state cases fall into one of three categories. The Court, primarily from the 1890s into the 1970s, interpreted the due process clause in the Fourteenth Amendment to require the use of fair procedures in government deprivations of liberty or property, as discussed in chapter 6. The second category of good overrides of state law were the modern decisions issued under the equal protection clause voiding discriminations against minorities and women, including the opinions highlighted in this chapter. The third category consists of the Court's substantive due process applications of the First Amendment freedoms of religion, speech, press, and assembly and petition, although the good outcomes that involved no constitutional or policy ambiguity are accompanied by others where the best answer was just not clear.

Very few clearly good judicial overrides involved laws of Congress, and only one had more than a tangential impact.[30] This is a paltry record of achievement for more than 230 years of Supreme Court reviews of federal legislation. And more importantly, some of the misguided interpretations relating to Congress have had serious negative consequences for society and have distorted our understanding of the Constitution. This is especially true of the Court's effective removal of Congress from the Fourteenth Amendment.

Accordingly, the final chapter considers the reform options discussed by the Presidential Commission on the Supreme Court. They rely on a federal statute or constitutional amendment to transfer some policy-making power from the Supreme Court to Congress. The chapter ends with a proposed constitutional amendment to clarify that Congress has the authority to independently interpret the meaning of the Constitution, as amended, that the Fourteenth Amendment section five power of Congress to enforce the life, liberty, and property rights of persons does indeed extend to both private actors and state actions, and to stipulate that in the future no court has the authority to override a federal law unless the decision is affirmed by a unanimous vote of the Supreme Court. The Court would retain its position as the final arbiter in constitutional rights questions for both the states and the nation. However, the unanimous vote requirement would mean the laws of Congress will be enforced unless they clearly violate the Constitution.

NOTES

1. *Hylton*, 3 U.S. 171; *Stuart*, 5 U.S. 299; *Martin*, 14 U.S. 1; *McCulloch*, 17 U.S. 316; *Gibbons*, 22 U.S. 1; *Prigg*, 41 U.S. 539; and *License Tax Cases*, 72 U.S. 462. The one important exception to the general pattern of judicial deference was *Dred Scott v. Sandford* 60 U.S. 393 (1857), wherein the Court opined in dictum that Congress could not prohibit slavery in the territories under its constitutional authority to "make

all needful Rules and Regulations respecting the Territory [of] . . . the United States" because this would violate the due process property rights of slaveowners. Another override of Congress in the antebellum era, *Marbury v. Madison*, 5 U.S. 137 (1803), would assume importance later for Chief Justice John Marshall's justification of judicial review of federal law, but the issue addressed in the case was inconsequential—the failed delivery of some commissions to justices of the peace.

2. *Dewitt*, 46 U.S. 41; *United States v. E.C. Knight and Co*., 156 U.S. 1 (1895) ("commerce" does not include manufacturing); *Pollock v. Farmers' Loan and Trust Co*., 157 U.S. 429, affirmed and expanded 158 U.S. 1 (1895) (Congress cannot levy a federal income tax); *In re Heff*, 197 U.S. 488 (1905) (Congress cannot ban the sale of alcohol to Native American wards of the state); *Hammer v. Dagenhart*, 247 U.S. 251 (1918) (Congress cannot regulate child labor); *Adkins v. Childrens' Hospital*, 261 U.S. 525 (1923) (Congress cannot require a minimum wage for female and child employees); and William B. Glidden, *The Supreme Court versus Congress: Disrupting the Balance of Power, 1789–2014* (Santa Barbara: Praeger, 2015), 32–37 (nine New Deal cases in 1935–1936).

3. *Carolene Products*, 304 U.S. 144. Footnote 4 focused on the states under the Fourteenth Amendment, 304 U.S. at 146–47.

4. *Barnette*, 319 U.S. 624.

5. Quoted in Walter F. Murphy, James E. Fleming, and Sotorios A. Barber, *American Constitutional Interpretation* (Westbury, NY: Foundation Press, 2nd ed., 1995), 279.

6. Quoted in Max Farrand, ed., *The Records of the Federal Convention of 1787* (New Haven: Yale University Press, 1966), vol. 4, Appendix A, 424.

7. Todd Garvey, "The Take Care Clause and Executive Discretion in the Enforcement of the Law," September 4, 2014, 4–8, citing several cases. Congressional Research Service Report R43708. www.crs.gov.

8. Mark Tushnet, "Alternative Forms of Judicial Review," 101 *Michigan Law Review* 2781, 2782–83 (2003).

9. The Court's advocates who praised its preservation of democratic rule could point to some liberal Warren Court opinions issued in the 1960s, such as *Reynolds v. Sims*, 377 U.S. 533 (1964) (Alabama's apportionment scheme violates the equal protection clause; state legislative districts should be composed of roughly equal populations, if possible, to promote a one-person, one-vote principle), and *Harper v. Virginia Board of Elections*, 383 U.S. 663 (1966) (strikes down the state's poll tax as an unreasonable qualification imposed on the right to vote). It should be noted that these were state cases, not overrides of Congress. Moreover, in later cases the Court has been tolerant of state gerrymandering and voter dilution schemes. See generally Jesse H. Choper, Richard H. Fallon, Jr., Yale Kamisar, Steven H. Shiffrin, Michael C. Dorf, and Fre4derick Schauer, *Constitutional Law: Cases, Comments, and Questions* (St. Paul, MN: West Academic Publishing, 12th ed., 2019), 1551–97.

10. Alexander M. Bickel, *The Least Dangerous Branch: The Supreme Court at the Bar of Politics* c. 1962, 2nd ed., with a foreword by Harry H. Wellington (New Haven: Yale University Press, 1982), 16, 21.

11. Alfred H. Kelly, Wilfred A. Harbison, and Herman Belz, eds., *The American Constitution: Its Origins and Development* (New York: W.W. Norton & Co.), vol. 1, 7th ed., 1991. Appendix 3 has the constitutional amendments. *Oregon v. Mitchell*, 400 U.S. 112.

12. Gary May, *Bending Toward Justice: The Voting Rights Act and the Transformation of American Democracy* (New York: Basic Books, 2013); National Voter Registration Act, 107 Stat. 77, Pub. L. No. 103–31, May 20, 1993.

13. Fannie Lou Hamer, Rosa Parks, and Coretta Scott King Voting Rights Act Reauthorization and Amendment of 2006, Pub. L. No. 109–246; *Shelby County*, 570 U.S. 524; *Brnovich*, 594 U.S. ___; and *Rucho*, 588 U.S. ___.

14. Kelly et al., *Am Const.* Appendix One, U.S. Const. art I, sec. 8, article VI, and Amendment X.

15. E.g., *McCulloch v. Maryland*, 17 U.S. 316 (1819) (under the article I necessary and proper clause Congress has implied authority to incorporate a national bank, and Maryland cannot tax a federal instrumentality); *Martin v. Hunter's Lessee*, 14 U.S. 304 (1816) (the article VI supremacy clause combined with the 1789 Judiciary Act's grant of appellate jurisdiction gives to the Supreme Court the power to review decisions of the states' highest courts).

16. See the text at n.3 supra.

17. *Carolene Products*, 304 U.S. 144.

18. *Lopez*, 514 U.S. 549; *Morrison*, 529 U.S. 598; *New York*, 505 U.S. 144; *Printz*, 521 U.S. 899; *Seminole Tribe*, 517 U.S. 44; and *Alden*, 527 U.S. 706.

19. Jesse Choper, *Judicial Review and the National Political Process: A Functional Reconsideration of the Role of the Supreme Court* (Chicago: University of Chicago Press, 1980). Like the *Carolene Products* opinion, Choper argues the Court should focus on individual rights protection against government and leave the federalism issues to Congress.

20. See generally Choper, et al., *Const. Law*.

21. *Slaughterhouse Cases*, 83 U.S. 36 (1873).

22. See chapters 6 and 7 infra.

23. *Murdock*, 319 U.S. 105; *New York Times*, 376 U.S. 254; and *Torasco*, 367 U.S. 483.

24. *Brown*, 347 U.S. 483; *Loving*, 388 U.S. 1; *Reed*, 404 U.S. 71; *Graham*, 403 U.S. 365; *Lawrence*, 539 U.S. 558; and *Obergefeld*, 576 U.S.___.

25. *Plessy*, 163 U.S. 537; *Pace*, 106 U.S. 583; *Bradwell*, 83 U.S. 130; *Terrace*, 263 U.S. 197; and *Stanley*, 394 U.S. 557.

26. For example, a few days after the racial desegregation ruling in *Brown*, a Gallup Poll showed that 57 percent of Americans favored the decision, while 41 percent disapproved. See Race and Education 50 Years after *Brown v. Board of Education*, 8 (Approval Ratings on U.S. Supreme Court decision in *Brown v. Board of Education*, May 21–26, 1954). Of course, in the South there was "massive resistance" to desegregation until well into the 1960s. A Gallup Poll over several decades posed the question, "Do you approve of a married woman earning money in business or industry if she has a husband capable of supporting her?" In 1936, 72 percent said "no," and 18 percent said "yes." The lines crossed in 1963, and in 1969, 55 percent approved, while

41 percent disapproved, see Lydia Saad, Gallup Vault: A History of Resistance to See Women Working, 1–2. In a 1971 Gallup Poll, the year *Reed* was decided, two-thirds of Americans said they would vote for a woman as President. For this opinion survey, see Long-Term Gallup Poll Trends: A Portrait of American Public Opinion Through the Century, 2. Willingness to Support a Woman for President. A Gallup Poll Report, "U.S. Support for Same-Sex Marriage, 1996–2021," said that 27 percent of Americans supported same-sex marriage in 1996, and in 2015, on the eve of the Court's decision in *Obergefeld*, nearly 60 percent supported it, see Justin McCarthy, Record High 70% in U.S. Support Same-Sex Marriage, 1–3 (Gallup Poll data 1996–2021).

27. 1964 Civil Rights Act, codified at 42 U.S.C. sec. 2000 et seq.; 1965 Voting Rights Act, 79 Stat. 437, Pub. L. No. 89–110; Title VIII of 1968 Civil Rights Act (Fair Housing Act), codified at 42 U.S.C. sec. 3601 et seq.

28. *Harris*, 106 U.S. 629; *Civil Rights Cases*, 109 U.S. 3.

29. *City of Boerne*, 521 U.S. 507.

30. *Bolling v. Sharpe*, 347 U.S. 497 (1954), a companion case to *Brown v. Board of Education*, eradicated racial segregation in the public schools in the District of Columbia by reading into the Fifth Amendment due process clause an equal protection component. The Court in the 1970s relied on this precedent to overturn gender-based statutory discriminations in the federal government's social security and military benefit programs.

Chapter 2

The Drafting and Ratification of Our Constitution

The United States of America began as a group of thirteen sovereign republics, loosely held together by agreement in a governance document called the Articles of Confederation. During the 1780s a segment of the country's political elite became convinced that the Articles needed to be reformed or replaced in order to achieve a stronger federal government. With James Madison of Virginia playing a leading role, delegates from twelve of the thirteen states (all except Rhode Island) assembled in a convention in Philadelphia, and they worked through the summer of 1787 to draft a new Constitution. It embodied a set of compromises designed to achieve a balance among three objectives: creation of a stronger federal government, reservation of appropriate powers to the states, and the safety of the rights and liberties of the people of the United States.

During the ratification campaign, the opponents of the Constitution, who became known as Anti-Federalists, worried about the powers being conferred on the new federal government. They argued that the "consolidated" government could tax and spend, regulate foreign commerce and commerce among the states, wage war, and ultimately do anything that it decided might be "necessary and proper" to promote the "general welfare" of the country. The Federalist framers and supporters of the Constitution defended it against such charges, saying that the federal government could exercise only those powers delegated to it by the document. Utilizing these powers, it would be able to do the country's business more effectively than the confederation form of government, but without endangering individual freedoms. In the performance of its assigned tasks, the government was structured in such a way as to ensure a deliberative and just operation. An extended republic with a multitude of interests, sects, and parties, a bicameral legislature, an independent executive with veto power, staggered and filtered elections, and an independent judiciary appointed by the President with the advice and consent of the Senate, all written down, constituted a set of screening mechanisms designed to preserve popular sovereignty while protecting private rights. Mediation, moderation, deliberation, and shared responsibilities were the hallmark features of the form of government created in 1787. For the founders of the republic, Daniel Elazar has summarized, "locating all sovereignty in the people as a whole, while dividing the exercise of sovereign powers among several governments, . . . was a means of checking despotic tendencies, majoritarian or otherwise, . . . while preserving the principle of popular government."[1]

Rhode Island and North Carolina rejected the Constitution, and a number of the other states submitted with their acceptances a set of recommendations for amendments once the new federal government was established. Bill of rights proposals became a common element of these requests for change. Although the Federalists did not believe a bill of rights was needed, some of them (including Madison) evolved to a conclusion that, once the Constitution was approved and the new federal government in place, it would be a good idea to propose a few modifications for the states to consider. They believed that the Constitution was not in need of repair, but some of the opposition might be won over to the strengthened national framework if their concerns about the preservation of local self-government and individual liberties could be ameliorated without changing the basic structure and character of the government.

THE STATES' ARTICLES OF CONFEDERATION

The American colonies, in their evolving struggles with King George III and Parliament, decided to send delegates to the First Continental Congress in 1774 to obtain improved coordination and communication of the colonies' demands for greater local autonomy within the British Empire. This Congress asserted that the colonists had all the rights of English subjects, and that their elected assemblies should enjoy the exclusive right to legislate on all matters of taxation and domestic commerce, subject only to the veto of the king.

The Second Continental Congress began holding meetings in May 1775, after the colonists had engaged in military skirmishes with British forces in Lexington and Concord, Massachusetts, and in Virginia, with the Battle of Bunker Hill in Boston soon to follow. In the early stages of the American Revolution that ensued, the Second Continental Congress issued its Declaration of Independence, severing the bonds between the "united States of America" and the mother country, called upon the states to establish new governments, and drafted the nation's first constitution, the Articles of Confederation, sent to the states in 1777 and ratified by them four years later.[2]

The Declaration of Independence, July 4, 1776, and the state constitutions adopted pursuant to the call of Congress, reflected the natural law and natural rights doctrine that had attained a prominent position in American political thought. Penned primarily by Thomas Jefferson, the Declaration explained that the people of the "Thirteen United States of America" were assuming among the powers of the earth a separate and equal station to which the "Laws of Nature and of Nature's God" entitled them. Famously, the document announced to the world the new nation's foundational principles: "We hold these truths to be self-evident, that all men are created equal, that they are endowed by their Creator with certain unalienable Rights, that among these are Life, Liberty, and the pursuit of Happiness. That to secure these rights, Governments are instituted among Men, deriving their just powers from the consent of the governed." John Adams later said that every idea in the Declaration of Independence "had been hackneyed in Congress for two years before," and Jefferson in private correspondence indicated that he had merely attempted to convey an "expression of the American mind," to reflect the "harmonizing sentiments of the day."[3]

Most of the state constitutions adopted between 1776 and 1784 reflected the same basic natural law philosophy, and the republican political understanding that the people are sovereign, with the result that any government, to remain legitimate, must protect their fundamental rights. Virginia was the first to act, in 1776, and section one of its bill of rights was typical: "All men are by nature equally free and independent, and have certain natural, inherent and inalienable rights, amongst which are, the enjoying and defending life and liberty, acquiring, possessing and protecting property, and pursuing and obtaining happiness and safety." New Hampshire (1784) was the last to act in this sequence of early state constitution-making, and the product was also typical. Its bill of rights began with this assertion: "Article I. All men are born equally free and independent; therefore, all government of right originates from the people, is founded in consent, and instituted for the general good. II. All men have certain natural, essential, and inherent rights; among which are—the enjoying and defending of life and liberty—acquiring, possessing and protecting property—and in a word, of seeking and obtaining happiness." When men "enter into a state of society, they surrender up some of their natural rights to that society, in order to insure the protection of others; and, without such an equivalent, the surrender is void."[4]

Donald Lutz has summarized the core set of assumptions and principles that American political thinkers broadly shared in the founding era, and that came to fruition in the early state constitutions. Basic to the theory of popular control were these propositions: Humans develop and maintain their highest levels of moral and material existence while living in communities. A community is defined by a commonly held set of values, interests, and rights distributed through a limited population. The community and its government originate in the consent of the people. All men can give or withhold their consent, a capacity they share equally (regardless of other differences). Since all civil rights derive from the basic right to give or withhold consent, and since all men have the same capacity for such choice, everyone has the same rights in equal amounts. The people in a community have a common interest in protecting and preserving their shared values, interests, and rights. The legislature is elected by the majority, and therefore it represents the community. Government should be based upon and beholden to the deliberate sense of the community. The legislature determines the deliberate sense of the community, so it should predominate in the government. The primary political virtue of society is its willingness and ability to seek the common good. Popular elections filter upward men of greater virtue, on average, than are found in the general population. In its deliberations the legislature should seek the long-term common good of the community. In order to effectively seek the common good, the legislature should reflect in its membership all interests within the community in due proportion. Both the wealth and the rights of the community should be protected.[5]

After issuing the Declaration of Independence and encouraging the states to establish new governments, the Continental Congress drafted the nation's first constitution. Titled the "Articles of Confederation and Perpetual Union between the States," this form of government was so weak at its center that it offered little more than a mechanism to solicit some enhanced cooperation among thirteen separate republics. Article II, for example, stipulated that each of the states "retains its sovereignty, freedom and independence, and every power, jurisdiction, and right, which is not by this Confederation expressly delegated to the United States, in Congress assembled." Article III said the states were entering into a "league of friendship with each other, for their common defense, the security of their liberties, and their mutual and general welfare." The Confederation Congress consisted of equal state delegations with one vote each, and the assent of nine states was needed before Congress could conduct war, engage in diplomatic relations, requisition taxes from the states, appropriate money, or indeed do anything of significance. The confederate government acted upon states, not individuals, and Congress had no institutional means, no executive or judicial branch, to enforce its directives once they were issued.[6]

During the 1780s it became increasingly difficult for the Confederation Congress to conduct foreign relations, honor its obligations, or generate workable arrangements among the states on issues of regional or national significance. Various states refused to comply with tax requisitions of Congress, imposed discriminatory burdens on interstate commerce, entered illegal compacts, violated national treaties, waged war with the Indians, and pursued land acquisitions in the disputed western territories. Within their own borders, states sometimes encroached upon the rights of minorities and individuals, such as merchants and creditors. For example, they enacted paper money laws, or debtor relief acts, or refused to carry out treaty obligations on Tory property confiscated during the war. No central authority existed to counteract these republican mischiefs.[7]

James Madison in his April 1787 memorial, *Vices of the Political System of the United States*, complained about the weakness of the confederation government to conduct national affairs, and the "multiplicity," "mutability," and "injustice" of the laws of the states. He spoke from close-up experience, having been a member of the Confederation Congress (1780–1783) and the Virginia House of Delegates (1783–1786). This injustice in the states, he said, is the greater evil "because it brings into question the fundamental principle of republican Government, that the majority who rule . . . are the safest guardians of both public Good and of private rights." Madison then posed his main question: "Whenever . . . an apparent interest or common passion unites a majority what is to restrain them from unjust violations of the rights and interests of the minority, or of individuals?" One component of his answer was a stronger union with a functioning national government at its head. While small republics tend not to be sufficiently neutral among the different interests and factions in society, "an extensive Republic meliorates" this condition.[8]

THE PHILADELPHIA CONVENTION DRAFTS A NEW CONSTITUTION

Little more than a month later, in response to a request from the Confederation Congress, a convention of delegates assembled in Philadelphia to develop some reform suggestions for the states to consider. They soon moved beyond the idea of reforming the Articles of Confederation and proceeded during the long hot summer to draft a new Constitution with a real government at its center. The framers said in the Constitution's Preamble that the new form of government was being ordained by "We the People of the United States," in order to form a more perfect union, establish justice, ensure domestic tranquility, provide for the common defense, promote the general welfare, and secure the blessings of liberty for themselves and their posterity. Notice the transition being made from sovereign states (members of a league for their mutual benefit) to the sovereign people of the United States.

The Constitution creates a set of separated but overlapping powers between the states and the federal government, and among the three branches within the federal government. Article I vests the legislative power of the nation in a bicameral Congress, the House of Representatives composed of members chosen every second year by the people of the states, and the Senate composed of two senators from each state, chosen by the legislatures thereof for six-year terms. Every two years one-third of the Senate seats are up for reelection. Article I, section eight of the Constitution sets forth the specific powers of Congress. It can lay and collect taxes to pay the debts and provide for the common defense and general welfare of the United States; borrow money; regulate commerce with foreign nations and among the states; coin money; establish post offices and roads; promote the progress of science and the arts; declare war; raise and support military forces; exercise exclusive legislation over the nation's capital; and make laws "necessary and proper for carrying into Execution the foregoing Powers, and all other Powers vested . . . in the Government of the United States, or in any Department or Officer thereof."

Article II of the Constitution vests the executive power in the President, who is charged with taking care that the laws are faithfully executed. He is commander-in-chief of the armed forces, and with the advice and consent of the Senate can make treaties and appoint certain public officials. The President and Vice President are chosen for four-year terms by electors appointed by the states in such a manner as their legislatures may direct.

Article III of the Constitution vests the judicial power in "one Supreme Court, and in such inferior Courts as the Congress may from time to time ordain and establish." The judicial power extends to all cases arising under the Constitution, laws, and treaties of the United States; cases affecting ambassadors and other public ministers; admiralty and maritime cases; controversies to which the United States is a party; controversies between two or more states; and controversies between a state or its citizens and foreign states, citizens, or subjects. The Supreme Court has original jurisdiction in cases affecting ambassadors and other public ministers, and those in which a state is a party. In all other cases mentioned, it has "appellate Jurisdiction . . . with such Exceptions, and under such Regulations as the Congress shall make." The President, with the advice and consent of the Senate, appoints judges to the supreme and inferior courts, who hold their offices during good behavior.

Article VI says that the members of Congress and the state legislatures, and all executive and judicial officers of the United States and the states, shall be bound by oath or affirmation to support the Constitution.[9] This oath clause imposes on each department of government an obligation to make sure its actions are constitutional. To help ensure that the laws of the nation and the states stay within constitutional limits, James Madison proposed to his fellow delegates in the convention a congressional negative on state laws, and a council of revision to review bills of Congress. Specifically, he wanted to give Congress the power to negate all state laws that in its opinion contravened the articles of union, and within the federal government, he wanted the executive and a convenient number of the national judiciary to form a council of revision with authority to review bills of Congress, including congressional negatives of state law, before the bill or congressional negative could become final.[10]

Instead of authorizing Congress to negative state laws, the Constitution in article VI provides that the Constitution, laws, and treaties of the United States are the "supreme Law of the Land," and the judges in every state shall be bound thereby, "any Thing in the Constitution or laws of any State to the Contrary notwithstanding." This supremacy clause is a call for state judges in their decisions to ensure that state laws and actions presented to them for enforcement comply with the Constitution and laws of the United States. In lieu of the complicated executive-judicial council of revision procedure for bills of Congress, article II of the Constitution authorizes the President to veto bills presented to him, which veto can be overridden by a two-thirds vote of both houses of Congress.[11]

The framers discussed the congressional negative and council of revision plans on several occasions in June, July, and August, and the debates reveal a lot about their views concerning federal-state relations and the federal judicial role vis-à-vis Congress. I will cover first the congressional negative and then follow with the council of revision. On June 8 Charles Pinckney of South Carolina proposed that the national legislature should have the authority to "negative all [state] laws which they should judge to be improper." This went beyond Madison's initial plan, which merely authorized Congress to negative state laws that contravened the articles of union. Pinckney said the experience of the Articles of Confederation showed that such a universality was needed to keep the states in due subordination to the nation. Madison seconded Pinckney's motion. He regarded "an indefinite power to negative legislative acts of the States as absolutely necessary to a perfect system. Experience had evinced a constant tendency in the States to encroach on the federal authority; to violate national Treaties; to infringe the rights and interests of each other; and to oppress the weaker party within their respective jurisdictions. A negative was the mildest expedient that could be devised for preventing these mischiefs." Hugh Williamson of North Carolina wanted to let the states control their own policies. Elbridge Gerry of Massachusetts likewise objected that this congressional negative power would "enslave the states," all of which have their own separate interests. Roger Sherman preferred to define the cases when the negative could be used, but James Wilson of Pennsylvania thought this would be "impractical." We are one nation and must bury local interests. Gunning Bedford of Delaware worried that the large states would crush the smaller states in the Congress. Madison responded that the convention could lodge the negative power in the Senate, where the states have equal representation, to obviate this concern. The state delegations voted down

Charles Pinckney's motion for a congressional negative in all cases, three yeas to seven nays, with Delaware divided.[12]

Later in June, John Lansing of New York opposed the congressional negative for three reasons: (1) Congress would not have the leisure time to review all state laws. (2) The members would not be competent judges. "Will a gentleman from Georgia be a Judge of the expediency of a law which is to operate in N. Hampshire?" (3) The states will "never feel a sufficient confidence in the general Government to give it a negative on state laws."[13]

On July 17 the delegates again considered the congressional negative. Gouverneur Morris opposed it as being "terrible to the states." Such a power would not be necessary if sufficient legislative authority were given to the general government. Luther Martin of Maryland considered the negative to be improper. "Shall all the laws of the States be sent up to the General Legislature before they shall be permitted to operate?" Madison argued that the power was "essential to the efficacy and security of the General Government." We cannot rely on state tribunals to be guardians of the national authority and interests, as some delegates were suggesting. In all the states they are "more or less dependent on the Legislatures." A power to negative the improper laws of the states is the "most mild and certain means of preserving the harmony of the system." Morris reiterated his opposition. A law that ought to be negatived will be set aside in the courts, and if that security should fail, it may be repealed by a national law. The state delegations voted down the congressional negative, seven to three. Luther Martin then moved a resolution that the legislative acts and treaties of the United States shall be the "supreme law of the respective jurisdictions," so far as those acts and treaties relate to the states or their citizens, and the state judiciaries shall be bound thereby in their decisions, anything in the laws of the individual states to the contrary notwithstanding. The state delegations agreed to this unanimously.[14]

On August 23 Charles Pinckney reopened the subject with a motion that the Congress should be able to negative state laws that in its opinion interfere with the "general interests and harmony" of the union, if two-thirds of both houses agree. Roger Sherman said this was unnecessary because the laws of the general government will be supreme, as the drafted Constitution now stands. James Wilson supported Pinckney's proposal because the "firmness" of the state judges to strike down state laws which are in violation of the national Constitution is "not sufficient," and it is better to prevent the passage of an "improper law" than to declare it void later. The state delegations voted down Pinckney's motion for this revised form of a congressional negative on state laws, six to five. What survived instead was the Constitution's supremacy clause to be enforced by the judges in the states.[15]

At the beginning of the debate on the proposed council of revision, whereby the executive and some of the judiciary would be able to exercise a revisionary power over federal legislation, subject to a supermajority override in both houses of Congress, James Wilson and New York's Alexander Hamilton moved to instead give the executive an "absolute negative" on the laws. Benjamin Franklin of Pennsylvania objected to this, observing that in his state the governor had regularly used his negative to extort money for his own benefit. Franklin worried that if a negative should be adopted as proposed, "more money and power would be demanded, till at last enough would be gotten to influence and bribe the Legislature into a complete subjection to the will of the Executive." Roger Sherman spoke against "enabling any one man to stop the will of the whole. No man could be found so far above all the rest in wisdom." Madison supposed that if a proper proportion of each branch of the legislature should be required to overrule the objections of the executive, it would "answer the same purpose as an absolute negative." Gunning Bedford opposed having any check on the legislature. It would be a sufficient security for the rights of the other departments to mark out in the Constitution the boundaries of the legislative authority. The representatives of the people are the best judges of what is for their interest. "The two branches would produce a sufficient control within the Legislature itself." The state delegations ultimately voted unanimously against an absolute executive negative.

Following this initial colloquy, two main views contended for support. James Madison and James Wilson most persistently, joined by Gouverneur Morris, George Mason, and John Mercer of Maryland, argued for a combined executive-judicial revisionary power with a legislative override. They wanted to reinforce the executive with the influence of the judicial department. Madison said whether the object is to restrain the legislature from encroaching on the other departments, or on the rights of the people, or from passing laws unwise in principle or improper in form, annexing the wisdom and weight of the judiciary to the executive is a good idea. This would help to preserve a "consistency, conciseness, perspicuity and technical propriety in the laws," ingredients shamefully wanting in our republican codes. Even with this executive-judicial cooperation the legislature might still be "an overmatch for them. Experience in all the States had evinced a powerful tendency in the Legislature to absorb all power into its vortex." This was the "real source of danger to the American Constitutions; and suggested the necessity of giving every defensive authority to the other departments that was consistent with republican principles." When someone objected that the participation of the judiciary in the legislative process would violate the principle of separate powers, Madison answered that a strengthened veto would be an "auxiliary precaution in favor of the maxim." Moreover, a rigid separation of powers theory was already compromised by the proposal for an executive veto power over legislation.

James Wilson noted that although it had been said the judges, as "expositors" of the laws, could defend their constitutional rights, this would be insufficient because laws may be unwise, unjust, dangerous, or destructive, and yet "may not be so unconstitutional as to justify the Judges in refusing to give them effect." Gouverneur Morris "concurred in thinking the public liberty in greater danger from Legislative usurpations than from any other source." Emissions of paper money, a remission of debts, and other "largesses to the people" will sometimes be popular and pushed for that reason. George Mason noted that, notwithstanding the precautions which have been taken, the constitution of the national legislature so much resembles that of the individual states that it "must be expected frequently to pass unjust and pernicious laws." A restraining power is therefore needed. It has been said the judges will have a double negative if they are joined up front with the executive to check proposed legislative enactments and then can strike down enacted laws in deciding cases. This is not true because in their expositions of the laws, they can declare a law void only if it is "plainly unconstitutional." All other laws, "however unjust oppressive or pernicious," the courts will be obliged to enforce. John Mercer supported the idea that judges should be allowed to participate up front in the revisionary power. "He disapproved of the Doctrine that the Judges as expositors of the Constitution should have authority to declare a law void," believing instead that "laws ought to be well and cautiously made, and then to be uncontrollable."

The convention eventually settled upon a rival plan pushed by Elbridge Gerry, an executive veto unsupported by the judiciary, with Congress having the ability to override the veto by two-thirds majorities in both houses. Gerry said the judiciary would have a sufficient check against encroachments on their own department by their exposition of the laws, "which involved a power of deciding on their Constitutionality. In some States the Judges had actually set aside laws as being against the [State] Constitution. This was done too with general approbation. It is quite foreign from the nature of their office to make them judges of the policy of public measures." The object of the revisionary power is to allow the executive to defend his department against legislative encroachment, which he can do on his own. The council of revision "was combining and mixing together the Legislative and the other departments. . . . It was making Statesmen of the Judges; and setting them up as the guardians of the Rights of the people." Gerry instead preferred to rely on the elected representatives of the people to be the "guardians of their Rights and interests." Do not make "the Expositors of the laws, the Legislators" too.

Rufus King of Massachusetts preferred that the executive act alone in order to preserve his "responsibility." His fellow state delegate Nathaniel Gorham did not see the advantage of employing the judges in the exercise of the revisionary power, as they "are not to be presumed to possess any peculiar knowledge of the mere policy of public measures." Luther Martin considered the association of the judges with the executive a "dangerous innovation" which could claim no advantage. "A knowledge of Mankind, and of Legislative affairs cannot be presumed to belong in a higher degree to the Judges than to the Legislature. And as to the Constitutionality of laws, that point will come before the Judges in their proper official character. In this character they have a negative on the laws. Join them with the Executive in the Revision and they will have a double negative." In one final failed effort, on August 15, Madison moved "that all acts before they become laws should be submitted both to the Executive and Supreme Judiciary Departments, that if either of these should object two-thirds of each House, if both should object, three-fourths of each House, should be necessary to overrule the objections and give to the acts the force of law." Elbridge Gerry said the motion came to the same thing as what had already been rejected more than once, and the convention agreed with him, eight to three.[16] The Constitution accepts the bicameral legislature and the executive veto as sufficient protections to keep Congress within the limitations of the Constitution.

SOME CONTROLS AND PROHIBITIONS BUT NO BILL OF RIGHTS

In addition to resolving the major issues of government power, structure, and representation, and addressing relations among the three federal branches and between the general government and the states, the framers in the Philadelphia convention adopted some specific controls and prohibitions on government. They placed several provisions in article IV of the Constitution to control the conduct of the states in their interactions with each other. Article IV, section one requires that full faith and credit be given in each state to the laws and judicial proceedings of every other state. Section two contains three requirements. The citizens of each state shall be entitled to the privileges and immunities of citizens in the several states. A person charged with crime in any state who flees from justice, and is found in another state, shall upon request be returned to the state from which he has fled. No person "held to service or Labor" in one state, under the laws thereof, escaping into another, shall be discharged from such service or labor under the laws of that other state, but "shall be delivered up on claim of the Party to whom such Service or Labor may be due." These article IV clauses deal with the subjects of full faith and credit, citizen privileges and immunities, criminal extraditions, and fugitive slaves, respectively.[17]

As for prohibitions, article I, section nine applies to the federal government. Among other things, it stipulates that the privilege of the writ of habeas corpus shall not be suspended unless the public safety requires it in a case of rebellion or invasion; no bill of attainder or ex post facto law shall be passed; no exports from any state shall be taxed; no money shall be drawn from the treasury except in consequence of appropriations made by law; and no title of nobility shall be conferred.

Article I, section ten provides that no state shall enter any treaty or alliance; coin money; emit bills of credit; make anything but gold and silver coin a tender of payment of debts; pass a bill of attainder, ex post facto law, or law impairing the obligation of contracts; or grant any title of nobility. No state shall, without the consent of Congress, lay any duties on imports or exports except what may be necessary for executing its inspection laws. No state shall, without the consent of Congress, keep troops or ships of war in time of peace, enter a compact with any other state or with a foreign power, or engage in war unless invaded or in such imminent danger as will not admit of delay.[18]

These are the conditions and prohibitions on government that the convention delegates agreed to put in the Constitution. Others failed to make the cut. In the final days at Philadelphia, on September 12, George Mason said he wished the plan had been prefaced with a bill of rights, and he would second a motion if made for the purpose. "It would give great quiet to the people, and with the aid of the State declarations, a bill might be prepared in a few hours." Elbridge Gerry moved for a committee to prepare a bill of rights, and Mason seconded the motion. Roger Sherman said the state declarations of rights are not repealed by this Constitution, and being in force are sufficient. Mason replied that the laws of the United States are to be paramount to state bills of rights. On the question for a committee to prepare a bill of rights, the state delegations at the convention unanimously voted "no." Two days later, Charles Cotesworth Pinckney of South Carolina and Gerry moved to insert into the article I, section nine, prohibitions on Congress a declaration "that the liberty of the Press should be inviolably observed." Sherman remarked, "It is unnecessary. The power of Congress does not extend to the Press." On the question, the motion was defeated, seven states to four, the "ayes" being Massachusetts, Maryland, Virginia, and South Carolina.[19]

Three of the delegates refused to sign the completed Constitution. Governor Randolph feared the indefinite and dangerous powers of Congress, and made a motion that some provision should be made for the state ratification conventions to offer amendments to be submitted to and decided on by a second general convention. His Virginia colleague George Mason seconded the motion, commented on the dangerous power and structure of the government, and concluded that it would probably end either in a monarchy or a tyrannical aristocracy. This convention had been formed without the knowledge or idea of the people; a second one would know more of the sense of the people and be able to provide a system "more consonant with it." Elbridge Gerry followed with eleven objections to the plan, and like Randolph and Mason, said that he could not sign the document without a stipulation for a second convention. All the state delegations answered "no" to Randolph's motion for a provision calling for state conventions to offer amendments in preparation for a second convention, answered "aye" to the Constitution, and adjourned.[20]

ELEVEN STATES RATIFY, INCLUDING SOME THAT PROPOSE AMENDMENTS

The Confederation Congress received the proposed new Constitution and submitted it to the states for their consideration. This in turn generated a variety of responses. Supporters of the Constitution became generally known as Federalists, and the opponents, Anti-Federalists. In a referendum the people of Rhode Island rejected the Constitution, 2,711 to 239. The other twelve states decided to hold conventions, and all of them except North Carolina voted to accept the Constitution. Delaware ratified first, December 7, 1787 (30 to 0), followed by Pennsylvania, December 12, 1787 (46 to 23); New Jersey, December 18, 1787 (38 to 0); Georgia, December 31, 1787 (26 to 0); Connecticut, January 9, 1788 (128 to 40); Massachusetts, February 6, 1788 (187 to 168); Maryland, April 26, 1788 (63 to 11); South Carolina, May 29, 1788 (149 to 73); New Hampshire, June 21, 1788 (57 to 47); Virginia, June 25, 1788 (89 to 79); and New York, July 26, 1788 (30 to 27).[21]

Several of the state conventions ratified the Constitution without engaging in public debate or recommending any changes. Others debated the Constitution, and in one form or another they proposed amendments for future consideration. In Pennsylvania, the minority offered fourteen amendments which they wanted to be part of the state's conditional approval of the Constitution. When the convention rejected this plan for a ratification conditioned upon the acceptance of the desired modifications, the minority published their amendments in the local press. In Maryland too, the Anti-Federalist minority failed to obtain support for a conditional approval based on their twenty proposed amendments, which they then published in the press.

In Massachusetts, the Federalist leadership participated in drafting nine amendments to procure the delegates' acceptance of the Constitution. The convention adopted the amendments not as a prior condition for ratification of the Constitution, but to be taken up by the new federal government once it was established and in operation. Other closely divided state conventions followed the Massachusetts formula by ratifying the Constitution without condition, and then including with their decision documents amendments for Congress to consider. New Hampshire copied the nine Massachusetts amendments and added three of its own. Virginia proposed a bill or declaration of rights consisting of twenty articles and accompanied it with a set of twenty-one additional amendments. New York developed two groups of amendments, twenty-four and thirty-two in number. Finally, on August 2, 1788, North Carolina copied for its own use the Virginia declaration of rights (twenty articles), and withheld its ratification pending the nation's adoption of proposed changes.

All told, according to one compilation, eight states submitted a total of 210 amendments, and with duplications omitted, these included nearly one hundred different substantive provisions. Some of the proposals targeted the plan of government, decisions the framers had made about powers and structure and representation; others wanted to build in guarantees for the states; and still others suggested protections for individual rights and liberties. New York in a circular letter to the states, and Virginia and North Carolina in their submissions to the Confederation Congress, requested that a second national convention be called to overhaul the Constitution.[22] The struggle to gain acceptance of the Constitution in the state conventions and among the general population was protracted and intense.

THE FEDERALISTS' RESPONSE: THE CONSTITUTION NEEDS NO BILL OF RIGHTS

The Federalists in the state conventions and in the press responded to the Anti-Federalist arguments against the Constitution, including their demands for a bill of rights. Leading Federalists such as James Wilson and Thomas McKean in the Pennsylvania convention, Oliver Ellsworth in Connecticut, and James Iredell in North Carolina, among others, argued that a bill of rights was both unnecessary and potentially dangerous. It was unnecessary because, in contrast to the states, where the people vested in their governments all powers and rights which they did not reserve to themselves in a statement of their rights, the federal government can exercise only those powers which are delegated to it. Everything not given up is retained by the states or the people. Moreover, a bill of rights could be dangerous, because any enumeration of the rights reserved to the people necessarily would be incomplete, and whatever is not included in the list would be presumed to be powers given to the government.[23]

The *Federalist Papers*, written mostly by Madison and Hamilton, constituted the most elaborate and sophisticated analysis and defense of the Constitution. Eighty-five in number, written anonymously under the pseudonym of "Publius," and addressed to the people of New York, the major themes of the *Federalist Papers* were federalism, checks and balances, separated powers, pluralism, and representation. In sequence from October 1787 to May 1788 Publius described the deficiencies of the Articles of Confederation form of government, characterized the Constitution as a product of compromise, explained and justified the federal government's quantity of powers, the separation of powers, the House of Representatives, the Senate, and the executive and judicial departments, and finished with Hamilton's essay on why no bill of rights was needed.[24]

In *Federalist Paper No. 38* Madison reviewed the numerous objections to the plan with some exasperation:

> This one tells us that the proposed constitution ought to be rejected because it is not a confederation of States, but a Government over individuals. Another admits that it ought to be a government over individuals, to a certain extent, but by no means to the extent proposed. A third does not object to the Government over individuals, or to the extent proposed, but to the want of a bill of rights. A fourth concurs in the absolute necessity of a bill of rights, but contends that it ought to be declaratory not of the personal rights of individuals, but of the rights reserved to the States in their political capacity. A fifth opinion is that a bill of rights of any sort would be superfluous and misplaced, and that the plan would be unexceptionable, but for the fatal power of [Congress] regulating the times and places of election [in the states]. An objector in a large State exclaims loudly against the unreasonable equality of representation in the Senate. An objector in a small State is equally loud against the dangerous inequality in the house of representatives. . . . A patriot in a State that does not import or export, discerns insuperable objections against a direct tax. A patriot in a State of great export and imports is no less dissatisfied that the whole burden of taxes may be thrown on consumption. This Politician discovers in the constitution a direct and irresistible tendency to monarchy. That is equally sure, it will end in aristocracy.

Madison added more examples to the list, and concluded that it was a matter of "wonder and regret" that those who raised many objections against the new Constitution seemed to ignore the defects of the current one. It is unnecessary that the Constitution should be perfect, only that it be better than the one it will replace.[25]

In *Federalist Papers No. 10 and 51* Madison explained why the federal government would not endanger the rights of minorities and individuals. *No. 10* noted that a well-constructed union breaks and controls the violence of faction. A faction means citizens who are united and activated by some common passion or interest adverse to the rights of other citizens or to the aggregate interests of the community. The causes of faction cannot be removed while the people enjoy liberty, so relief must be sought by controlling its effects. If a faction consists of less than a majority, relief is supplied by the republican principle of majority rule. When a majority forms a faction, to secure the public good and private rights against such a faction, and at the same time preserve the spirit and form of popular government, is the great object to be pursued. Extend the sphere, and you take in a greater variety of parties and interests, you make it less probable that a majority of the whole will have a common motive to invade the rights of other citizens. The advantage which a republic has over a democracy, in controlling the effects of faction, is enjoyed by a large over a small republic, and is enjoyed by the union over the states composing it. A rage for paper money, for an abolition of debts, for an equal division of property, or for any other improper or wicked project will be less apt to pervade the whole body of the union than a particular member of it. In the extent and proper structure of the union we behold a republican remedy for the diseases most incident to republican government.

No. 51 observed that in the "compound republic of America" the power surrendered by the people is divided between two governments, state and federal, and within each is subdivided among distinct and separate departments. "Hence a double security arises to the rights of the people." It is important not only to guard society against the oppression of its rulers, but to guard one part of society against the injustice of the other part. In the federal republic of the United States, while all authority is derived from and dependent on society, the society itself will be divided into so many parts, interests, and classes of citizens, that the rights of individuals or the minority will be in little danger from interested combinations of the majority. Notwithstanding the contrary opinions which have been entertained on the subject, in fact the larger the society, the more capable it will be of self-government. "And happily for the *republican cause*, the practicable sphere may be carried to a very great extent by a judicious modification and mixture of the *federal principle*" (emphasis in the original).[26]

In *Federalist Paper No. 84* Hamilton directly addressed the objection that the plan of the Philadelphia convention contained no bill of rights. Some of the states have no bill of rights, and they are as free as those that do. The Constitution does contain some provisions, mostly in article I, section nine, and in article III, that offer security to liberty and republicanism. In their origins bills of rights are stipulations between kings and their subjects. Such was Magna Carta, obtained by the barons from King John. Such was the declaration of rights presented by the English Parliament to William of Orange in 1688, and afterward "thrown into an act of parliament, called the bill of rights." But in a Constitution "founded upon the power of the people, and executed by their immediate representatives and servants," continued Hamilton, the people retain everything and have no need of particular reservations. Bills of rights are "not only unnecessary in the proposed constitution, but would even be dangerous. They would contain various exceptions to powers which are not granted, and on this very account, would afford a colorable pretext to claim more than were granted." For why declare that things shall not be done when there is no power to do them? A related problem is definition and scope. What signifies a declaration that "liberty of the press shall be free?" for example. Who can give it any definition that would not leave the "utmost latitude for evasion?" Hamilton concluded with a flourish: The Constitution is "in every rational sense, and to every useful purpose, A BILL OF RIGHTS."[27]

MADISON AND JEFFERSON DISCUSS RIGHTS

Madison's thoughts about the Constitution and his movement from indifference to support for a bill of rights can be traced in his correspondence with Jefferson, who was serving as the United States' minister to France and living in Paris at the time. In an October 24, 1787 letter, Madison summarized the main points of the Constitution recently drafted in Philadelphia. It was generally agreed that the objects of the union could not be achieved by any system founded on the principle of a confederation of sovereign states. Hence was embraced the alternative of a government which instead of operating on the states would operate on the individuals composing them. This groundwork being laid, the great objects to be achieved were to write a proper energy in the executive and a proper stability in the legislature, with the essential character of a republic, and to give the general government every power requisite for general purposes, leaving to the states every power which might be beneficially administered by them. He noted the difficult compromises that had to be made to procure agreement, his strong disappointment at failing to achieve a congressional "negative on the laws of the states," his often-repeated argument that private rights would be more secure under the guardianship of the checked-and-balanced and extended regime of the general government than under the more compact spheres of the state governments, and concluded by saying that he hoped for success in the ratification campaign.

Jefferson replied that he liked the general idea of framing a government which could operate peacefully "without needing the continued recurrence to the States," the organization into legislative, executive, and judicial branches, the power given to the legislature to levy taxes, and the negative given to the executive with a third of either house. However, he did not like the omission of a bill of rights providing "clearly . . . for freedom of religion, freedom of the press, protection against standing armies, restriction on monopolies, the eternal and unremitting force of the habeas corpus laws, and trial by jury in all matters of fact triable by the laws of the land." A "bill of rights is what the people are entitled to against every government on earth, general or particular, and what no just government should refuse, or rest on inference."[28]

Following the successful ratification campaign, in an October 17, 1788, letter to Jefferson, Madison enclosed a pamphlet to give a "collective view" of the many alterations that had been proposed for the new Constitution. Not a few people, particularly in Virginia, have contended for amendments "from the most honorable and patriotic motives," and among the advocates for the Constitution "there are some who wish for further guards to public liberty and individual rights." Madison was willing to support a bill of rights because it is desired by others, and "if properly executed could not be of disservice." At the same time, he gave four reasons why he had not viewed this in an important light:

> 1. Because I conceive that in a certain degree . . . the rights in question are reserved by the manner in which the federal powers are granted. 2. Because there is great reason to fear that a positive declaration of some of the most essential rights could not be obtained in the requisite latitude. . . . 3. Because the limited powers of the federal Government and the jealousy of the subordinate Governments, afford a security which has not existed in the case of the State Governments, and exists in no other. 4. Because experience proves the inefficacy of a bill of rights on those occasions when its control is most needed. Repeated violations of these parchment barriers have been committed by overbearing majorities in every State.

In our governments, Madison continued, the real power lies with the majority in the community, not with their elected officials. Even so, he could see two uses for a bill of rights. First, political truths declared in a solemn manner may "become incorporated with the national sentiment, [and thereby] counteract the impulses of passion and interest." Second, there may be occasions where the evil springs from the government itself, and then "a bill of rights will be a good ground for an appeal to the sense of the community."[29]

In his belated reply of March 24, 1789, Jefferson added one more argument to the two points Madison had mentioned in his lukewarm support for a bill of rights: "the legal check which it puts into the hands of the judiciary." He then gave brief answers to Madison's four reasons why a bill of rights was not important. 1. The rights in question are reserved by the way the federal powers are granted. Answer: While the federal government has limited powers, we should guard against "their abuses of power within the field submitted to them." 2. "A positive declaration of some essential rights could not be obtained in the requisite latitude." Answer: "Half a loaf is better than no bread." 3. The jealousy of the states will afford protection against federal abuses. Answer: The state governments are only agents. "They must have principles furnished them whereon to found their opposition." 4. Experience proves the inefficacy of a bill of rights. Answer: "True. But though it is not absolutely efficacious in all circumstances, it is of great potency always, and rarely inefficacious."

By this time Jefferson knew that Madison had become committed to the project of a federal bill of rights. Madison had said as much in public letters he had issued during his successful campaign in Virginia for a seat in the House of Representatives. Therefore, Jefferson concluded his letter with the observation that he was "pleased with the prospect that a declaration of rights will be added" and hoped it will be done in a way "which will not endanger the whole frame of government, or any essential part of it."[30] Regarding this last point about preserving the essence of the Constitution, we will see that in his push for some constitutional amendments in the First Congress, Madison would be careful to protect and preserve the delegated powers, structure, and representation principles of government embodied in the Constitution of 1788. He would work to ameliorate the fears of some Anti-Federalists but would not compromise or modify any element of the strengthened federal authority.

NOTES

1. Daniel J. Elazar, "Our Thoroughly Federal Constitution," in Robert A. Goldwin and William A. Schambra, eds., *How Federal is the Constitution?* (Washington, DC: American Enterprise Institute, 1987), 56.

2. Alfred H. Kelly, Winifred A. Harbison, and Herman Belz, *The American Constitution: Its Origins and Development* (New York: W.W. Norton & Co., 7th ed., vol. 1, 1991), 56–61.

3. Ibid., 59, 60, and Appendix 1; Donald S. Lutz, *The Origins of American Constitutionalism* (Baton Rouge: Louisiana State University Press, 1988), 113; George Anastaplo, "The Declaration of Independence," 9 *Saint Louis University Law Journal* 390, 391(1965).

4. Francis N. Thorpe, ed., *The Federal and State Constitutions, Colonial Charters, and Other Organic Laws of the United States* (Washington, DC: Government Printing Office, 7 vols., 1909), 3812–13 (Virginia), 2453–54 (New Hampshire).

5. Lutz, *Origins of Am. Constitutionalism*, 94–95.

6. Kelly et al., *Am. Const.* Appendix Two.

7. For the history of the Confederation era, see Merrill Jensen, *The New Nation: A History of the United States during the Confederation, 1781–1788* (New York:

Alfred A. Knopf, 1950); Gordon S. Wood, *The Creation of the American Republic, 1776–1787* (Chapel Hill: University of North Carolina Press, 1969).

8. *Vices*, reprinted in Jack N. Rakove, comp., *James Madison Writings* (New York: Library Classics of the United States, Inc., 1999), 69–80.

9. Kelly et al., *Am. Const.* Appendix Three has the Constitution.

10. Adrienne Koch, ed., *Notes on Debates in the Federal Convention of 1787 Reported by James Madison* (New York: W.W. Norton & Co., 1987), 30–32, has the congressional negative and the council of revision plans, resolutions six and eight, respectively, in the Virginia Plan, which was written by Madison.

11. U.S. Const., arts. II and VI, in Kelly et al., *Am. Const.* Appendix Three.

12. Koch, ed., *Madison's Notes on Convention,* 88–92.

13. Ibid., 121–22, 156–57.

14. Ibid., 302–7.

15. Ibid., 518–19.

16. The debates on the council of revision occurred on June 4 and 6, July 21, and August 15. See ibid., 61–67, 79–81, 336–43, and 461–62.

17. U.S. Const., art. IV, secs. 1 and 2, in Kelly et al., *Am. Const.* Appendix Three. Three of the clauses—full faith and credit, privileges and immunities, and criminal extradition—were drawn from article IV of the Articles of Confederation. Only the fugitive slave clause was new. The framers of the Constitution carefully avoided any mention of "blacks" or "slaves" in the document. This is evidenced in the wording of the fugitive slave clause, as well as several other provisions which deal directly or indirectly with slavery.

18. Most of the provisions in article I, sections 9 and 10, were drafted in the convention's five-member committee of detail, after that body received a referral on August 20 of a proposed set of limitations on government from Charles Cotesworth Pinckney. Koch, ed., *Madison's Notes on Convention*, 485–87. Kelly et al., *Am Const.* Appendix Three, Constitution art. I, secs. 9 and 10.

19. Koch, ed., *Madison's Notes on Convention*, 630, 640.

20. Ibid., 650–51. A few others, such as Richard Yates and John Lansing of New York and Luther Martin of Maryland, had earlier left the convention when they became dissatisfied with the direction it was headed, shifting substantial power from the states to the federal government.

21. Michael G. Kammen, ed., *The Origins of the American Constitution: A Documentary History* (New York: Penguin Press, 1986), xxvii–ix.

22. Carol Berkin, *The Bill of Rights: The Fight to Secure America's Liberties* (New York Simon & Schuster, 2017), 26–31; Bernard Bailyn, ed., *The Debate on the Constitution: Federalist and Antifederalist Speeches, Articles, and Letters During the Struggle over Ratification* (New York: Library of America, 1999), Part One, 526–52, and Part Two, 536–72. Bernard Schwartz, ed., *The Bill of Rights: A Documentary History* (New York: Chelsea House Publishers, vol. 2, 1971), 983 presents the numbers on the Anti-Federalists' amendments.

23. Leonard W. Levy, *Seasoned Judgments: The American Constitution, Rights, and History* (New Brunswick (USA): Transaction Publishers, 1995), 3–5, discusses the Federalist position on a bill of rights.

24. Garry Wills, ed., *The Federalist Papers by Alexander Hamilton, James Madison and John Jay* (New York: Bantam Books, 1982), vii–xxvii.

25. Ibid., 182–89.

26. Ibid., 42–49, and 261–65.

27. Ibid., 434–43.

28. Kammen, ed., *Origins of Const.*, 65–71 (Madison letter), 90–93 (Jefferson reply, December 20, 1787).

29. Ibid., 367–71.

30. Ibid., 376–78. In a December 8, 1788, letter to Jefferson, Madison had written that the "friends of the Constitution, some from an approbation of particular amendments, others from a spirit of conciliation, are generally agreed that the System should be revised. But they wish the revisal to be carried no farther than to supply additional guards for liberty, without abridging the sum of power transferred from the States to the general Government." Those who have opposed the Constitution, on the other hand, are "zealous for a second Convention." They seek sweeping changes, extending "at least as far as alterations have been proposed by any State." Ibid., 374–76. During his campaign for election to the House of Representatives, in January 1789, Madison had written several public letters explaining his moderate federalism and his approval of the concept of amendments incorporating a bill of rights. See Ralph Ketchum, *James Madison, A Biography* (Charlottesville: University Press of Virginia, 1990), 176.

Chapter 3

The Original Meaning of the Bill of Rights

This chapter considers the legislative history of the Bill of Rights, drafted by the First Congress in 1789 and ratified by the states over the next two years. This history sheds light on the original meaning and purpose of the amendments, both in their entirety as a project, and in some of the provisions, such as the First and Second Amendments, the Fifth Amendment due process of law clause, the Eighth Amendment cruel and unusual punishment clause, and the Ninth and Tenth Amendments. Just as James Madison has been called the Father of the Constitution because of his influential role in the Philadelphia convention which drafted it, he can rightfully be called the Father of the Bill of Rights because of his work in the First Congress.

Madison accomplished a lot, but not everything he wanted, in each situation. In the constitutional convention (1787), he failed to gain approval for a congressional supervisory and veto power over the laws of the states. And in the First Congress, his proposed amendment to the Constitution, stipulating that "No State shall abridge the right of trial by Jury in criminal cases, nor the rights of conscience, nor the freedom of speech, or of the press," passed in the House but was deleted by the Senate. Madison's desire for a congressional supervisory and veto power over the laws of the states, which the constitutional convention voted down, would later be embodied in section five of the Fourteenth Amendment (1868), adopted in the wake of the Civil War. The rights embodied in his only amendment intended to control the actions of the states, which the First Congress refused to include in the Bill of Rights package, eventually would be applied to the states by the courts under section one of the Fourteenth Amendment.

MADISON'S MILD JUSTIFICATION FOR AMENDMENTS

In his opening message to the Federalist-dominated First Congress, April 30, 1789, President George Washington said it will remain in your judgment to decide how far the exercise of the amendment power in article V of the Constitution is rendered expedient by the "nature of objections which have been urged against the system, or by the degree of inquietude which has given birth to them." While you avoid every alteration which might endanger effective government, or which should await future experience, "a reverence for the characteristic rights of freemen, and a regard for public harmony," will influence your deliberation on the question of how the rights can be fortified, or the harmony be safely promoted.[1]

Meanwhile, Madison was studying the state ratification conventions' proposals for change in his preparation of a group of amendments he would ask Congress to incorporate into the preamble and body of the Constitution, mostly as additions to article I, section nine, and article III. Commentators have found considerable overlap between the recommendations from the state conventions and the first ten amendments to the Constitution, amendments which in the twentieth century would become known collectively as the Bill of Rights. According to Bernard Schwartz, for example, all eight states which proposed amendments recommended a provision like the one ultimately included in the Tenth Amendment, reserving to the states or the people powers not delegated to the federal government. Seven states wanted a guarantee of jury trial in civil cases. Six asked for protection for religious freedom. Five sought guarantees of freedom of the press (with three of them adding freedom of speech). Five asked for confirmation of the right to bear arms; a right to trial by jury in the local district; a prohibition against compelled quartering of troops; and a right against unreasonable searches and seizures. Four states requested protection for the following rights: no abridgement of any person's life, liberty, or property except by the "law of the land" (proposed by three states), or by due process of law (proposed by New York); speedy public trial; assembly and petition; and against excessive bail and fines and cruel and unusual punishment. Of the twenty-two amendments supported by four or more states, fourteen were incorporated by Madison into his recommendations to Congress.[2]

In his major speech to the House of Representatives, June 8, 1789, Madison gave his reasons for seeking revisions to the Constitution during the very first session of Congress. He wanted to "render it as acceptable to the whole people of the United States as it has been found acceptable to a majority of them." Notwithstanding the ratification of the Constitution by eleven states, some unanimously and others by large majorities, still many constituents are dissatisfied with it, "among whom are many respectable for their talents, their patriotism, and respectable for the jealousies they have for their liberty, which, though mistaken in its object, is laudable in its motive." If all power is subject to abuse, then abuse of the federal government's powers may be "guarded against in a more secure manner than is now done, while no one advantage arising from the exercise of that power shall be damaged or endangered by it." We have something to gain, and if we proceed with caution, nothing to lose. It is necessary to proceed with caution because "we must feel for the Constitution itself, and make that revisal a moderate one."

Madison offered his amendments, gave justifications for some of them, countered the mainstream Federalist objections to a bill of rights (including previous ones of his own), and added a few other observations. The greatest danger to liberty in a system like ours is "not found with the executive or legislative departments of government, but in the body of the people, operating by the majority against the minority." It may be thought "all paper barriers against the power of the community are too weak to be worthy of attention." Yet they are not useless. As they "have a tendency to impress some degree of respect for them, to establish the public opinion in their favor, it may be one mean to control the majority from those acts to which they might be otherwise inclined." He drew on Thomas Jefferson's argument to say that if a bill of rights is incorporated into the Constitution, "independent tribunals of justice will consider themselves . . . the guardians of those rights." There is also a "great probability that such a declaration in the federal system would be enforced because the state legislatures will jealously and closely watch the operations of this government." They will be able to resist "with more effect every assumption of power than any other power on earth can do." Thus, "if we can make the Constitution better in the opinion of those who are opposed to it, without weakening its frame, or abridging its usefulness, in the judgment of those who are attached to it, we act the part of wise and liberal men to make such alterations as shall produce the effect."[3]

THE FIRST CONGRESS ENACTS AMENDMENTS FOR THE STATES TO CONSIDER

In presenting his amendments and asking for prompt consideration by the House, Madison faced opposition to quick action from many Federalist members. Some saw no need for amendments; some wanted to focus on the necessary business of organizing the government, raising revenue, and establishing several executive departments and the judiciary; and some preferred to await the passage of time until experience could demonstrate what if any changes needed to be made to the system. The Anti-Federalists for their part wanted to overhaul the federal government in major ways and to reinvigorate states' rights, perhaps at a second federal convention. Just as Madison hoped by his proposed amendments to win over many of the opposition forces, including in the two states yet to join the union, it was tempting for the Anti-Federalists in Congress to delay or obstruct rights measures whose acceptance could undermine support for more basic change.[4]

The House received Madison's amendments and set them aside, not to be brought up again until July 21. On that day the House referred Madison's amendments and all the other state-proposed amendments to a special committee of eleven, consisting of one representative from each state. Madison served as the member from Virginia. The committee reported back a week later, and on August 13–22 the House debated the amendments, modified some of the provisions, and sent the package to the Senate. In early September the Senate spent a week on the seventeen amendments it had received from the House, reduced them to twelve in number, made various changes of style and substance, and on September 14 sent its revision back to the House. A week later a conference committee of six convened to resolve the differences. All six of the members were Federalists, and Madison was among them. Three days later (September 24) the conference committee issued its report, approving the Senate version with two changes. The House and Senate accepted the committee's report, and President Washington sent the twelve amendments to the states for ratification.[5]

When Madison introduced his articles of amendment in the House, his plan was to incorporate them into the Constitution, not add them as a separate supplement. But in the August debate, Roger Sherman of Connecticut said he did not want to "interweave our propositions into the work itself, because it will be destructive of the whole fabric." It would make the document confusing to incorporate such "heterogeneous articles." Also, it is questionable whether the Congress has the right to propose amendments in this way. The Constitution is the act of the people, and it should remain entire. The amendments will be the act of the state governments. Madison replied that it would be easier to understand the amendments if they are interwoven into the parts to which they relate. After some arguments on both sides of this form issue, the House decided to place the amendments as a supplement to the Constitution.[6]

The Senate reduced the House's articles of amendment from seventeen to twelve by deleting two of them and combining others. It deleted the fourteenth and sixteenth articles. In contrast to the House, the Senate did not record its debates, so at best we can make only educated guesses as to why the deletions were made. Article fourteen provided that "No State shall infringe the right of trial by Jury in criminal cases, nor the rights of conscience, nor the freedom of speech, or of the press." When the House briefly considered this state-focused amendment, Thomas Tucker, an Anti-Federalist representative from South Carolina, moved to strike out these words. He wanted to "leave the State Governments to themselves, and not to *interfere* with them more than we already do" (Tucker's emphasis). Madison responded that he "conceived this to be the most valuable amendment on the list." It is easy to see why Madison considered this to be the most important of his amendments, for two reasons. First, he did not believe the other amendments changed the nature and operation of the federal government as it had been created in the Constitution. It had no authority to do any of the things that the general list of guarantees and restraints said could not be done. Second, he thought the state governments posed the most danger to minority and individual rights, rather than the extended, checked-and-balanced, and filtered federal government, with its limited, delegated powers. To impose duties on the states in the important matters of jury trial in criminal cases, the rights of conscience, and the freedoms of speech and press would represent a meaningful change in the constitutional relationship between individuals and their government. The House rejected Tucker's motion without more debate. Presumably the Senate was responsive to states' rights sentiment when it rejected the fourteenth article.[7] After all, its members were chosen by the state legislatures.

The sixteenth article reiterated the separation of powers principle already embodied in the Constitution: "The powers delegated by the Constitution to the Government of the United States shall be exercised as therein appropriated, so that the Legislative shall never exercise the powers vested in the Executive or Judicial; nor the Executive the powers vested in the Legislative or Judicial; nor the Judicial the powers vested in the Legislative or Executive." In the House Roger Sherman conceived the amendment to be "altogether unnecessary inasmuch as the constitution assigned the business of each branch of the Government to a separate department." Madison in response "supposed the people would be gratified with the amendment, as it was admitted that the powers ought to be separate and distinct; it might also tend to an explanation of some doubts that might arise respecting the construction of the constitution." Without further argument the House agreed to retain this article confirming the separation of powers among the three branches of the federal government. Presumably, in removing the article the Senate agreed with Sherman that it was superfluous, merely stating something that was already provided in the instrument.[8]

TEN AMENDMENTS ARE RATIFIED

Although the Congress sent out to the states twelve articles of amendment, the states failed to ratify the first two. The first article allowed Congress to regulate the amount and ratio of representation in the House of Representatives. After the first census, there would be at least one hundred representatives (and at least one representative for every forty thousand persons), until the number of representatives reached two hundred, after which there would be at least two hundred representatives (and at least one representative for every fifty thousand persons). The second article stipulated that any increase in compensation that members of Congress voted for themselves could not take effect until after the next election.[9] The remaining ten articles were ratified, and they read as follows:

> First Amendment: Congress shall make no law respecting an establishment of religion, or prohibiting the free exercise thereof, or abridging the freedom of speech, or of the press, or the right of the people peaceably to assemble and to petition the government for a redress of grievances.
>
> Second Amendment: A well regulated Militia, being necessary to the security of a free State, the right of the people to keep and bear Arms, shall not be infringed.
>
> Third Amendment: No Soldier shall in time of peace be quartered in any house without the consent of the Owner, nor in time of war, but in a manner to be prescribed by law.
>
> Fourth Amendment: The right of the people to be secure in their persons, houses, papers and effects against unreasonable searches and seizures shall not be violated, and no Warrants shall issue, but upon probable cause supported by Oath or affirmation, and particularly describing the place to be searched, and the persons or things to be seized.
>
> Fifth Amendment: No person shall be held to answer for a capital or otherwise infamous crime, unless on a presentment or indictment of a Grand Jury, except in cases arising in the land or naval forces, or in the Militia, when in actual service in time of war or public danger; nor shall any person be subject for the same offence to be twice put in jeopardy of life or limb; nor be compelled in any criminal case to be a witness against himself, nor be deprived of life, liberty, or property without due process of law; nor shall private property be taken for public use without just compensation.
>
> Sixth Amendment: In all criminal prosecutions, the accused shall enjoy the right to a speedy and public trial, by an impartial jury of the state and district wherein the crime shall have been committed, which district shall have been previously

ascertained by law, and to be informed of the nature and cause of the accusation; to be confronted by the witnesses against him; to have compulsory process for obtaining witnesses in his defense, and to have the Assistance of Counsel for his defense.

Seventh Amendment: In suits at common law, where the value in controversy exceeds twenty dollars, the right of trial by jury shall be preserved, and no fact tried by the jury shall be otherwise re-examined in any Court of the United States, than according to the rules of the common law.

Eighth Amendment: Excessive bail shall not be required, nor excessive fines imposed, nor cruel and unusual punishments inflicted.

Ninth Amendment: The enumeration in the Constitution, of certain rights, shall not be construed to deny or disparage others retained by the people.

Tenth Amendment: The powers not delegated to the United States by the Constitution, nor prohibited by it to the States, are reserved to the States respectively, or to the people.[10]

THE THIRD, FOURTH, SIXTH, AND SEVENTH AMENDMENTS

Little need be said about the Third, Fourth, Sixth, and Seventh Amendments. They generated little debate in the Congress that enacted them, and are self-evident as to their meaning. The Third Amendment prohibits in peacetime the quartering of soldiers in any house without the owner's consent. This was a response to the Quartering Acts Parliament had passed in the years leading up to the American Revolution, which allowed the British army to lodge soldiers in private inns and residences. The Declaration of Independence cited the quartering of troops as one of the colonists' grievances.[11]

The Fourth Amendment search and seizure provisions also were influenced by prerevolution events. When the colonists began smuggling operations to circumvent the British customs duties, King George III employed "writs of assistance." These were search warrants broad in scope. British agents used them to enter people's homes and shops without reason or notice and to interrogate anyone about their use of goods possibly acquired without paying taxes due.[12] The Fourth Amendment bans "unreasonable" searches and seizures. Literally, warrantless searches and seizures would seem to be lawful if they are reasonable in the circumstances. The amendment goes on to say that if a warrant is used, it must be based on probable cause and describe the place to be searched and the persons or things to be seized.

The founding generation believed that the local jury trial was an important safeguard for the people against oppressive government acts. The Constitution in article III, section two specifies that all crimes except for impeachment shall be tried by a jury in the state where the crime was committed. The Sixth Amendment essentially repeats this local jury trial provision in criminal cases and adds several other fair trial requirements to accompany the protection: in all criminal prosecutions the accused shall enjoy the right to a speedy and public trial by an impartial jury in the state and district wherein the crime was committed, etc. The Seventh Amendment guarantees a jury trial in civil cases where the amount in controversy exceeds twenty dollars. As we move on from these four explicit amendments, the legislative history of the Bill of Rights' enactment offers significant insights into the original meaning and purpose of the other six amendments.

THE FIRST AMENDMENT

Let us begin with the religion clauses. Madison's proposal on June 8 stated that "The civil rights of none shall be abridged on account of religious belief or worship, nor shall any national religion be established, nor shall the full and equal rights of conscience be in any manner, or on any pretext, infringed." The committee of eleven offered a shortened version in its July 28 report: "No religion shall be established by law, nor shall the equal rights of conscience be infringed." In the House's August debate Peter Silvester of New York worried that the committee's language "might be thought to have a tendency to abolish religion altogether." Benjamin Huntington of Connecticut also was concerned that the words might be taken in such latitude as to be "hurtful to the cause of religion." Ministers and churches "to the Eastward"—he was referring to New Hampshire, Massachusetts, and Connecticut—relied on contributions from their members. If a suit was brought in federal court, under the committee's language the person who had failed to perform his engagement could not be compelled to do it because "a support of ministers, or building of places of worship might be construed into a religious establishment."[13]

Madison said the meaning was that "*Congress* should not establish a religion . . . nor compel men to worship God in any manner contrary to their conscience" (my emphasis). The amendment did not speak to what the states could do. He moved to reinsert the word "national" before religion being established, as had been the case in his original June 8 proposal, to remove any doubt on this point. Following some further discussion, the House accepted the language proposed by Samuel Livermore of New Hampshire: "Congress shall make no laws touching religion, or infringing the rights of conscience." The religion clauses went through a few more iterations before their final settlement in the First Amendment. From Livermore's version onward one message was clear: Congress must not be involved with matters of religion in the states.[14]

The rest of the clauses in the First Amendment began as two separate propositions in Madison's June 8 recommendations: The first one read, "The people shall not be deprived or abridged of their right to speak, or write, or to publish their sentiments; and the freedom of the press, as one of the great bulwarks of liberty, shall be inviolable." Another proposal stipulated that, "The people shall not be restrained from peaceably assembling and consulting for their common good; nor from applying to the Legislature by petitions, or remonstrances, for their grievances." The committee of eleven combined these two propositions into a single, slightly revised one: "The freedom of speech, and of the press, and the right of the people peaceably to assemble, and consult for their common good, and to apply to the Government for redress of grievances, shall not be infringed." The House said nothing about the freedoms of speech and press. However, Thomas Tucker's motion to buttress the assembly and petition clauses by adding a right for the people to deliver binding instructions to their representatives generated some comment. Several Federalist members insisted that a provision authorizing the people to issue binding instructions to their congressmen would be a bad idea, that it would undermine the advantages to be derived from a deliberative, representative government seated at the head of the expanded American republic.[15]

Thomas Hartley of Pennsylvania said the members of Congress presumably know the interests and circumstances of their constituents. If they forfeit the confidence of the people, they will be removed at the next election. Representation is the principle of our government and is inconsistent with the receipt of binding instructions from the people back home. When the passions of the people are excited, and instructions are issued for party purposes, we want our government to be composed of men of firmness and wisdom, able to discover and resist popular error. Can it be supposed that the inhabitants of a single state district are better informed with respect to the interests of the union than a select body assembled from every part? Congress will be the best judges of sound policy. George Clymer, also of Pennsylvania, added that to make legislators bound by the instructions of their constituents would be a dangerous proposition, destructive of all ideas of an independent and deliberative body which are essential to the legislatures of free governments. Binding instructions would "prevent men of abilities and experience from rendering those services to their community that are in their power, destroying the objective contemplated by establishing an efficient General Government, and rendering Congress a mere passive machine."

Roger Sherman observed that the right of the people to consult for their common good can go no further than to petition the legislature, or apply for a redress of grievances. It is the duty of a good representative to inquire what measures are most likely to promote the general welfare, and after he has discovered them, to give them his support. James Jackson of Georgia predicted that establishing the doctrine of instructions would necessarily drive the House into a number of factions. Maryland's Michael Stone did not want to change our government from a representative one to a democracy using binding instructions. Finally, New York's John Lawrence said that every member on this floor should consider himself the representative of the whole union, not of a particular district which has chosen him. The House did not change the committee's language to include a right of instruction.[16]

The Senate rewrote slightly the freedom of speech, press, and assembly and petition clauses, as they had come over from the House, and combined them in a single amendment to follow the religion clauses. By placing the religion, speech, press, and assembly and petition clauses in the First Amendment, which begins, "Congress shall make no law," the framers made it clear that whatever these rights might entail, Congress could not pass a law to abridge them. How the states might deal with these matters remained untouched.

THE SECOND AMENDMENT

Like the First Amendment, the Second Amendment is primarily a states' rights provision. It is intended to insulate state militias from undue federal interference. Article I, section eight, in clauses twelve, thirteen, and fifteen of the Constitution, empowers Congress to raise and support an army, provide and maintain a navy, and call forth the state militias to execute the laws of the union, suppress insurrections, and repel invasions. Article I, section eight, clause sixteen allows Congress to organize, arm, and discipline the militias, and to govern such part of them as may be employed in the service of the United States, reserving to the states the appointment of officers, and the training of the militia according to the discipline prescribed by Congress. Many people opposed maintenance of a standing army as unnecessary and a danger to liberty; they preferred to rely on the various state militias to be their guardians against invasion or insurrection.[17]

Proposals from the state conventions (including those of the Pennsylvania and Maryland minorities published in the press) had sought some protection for the people's right to bear arms, mostly in the militia context. The statements from Virginia and North Carolina were the same for the most part, and they were typical: "That the people have a right to keep and bear arms; that a well regulated militia composed of the body of the people trained to arms is the proper, natural and safe defense of a free state. That standing armies in time of peace are dangerous to liberty, and therefore ought to be avoided, as far as the circumstances and protection of the Community will admit; and that in all cases the military should be under strict subordination to and governed by the civil power." North Carolina added a proviso that "any person religiously scrupulous of bearing arms ought to be exempted upon payment of an equivalent to employ another to bear arms in his stead."

The Pennsylvania minority and the New Hampshire convention did go beyond the militia context in their recommendations for an amendment. The Pennsylvania minority said "That the people have a right to bear arms for the defense of themselves and their own state, or the United States, or for the purpose of killing game; and no law shall be passed for disarming the people or any of them, unless for crimes committed, or real danger of public injury from individuals." In addition to bearing arms for the defense of the state or nation, this statement extended to self-defense and killing game. The New Hampshire convention offered the one proposal that bore no relation to the militia: "Congress shall never disarm any citizen unless such as are or have been in Actual Rebellion."[18]

Overlooking the proposals from Pennsylvania and New Hampshire, Madison and his colleagues in the First Congress focused exclusively on the militia context in their drafts and debates. Madison's June 8 recommendations included one on arms: "The right of the people to keep and bear arms shall not be infringed; a well armed and well regulated militia being the best security of a free country: but no person religiously scrupulous of bearing arms shall be compelled to render military service in person." The committee of eleven's version moved the militia to the first part of the sentence, thereby making it the center of attention, and this is where it would remain: "A well regulated militia, composed of the body of the people, being the best security of a free State, the right of the people to bear arms shall not be infringed; but no person religiously scrupulous shall be compelled to bear arms." This reference to religious scruples is intended to secure the public against the "mal-administration of the Government," said Elbridge Gerry of Massachusetts on the House floor. But he worried that the clause would give the "people in power" the opportunity to declare who have religious scruples, and prevent them from having to bear arms. The militias are to "prevent the establishment of a standing army, the bane of liberty." Under this provision, together with their other powers, Congress could undermine the militias and make a standing army necessary. If we give a discretionary power to exclude from militia duty those who have religious scruples, "we may as well make no provision on this head." Gerry wished the words to be confined to persons "belonging to a religious sect" scrupulous of bearing arms.[19]

James Jackson thought some of the state conventions had used better language to accommodate religious beliefs: "No one, religiously scrupulous of bearing arms, shall be compelled to render military service, in person, upon paying an equivalent." Roger Sherman thought that those who are religiously scrupulous of bearing arms "are equally scrupulous of getting a substitute, or paying an equivalent." He did not see the necessity of a clause of this kind. We do not live under an arbitrary government, and the states will control their militias except when they are called into federal service. Nor would it do to alter the language to "exclude the whole of any sect," as Gerry wanted, because there are men among the Quakers, for example, who would fight in defense of their country, notwithstanding the religious principles of the society. New York's Egbert Benson said he preferred to leave the question of religious scruples to the discretion of Congress, but at this point the House decided to leave the clause intact.[20]

Two days later the debate briefly resumed. Thomas Scott of Pennsylvania objected to the clause, "no person religiously scrupulous shall be compelled to bear arms." Under this language, such persons cannot be called upon for their services, nor can an equivalent be demanded. A militia could never be depended upon under such conditions, said Scott, and recourse to a standing army will be necessary. The House retained the clause but added "in person" at the end of it, thereby preserving the right of states to require a religious objector to pay for a replacement to serve if he did not want to bear arms himself: "A well regulated militia, composed of the body of the People, being the best security of a free State, the right of the People to keep and bear arms, shall not be infringed; but no one religiously scrupulous of bearing arms, shall be compelled to render military service in person." The Senate made some style changes and dropped the religious exemption, and the House acquiesced to the Senate's version: "A well regulated Militia, being necessary to the security of a free State, the right of the people to keep and bear Arms, shall not be infringed." During the entire drafting process, the focus remained on the right and the duty of people to bear arms in the context of militia regulation. In the end Congress retained discretion for itself to deal with the subject of religious objectors being exempted from having to bear arms in the state militias.[21]

THE EIGHTH, NINTH, AND TENTH AMENDMENTS

Unlike most of the Bill of Rights amendments, which underwent changes during the drafting process, the Eighth Amendment passed exactly as Madison had written it: "Excessive bail shall not be required, nor excessive fines imposed, nor cruel and unusual punishments inflicted." William Smith of Maryland did think the reference to "cruel and unusual" punishments was too indefinite. Samuel Livermore said the proposition in general had no meaning, and so was not needed. What is meant by "excessive" bail or fines? Who is to judge? As for cruel and unusual punishments, it is sometimes necessary to hang a person. There are whippings, and ears cut off. Are these "cruel"? We should not restrain ourselves. With no more discussion, a large majority of the House members then accepted the amendment as worded, and it did not come up for further debate.[22]

The Ninth Amendment is merely an interpretive guide to the Bill of Rights. Unlike the first eight amendments, it does not guarantee any rights to the people or impose any restraints on government. What it does do is solve the Federalists' concern that an enumeration of personal liberties and rights in any conceivable declaration that might be made would never be comprehensive enough to cover all the rights the people should enjoy. The Ninth Amendment's statement that the enumeration in the Constitution of certain rights shall not be construed to deny or disparage others retained by the people clearly leaves the retained rights of the people fully in place, whatever those rights may be, unlimited by anything said in the first eight amendments. It states a truism. The history which leads us to discover the original meaning and purpose of the Ninth Amendment is based upon our understanding of the arguments against having a bill of rights, previously expressed by the Federalists in some of the state ratifying conventions, and by Alexander Hamilton in *Federalist Paper No. 84*. The deliberations of the First Congress did not include a discussion of this amendment.

The Tenth Amendment was intended to reassure the people worried about the powers being delegated to the federal government by the Constitution, which had recently replaced the Articles of Confederation. The issue became how much reassurance to give the opposition versus how much latitude to preserve for the United States. Recall that article II of the Confederation's constitution said the states retain every power "not expressly delegated" to the United States in Congress assembled. Several of the proposals from the state ratification conventions stipulated that all the powers not "expressly" delegated to the federal government by the Constitution should be reserved to the states. But Madison and his colleagues in the First Congress chose not to limit the federal authority to expressly delegated powers, leaving it space and discretion to fill out details of the government's operation in the future. Twice in the House Anti-Federalist members tried to place the word "expressly" before delegated powers. For example, Thomas Tucker of South Carolina moved to add the word "expressly" so that the Tenth Amendment sentence would read "the powers not *expressly* delegated" by the Constitution to the United States are reserved to the states (my emphasis). Madison objected to this because it was impossible to confine a government to the exercise of express powers. There must be admitted "powers by implication unless the constitution descended to recount every minutia." Roger Sherman agreed with Madison, observing that corporate bodies are supposed to possess "all powers incident to a corporate capacity, without being absolutely expressed." Tucker's motion was voted down without further discussion.[23]

Like the Ninth Amendment, the Tenth Amendment does not guarantee any rights to the people or restrain any powers of government. It too is an interpretive guide to understanding the Constitution, and it merely states a truism. The powers delegated to the federal government by the Constitution obviously cannot be powers reserved to the states or the people. Conversely, powers not delegated to the federal government by the Constitution are necessarily powers reserved to the states or the people. There does remain an interpretive issue to sort out. What is the scope of the federal government's implied powers, i.e., those not expressly delegated? This question has been contested in the political branches of the government and litigated in the courts ever since 1791. The legislative history of the Tenth Amendment does suggest that the powers of the United States government—particularly the article I delegated powers of Congress—should be allowed to grow over time as a response to the evolving and expanding needs of the republic.

THE FIFTH AMENDMENT, ESPECIALLY THE DUE PROCESS CLAUSE

The Fifth Amendment's due process clause is the final provision to consider here for original meaning analysis, and along with the First Amendment is the most important guarantee in the Bill of Rights because of the Supreme Court's future rulings under it. The clause traced its origins to Magna Carta (1215) in old England, wherein under duress King John promised his barons that "no free man shall be taken or imprisoned or dispossessed, or outlawed, or banished, or in any way destroyed, . . . except by the legal judgment of his peers or by the law of the land." Later confirmations and interpretations of the Great Charter of Liberties established a link between the law of the land and due process phrases. For example, Parliament's Petition of Right (1628) repeated Magna Carta's law of the land provision and followed with a recital from the laws of Edward III, "no man of what estate or condition that he be, should be put out of his land or tenements, nor taken nor imprisoned, nor disinherited, nor put to death without being brought to answer by due process of law." Sir Edward Coke's *Institutes of the Laws of England* (1628–1644) similarly equated due process with a procedural judicial safeguard when he said: "that no man be taken, imprisoned, or put out of his freehold without process of the law, that is, by indictment or presentment of good and lawful men, where such deeds be done in due manner, or by writ original of the common law."[24]

In the American founding era, the state constitutions used the Magna Carta language. Thus, New Hampshire (1783), Massachusetts (1780), New York (1777), Pennsylvania (1776 and 1790), Maryland (1776), Virginia (1776), North Carolina (1776), and South Carolina (1778 and 1790), all employed a close variant of the guarantee that no person, or no freeman, shall be taken or imprisoned, or deprived of his life, liberty, or property, except by the judgment of his peers, or by the law of the land.[25] New York was the one state that departed from this standard law of the land phraseology (which was already in its constitution) when the legislature enacted a bill of rights in 1787 that used due process language in four separate criminal law procedures: Second, no citizen shall be taken or imprisoned, or otherwise destroyed, "but by lawful Judgment of his or her Peers, or by due Process of Law." Third, no citizen shall be taken or imprisoned for any offense, unless it be by indictment or presentment of good men of the neighborhood where such deeds be done, "in due Manner, or by due Process of Law." Fourth, no person shall be put to answer without presentment before justices, "or Matter of Record, or due Process of Law, according to the Law of the Land." And fifth, no person "shall be taken, or imprisoned, or disinherited, or put to death, without being brought to answer by due Process of Law."[26]

In the same session that the New York legislature enacted its statutory due process clauses, it considered a bill to prevent privateers from holding public office. Speaking in opposition to the measure, Alexander Hamilton cited the state constitution's mandate that nobody "shall be disfranchised, or deprived of any of the Rights or Privileges secured to the Subjects of this State by this Constitution, unless by the law of the land, or the Judgment of his Peers." Although some gentlemen "hold that the law of the land will include an act of the legislature," the English luminary Lord Coke, in his comment on a similar clause in Magna Carta, interprets the law of the land to mean "presentment and indictment, and process of outlawry," in contradistinction to a trial by jury. But if there were any doubt about the meaning of the constitution, Hamilton continued, our statutory bill of rights removes it by declaring that "no man shall be disfranchised or deprived of any right, but by *due process of law*, or the judgment of his peers. The words '*due process*' have a precise technical import, and are only applicable to the process and procedures of the courts of justice; they can never be referred to an act of legislature."[27] Hamilton was saying in effect that if the state wanted to deprive someone of his rights, in this circumstance the right of a privateer to hold public office, it could do so only by means of a judicial proceeding.

Three state conventions offered "law of the land" amendments to be considered by the First Congress. The Pennsylvania minority recommended: "That in all capital and criminal prosecutions, a man has a right to demand the cause and nature of his accusation, . . . to be heard by himself or his counsel, to be confronted with the accusers and witnesses, to call for evidence in his favor, and a speedy trial, by an impartial jury of the vicinage . . . ; that no man be deprived of his liberty, except by the law of the land or the judgment of his peers." Virginia and North Carolina proposed identical articles in old English style: "That no freeman ought to be taken, imprisoned, or disseised of his freehold, liberties, privileges or franchises, or outlawed or exiled, or in any manner destroyed or deprived of his life, liberty or property but by the law of the land." New York offered a due process of law amendment from its recent statutory bill of rights: "That no Person ought to be taken or disseised of his freehold, or be exiled or deprived of his Privileges, Franchises, Life, Liberty or Property but by due process of Law."[28]

When Madison picked among the proposed amendments from the state conventions for his June 8 presentation to the First Congress, he decided to offer a shortened version of New York's due process clause rather than the law of the land clause that was prevalent in the state constitutions. He may have made this choice because the federal Constitution already had a law of the land clause in it, in article VI, stating that the Constitution and laws and treaties of the United States shall be the "supreme Law of the Land." In any event, Madison included his due process language as part of a four-clause proposition: "No person shall be subject, except in cases of impeachment, to more than one punishment or one trial for the same offence; nor shall be compelled to be a witness against himself; nor be deprived of life, liberty, or property, without due process of law; nor be obliged to relinquish his property, where it may be necessary for public use, without a just compensation." Compare this with the final Fifth Amendment as ratified by the states: "No person shall be held to answer for a capital, or otherwise infamous crime, unless on a presentment or indictment of a Grand Jury, except in cases arising in the land or naval forces, or in the Militia, when in actual service in time of War or public danger; nor shall any person be subject for the same offence to be twice put in jeopardy of life or limb; nor shall be compelled in any criminal case to be a witness against himself, nor be deprived of life, liberty, or property, without due process of law; nor shall private property be taken for public use, without just compensation."

In modern parlance these clauses in the Fifth Amendment may be referred to as the grand jury clause, the double jeopardy clause, the self-incrimination clause, the due process clause, and the just compensation clause.[29] The grand jury clause passed as a separate provision in the House, and it was moved over by the Senate to be the first clause in the Fifth Amendment. The Senate rewrote the House's no more than one trial or punishment clause to be the double jeopardy clause. The House narrowed the self-incrimination clause so that it applied only to criminal cases. It did this on a motion from John Lawrence, unanimously and without discussion, an indication that the decision to narrow the scope of the clause was widely accepted.[30] The due process clause followed the self-incrimination clause, and it was not changed or even discussed during the House and Senate considerations. Madison proposed the just compensation clause even though no state convention had recommended it. This was the one proposition he introduced on his own initiative.[31]

The first four clauses in the Fifth Amendment, including the due process clause, are procedural in nature and generally relate to criminal cases. The due process clause also can be implicated in a person's civil property dispute with the government or a private party. Only the final clause, requiring the payment of just compensation upon the taking of private property for public use, explicitly guarantees a substantive right in a noncriminal and non-litigation setting.

We may place the due process clause in a broader Bill of Rights context. The first three amendments guarantee substantive rights: the freedoms of religion, speech, press, and assembly; keeping and bearing arms; and home security from soldier occupancy. They say nothing about procedures. The Fourth Amendment is a hybrid provision that involves both substance and procedure. The requirements that government searches and seizures must be "reasonable," and that any warrants issued must be based upon probable cause, imply the existence of a substantive right of privacy, and prescribe procedures to be followed if that privacy is to be invaded. The Fifth Amendment's just compensation clause confers a substantive right to just compensation but does not spell out procedures for the taking of private property for public use. The rest of the Fifth Amendment, and the Sixth and Seventh Amendments, specify some procedures which government must follow in order to deprive someone of life, liberty, or property. The Eighth Amendment confers substantive rights on suspected criminals awaiting trial (no excessive bail) and on convicted criminals (no excessive fine or cruel and unusual punishment). Like the first three amendments and the just compensation clause, it does not deal with procedure.

Focusing precisely upon the due process clause, the question it poses is explicit: what process is due for the government to deprive a person of life, liberty, or property? Although compliance with process requirements primarily rests with the executive and judicial departments of government, the legislature is implicated as well. It establishes through statutes what process the other departments will apply in law enforcement actions and in court cases. Process relates to the procedure by which a substantive right may be deprived by government. It does not describe or embody a substantive right.

From the general context of Magna Carta and subsequent interpretations in England, to the American state constitutions in the founding era, the state conventions' proposals for amendment of the Constitution during the ratification process, the drafting history of the clauses in the Fifth Amendment, the interrelationship among the executive-judicial procedural guarantees in the Fourth through the Seventh Amendments, and finally by a literal and focused reading of the due process clause itself, one clear message about the original meaning of the due process clause comes into view: everyone's life, liberty, and property should be secure until the government has reason to take an adverse action against a person. Before the government deprives that person of life, liberty, or property in a criminal prosecution, or of property in a civil proceeding, it must provide notice and make available a hearing on the facts, in compliance with the Constitution as amended, the predicate statute on which the action is based, and the common law (prior court decisions). The due process clause does not pertain to substantive policy decisions embodied in statutes, including statutes regulating people's life, liberty, and property.

THREE BILL OF RIGHTS DECISIONS IN THE FIRST EIGHTY YEARS

Only three times in the first eighty years of the republic did the Supreme Court give serious consideration to the meaning and application of the Bill of Rights. In his last major decision for the Court, Chief Justice John Marshall in *Barron v. Mayor and City Council of Baltimore* (1833) held that the Bill of Rights amendments do not apply to the states. The plaintiff owned a wharf in the harbor of Baltimore, and the city's roadbuilding and diversion of streams near the waterfront rendered the wharf of little or no value. Mr. Barron sought to recover damages under the Fifth Amendment's just compensation clause. The Constitution was ordained by the people of the United States for themselves, for their own government, said Marshall, not for the governments of the individual states. The powers and limitations the people conferred on the United States apply only to that government, and not to the governments of the individual states, which were framed by different persons and for different purposes. A comparison of sections nine and ten in article I of the original Constitution, each of which is a miniature bill of rights, demonstrates the difference between limitations being imposed on the federal government and those imposed on the states. The clauses in section nine sometimes refer to Congress and sometimes use general language. An example of the latter is the statement that "No Bill of Attainder or ex post facto Law shall be passed." However comprehensive this language, it contains no restriction on the states. Each of the clauses in section ten, by contrast, begins "No State shall . . . ," thereby identifying the subject of the restraints. There is no similar language in the Bill of Rights amendments.[32]

Murray's Lessee v. Hoboken Land and Improvement Co. (1856) upheld against a Fifth Amendment due process clause challenge the Treasury Department's use of a distress warrant to summarily seize and dispose of property for money allegedly owed to the government by the New York collector of customs. That the warrant is a "legal process" is not denied, said the Court, but is it "due process of law?" The Constitution "contains no description of those processes which it was intended to allow or forbid," but clearly the legislative power "cannot enact any process which might be devised. The article is a restraint on the legislative, as well as on the executive and judicial, powers of the government, and cannot be construed as to leave Congress free to make any process 'due process of law,' by its mere will." The Supreme Court's assumption that the due process clause applies to the entire government including the legislature seems sound. If Congress could prescribe, without limitation, any procedure it wished to deprive a person of life, liberty, or property, the guarantee would be meaningless. This conclusion is also consistent with the fact that when Madison proposed to insert his amendments into the body of the Constitution, he planned to put the due process clause in article I, section nine, which includes limitations on Congress, rather than in article II or III, which cover the executive and judicial authorities.

The Court in *Murray's Lessee* found that in the circumstances of the case the warrant was the only process that was due. The Court engaged in a two-step analysis to reach this result. First it asked whether the Treasury Department's summary procedure conflicted with any of the Constitution's provisions. Finding no constitutional prohibition on the use of distress warrants, it then looked to Anglo-American history for an answer. Tested by the common and statute law of England prior to the emigration of our ancestors, and the laws of many states at the time of the Fifth Amendment's adoption, said the Court, the proceedings authorized by the federal law are due process when applied to the ascertainment and recovery of balances due to the government from a collector of customs. Though "due process of law" generally implies regular allegations, an opportunity to answer, and a trial, this is not "universally true." There have been cases in the history of England and America in which process "in its nature final, issues against the body, lands, and goods of certain public debtors" without any such trial. The statute passed by Congress authorizes a lawsuit to be filed challenging the facts as alleged, but unless and until this happens, "the action of the executive power in issuing the warrant, . . . is conclusive evidence of the facts recited, and of the authority to make the levy."[33]

In *Dred Scott v. Sandford* (1857), Chief Justice Roger Taney for the Supreme Court attempted to resolve two political controversies that had long plagued the nation: Did free Black people have the status of "citizens" under the Constitution, and could Congress ban slavery in the territories? Dred Scott's Missouri slaveholder had taken him to live for two years in the free state of Illinois, and for two more years in the free territory of Wisconsin, and then had brought him back to Missouri, wherein he was later sold to Mr. Sandford, a resident of New York. Dred Scott then sued for his freedom in federal court. His right to sue Sandford in federal court rested on his claim to be a citizen within the coverage of article III of the Constitution, which grants the federal courts jurisdiction to hear controversies "between citizens of different States." The Court held that Black people could not be considered citizens within the meaning and protection of the Constitution, and so dismissed the case. After resolving the citizenship issue, Taney went on to opine that Scott's two-year residence in the free state of Illinois did not make him a free man unless that was the law in the slave state of Missouri, his place of return.

Scott's residence in the free territory of Wisconsin inspired Taney to also consider the question of slavery in the territories and the power of Congress relating thereto. He concluded that Congress could not ban slavery in the territories. The federal government acts as the agent for all the people in all the states—slave and free states—in obtaining and administering the territories. Moreover, Congress must operate within the constraints of the Constitution and the Bill of Rights in the territories. This includes the Fifth Amendment mandate that no person shall be deprived of life, liberty, or property without due process. An "act of Congress which deprives a citizen of the United States of his liberty or property, merely because he came himself or brought his [slave] property into a particular Territory of the United States, and who has committed no offense against the laws, could hardly be dignified with the name of due process of law."

This was the first time the Supreme Court employed an approach under the due process clause that went beyond a question of procedure to delve into a substantive policy decision of Congress. In this case it was a disaster. Article IV, section three of the Constitution states that Congress "shall have Power to . . . make all needful rules and Regulations" respecting the territories of the United States. Congress in the 1820 Missouri Compromise had made the decision to exclude slavery from the territories to the north and west of the southern border of Missouri, and Taney did not agree with that result.[34] Rather than putting the issue to rest, his opinion in the *Dred Scott* case stoked the anxieties of the northern Republican antislavery forces and gave the southern slaveholding hard-liners legal support for their aggressive expansion plans. The Court's use of the due process clause in the Fifth Amendment to overrule policy judgments of Congress has been given a name in the modern era—it is called "substantive due process" analysis.

NOTES

1. *Annals of Congress* 1789, 1st sess., 27–29.

2. Bernard Schwartz, *The Bill of Rights: A Documentary History* (New York: Chelsea House Publishers, vol. 2, 1971), 983. Neil H. Cogan, ed., *The Complete Bill of Rights: The Drafts, Debates, Sources, and Origins* (New York: Oxford University Press, 2nd ed., 2015) offers a more extensive summary of the state conventions' proposals, including those offered by the Pennsylvania and Maryland minorities in the press, and proposals later offered from Rhode Island in 1790. He moved through the Bill of Rights in order, and matched them with the recommendations from the states, as follows: Eight states proposed amendments relating to the establishment clause and the free exercise of religion; seven on free speech and free press; six on assembly and petition; eight on bearing arms; six on quartering soldiers; six on search and seizure; three on the Fifth Amendment grand jury clause; two on double jeopardy; five on the self-incrimination clause; four on law of the land or due process; none on the just compensation clause; six on the Sixth Amendment criminal trial; eight on the Seventh Amendment civil jury trial; five on the Eighth Amendment bail and punishment clauses; three on the Ninth Amendment; and eight on the Tenth Amendment. See Cogan, 12–13, 157–58, 227–28, 275–76, 317–18, 342–43, 423–24, 476, 504–5, 540–41, 584, 612–13, 805–7, 921, 1041–42, and 1078–79.

3. Madison speech of June 8, 1789, in Jack N. Rakove, comp., *James Madison Writings* (New York: The Library of America, 1999), 437–52.

4. Madison addressed the politics of the situation more pointedly in an August 19, 1789, letter he dashed off to Richard Peters, the Speaker of the Pennsylvania Assembly, pending the outcome of the "noxious project of amendments." The House was "so deep in them now" that Madison was hopeful something would be done. It was worth the effort because a constitutional provision in favor of essential rights "is a thing not improper itself. . . . It may not be necessary in a republic . . . but it is in some degree rational in every Government." Many states had adopted the Constitution under a "tacit compact" in favor of some subsequent modifications. In Virginia if Federalist candidates for the House of Representatives (including Madison himself) had not "taken this conciliatory ground," they would not have been elected. If amendments had not been proposed from the federal side of the house, the proposition would have come "*within three days*, from the adverse side." (emphasis in the original) If successful "it will kill the opposition everywhere." Without some amendments being proposed, the antifederal leaders will say to the people—we told you not to ratify the constitution until all necessary changes are made. Failure to act now will be a pretext at the fall sessions of the state legislatures "to blow the trumpet for a second Convention." Ibid., 471–73.

5. Carol Berkin, *The Bill of Rights: The Fight to Secure America's Liberties* (New York: Simon & Schuster, 2015), chs. 5–11; 1 *Annals* 1789, 440–68, 685–91, 730–92, 795–808, and 948; Linda Grant De Pauw, ed., *Documentary History of the First Federal Congress 1789–1791, Volume 1, Senate Legislative Journal* (Baltimore: Johns Hopkins University Press, 1972), 135–39, 150–68, 181–83, and 185–86.

6. 1 *Annals* 1789, 734–44, 795.

7. Ibid., 784; De Pauw, ed., *Sen. Legis. Journal*, 138, 158.

8. 1 *Annals* 1789, 789–90; De Pauw, ed., *Sen. Legis. Journal*, 159.

9. De Pauw, ed., *Sen. Legis. Journal*, 136 has articles the first and second.

10. Alfred H. Kelly, Winfred A. Harbison, and Herman Belz, *The American Constitution: Its Origins and Development* (New York: W.W. Norton & Co., vol. 1, 7th ed., 1991), Appendix Three, U.S. Constitution.

11. Akil Reed Amar, *The Bill of Rights: Creation and Reconstruction* (New Haven: Yale University Press, 1998), 59–64; Berkin, *Bill of Rights*, 74–75.

12. Berkin, *Bill of Rights*, 74.

13. Cogan, ed., *Complete Bill of Rights*, 1–2; 1 *Annals* 1789, 757–58.

14. 1 *Annals* 1789, 757–59; Berkin, *Bill of Rights*, 150; DePauw, ed., *Sen. Legis. Journal*, 136; Alan Brownstein, ed., *The First Amendment: The Establishment of Religion Clause—Its Constitutional History and the Current Debate* (Amherst, NY: Prometheus Books, 2008), 67–68.

15. Berkin, *Bill of Rights,* 150; 1 *Annals* 1789, 759–60.

16. 1 *Annals* 1789, 760–68.

17. Kelly et al., *Am Const*. Appendix Three, U.S. Constitution art. I, sec. 8, cls. 12–13, 15, 16; Amar, *Bill of Rights*, 46–59.

18. Cogan, ed., *Complete Bill of Rights*, 275–76.

19. Berkin, *Bill of Rights*, 150; 1 *Annals* 1789, 778–79.

20. 1 *Annals* 1789, 779–80.

21. Ibid., 796.

22. Berkin, *Bill of Rights*, 150 for Madison's proposal; 1 *Annals* 1789, 782–83 (Smith and Livermore).

23. 1 *Annals* 1789, 790. Cogan, ed., *Complete Bill of Rights*, 1078–79, has the proposals from the state conventions. The Pennsylvania and Maryland minorities, and Massachusetts, New Hampshire, and South Carolina offered some version of the sentiment that powers not "expressly" delegated to the federal government should be reserved to the states.

24. Richard L. Perry, ed., *Sources of Our Liberties: Documentary Origins of Individual Liberties in the United States Constitution and Bill of Rights* (New York: American Bar Association, 1959), 17, 74. Coke is quoted in Edward Keynes, *Liberty, Property, and Privacy: Toward a Jurisprudence of Substantive Due Process* (University Park: Pennsylvania State University Press, 1996), 12.

25. For the early state constitutions and bills of rights, see generally Francis N. Thorpe, ed., *The Federal and State Constitutions, Colonial Charters, and Other Organic Laws of the United States* (Washington, DC: Government Printing Office, 7 vols, 1909).

26. Cogan, ed., *Complete Bill of Rights*, 541–46.

27. Hamilton is quoted in James W. Ely Jr., "The Oxymoron Reconsidered: Myth and Reality in the Origins of Substantive Due Process," 16 *Constitutional Commentary* 315, 325–26 (1999).

28. Ibid., 540–41.

29. What I have called the self-incrimination clause, and the just compensation clause, respectively, are also commonly referred to as the privilege against self-incrimination clause, and the takings clause.

30. 1 *Annals* 1789, 782.

31. Leonard W. Levy, *Seasoned Judgments: The American Constitution, Rights, and History* (New Brunswick, NJ: Transaction Publishers, 1995), 239. Levy does point out that Massachusetts and Vermont did have such a provision in their constitutions.

32. *Barron*, 32 U.S. 243, 244, 247–51.

33. *Murray's Lessee*, 59 U.S. 272, 274–81, 285.

34. *Dred Scott*, 60 U.S. 393, 406–54.

Chapter 4

The Original Meaning of the Fourteenth Amendment

Eleven southern slave states seceded from the union over the issue of slavery, and four bloody years of military conflict followed. In the aftermath of the Civil War, the Republican Party–dominated Thirty-ninth Congress, in its first session, from December 4, 1865, to July 28, 1866, assumed the momentous task of reconstructing the union, reforming the Constitution, and dealing with the chaos in the South. The Senate and House Judiciary Committees, chaired by Senator Lyman Trumbull of Illinois and Representative James Wilson of Iowa, respectively, drafted and ushered through to passage the Civil Rights Act of 1866, based primarily upon the authority of the Thirteenth Amendment (1865), which abolished slavery and empowered Congress to enforce it by appropriate legislation. Directed at the Black Codes being enacted in the southern states to maintain control over the former slaves, the Civil Rights Act declared all persons born in the United States to be citizens of the United States, and mandated that all such citizens in the states without regard to their race or color shall have the same rights to make and enforce contracts, to sue, be parties, and give evidence in court, to inherit, purchase, lease, hold, and sell real and personal property, and to have the "full and equal benefit of all laws and proceedings for the security of person and property, as is enjoyed by white citizens." Persons who acted under any state law or custom to violate this mandate could be fined and imprisoned.[1]

In addition to the Judiciary Committees of the House and Senate, another center of power in the Congress was the Joint Committee on Reconstruction, established in the opening days of the session to determine when and under what conditions the eleven defeated southern states should be restored to their representation in Congress. This committee was chaired by House leader Thaddeus Stevens of Pennsylvania and Senator William Fessenden of Maine, and its fifteen members included Representative John Bingham of Ohio, who would write the key provisions of the Fourteenth Amendment. The Joint

Committee drafted and sent to Congress in sequence three proposed constitutional amendments. First it submitted an amendment to revise the basis of the states' representation in the union, which passed the House but was defeated in the Senate. Next it submitted an amendment authored by Bingham, which the House debated in late February and postponed for later consideration. Finally, it submitted a proposal that became the Fourteenth Amendment, following its enactment in the Congress and ratification in the states.[2]

An important link between the founding era of the republic and the 1866 Congress in its enactments of the Civil Rights Act and the Fourteenth Amendment was article IV, section two of the Constitution, which stipulated that the "Citizens of each State shall be entitled to all Privileges and Immunities of Citizens in the several States," as this clause was interpreted in the leading case of *Corfield v. Coryell* (1823), by Supreme Court Justice Bushrod Washington while sitting on circuit. Washington was a nephew of George Washington and had participated in the Virginia state convention which ratified the Constitution. In holding that New Jersey could limit fishing rights in its oyster beds to its own residents without violating the rights of a citizen from another state, Washington reasoned that article IV, section two, of the Constitution protects only fundamental rights, and that fishing for oysters was not a fundamental right. He then proceeded to summarize the fundamental rights of citizens, the privileges and immunities of citizenship, which no state could lawfully abridge:

The inquiry is, what are the privileges and immunities of citizens in the several states? We feel no hesitation in confining these expressions to privileges and immunities which are, in their nature, fundamental, which belong, of right, to the citizens of all free governments, and which have, at all times, been enjoyed by the citizens of the several states. . . . What these fundamental principles are, it would perhaps be more tedious than difficult to enumerate. They may, however, be all comprehended under the following general heads: Protection by the government; the enjoyment of life and liberty, with the right to acquire and possess property of every kind, and to pursue and obtain happiness and safety; subject nevertheless to such restraints as the government may justly prescribe for the general good of the whole. The right of a citizen of one state to pass through or to reside in any other state for purposes of trade, agriculture, professional pursuits, or otherwise; to claim the benefit of the writ of habeas corpus; to institute and maintain actions of any kind in the courts of the state; to take, hold, and dispose of property, either real or personal; and an exemption from higher taxes or impositions than are paid by the other citizens of the state; may be mentioned as some of the particular privileges and immunities of citizens, which are clearly embraced by the general description of privileges deemed to be fundamental; to which may be added, the elective franchise, as regulated and established by the laws or constitution of the state in which it is to be exercised. These, and many others which might be mentioned, are, strictly speaking, privileges and immunities, and the enjoyment of them by the citizens of each state, in every other state, was manifestly calculated.[3]

Notice several things about the clause and the interpretation. First, Justice Washington limits the rights being protected for out-of-state citizens within the host state to "fundamental rights," whereas the clause protects all privileges and immunities of citizens without any limitation. Second, though, the interpretation does not impose much of a limitation, since it broadly defines fundamental rights to include protection by the government in the enjoyment of life and liberty, with the right to acquire and possess property, and to pursue and obtain happiness and safety, subject only to such restraints as the government may justly prescribe for the general good of the whole. Third, Washington obviously looks to the nation's Declaration of Independence and to the states' natural rights–based constitutions as the source for his fundamental rights definition. Fourth, *Corfield* effectively establishes a national minimum standard for citizens' rights. Every citizen, wherever he might go or be in the United States, is entitled to government protection in his fundamental rights of life, liberty, property, and the pursuit of happiness, subject only to such restraints as the government may justly impose for the general good of the whole. This is the way the Republicans understood the opinion, and spoke about it, in 1866.

The Senate and House Judiciary Committees based the Civil Rights Bill on the explicit enforcement authority in the Thirteenth Amendment, and in some speeches, members also relied on an implicit authority to enforce the article IV, section two privileges and immunities clause as interpreted in *Corfield.* They quoted from *Corfield* to describe the rights of citizenship they wanted to protect, and could protect. John Bingham was a reluctant outlier on this. A member of Congress from 1855 to 1863, he had been absent from the Thirty-eighth Congress, which enacted the Thirteenth Amendment on March 2, 1865, in a lame duck session, after months of spirited political and constitutional debate between the Republicans and the Democratic Party opposition, most of whom opposed the amendment because they believed it would prolong the war and represent a massive federal intrusion into the rights of the states to govern their own affairs. Now returned to a leadership position in his party, Bingham was one among a handful of Republicans who believed that Congress possessed no authority, neither under its express enforcement power in section two of the Thirteenth Amendment, nor an implied authority under article IV, section two of the Constitution, to protect the rights, privileges, and immunities of all citizens in the states. Therefore, Bingham spoke in opposition to the Civil Rights Bill and worked to obtain support for a constitutional amendment that would grant to Congress clear authority to enforce protection for the life, liberty, and property rights of all citizens and persons in the states. The Fourteenth Amendment would provide this authority.[4]

THE CIVIL RIGHTS ACT

In the opening days of the Thirty-ninth Congress, in December 1865, Senator Henry Wilson of Massachusetts introduced a bill to support the freedom of all the Black people who had been released from bondage under President Lincoln's Emancipation Proclamation. Wilson's bill would render null and void any law wherein any inequality of civil rights or immunities was recognized or maintained by reason of race, color, or previous condition of slavery. John Sherman of Ohio sympathized with Wilson's purpose, but he wanted to wait until the Thirteenth Amendment was announced as ratified and added to the Constitution. Then Congress would have clear authority to enact a protective statute for the entire country, not just for the southern states covered by Lincoln's proclamation. Sherman said that the new amendment's first section, abolishing slavery, "secures to every man in the United States liberty in its broadest terms." And the second section, giving Congress the power to enforce the article, meant that there would be "not only a guaranty of liberty to every inhabitant of the United States, but an express grant of power to secure this liberty by appropriate legislation."

The authors of the Thirteenth Amendment had given the enforcement power to Congress because of the country's experience with the privileges and immunities clause in article IV of the Constitution, continued Sherman. There had never been any doubt as to the meaning of this clause. The person who was recognized as a citizen in one state had the right to go into any other state "and exercise the immunity of a citizen of the United States; but the trouble was in enforcing this constitutional provision." In a celebrated case before the war, Samuel Hoar, a Massachusetts attorney who had gone to South Carolina to file a lawsuit, "was driven out, although he went there to exercise a plain constitutional right, and although he was a white man of undisputed character. This constitutional provision was in effect a dead letter to him" because Congress had no express power to secure the right.[5]

A brief history of the Hoar incident will clarify Sherman's reference and give a context to his remarks. In response to a slave insurrection led by a local Black sailor, South Carolina in the 1830s required that all Black people who entered its ports aboard a ship from a foreign country, or from another state in the United States, be confined until the vessel departed. Half a dozen other southern coastal states passed similar laws in an effort to quarantine dangerous influences or ideas. In 1843 a committee of Boston merchants urged Congress to overturn the Black seamen laws of the southern states, arguing that they violated the privileges and immunities clause. The free Black people in Massachusetts were citizens, the petitioners said, and as such were entitled under the Constitution to be protected in their enjoyment of all the privileges and immunities of citizens in any of the states to which they might go. While the House of Representatives committee that considered the request agreed with the legal analysis, they said that any relief would have to come from the southern states themselves, in their legislatures or courts. The Boston merchants then hired Samuel Hoar, a former congressman and a prominent attorney, to go down to South Carolina to challenge the constitutionality of the Black seaman law. Upon going there, he was chased out of the state by threatened mob violence. The merchants also sent attorney Henry Hubbard down to New Orleans for the same purpose, and with the same result. Incidents such as these helped to convince people in the North that they could not safely venture south of the Mason-Dixon Line and continue to enjoy their rights as citizens of the United States.[6]

After the Christmas holidays, the Thirteenth Amendment having been ratified, Senate Judiciary Committee Chairman Lyman Trumbull of Illinois reported out a bill to "protect all persons in their civil rights, and furnish the means of their vindication." On January 29 he opened Senate debate on his Civil Rights Bill. He proposed to give all persons "practical freedom," and to fulfill the promise of the Thirteenth Amendment. Past declarations of abstract truths and principles had been adopted by the nation but not enforced by the states. Of what avail had been the Declaration of Independence announcement of the founding principles of the new nation when state governments treated Black people as slaves? Of what avail had been the privileges and immunities clause to the distinguished citizen of Massachusetts who had gone to South Carolina to enforce a constitutional right in court? And of what avail will it be now that the Constitution declares slavery shall not exist if states are allowed to pass and administer laws depriving persons of privileges "essential to freedmen"?[7]

The Thirteenth Amendment says slavery shall not exist in the United States, and the Republicans read this as a guarantee of liberty for all persons, which Congress could enforce. They also had a broad conception of citizen rights in the article IV privileges and immunities clause in the original Constitution, as it had been interpreted in *Corfield v. Coryell* (1823). They regularly quoted from the case to show the comprehensive nature of citizen rights that had existed and should have been protected under the Constitution since the beginning of the republic. Government protection in life, liberty, property, and the pursuit of happiness—this guarantee being available under the article IV privileges and immunities clause, said Trumbull, "how much more are the native-born citizens of the State itself entitled to these rights!" When a Democratic opponent of the Civil Rights Bill said that article IV is limited in its protective features to a citizen of one state going into another state, Trumbull replied that of course he knew this. He was merely using the case to describe the basic minimum rights that all citizens possess by virtue of their status as citizens and members of the republic.[8]

House Judiciary Committee Chairman James Wilson of Iowa said that if the states would practice the declaration in the Constitution that the "citizens of each State shall be entitled to all privileges and immunities of citizens in the several States," and enforce it as meaning that the citizen has the "right of protection by the Government, the enjoyment of life and liberty, with the right to acquire and possess property of every kind, and to pursue and obtain happiness and safety, " as *Corfield* had explained is the entitlement of all citizens, then the subject matter of the Civil Rights Bill could be left with the states, particularly if "the States would admit, and practice the admission, that a citizen does not surrender these rights because he may happen to be a citizen of the State which would deprive him of them. . . . But, sir, the practice of the States leaves us no avenue of escape, and we must do our duty by supplying the protection which the States deny." Just as Trumbull had done in the Senate, Wilson was describing on the House floor the fundamental rights that all citizens had possessed under the Constitution from the time of its adoption. While the description was based on Justice Washington's interpretation of the article IV privileges and immunities clause, it is relevant to all citizens, not just those who leave their home state to enter another state's jurisdiction.[9]

As the Civil Rights Bill passed the Senate, it guaranteed all inhabitants the right to make and enforce contracts, etc., and to enjoy full and equal civil rights and immunities. The House Judiciary Committee reported the bill out with two changes. First, it narrowed the protected class from "inhabitants" to "citizens of the United States." Chairman Wilson explained that there was some doubt among his committee members whether the federal government had the authority to protect persons who were not citizens of the country. Second, the committee changed the rule from one granting all inhabitants full and equal civil rights to one granting all citizens the same civil rights as white citizens. Wilson said that making white citizens the reference point for the protection of civil rights would mean that women and children could be treated differently from men. Only discrimination based upon race or color would be outlawed.[10]

John Bingham was one of a half dozen Republicans who spoke in reluctant opposition to the Civil Rights Bill in the House. In a widely publicized speech, he presented two constitutional objections. Specifically, the House had changed the bill's protected class from "inhabitants" to "citizens," thereby implying that discrimination against aliens would be permissible. Are we not committing the "terrible enormity of distinguishing here in the laws in respect to life, liberty, and property between the citizen and the stranger within your gates . . . ? Sir, that is forbidden by the Constitution." The Fifth Amendment provides that no "person," not no "citizen," shall be deprived of life, liberty, or property without due process of law. The founding fathers recognized and embodied in the Constitution the higher law principle that requires the equality of all persons in their basic rights. Congress would violate the Fifth Amendment if it so much as implied that the "stranger" could be put beyond the protection of equal laws.

More generally, even if this discrimination were removed, Bingham doubted the power of Congress to pass the bill. "The care of the property, the liberty, and the life of the citizen, under the solemn sanction of an oath, imposed by your Federal Constitution, is in the states, and not in the Federal Government." The Tenth Amendment says that the powers not delegated to the United States are reserved to the states or the people. The Constitution does not delegate to the United States the power to punish offenses against the life, liberty, or property of the citizens in the states, nor does it prohibit that power to the states, but leaves it as the reserved power of the states. Bingham agreed with the bill's purpose and said that the "law in every State should be just." It has long been otherwise in many parts of the union. However, this situation should be remedied not by an arbitrary assumption of power by Congress, but instead by amending the Constitution to expressly prohibit the states from such abuses of power in the future.[11]

House Judiciary Committee members Samuel Shellabarger of Ohio and Chairman Wilson responded to Bingham's speech with common Republican arguments in defense of the bill. The Thirteenth Amendment promises liberty for all persons in the country, and empowers Congress to enforce it with appropriate legislation. The United States demands allegiance from its citizens and owes them protection in return. The Constitution enumerates rights which the United States must be able to protect in the states, or it is "no nation." These and other arguments prevailed, and the Republicans in both houses in early April passed the Civil Rights Act by two-thirds majorities over President Andrew Johnson's veto.[12]

BINGHAM'S FEBRUARY AMENDMENT

Let us retrace our steps to consider the initiatives coming out of the Joint Committee on Reconstruction, beginning with its basis of representation constitutional amendment. In one of the compromises on slavery, the Constitution apportioned membership in the House of Representatives among the states according to their respective populations, determined by adding to the "whole Number of free Persons . . . three fifths of all other Persons." With slavery abolished by the Thirteenth Amendment, this three-fifths of a person formula no longer applied, and unless something was done, the former slave states would have a stronger presence in the federal government than they had ever enjoyed, based upon their freedmen now counting as whole persons. The Joint Committee's proposed constitutional amendment still based the states' representation on population, but with a proviso that eliminated from the count any class of citizens denied the elective franchise on account of race or color. This would give the southern states a choice—enfranchise their Black citizens on equal terms with whites, or suffer a loss in power within the union. Of course, the Democrats in Congress opposed the measure—they wanted to restore the southern states to the union immediately and without any preconditions or constitutional changes—but two groups of Republicans opposed it as well. Some wanted to guarantee the right of citizens to vote without regard to race or color, and others wanted to base the states' representation on legal voters rather than population. Both groups criticized the committee's plan with its proviso, reducing a state's numbers for denying the elective franchise on account of race or color, because this implied that such class disfranchisement was constitutionally permissible. Admittedly, every state applied suffrage qualifications, and they would continue to do so, but the Republican opponents of the basis of representation amendment did not want to suggest in the words of the Constitution that race might be a legitimate ground for exclusion. The House passed this proposed constitutional amendment but the Senate voted it down.[13]

After submitting its basis of representation amendment to Congress on January 31, the Joint Committee on Reconstruction next sent to the Congress on February 10 John Bingham's constitutional amendment: "The Congress shall have power to make all laws which shall be necessary and proper to secure to the citizens of each State all privileges and immunities of citizens in the several States (Art. 4, Sec. 2); and to all persons in the several States equal protection in the rights of life, liberty and property (5th Amendment)." Bingham has indicated his constitutional sources in the parentheses. He has copied from the privileges and immunities clause and from the life, liberty, and property rights premise of the Fifth Amendment due process clause to describe the rights of persons and citizens he wants to empower Congress to secure and protect. Life, liberty, and property rights for all persons are very broad. What additional rights—privileges and immunities—do citizens possess? From a speech given by Bingham years earlier we know that he believed all persons in the United States are entitled to be equally protected in their life, liberty, and property rights, and in addition, citizens have political rights (the right to vote was mentioned).[14] Why does this distinction between all persons' rights and citizens' political rights not appear in the February amendment submitted to Congress?

Bingham had elaborated the distinction clearly in an earlier version of his amendment, considered in the Joint Committee: "Congress shall have power to make all laws necessary and proper to secure to all citizens of the United States, in every State, the same political rights and privileges; and to all persons in every State equal protection in the enjoyment of life, liberty and property." This formulation was straightforward in the identification of what Congress would be able to secure—life, liberty, and property rights for all persons including aliens, and, in addition, political rights for citizens. Bingham changed his language once the committee sent to Congress the basis of representation amendment, with its proviso allowing states to continue to discriminate in the elective franchise on account of race or color if they were willing to suffer a diminution of their representation in the House. Giving Congress the power to enforce equal political rights for citizens in the states would be incompatible with the states' control of suffrage qualifications allowed by the basis of representation amendment.[15] Bingham's incorporation of the article IV privileges and immunities clause language in his amendment introduced ambiguity on political rights and avoided conflict with the basis of representation amendment. Justice Washington's opinion in *Corfield* had included in his list of the fundamental rights of citizens, "the elective franchise, as regulated and established" by the laws of the state in which it is to be exercised.[16]

The House debated Bingham's amendment giving Congress power to secure to citizens all the privileges and immunities of citizens, and to all persons, equal protection for the rights of life, liberty, and property, in late February. In his brief introduction Bingham said every word of the amendment is in the Constitution, in article IV, section two, and the Fifth Amendment due process clause, except for the words granting to Congress the power of enforcement. It is clear by contemporaneous construction, and continued legislative, executive, and judicial construction, that "this immortal bill of rights embodied in the Constitution, rested for its execution and enforcement upon the fidelity of the States." The amendment "would not impose on any state or citizen any obligation which is not now enjoined upon them by the very letter of the Constitution." The amendment gives to the whole people the care of the unity of the government which constitutes us one people, and without which American nationality would cease to be.[17]

Several Republicans who spoke believed that Congress already possessed the implied power to legislate protection for all citizens in the enjoyment of their privileges and immunities, and for all persons in their rights of life, liberty, and property. They supported the amendment as a useful summary and clarification. As William Higby of California put it, virtually all the words in the amendment are in the existing Constitution, in articles I and IV and the Fifth Amendment, but they are "so scattered through different portions of it" as to be without energy or life. Frederick Woodbridge of Vermont agreed with Bingham that the nation must be able to protect its citizens in the "natural rights which necessarily pertain to citizenship." He was inclined to think it could be done by legislation, but since President Johnson had expressed doubts, "it was better to submit the proposition to the people."[18]

In a discordant note among the Republicans, Representatives Robert Hale and Thomas Davis of New York opposed the proposal because it gave too much power to Congress, which could regulate life, liberty, and property in all of the states, in any manner it decides is proper, the only limitation being that the law must be equal. Protection for individual rights might be enhanced, or it might be circumscribed and limited, if only it be equal. Hale also said the current Constitution is "sufficient" and the amendment unnecessary because the Fifth Amendment limits the "power of Federal and State legislation." Any person who is denied his liberty or property rights in a state can pursue his remedy in court. When Bingham interjected to ask if Hale could name a case where a party aggrieved in his personal rights had been able to procure a remedy by filing a suit in court, Hale said he could not now do so. When a Democratic opponent of the measure asked if Bingham had found or heard of a case in which the Constitution "has been pronounced to be insufficient," Bingham replied that he could cite such cases but would let Hale finish his remarks.[19]

The next day Bingham responded to the concerns of Hale and Davis and reiterated the need for a new delegation of power to Congress, in a speech entitled "One Nation, One People, One Constitution," that was published and widely distributed. He began by saying his object was a limited one of protecting individuals whose constitutional rights are not being honored by their state government.

> Gentlemen admit the force of the provisions in the bill of rights, that the citizens of the United States should be entitled to all the privileges and immunities of citizens of the United States in the several States, and that no person shall be deprived of life, liberty or property without due process of law, but they say, "We are opposed to its enforcement by act of Congress under an amended Constitution, as proposed." Why are gentlemen opposed to the enforcement of the bill of rights, as proposed? Because they aver it would interfere with the reserved rights of the states! What state has reserved the right to withhold from any citizen within its limits any of the privileges and immunities of citizens? Gentlemen say we are not opposed to "the bill of rights that all shall be protected alike in life, liberty and property; we are only opposed to enforcing it by national authority." Representative Hale thinks all persons could have remedies for all violations of their life, liberty, and property rights in the federal courts. I asked him yesterday to name such a case. A gentleman on the other side asked if I could cite a decision showing that the federal courts are unable to enforce

> "the bill of rights under the articles of amendment to the Constitution." Yes, I can, and such decisions make plain the need for this amendment. The Supreme Court in *Barron v. Baltimore* (1833) and in *Livingston v. Moore* (1833) settled that the bill of rights does not apply to the states. By these decisions the people are without remedy.

The Constitution is the "supreme law of the land," continued Bingham, which state officials are bound by their solemn oath to support, and which state judges have to apply, notwithstanding contrary state law provisions. Given these protections, it is not surprising that the founding fathers failed to grant Congress an express power to "enforce by penal enactment these great canons of the supreme law, securing to all the citizens in every State all the privileges and immunities of citizens, and to all the people all the sacred rights of person—those rights dear to freemen and formidable only to tyrants." The founders expected state officers to obey these constitutional mandates. Bingham then offered a second reason for the original failure to grant the federal government the power to enforce all the provisions of the Constitution in the states. Such a power would have been incompatible with slavery in any state, "for although slaves might not have been admitted to be citizens, they must have been admitted to be persons." The fathers had to accommodate the institution of slavery in order to achieve the necessary consensus for the new union under the Constitution. Passing the antislavery amendment, is anyone prepared to say the "bill of rights confers express legislative power on Congress to punish State officers for a willful and corrupt violation of their oaths, and oppressive and flagrantly unjust violations of the declared rights of every free citizen and every free man in every free State?" When the rebel states are restored to the union, how can the government of the United States intervene, except as to slavery, under the Constitution as it now stands, to protect the freed Blacks and the loyal white minority within their borders? The loyal minority of white citizens and the disenfranchised free Black citizens will be "utterly powerless" to protect themselves. There is no remedy without an amendment of your Constitution.[20]

Giles Hotchkiss of New York followed Bingham to the floor and brought the debate to a dramatic conclusion. He was unwilling that Congress shall have the power to establish uniform laws throughout the country upon the subject named, the protection of life, liberty, and property. The object of a constitution is not only to confer power on the majority, but to restrict the power of the majority and protect the rights of the minority. The amendment leaves "to the caprice" of Congress the protection of life, liberty, and property. Should the power of this government, as the gentleman from Ohio fears, pass into the hands of the rebels, I do not want rebel laws to govern and be uniform throughout the union.

Hotchkiss offered a second objection, complaining that the amendment was not as strong as the Constitution now is. The Constitution gives equal rights to a certain extent to all our citizens, whereas the amendment merely provides that Congress may pass laws to secure these rights. Why not stipulate by an amendment to the Constitution that no state shall discriminate against any class of citizens, and let that amendment stand as a part of the organic law of the land, subject only to be defeated by another constitutional amendment. "We may pass laws here today, and the next Congress may wipe them out. Where are your guarantees then?" I want to secure the very rights for which the gentleman [Bingham] is contending, but I want to secure them by a constitutional amendment that legislation cannot override. "Then if the gentleman wishes to go further, and provide by laws of Congress for the enforcement of these rights, I will go with him." Following this speech, the Republicans (including Bingham) voted to postpone the measure to the second Tuesday in April.[21]

THE FOURTEENTH AMENDMENT

After a quiet period, the Joint Committee on Reconstruction in the last week of April drafted the Fourteenth Amendment in five sections. Sections one and five are Bingham's revision of his February amendment. The committee developed the middle three sections from various sources and they have long been irrelevant. Section two is a revised version of the basis of representation amendment; section three disqualifies men who had voluntarily participated in the rebellion from voting in federal elections prior to July 4, 1870; and section four states that the public debt of the United States shall not be questioned, but neither the United States nor any state shall pay any debt incurred in aid of the rebellion, or any claim for loss of any slave.

Section two apportions representation among the states according to their respective numbers, counting the whole number of persons in each state. But whenever a state denies the elective franchise to any portion of its adult male citizens for any reason other than participation in rebellion or other crime, the basis of representation in such state shall be reduced in the proportion which the number of such male citizens bears to the whole number of adult male citizens. This obfuscating language reduces a state's basis of representation if it denies the vote to its adult Black male citizens but does not mention race or color, thereby satisfying the Republican critics in Congress who opposed the earlier basis of representation amendment's penalty for denying the elective franchise on account of race or color because this would imply, in the words of the Constitution, that race might be a legitimate ground for exclusion. Section two lost its relevance when the United States adopted the

Fifteenth Amendment (1870), which provides that the right of citizens of the United States to vote shall not be denied or abridged by the United States or any state on account of race or color. Sections three and four of the measure in committee, relating to rebel voters, and non-payment of rebel debts and claims for the loss of any slave, may have historical interest but require no further discussion.[22]

Bingham's rewritten section one provides: "No State shall make or enforce any law which shall abridge the privileges or immunities of citizens of the United States; nor shall any State deprive any person of life, liberty, or property without due process of law; nor deny any person within its jurisdiction the equal protection of the laws." And section five: "The Congress shall have the power to enforce, by appropriate legislation, the provisions of this article."

This revised version responds to the two Republican objections that had been leveled against the February amendment. As Hale, Davis and Hotchkiss wanted, primary responsibility for the protection of life, liberty, and property rights of persons, and for the privileges and immunities of citizens, will remain with the states. Only if states fail to provide that protection will the section five enforcement authority be triggered. Instead of an open-ended power to regulate life, liberty, and property, and citizen privileges and immunities, without regard to what the states are doing, Congress will have a more narrowly focused power, to intervene with legislation only if states abridge privileges or immunities of citizens, deprive persons of life, liberty, or property without due process of law, or deny equal protection of the laws to persons and citizens subject to their jurisdiction.

Second, as Hotchkiss wanted, the guarantee of individual rights is being placed in the Constitution (in section one of the Fourteenth Amendment), and is not left dependent upon congressional action to secure rights. Imposing on the states the constitutional requirement to provide (not deny) equal protection of the laws for rights, privileges, and immunities is both stronger and less centralizing than was the February proposition. Such an imposition of responsibility on the states is stronger than merely authorizing Congress to pass laws to secure rights. Congress might not pass laws, and if it does, they can be overturned by subsequent legislation. Now, as a constitutional obligation imposed on the states, the section one mandate cannot be overturned or weakened by subsequent federal legislation. It is less centralizing because Congress has no authority to act unless states do not fulfill their constitutional obligations. Only then can it bring the resources of the federal government to bear upon the specific, identified problem. Congress can pass a law to provide equal protection for some aspect of the people's life, liberty, or property rights, or for some privilege or immunity of citizenship, if it decides there is a need to either change or strengthen what the states are doing. Bingham, in looking back upon his drafting efforts, could truly assert that his later amendment was "more comprehensive" than the draft which the House rejected in February, that it accomplished "all and more than did the February proposition."[23] The states would be required, and Congress would be authorized, to secure just and equal protection for individual rights.

Thaddeus Stevens introduced the measure in the House with the statement that the principles had all been asserted in the Declaration of Independence and the organic law of the nation, but the Constitution did not limit the actions of the states. The amendment would supply that defect, and enable Congress to correct the unjust legislation of the states, so that the law that operates on one person would operate on all. James Garfield of Ohio characterized the amendment as holding over "every citizen . . . the protecting shield of the law." Thomas Eliot of Massachusetts thought Congress probably already had the authority to prohibit state legislation that discriminated against classes of citizens or deprived persons of life, liberty, or property without due process, or denied to any person the equal protection of the laws, but he supported the amendment to remove any doubt. In his final summing-up speech on the House floor, Bingham covered familiar themes. He said that his amendment would supply the power in the "whole people of the United States . . . to do that by congressional enactment which hitherto they have not had the power to do. . . . To protect by national law the privileges and immunities of all the citizens of the Republic and the inborn rights of every person within its jurisdiction whenever the same shall be denied by the unconstitutional acts of any State."[24]

In his presentation of the Fourteenth Amendment to the Senate, on behalf of the Joint Committee on Reconstruction which had drafted it, Jacob Howard of Michigan gave a detailed explanation of the amendment's meaning in a speech so widely excerpted in the nation's press that it was called the "Howard Amendment." He focused on the privileges and immunities clause, as it was being copied from the existing Constitution and placed in the Fourteenth Amendment. Howard quoted the list of fundamental rights of citizenship, which had been compiled and presented by Justice Washington in *Corfield v. Coryell* (1823) under the general headings of protection by the government in life, liberty, property, and the pursuit of happiness, in order to give some intimation of what the opinion of the judiciary would probably be. To these privileges and immunities, "which cannot be defined in their entire extent and precise nature—to these should be added the personal rights guaranteed and secured by the first eight amendments of the Constitution." This "mass of privileges, immunities, and rights," continued Howard, some secured by article IV and some by the first eight amendments, could not then be enforced by Congress. They stand simply as a "bill of rights in the Constitution, without power on the part of Congress to give them full effect; while at the same time the States are not restrained from violating the principles embraced in them." The great object of section one of the Fourteenth Amendment, concluded Howard, is to "restrain the power of the States and compel them to respect these great fundamental guarantees." Section five would give Congress the power "to carry out all the principles of all these guarantees." The states should protect citizens in their life, liberty, property, and pursuit of happiness, and comply with the Bill of Rights, and Congress under section five could monitor the situation and make sure that this protection is provided in fact as it is recognized as a duty in theory.[25]

A brief discussion ensued in the Senate, focusing on suffrage. Ben Wade of Ohio complained that section three's disfranchisement of former rebels in federal elections until July 4, 1870, would not prevent them from remaining in control of their state governments. Granting to Black people the right to vote would be better, and he was convinced that the loyal states would accept this suffrage extension as part of the Fourteenth Amendment. William Stewart of Nevada added that the "Union party are agreed that all men are entitled to life, liberty, and the pursuit of happiness, and that they will indorse any necessary means to secure these inalienable rights to every American citizen." The right to vote is one of those means. He therefore proposed that the Fourteenth Amendment be modified to require impartial suffrage, and to accompany this with an offer of amnesty for the former rebels.[26]

The Senate Republicans then caucused for five days, and upon their return they added the first sentence to the Fourteenth Amendment, providing that all persons born or naturalized in the United States are "citizens of the United States and of the State wherein they reside." When the Republicans discussed the suffrage question in their caucus, perhaps their attention was drawn to the Supreme Court's *Dred Scott* (1857) decision, holding that Black people could not be citizens of the United States entitled to sue in federal courts in a diversity case. Moreover, the slave states had excluded Black people from being citizens of the state. The definition of citizenship in the Fourteenth Amendment resolved these national and state citizenship issues.

In the resumed floor discussion in the Senate, Luke Poland of Vermont observed that with the whole people of the nation now standing upon the basis of freedom, there should be no objection to granting Congress the power to enforce the privileges and immunities of citizens, rights already embodied in the Constitution. The due process and equal protection clauses as well are the "spirit and inspiration of our system of government, the absolute foundation upon which it was established. It is essentially declared in the Declaration of Independence and in all the provisions of the Constitution." William Stewart reiterated that the amendment "declares that all men are entitled to life, liberty, and property protection, and imposes upon the Government the duty of discharging these solemn obligations."[27]

As the Senate was concluding its deliberations, the Joint Committee on Reconstruction issued its report on the proposed amendment. The report said that this proposal was an effort based upon compromise, and was designed to achieve a timely and fair reconstruction of the states and the nation. The country could not abandon Black people without securing to them their rights as free men and citizens. It was important to inquire what could be done "to secure their rights, civil and political." There were doubts about whether Congress under the Thirteenth Amendment could prescribe voter qualifications in the states. It was also doubtful that the states would consent to surrender their control over suffrage qualifications. The amendment's section two reduction of representation in Congress for states which discriminated would be "in its nature gentle and persuasive, and would lead, it was hoped, . . . to an equal participation of all without distinction, in all the rights and privileges of citizenship, thus affording a full and adequate protection to all classes of citizens, since all would have, through the ballot-box, the power of self-protection."[28]

The Republicans and Democrats pressed their arguments for and against the Fourteenth Amendment during the drive for ratification. The Republicans made securing the ratification of the amendment the main theme of their fall election campaign, and President Johnson and the Democrats urged its defeat for standard states' rights reasons. Newspaper commentary, political speeches, governors' messages, and state legislative proceedings in connection with the ratification question carried forward the same general debate that had preoccupied the first session of the Thirty-ninth Congress.

The Democrats in the North and South warned that adoption of the amendment would intrude upon the traditional responsibilities of the states, establish social and political equality between the races, and consolidate power in the federal government to deal with all matters affecting the life, liberty, and property of the people. The Democratic minority in the Tennessee Senate unsuccessfully offered a resolution that ratification of the amendment should not be construed to confer on Black people the rights to suffrage, hold public office, or sit on juries, or to intermarry with whites. The Democratic-controlled legislature in New Jersey in 1867, in the process of defeating the amendment, complained that it would if adopted give to the federal judiciary jurisdiction over every state law and every principle of the common law relating to life, liberty, and property. The Democratic minority in Indiana said the amendment confers on Black people the same political and civil rights as whites and would lead to integrated schools.

Congress would be the protector of life, liberty, and property, the guarantor of equal protection of the laws, and would be able to declare a system of rights and remedies to be enforced in the federal courts, warned the North Carolina governor's message. The legislature agreed that the proposal would enable the federal government to come between the states and their citizens in almost all conceivable cases. The Florida governor observed that sections one and five of the amendment confer on Congress the power to legislate in all cases touching citizenship, and the life, liberty, and property of every individual. These are representative samples of the Democratic argument during the Fourteenth Amendment's consideration and ultimate ratification. Benjamin Cregan, a member of the New York State Assembly who was nicknamed "Tom Thumb" because of his small size, was the only Democratic state legislator throughout the entire country in 1866 or 1867 who voted to ratify the amendment.[29]

The congressional Republicans continued to stress the need to protect constitutional rights in the states. Many said the Fourteenth Amendment incorporates the Civil Rights Act, grants Congress the power to define and secure the privileges of citizens, and guarantees the inalienable rights of life, liberty, and property of all persons, but it does not confer political or social rights. Bingham characterized his proposal as the embodiment of Christianity and the Golden Rule, the grant of power to each citizen to correct any state wrong by judicial process, and the promise of "equal laws and equal and exact justice . . . secured within every State . . . by the combined power of all the people of every State." House Speaker Schuyler Colfax of Indiana said the amendment places the Declaration of Independence "in our Constitution."[30]

Republican governors and state legislators spoke in similar sweeping terms. Indiana Governor Morton explained that the first section of the amendment prohibits any state from abridging the rights of United States citizenship, and the due process clause is "intended to throw the equal protection of the laws around every person who may be within the jurisdiction of any State, whether citizen or alien, and without regard to condition or residence, not only as to life and liberty, but also as to property." In presenting the amendment to his legislature, Governor Cox of Ohio said it grants the national government power to protect the citizens of the United States in their legal privileges in case any state attempts to oppress any individual citizen or class of citizens, or to deny equal protection to anyone. The necessity for this had been demonstrated in the South, where freedom of speech and discussion had not been tolerated for many years prior to the war. According to Governor Fletcher of Missouri, section one of the amendment "secures to all persons equality in protection of life, liberty, and property, under the laws of the State." Equal rights and impartial liberty are the main idea, said Vermont Governor Dillingham.[31]

As the state legislatures considered the Fourteenth Amendment for ratification, only Pennsylvania and Massachusetts held extensive, recorded debates. In Pennsylvania, one advocate said the amendment enabled the federal government to achieve the object for which the founders of the republic had declared all governments are established, namely, to protect all citizens in their rights of life, liberty, and property. Another said it was necessary to adopt the proposal to secure peace and freedom, including the freedom of speech. Still another declared it proposes to write the Civil Rights Act into the Constitution, and to put the inalienable rights enunciated in the Declaration of Independence into the organic law of the land.

The Massachusetts legislature's Joint Committee on Federal Relations included majority and minority reports, both authored by Republicans, in preparation for the ensuing debate. The majority report recommended that ratification be deferred because the protections secured by section one of the amendment are already in the Constitution, in the Preamble, in article IV's citizen privileges and immunities clause and the republican guarantee clause, and in the First, Second, Fifth, Sixth, and Seventh Amendments. Although the equal protection clause does not appear explicitly in the Constitution, it is there by inference. Adopting the amendment would imply that the basic rights of man had never been guaranteed by the supreme law of the land, and this would be a mischievous admission. The majority report also wanted to establish Black suffrage in all the states, something the amendment does not do directly and unambiguously. The minority report, whose recommendation for ratification the legislature accepted, argued that the proposal is a "declaration of the true intent and meaning of American citizenship," and that it advances in the direction of unrestricted popular rights "which, when completed, will make our Constitution and laws accordant with the highest principles of free civil organization."[32]

Life, liberty, and property rights protection for the American people were the subjects of profuse and animated discussion in Congress and the states during the enactment and ratification of the Fourteenth Amendment. The Republican supporters wanted to clearly require the states to honor and secure these basic rights, subject to review in the courts under section one, and legislative response in Congress under section five. The Democratic opposition by contrast wanted to leave this responsibility for the regulation of life, liberty, and property rights within the exclusive control of the states, not subject to federal government review or intervention.

CONGRESS ENFORCES THE FOURTEENTH AMENDMENT

Following the adoption of the Fourteenth Amendment in 1868, the Republicans in Congress enacted three major laws under their section five authority which shed further light on their understanding of the amendment's terms and promise: section six of the Enforcement Act of May 30, 1870, the Ku Klux

Klan Act of April 20, 1871, and the Civil Rights Act of 1875. The 1870 Enforcement Act passed the House as a measure to enforce the Fifteenth Amendment's ban on racial discrimination in voting. Senator John Pool of North Carolina convinced the Senate to add a new section six to the bill, aimed at combating the activities of the hooded knights of the Ku Klux Klan and other white terrorist organizations operating in many parts of the South. Section six provided that if two or more persons conspired together, or went in disguise upon the public highway, or upon the premises of another, with the intent to violate the act, or to injure, oppress, threaten, or intimidate any citizen with the intent to prevent or hinder his free exercise and enjoyment of any right or privilege granted or secured to him by the Constitution or laws of the United States, the conspirators upon conviction could be fined and imprisoned.[33]

Pool laid out his analysis of Congress's power under the Fourteenth Amendment to legislate against such conspiracies in the states. This amendment says the states shall not "deny" equal protection of the laws. The denial might take the form of an oppressive act, or it might consist of a failure to act. If the state allows by inaction some of its citizens to infringe the rights of others, then it is effectively denying protection to those others. Pool compared the equal protection clause and the privileges or immunities clause which precedes it. The state shall not "make or enforce any law" that abridges the privileges or immunities of citizens. This contemplates a positive act by the state, the making or enforcement of a law. Such action can be held unconstitutional, and therefore be voided, in the courts. If the state denies equal protection to its citizens by an oppressive act, this too can be remedied by the courts. But when the state denies equal protection by inaction, this triggers the section-five congressional authority to enforce individual rights, to secure people against the harmful acts of others, by appropriate legislation. Pool concluded: "The legislation of Congress must be to supply acts of omission on the part of the States." [34]

The dominant white community in many parts of the South continued to harass, oppress, and commit outrages on Black people and white Republicans. In the early months of 1871, a select committee of the Senate held hearings on the activities of the Ku Klux Klan in North Carolina. Based upon the evidence collected and testimony received, John Sherman proposed a resolution: "Resolved, That as organized bands of lawless and desperate men, mainly composed of soldiers of the late rebel armies, armed, disciplined, and disguised, and bound by oaths and secret obligations, are proven to exist" in North Carolina, and have defied civil authority in that state, "and by organized perjury have rendered the courts powerless to punish crimes they have committed, thus overwhelming the safety of person and property, and the rights which are the primary basis of civil government, and which are guaranteed by the Constitution of the United States to all its citizens," and as there is good reason to believe that similar activities are being engaged in throughout the South, the Senate Judiciary Committee should be asked to report a bill to execute the laws, punish and prevent such organized violence, and secure to all citizens the rights so guaranteed to them.[35]

Meanwhile, President Ulysses S. Grant sent a message to Congress, asking it to consider passing new legislation to "effectively secure life, liberty, and property, and the enforcement of law" in all parts of the United States. Congress responded with the Ku Klux Klan Act of 1871, which addressed private conspiracies. If two or more persons conspired to oppose by force the authority of the government of the United States, or by force or intimidation to hinder the execution of any law of the United States, or deter any party or witness from attending and testifying truthfully in any court of the United States, or influence the verdict of any juror in any court of the United States, or if two or more persons conspired together "for the purpose . . . of depriving any person or any class of persons of the equal protection of the laws, or of equal privileges and immunities under the laws," or to prevent or hinder the constituted authorities of any state from giving to all persons within such state the equal protection of the laws, the members of the conspiracy could be fined and imprisoned, and they could be sued for damages by any person injured in his person or property.[36]

To the Democrats' argument that the Fourteenth Amendment merely imposes a set of negatives against the states, and that therefore the enforcement power of Congress is limited to countering the discriminatory laws and actions of the states, the Republicans in their enactment of the Klan Act gave a detailed, precise response, with the equal protection clause playing a prominent role. For example, Representative George Hoar of Massachusetts said that although it is sometimes suggested that the first section of the Fourteenth Amendment aims solely at unlawful acts by state authorities, in fact Congress is empowered to interfere by appropriate legislation in the case of a state denial of equal protection. If it had been the purpose to provide merely for the case of an affirmative, formal exercise of state power in derogation of civil rights, the first clause, saying that no state shall make or enforce any law that abridges the privileges or immunities of citizens would have covered the point. But the section goes on to require equal protection. If the jurors of South Carolina will not do justice on behalf of Black victims of crime, and the state authorities fail to intervene to afford a remedy, this is a denial of the equal protection of the laws, and the federal government can step in and fill the gap.[37]

If section one was a mere veto of state acts, observed Representative David Lowe of Kansas, there would be no room for the appropriate legislative authority of section five. The section one provisions would exhaust themselves by the prohibitions and leave nothing for active legislation. Taking the first and fifth sections together, the intention was to enable Congress to secure to citizens the actual enjoyment of the rights and privileges guaranteed for them. The federal government could not serve a writ of mandamus on state executives and state courts to compel them to recognize and protect the rights of citizens. The United States must resort to its own agencies to carry its authority into execution. Dozens of Republican members in both houses of Congress made statements of similar import during the development and enactment of the Ku Klux Klan Act.[38]

Since he was the author of the key words in the Fourteenth Amendment, it is worth pausing to consider Bingham's statement made early in the Klan debates. When Republican Representative John Farnsworth of Illinois asked why he had changed his amendment from the February form, which had affirmatively empowered Congress to directly secure the privileges and immunities of citizens and equal protection for the life, liberty, and property of persons, to its final form with negatives against the states, Bingham explained that after returning from the House debate he had re-examined Chief Justice Marshall's Supreme Court opinion in *Barron v. Baltimore* (1833), and noted, as never before, the statement that if the framers of the Bill of Rights amendments had intended them to apply to the states, they would have expressed that intent, just as the framers of the Constitution had done in article I, section ten, when they said "No State shall emit bills of credit," etc. So, Bingham began his revised amendment in section one with the words "No State shall" to make it clear that the protections for citizens' and persons' rights are being imposed upon the states as a constitutional obligation. Before the ratification of the Fourteenth Amendment, the states denied trial by jury, they took property without compensation, they denied freedom of the press, and there was no remedy. "Who dare say, now that the Constitution has been amended, that the nation cannot by law provide against all such abuses and denials of right as these in States and by States?" It is now competent for Congress to declare that no man shall be held to answer in the tribunals of any state for any act made criminal by the laws of the state without a fair and impartial trial by a jury, or to declare that no state shall make or enforce any law which shall abridge the freedoms of speech or press or to peaceably assemble and petition for a redress of grievances. The Fourteenth Amendment is "more comprehensive" than the draft rejected in February; it accomplishes "all and more than did the February proposition."

Bingham went on to say the Fourteenth Amendment allows Congress to provide for the "better enforcement of the Constitution and laws of the United States and the better security of the life, liberty and property of the citizens of the United States" in the states. Although the Constitution is the supreme law of the land, it is "not self-executing." The federal government would not be worth much "if it must rely on States to execute" the Constitution's "grants of power, its limitations of power upon States, and its express guarantees of rights to the people." The states possess "concurrent power" to enforce the Constitution, but this does not mean that the nation must wait for their action, Bingham concluded. Laws can be "preventive . . . as well as remedial and punitive."[39]

Another particularly clarifying statement came from Republican Representative James Garfield, made several days after his colleague Bingham spoke. The remarks of Hoar, Lowe, Farnsworth, and Bingham, recited above, came early in the debate, when the Klan Bill swept broadly to provide that if two or more persons conspired or combined together to do any act in violation of the rights, privileges, or immunities of any person which, if committed within the sole or exclusive jurisdiction of the United States, would constitute the crime of murder, manslaughter, mayhem, burglary, robbery, assault and battery, perjury, arson, larceny, criminal obstruction of process, or resistance of officers in the discharge of official duty, the persons engaged in the act or acts shall be guilty of a felony and upon conviction be subject to fine and imprisonment.[40] This was a massive intrusion into the police power of the states, Farnsworth had complained, the type of direct regulation of life, liberty, and property which the rejected February amendment would have empowered Congress to do, and not within the scope of the revised Fourteenth Amendment, which only gets at the acts of the states.

Garfield expanded upon Farnsworth's point. He recited the history of the February proposal, the objections against it, and the revised Fourteenth Amendment, with its focus on the actions of the states. He quoted from remarks of Thaddeus Stevens and Bingham, made during the House's passage of the amendment. House leader Stevens opened with a statement that section one would enable Congress to correct the unjust legislation of the states, and Bingham closed by saying Congress could protect rights when they are denied by the unconstitutional acts of any state. Placing section five first, Garfield said that it allows Congress to enforce the section one negatives on the states.

Garfield then moved on to explain how the Congress could and should deal with the conditions in the South. The states' laws are fine; they are just not being enforced effectively. The provision in the Fourteenth Amendment that the state shall not "deny" equal protection of the laws means that it "must afford" such protection. By the states' inaction, equal protection is being denied to people, and Congress can intervene to provide that protection without violating the local laws. Amendments to the Klan Bill are now being prepared to accomplish this very goal, Garfield concluded. As enacted, the revised Klan Act mainly punished organized criminal interference with federal or state law enforcement efforts, and their deprivations of persons' enjoyment of the equal protection of the laws. Both Farnsworth and Garfield voted for it.[41]

Nearing the end of the Reconstruction Era, Congress enacted the 1875 Civil Rights Act. Based upon the premise that "it is essential to just government we recognize the equality of all men before the law, and hold that it is the duty of government in its dealings with the people to mete out equal and exact justice to all, of whatever nativity, race, color, or persuasion, religious or political, and it being the appropriate object of legislation to enact great fundamental principles into law," the act mandated that all citizens shall be entitled to the full and equal enjoyment of inns, public conveyances on land and water, theaters, and other places of public amusement, without regard to their race or color. Any person who denied such accommodations or privileges could be sued for damages by the injured party, in federal court, and could be fined or imprisoned.[42]

THE STATES MUST (AND CONGRESS CAN) PROTECT LIFE, LIBERTY, AND PROPERTY RIGHTS

The core original meaning of the Fourteenth Amendment is that the states have an obligation, and Congress has the power, to protect we the people's life, liberty, and property. Bingham disclosed in the Klan Bill debate that he had rewritten his February amendment into a set of negatives on the states with Chief Justice Marshall's *Barron v. Baltimore* opinion in mind, to clearly embody in the Constitution the states' duty to deliver protection for people's rights. Recall that Marshall said if the framers of the Bill of Rights intended it to apply to the states, they would have begun with the statement "No State shall," as the framers of the Constitution had done in article I, section ten. Bingham could have achieved his stated goal without the introductory "No State shall" language. He could have said in section one, for example, that the states shall provide equal protection of the laws for citizens' privileges and immunities and for persons' life, liberty, and property. This would have avoided the Supreme Court's unfortunate development of the state action doctrine in two 1883 cases, applied to constrain Congress's section five authority. The negative formula gave the courts plenty to work with in section one, in terms of telling state governments what they could not do, what actions would abridge citizen privileges or immunities, or deprive persons of their life, liberty, or property without due process of law, or deny equal protection, but it came at the expense of a correct understanding of the potential embodied in section five for Congress to provide positive and proactive government protections for people's rights. Only by boring into the details of the Fourteenth Amendment's framing, discussion, passage, ratification, and early legislative implementation, can we discover the states' affirmative section-one duty to act, and the concurrent congressional lawmaking authority in section five.

By exploring the history of the Fourteenth Amendment's adoption and early legislative enforcement, we know why the Republicans in Congress wrote it in the way they did. They intended to require the states to protect the life, liberty, and property of all persons within their jurisdiction, and to empower Congress to ensure that appropriate equal protection for these rights is provided (not denied). Affirmative government protection for our life, liberty, and property is the primary focus and concern of the amendment. The substantive and procedural guarantees in the first eight amendments are relevant to this enterprise, and can be enforced in the states by the courts under section one, and by Congress under section five, to the extent they are deemed to provide some specific supports for life, liberty, and property rights.

NOTES

1. See generally, e.g., Herman Belz, *Emancipation and Equal Rights: Politics and Constitutionalism in the Civil War Era* (New York: W.W. Norton & Co., 1978); Eric Foner, *Reconstruction: America's Unfinished Revolution 1863–1877* (New York: Harper & Row, 1988); and William B. Glidden, *Congress and the Fourteenth Amendment: Enforcing Liberty and Equality in the States* (Lanham: Lexington Books, 2013). The Civil Rights Act is printed in *Congressional Globe*, 39th Cong., 1st sess. (1866) (hereafter CG 39:1) Appendix IC 30–33.

2. Glidden, *Fourteenth Amendment*, ch.3; Benjamin R. Kendrick, *The Journal of the Joint Committee of Fifteen on Reconstruction: 39th Congress, 1865–1867* (New York: Columbia University Press, 1914) Reprint by Negro Universities Press, 1969, 37–129.

3. *Corfield*, 6 Fed. Cas. 546 (No. 3,230) (C.C.E.D.Pa.).

4. Glidden, *Fourteenth Amendment*, chs. 2–3; Jacobus tenBroek, *Equal Under Law* (New York: Collier Books, enlarged edition, 1965); and Michael Vorenberg, *Final Freedom: The Civil War, the Abolition of Slavery, and the Thirteenth Amendment* (New York: Cambridge University Press, 2001).

5. CG 39:1, 2, 39–41 (Sen. Wilson's bill introduced Dec. 5 and discussed Dec. 13, 1865); CG 39:1, 41–42 (Sen. Sherman, Dec. 13, 1865).

6. For the Black seamen laws, and the citizenship controversy that surrounded them, see Don E. Fehrenbacher, *The Dred Scott Case: Its Significance in American Law and Politics* (New York: Oxford University Press, 1978), 69–73; William M. Wiececk, *The Sources of Antislavery Constitutionalism in America, 1760–1848* (Ithaca: Cornell University Press, 1977), 131–40.

7. CG 39:1, 474–76.

8. CG 39:1, 600 (Exchange between Sen. Trumbull and a Democrat, Feb. 2, 1866).

9. CG 39:1, 1115–19 (Rep. Wilson, Mar. 1, 1866).

10. Ibid.

11. CG 39:1, 1290–93 (Rep. Bingham, Mar. 9, 1866).

12. CG 39:1, 1293–94 (Rep. Shellabarger, Mar. 9, 1866), 1294–95 (Rep. Wilson, Mar. 9, 1866). The bill passed the House on March 13, 1866, CG 39:1, 1367, was vetoed by President Johnson on March 27. 1866 (the veto message is printed in CG 39:1, 1679–81), and the veto was overridden by the Senate on April 6, and by the House on April 9, 1866, CG 39:1, 1809 and 1861.

13. Glidden, *Fourteenth Amendment*, 130–32.

14. Ibid., 32–33; Kendrick, *Journal of Joint Committee*, 60–63. For example, in an 1859 speech Bingham opposed the admission of the Oregon territory as a state in part because it allowed aliens to vote. All persons "are equally entitled to the enjoyment of the rights of life, liberty, and property," said Bingham, but only citizens should be eligible to vote. Alfred Avins, *The Reconstruction Amendments' Debates: The Legislative History and Contemporary Debates in Congress on the 13th, 14th, and 15th Amendments* (Richmond: Virginia Commission on Constitutional Government, 1967), 15–18, has Bingham's Oregon speech.

15. Kendrick, *Joint Committee Journal*, 43, 46, and 50–63.

16. *Corfield*, 6 Fed. Cas. 546 (No. 3,230) (C.C.E.D.Pa.) In 1871 Bingham, in a report from the House Judiciary Committee rejecting the memorial request of Virginia Woodhull that Congress declare the right to vote "without regard to sex" under the Fourteenth Amendment's privileges or immunities clause, cited *Corfield* for the proposition that the right to vote is "established and regulated" by the states, with the exception that the Fifteenth Amendment prohibits the states from denying the right to vote on account of race or color. House Report No. 22, Jan. 30, 1871.

17. CG 39:1, 1033–34 (Rep. Bingham introduces his amendment, Feb. 26, 1866).

18. CG 39:1, 1054–56 (Rep. Higby, Feb. 27, 1866); CG 39:1, 1088 (Rep. Woodbridge, Feb. 28, 1866). Higby tied together the language in article I, section eight, which says in the first clause, "the Congress shall have power," and in the last clause of the section, "to make all laws which are necessary and proper," with the article IV, section two privileges and immunities clause, and the Fifth Amendment due process clause. For other supporting speeches see, e.g., CG 39:1, 1057–58; 1062–63 (Rep. Kelley, Feb. 27, 1866), and CG 39:1, 1066–67 (Rep. Price, Feb. 27, 1866).

19. See CG 39:1, 1063–65 and 1083, 1087 for the statements of Reps. Hale and Davis, respectively, Feb. 27 and 28, 1866; CG 39:1, 1065 for the exchange among Reps. Hale, Bingham, and Dem. Rep. Eldridge on the "sufficiency" of the Constitution through the courts to protect people in the states, Feb. 27, 1866.

20. CG 39:1, 1088–94 (Rep. Bingham, Feb. 28).

21. CG 39:1, 1094–95 (Rep. Hotchkiss, Feb. 28); CG 39:1, 1095 (vote to postpone).

22. Kendrick, *Joint Committee Journal*, 82–120.

23. *Congressional Globe*, 42nd Cong., 1st sess. (1871) (hereafter CG 42:1) Appendix, 81–85 (Rep. Bingham, Mar. 31, 1871).

24. CG 39:1, 2459–60 (Rep. Stevens, May 8, 1866); CG 39:1, 2462–63 (Rep. Garfield, May 8, 1866); CG 39:1, 2511–12 (Rep. Eliot, May 9, 1866); and CG 39:1, 2541–43 (Rep. Bingham, May 10, 1866). Some of the Republicans criticized sections two and three of the amendment, and said they would prefer to directly and

unambiguously guarantee the right to vote without regard to race or color. Bingham admitted the section two basis of representation provision excluded the conclusion that by the first section suffrage "is subjected to congressional law." For the complete House discussion, see CG 39:1, 2459–71, 2498–2515, and 2530–43 (May 8–10, 1866).

25. 39 CG:1, 2764–68 (Sen. Howard, May 23, 1866). Horace E. Flack, *The Adoption of the Fourteenth Amendment* (Baltimore: Johns Hopkins University Press, 1908), 157, notes the common references to the "Howard Amendment."

26. CG 39:1, 2768–70 (Sen. Wade, May 23, 1866); CG 39:1, 2798–2801 (Sen. Stewart, May 24, 1866).

27. CG 39:1, 2961 (Sen. Poland, June 5, 1866).

28. Senate Report No. 112, "Report of the Joint Committee on Reconstruction," June 8, 1866, 39 CG:1, 1–15.

29. Main reliance for the ratification campaign is placed upon Flack, *Adoption of Fourteenth Amendment*, chs. 3–4; Charles Fairman, "Does the Fourteenth Amendment Incorporate the Bill of Rights? The Original Understanding," 2 *Stanford Law Review* (1949) 5, 68–126; Joseph B. James, *The Framing of the Fourteenth Amendment* (Champaign: University of Illinois Press, 1965), ch. 12; Joseph B. James, *The Ratification of the Fourteenth Amendment* (Macon: Mercer University Press, 1984); and Michael Kent Curtis, *No State Shall Abridge: The Fourteenth Amendment and the Bill of Rights* (Durham: Duke University Press, 1986), ch.5. Flack, *Adoption of Fourteenth Amendment*, 95, concluded from the debates in Congress that the framers intended to make the Bill of Rights applicable to the states, give validity to the 1866 Civil Rights Act, and declare who are citizens of the United States. He found nothing in the states' ratifications to alter these three objectives. See Flack, *Adoption of Fourteenth Amendment*, 163–164 (Tennessee Democratic minority resolution), 166 (New Jersey legislature), and 167 (Ben Cregan); Fairman, "Original Understanding," 82 (Tennessee Democratic minority resolution, 93–94 (North Carolina governor and legislature), and 104 (Indiana Democratic minority). James, *Framing of Amendment*, 165, and Curtis, *No State Shall Abridge*, 152, have the Johnson administration's efforts against ratification.

30. See generally sources cited in n. 29, supra; James, *Framing of Fourteenth Amendment*, 160 (Bingham); Fairman, "Original Understanding," 73 (Colfax).

31. James, *Ratification of Fourteenth Amendment*, 42 (Morton); Flack, *Adoption of Fourteenth Amendment*, 169 (Cox), and 172 (Fletcher); Fairman, "Original Understanding," 90 (Dillingham).

32. Curtis, *No State Shall Abridge*, 147–49, 149–51 (Pa. and Mass. debates).

33. Herbert Wechsler, *The Nationalization of Civil Liberties and Civil Rights*. Published as a Supplement to the *Texas Quarterly*, vol. XII, no. 2, 1969 Appendix: "Survival and Repeal of Civil Rights Laws Enacted During the Period 1866 to 1875," has the 1870 Enforcement Act, the 1871 Ku Klux Klan Act, and the 1875 Civil Rights Act.

34. *Congressional Globe*, 41st Cong., 2nd. sess. (1870) 3503–4 (House passage of bill, May 16, 1870), and 3611–13 (Sen. Pool's section six and supporting speech, May 18, 1870).

35. 42 CG:1, 236 (Sen. Sherman resolution).

36. President Grant's message was read in the House, 42 CG:1, 244–45, and the Senate, 42 CG:1, 236, on March 23, 1871. Wechsler, *Civil Liberties and Civil Rights* has the Klan Act.

37. CG 42:1, 332–35 (Rep. Hoar, Mar. 29, 1871).

38. CG 42:1, 374–76 (Rep. Lowe, Mar. 31, 1871). For the main Republican speeches on the Klan Bill, see CG 42:1, 319–22, 339, 367–70, 374–76, 389–96, 413–14, 425–29, 434–35, 439, 441–42, 448–50, 456–57, 459–61, 486–88, 498–506, 511–12, 514, 604–9, 691–98, and CG 42:1 Appendix, 40, 68–71, 79–85, 113–17, 141–42, 149–55, 165, 180–83, 187–90, 196, 228, 247–51, 261–63, 273–77, 283–85, 299–300, 307–11, and 312–16. For the Democratic position, see the speeches in CG 42:1, 335–38, 353–57, 371–74, 395–97, 429–32, 441–46, and CG 42:1 Appendix, 86–87, 218–22, 231, and 242–44.

39. CG 42:1 Appendix, 113–15 (Rep. Farnsworth, Mar. 31, 1871); CG 42:1 Appendix, 81–86 (Rep. Bingham, Mar. 31, 1871). Bingham's disclosure in the Klan Bill debate that he had rewritten his February amendment into a set of negatives on the states with Chief Justice Marshall's *Barron v. Baltimore* opinion in mind is confirmed by the fact that his initial revision of the February amendment in late April 1866, within the Joint Committee on Reconstruction, said that no state shall "deny to any person within its jurisdiction the equal protection of the laws, nor take private property for public use without just compensation." The ban on taking property without compensation was the provision in the Bill of Rights that had been litigated in *Barron*. The committee voted down this statement, presumably because it was too narrow in scope, and then later in the day accepted Bingham's three-clause sentence for section one of the Fourteenth Amendment. Kendrick, *Journal of Joint Committee*, 82–89, has the April 21 deliberations.

40. CG 42:1, 317, has the initial version of the Klan Bill, as introduced by Rep. Samuel Shellabarger.

41. CG 42:1 Appendix, 149–51 (Rep. Garfield, April 5, 1871). The Klan Bill passage vote in the House is at CG 42:1, 522.

42. Wechsler, *Civil Liberties and Civil Rights* has the 1875 Civil Rights Act.

Chapter 5

The Court Shreds Congress' Fourteenth Amendment Enforcement Power

In the early decades the Supreme Court's main interest in applying the broad terms of the Fourteenth Amendment was to protect states' rights against what it feared would become undue dominance from Congress and the federal courts. It therefore crafted restrictive interpretations of the three clauses in section one—the citizen privileges or immunities clause, the due process of law clause, and the equal protection of the law clause. While the Court would pour meaning into the due process and equal protection clauses in the twentieth century, the narrow reading of the citizen privileges or immunities clause turned out to be permanent, virtually erasing this clause from the Constitution. The Court also eviscerated the section five authority of Congress in some early cases, out of the same concern for states' rights, with the long-term result that the section five power to protect the people in their life, liberty, and property remains moribund today. The Court has effectively substituted itself for Congress as the designated federal enforcement agency for Fourteenth Amendment rights.

PROTECTING STATES' RIGHTS UNDER THE SECTION ONE CLAUSES 1873–1896

The *Slaughterhouse Cases* (1873) came first. When Louisiana granted an exclusive franchise to a company for the operation of a slaughterhouse within the city limits of New Orleans, the local butchers' trade association challenged the monopoly, arguing that the requirement that slaughtering be carried out only at the premises and with the permission of this single favored corporation violated the butchers' right to freely practice their occupation. In a five-to-four decision for the Court, Justice Samuel Miller rejected the claim, opining that the grant of the franchise was a legitimate exercise of the state's police power. Then he shredded the Fourteenth Amendment's citizens' privileges or immunities clause in a seemingly straightforward textual analysis. Miller observed that the amendment's first sentence creates a dual citizenship by its statement that "All persons born or naturalized in the United States . . . are citizens of the United States and of the State wherein they reside." The second sentence says that no state shall abridge the privileges or immunities of citizens of the United States, and it does not mention citizens of the states. The rights of citizens of the states, and the rights of citizens of the United States, are separate and distinct from each other, and the Fourteenth Amendment protects only the privileges and immunities which an individual enjoys as a result of his status as a citizen of the United States. Under the amendment, the privileges and immunities which the individual enjoys as a result of his status as a citizen of the state remain within the control of the state and beyond the reach of the federal government.

To identify the nature and scope of these state citizenship rights, Miller looked to article IV, section two, of the Constitution, which says that the "citizens of each State shall be entitled to all Privileges and Immunities of Citizens in the several States," as this clause was interpreted in the famous 1823 federal circuit court opinion of *Corfield v. Coryell*, authored by Supreme Court Justice Bushrod Washington while sitting on circuit. We have seen that in this case, holding that New Jersey could limit fishing rights in its oyster beds to its own residents without violating the rights of a citizen from another state, Justice Washington summarized the rights of the citizens of the several states, which no state could abridge, under the following heads: "Protection by the government; the enjoyment of life and liberty, with the right to acquire and possess property of every kind, and to pursue and obtain happiness and safety; subject nevertheless to such restraints as the government may justly prescribe for the general good of the whole." Justice Miller in the *Slaughterhouse Cases* in effect was saying that these fundamental rights of state citizenship, summarized in the 1823 case, remained under the exclusive control of the states so far as the Fourteenth Amendment's citizen privileges or immunities clause was concerned.

What came within the scope of the Fourteenth Amendment's citizen privileges or immunities clause, by contrast, were national citizenship rights that owed their existence to the "Federal government, its national character, its Constitution, or its laws." These were the rights of citizens of the United States which no state could abridge. A citizen of the United States has the right, for example, to travel to the seat of the national government and transact business with it; to peaceably assemble and petition the national government for a redress of grievances; to have the privilege of the writ of habeas corpus because this is a right established in the Constitution; to be protected in one's life, liberty, and property on the high seas and in foreign lands; to be a citizen of the state wherein one resides; and to enjoy the rights secured by the due process and equal protection clauses of the Fourteenth Amendment. None of this helped the butchers. Their right to engage in their trade did not owe its existence to the national government or Constitution, and so it could not be characterized as a privilege or immunity of national citizenship protected by the Fourteenth Amendment. The due process and equal protection clauses were not implicated either. Under no construction of the due process clause is the grant of the monopoly a deprivation of the butchers' property. As for the equal protection clause, "we doubt very much whether any action of a State not directed by way of discrimination against the negroes as a class, or on account of their race, will ever be held within the purview of this provision." The Court has held with a steady hand "the balance between State and Federal power," concluded Miller, and we trust this will remain true in the future.[1] The dual citizenship analysis of the *Slaughterhouse Cases* effectively erased the privileges or immunities clause from the Fourteenth Amendment, as is shown by the fact that in more than fifty Supreme Court cases decided under the clause during the next six decades, only one state law or action was found to be in violation of a national citizenship right, and that decision was overruled four years later.[2]

The due process and equal protection clauses also received narrow readings in the early cases. For example, *Walker v. Sauvinet* (1875) affirmed a $1,000 civil damage award that a state judge had rendered against Walker for refusing to serve Sauvinet, a man of color, at his coffeehouse in New Orleans, Louisiana, in violation of a state law banning racial discrimination at places of business. Walker appealed to the Supreme Court, contending that he had been denied his Seventh Amendment right to a jury trial. The Court said the Seventh Amendment jury trial right applies only to cases in the federal courts. The states, so far as the Seventh Amendment is concerned, are left to regulate trials in their own courts in their own way. "A trial by jury in suits pending in the state courts is not, therefore, a privilege or immunity of national citizenship which the states are forbidden by the Fourteenth Amendment to abridge." The Fourteenth Amendment also provides that a state cannot deprive a person of his property without due process of law, but this does not mean that all trials in the state affecting the property of persons must be by jury. "Due process of law is process according to the law of the land. The process in the States is regulated by the law of the State."[3]

Munn v. Illinois (1877) upheld a state law fixing maximum charges for the storage of grain in warehouses. The warehouses were sufficiently related to the public interest that they would be governed by the common law rule requiring charges to be reasonable, said the Court, and the reasonable price determination could be made legislatively rather than judicially. Rights of property cannot be taken away without due process,

> but the law itself, as a rule of conduct, may be changed at the will . . . of the legislature, unless prevented by constitutional limitations. . . . Indeed, the great office of statutes is to remedy defects in the common law as they are developed, and to adapt it to the changes of time and circumstances. We know that this is a power which may be abused, but that is no argument against its existence. For protection against abuses by legislatures, the people must resort to the polls, not the courts.[4]

In *Hurtado v. People of California* (1884), the Court expanded beyond *Walker*'s holding that the Seventh Amendment does not apply to the states to develop an analysis under the due process clause which logically meant that the entire Bill of Rights does not apply to the actions of the states. Mr. Hurtado, who had been convicted of murder and sentenced to death, appealed to the Supreme Court on the ground that he had been denied his right to be indicted by a grand jury, as the Fifth Amendment requires in capital cases. The Fifth Amendment consists of several clauses, said the Court, one of which calls for a grand jury hearing in capital cases, and another of which provides that no person shall be deprived of life, liberty, or property without due process of law. The inclusion of both instructions separately demonstrates that the framers of the Fifth Amendment did not think the concept of due process of law necessarily encompassed a grand jury element. If those responsible for the adoption of the Fourteenth Amendment had wanted to perpetuate the institution of the grand jury in all the states, they would have declared to that effect in the same way the founding fathers had done for the federal government. Since they did not do this, the grand jury requirement does not apply to the states. In his dissent, Justice John Marshall Harlan pointed out that the Court's redundancy analysis meant that none of the Bill of Rights guarantees could apply to the states, since every one of them is contained in a clause or article separate and distinct from the due process clause in the Fifth Amendment. Until 1925 the Supreme Court repeatedly did hold that none of the Bill of Rights applies to the states.[5]

The Court was similarly deferential under the equal protection clause, even when state laws made distinctions based on race. *Pace v. Alabama* (1883) upheld a statute which declared that "If any white person and any negro . . . intermarry or live in adultery or fornication with each other," upon conviction each may be imprisoned for up to seven years. There is no unlawful discrimination here, said the Court, because the law "applies the same punishment to both offenders, the white and the black." *Plessy v. Ferguson* (1896), the era's most important equal protection case, upheld a Louisiana requirement that all passenger trains must provide "equal but separate accommodations for the white and colored races." This is a "reasonable regulation," said the Court, thereby giving national legitimacy to the Jim Crow racial segregation laws just beginning to sweep across the South.[6]

THE COURT EVISCERATES CONGRESS'S SECTION FIVE AUTHORITY 1876–1883

Congress enacted the 1870 Enforcement Act, the 1871 Ku Klux Klan Act, and the 1875 Civil Rights Act to protect individual rights in the states, and the Supreme Court responded with an interpretive program designed to protect states' rights. It extended the dual citizenship doctrine of the *Slaughterhouse Cases* (1873) to the section five enforcement authority of Congress in *United States v. Cruikshank* (1876), leaving protection for the rights of citizens almost exclusively within state control and beyond the scope of federal law. Then in two cases decided in 1883, *United States v. Harris* and the *Civil Rights Cases*, it applied the state action doctrine, which the Democrats had employed in the Klan Bill debates, to hold that the private conduct of persons and businesses is beyond the reach of Congress under the Fourteenth Amendment.

Cruikshank dealt with a mass murder in Colfax, Louisiana, that occurred when upward of sixty Black Republicans assembled in a local courthouse to plan how to assume control of local government offices, based on the recent contested 1872 election results. A militia of more than one hundred white men, mostly former Confederate soldiers and members of the Klan or the White League, surrounded the courthouse, exchanged shots with the Black people inside, and murdered most of them following their surrender. The Justice Department prosecuted the leaders under section six of the 1870 Enforcement Act, for conspiring to deprive the victims of their rights and privileges "granted or secured . . . by the Constitution or laws of the United States," including their rights to assemble, to bear arms, to not be deprived of their lives and liberty without due process, to enjoy the full and equal benefit of all laws for the security of their person and property, and the right to vote in future elections. The Supreme Court dismissed the indictments.[7]

Citizens of the United States residing within any state are subject to two governments, said the Court in *Cruikshank*, one state and one national. There need be no conflict, however, because the power that one government possesses the other does not. The rights of state citizenship and of national citizenship are entirely different from each other; the states protect state citizenship rights, and the federal government protects national citizenship rights. None of the offenses charged in the indictment involved a right of national citizenship. The states have the exclusive power and responsibility to enforce their citizens' enjoyment of life and liberty, equality before the law, and the right to vote. These basic rights are beyond the authority of the United States to protect, and therefore fall outside the legitimate scope of the criminal conspiracy section of the 1870 Enforcement Act. Perhaps in order to avoid the absurd idea that no rights of national citizenship exist, the Court did note that the right of citizens to assemble to petition Congress, or to engage in an activity involving their relationship with the national government, is an attribute of national citizenship that could fall under the protection of the United States. But the indictment had not alleged that the victims had assembled to petition Congress, or that the murderers had intended to interfere with such a meeting. Following *Cruikshank*, the Court in future cases would identify only a few paltry rights of national citizenship that could be protected under section six of the 1870 Enforcement Act.[8]

The Supreme Court further shredded the section five congressional authority when it established the state action doctrine in two 1883 cases. *United States v. Harris* dealt with the Justice Department's indictment of twenty men in Crockett County, Tennessee, under section two of the Ku Klux Klan Act. As noted above, this section made it a crime for two or more persons to conspire together for the purpose of interfering with federal or state law enforcement efforts, or to deprive some person or persons of equal protection, privileges, or immunities under the law. Mr. Harris and his fellow conspirators had seized four Black men, who were being held in custody by a deputy sheriff for their alleged commission of certain crimes, and beat them to death. The Court said that the Fourteenth Amendment only limits the actions of the states, and here private parties had engaged in the wrongful conduct. Therefore, it dismissed the case.[9]

The *Civil Rights Cases* consolidated lawsuits from several states wherein Black people allegedly had been denied access to an inn, a theater, and a public conveyance on account of their race or color, in violation of the 1875 Civil Rights Act. The Supreme Court dismissed the lawsuits, holding that neither the Thirteenth Amendment nor the Fourteenth Amendment empowered Congress to pass this law. The Thirteenth Amendment did not apply because it was not slavery, or an incident or badge of slavery, for persons to be denied access to services on account of their race or color. The Fourteenth Amendment was of no help either because it deals exclusively with state governments and not with individuals. "Individual invasion of individual rights is not the subject-matter of the Amendment." Congress could correct the effects of a prohibited state law or action, but it could not create a code of municipal law to regulate the conduct of private persons and businesses.[10]

Justice John Marshall Harlan dissented in the *Civil Rights Cases*, relying on both the Thirteenth and the Fourteenth Amendment. He said the Thirteenth

Amendment makes all persons and races free, and grants Congress the power to make this freedom a reality in the states. Since slavery had been based on the alleged inferiority of the Black people held in bondage, "their freedom necessarily involved immunity from, and protection against, all discrimination against them." Federal law therefore could require equal access to public accommodations under the Thirteenth Amendment freedom guarantee.

The law also could be justified as appropriate legislation to enforce the Fourteenth Amendment. In an argument reminiscent of the statements of Republican originators, Harlan rejected the theory that the general government could not, in advance of hostile state laws or proceedings, actively interfere for the protection of Fourteenth Amendment rights. "It is said that such rights . . . are secured by way of prohibition against state laws and state proceedings, . . . and by power given to Congress for the purpose of carrying *such prohibitions* into effect" (Harlan's emphasis). But a section five of this character was not needed and serves no purpose. If it had been entirely omitted, the judicial power still could have nullified state laws and proceedings that violate Fourteenth Amendment rights. The power of congressional legislation cannot be so tied to the laws and actions of the states, concluded Harlan. "If . . . exemption from discrimination, in respect of civil rights, is a new constitutional right secured by the grant of state citizenship to colored citizens of the United States—and I do not see how this can now be questioned—why may not the Nation, by means of its own legislation of a primary character, guard, protect and enforce that right?" The country knew when it adopted the Fourteenth Amendment that the equal rights of citizenship might be threatened "by the hostile actions of corporations and individuals in the States," as well as by "unfriendly state legislation." The "great dissenter" Harlan spoke as a lone voice in the judicial wilderness on the subject of the Fourteenth Amendment section five enforcement power of Congress.[11]

THE MISCHIEVOUS ERRORS OF THE DUAL CITIZENSHIP AND STATE ACTION DOCTRINES

Until these early cases are overturned on the basis of the original meaning of the Fourteenth Amendment, our constitutional understanding will remain flawed. Superficially, the dual citizenship doctrine established by Justice Miller in his opinion in the *Slaughterhouse Cases*, under which the citizens of the state, as such, are excluded from the protective coverage of the Fourteenth Amendment, could derive some support from the constitutional text considered in the abstract. The first sentence in section one says that persons born or naturalized in the United States are citizens of the United States and of the state wherein they reside, while the second sentence merely says that the state shall not abridge the privileges or immunities of citizens of the United States, and does not mention citizens of the state. Thus, said Miller, only state abridgements of the rights of citizens of the United States, i.e., national citizenship rights, are subject to federal review and protection. The states retain exclusive control of state citizenship rights. The bifurcation of citizenship based upon this textual analysis loses force, however, when one realizes that Congress added the first sentence to define citizenship near the end of the enactment process. During the drafting in the Joint Committee on Reconstruction, House consideration and passage, and introduction in the Senate, the amendment contained no such introductory sentence. Out of an abundance of caution, the Republicans decided in their Senate caucus to overrule the *Dred Scott* decision on national citizenship, and the practice of slave states before the Civil War to exclude Black people from being citizens of the state. To remove any doubt, they put a definition of national and state citizenship into the Fourteenth Amendment.[12]

It is simply incredible to suggest that the Republicans at the last moment decided to dramatically transform the Fourteenth Amendment by placing the protection for citizens' enjoyment of their life, liberty, property, and pursuit of happiness—the rights that Justice Washington summarized in *Corfield v. Coryell*—outside the scope of the amendment, so as to leave them in the exclusive control of the states. Nobody in Congress or in the state ratifying legislatures expressed such an idea, and it makes no sense. Under the citizenship definition in the first sentence, a citizen of the United States is also a citizen of the state where he or she resides, pure and simple. Justice Stephen Field in his opinion for the four dissenting justices in the *Slaughterhouse Cases* made the point nicely: "A citizen of a State is now only a citizen of the United States residing in that State. The fundamental rights, privileges and immunities which belong to him as a free man and a free citizen now belong to him as a citizen of the United States, and are not dependent upon his citizenship of any State." These citizen rights do not derive their existence from the state's legislation, and they cannot be destroyed by its power, concluded Field.

History, logic, an accurate reading of article IV, section two and *Corfield*, and contemporary statements by the Republicans all compel this understanding about the nature and promise of the Fourteenth Amendment's citizenship definition and guarantee. Justice Miller in his opinion for the *Slaughterhouse Cases* majority misquoted the *Corfield* opinion to suit his own purpose. Article IV, section two says the "Citizens of each State shall be entitled to all privileges and immunities of Citizens *in* the several States." *Corfield* asked, "What are the privileges and immunities of citizens *in* the several States?" Justice Miller glossed over precise constitutional text and changed *Corfield*'s inquiry to be, "What are the privileges and immunities of citizens *of* the several states?" Referring to citizens *of* the several states, rather than to citizens *in* the several states, obviously supported the distinction he was making between state and national citizenship (my emphasis).[13]

The Republicans by contrast made it clear that a citizen of the state is a citizen of the United States residing in that state. For example, Bingham said in an 1862 speech in Congress, referring to article IV, section two, "Does not the constitution promise that the citizens of each State, being *ipso facto* citizens of the United States, shall be entitled to all privileges and immunities of citizens *in* the Several States?" The Constitution "does not read . . . that the citizens of each State should be entitled to the privileges and immunities of citizens of the several States. No, sir, the word used in the Constitution in this clause is not *of*, but *in*, the several States. All the privileges and immunities of citizens of the United States *in* the several States, is what is guaranteed by the Constitution" (Bingham's emphasis). In a January 9, 1866, speech Bingham again quoted the article IV clause with his ellipsis, "The citizens of each State (being *ipso facto* citizens of the United States) shall be entitled to all the privileges and immunities of citizens (supplying the ellipsis 'of the United States' in the several States.)" Citizenship is national, and ought to be protected by the national government.

In his presentation of the Fourteenth Amendment to the Senate, Jacob Howard said the first clause of section one involves the privileges and immunities of citizens of the United States. The term "citizen of the United States" appears twice in the constitution. The President and every senator shall be a "Citizen of the United States." Before the adoption of the Constitution, the citizens of each state were, in a sense, aliens in every other state. The states were sovereign governments, and they could naturalize foreigners as citizens of the state. They could also treat citizens of other states as aliens. To prevent such confusion, the Constitution included the article IV, section two privileges and immunities clause to make citizens of the several states equal with each other as to fundamental rights. The effect of the clause, Howard concluded, was to "constitute *ipso facto* the citizens of each one of the original States citizens of the United States." As one final example of the Republican understanding about the fused nature of an individual's national and state citizenship, James Garfield in the Klan Bill debates cited Chief Justice Marshall's Supreme Court opinion in *Gassie v. Ballou* (1832), which held that a citizen of the United States is also a citizen of the state in which he resides.[14] Overcoming this precedent and logic, the five-justice majority in the *Slaughterhouse Cases* divided citizenship into two separate components to protect the states against what they feared would be undue interference from the federal government.

In contrast to the dual citizenship theory, the state action doctrine does make sense for the courts when they are deciding cases under section one of the Fourteenth Amendment. The section one clauses address *state* abridgements, deprivations, and denials of rights. Absent some "state action," there is nothing for the court to do; it has no case or controversy to adjudicate. Once the state does act, then the court can assess whether the law enactment or enforcement abridges a citizen's privileges or immunities, deprives a person of life, liberty, or property without due process, or denies a person the equal protection of the laws. The court can judge whether the state's action is constitutional within the terms of the amendment.

But the logic of the state action doctrine collapses when it is extended to the section five enforcement authority of Congress. The states have an affirmative duty to protect people in their exercise and enjoyment of basic rights, a duty textually captured in the equal protection clause when read in conjunction with the two clauses that precede it in the section one sentence. All citizens have privileges and immunities (which cannot be abridged), and all persons have rights to life, liberty, and property (which cannot be deprived without due process). Saying that the state *shall not deny* the equal protection of the laws is equivalent to saying that it *shall provide* the protection. Protection in what? A logical reading of the sentence is that the states shall provide (not deny) equal protection of the laws to citizens in their privileges and immunities and to all persons in their life, liberty, and property. It is this state obligation to protect rights that Congress can enforce in section five. The people who wrote and supported the Fourteenth Amendment in 1866 and interpreted it in later debates in Congress consistently expressed this understanding of section one when read together with section five. Based upon this original meaning, Congress can protect people against private, as well as state-sponsored, harms and discriminations. Although the courts cannot address state failures to act, Congress can pass legislation to fill in the gaps.

PERMANENT CONSEQUENCES: THE SECTION FIVE POWER REMAINS LARGELY DORMANT

The early cases narrowly interpreting the section five congressional power to enforce the Fourteenth Amendment have never been overturned and remain "good law" today. When Congress in the 1960s finally returned to the project of granting equal protection for peoples' fundamental rights of life, liberty, property, and the pursuit of happiness, it mostly acted under its article I, section eight commerce and spending powers in the original Constitution. It relied on this source of authority, rather than section five of the Fourteenth Amendment, to avoid the state action doctrine, and the Supreme Court for a long time cooperated in the strategy. For example, Congress looked to article I, section eight to design and deliver the most important civil rights legislation since Reconstruction—the 1964 Civil Rights Act. Title II of the law banned discrimination on the basis of race, color, religion or national origin in any place of "public accommodation," defined as a hotel, motel, restaurant, movie house, etc. whose operations "affect commerce." Title VI outlawed similar discriminations in "federally assisted programs," such as schools and colleges, and Title VII guaranteed an equal opportunity in employment without regard to race, color, religion, sex, or national origin by the government or by private employers with twenty-five or more employees whose operations "affect commerce."

The liberal Warren Court upheld the public accommodations title as a permissible regulation of commerce in two 1964 cases. *Heart of Atlanta Motel v. United States* opined that the motel's refusal to serve Black people had a substantial effect on interstate commerce. This analysis enabled the Court to distinguish the *Civil Rights Cases* (1883) because the early precedent had not considered the commerce clause as a possible separate source of power for Congress to enact civil rights legislation. In a companion case decided the same day, *Katzenbach v. McClung*, the Court held that Congress had a rational basis for finding that racial discrimination in restaurants—in this instance Ollie's Barbecue, a family-owned restaurant in Birmingham, Alabama, which served few if any interstate travelers, but which did purchase food that moved across state lines—"adversely affected the free flow of commerce."

In a concurring opinion in the two cases, Justice William Douglas said he would have preferred the Court to base the statute upon the Fourteenth Amendment because this would have a "more settling effect, making unnecessary litigation over whether a particular restaurant or inn is within the commerce definition of the act or whether a particular customer is an interstate traveler." The means used were "appropriate" and "plainly adapted" to the end of the Fourteenth Amendment. Justice Arthur Goldberg, in his own concurring opinion, said that he agreed with Douglas that the primary purpose of the law was the "vindication of human dignity and not mere economics," and that this objective could be accomplished under section five of the Fourteenth Amendment. Justices Douglas and Goldberg had good instincts but they were unable to explain why the state action requirement need not be applied to constrain section five authority. A good history of the Fourteenth Amendment's original meaning would have given them a firm basis for their implicit abandonment of the state action doctrine as applied to laws of Congress.[15]

Other Fourteenth Amendment–type liberty and equal rights protections Congress enacted without reference to its section five power included the 1960 Civil Rights Act, the 1962 Work Hours and Safety Act, the 1963 Developmental Disabilities Assistance and Bill of Rights Act, the 1963 Equal

Pay Act, the 1967 Age Discrimination in Employment Act, the 1968 Fair Housing Act, the 1972 Equal Employment Opportunity Act, the 1974 Child Abuse Prevention and Treatment Act, the 1974 Equal Credit Opportunity Act, the 1978 Pregnancy Discrimination Act, the 1980 Privacy Protection Act, the 1980 Adoption Assistance and Child Welfare Act, the 1984 Victims of Crime Act, the 1987 Civil Rights Restoration Act, the 1988 Video Privacy Protection Act, the 1990 Americans with Disabilities Act, the 1990 Gun-free School Zones Act, the 1991 Civil Rights Act, the 1994 Driver's Privacy Protection Act, the 1994 Safe and Drug-free Schools and Communities Act, the 1994 Violence Against Women Act, and various amendments thereto.[16]

Just as some commentators were beginning to question whether the Constitution imposed any practical limits on the regulatory powers of Congress, aside from the restraints in the Bill of Rights, the Rehnquist Court struck down two of these laws as unconstitutional stretches of the commerce clause power. *United States v. Lopez* (1995), and *United States v. Morrison* (2000), each held that Congress could not reach conduct within the states that does not substantially affect interstate commercial or economic activity. *Lopez* reviewed the case of a senior in high school who carried a concealed handgun into his classroom in violation of the Gun-free School Zones Act, which made it a crime for anyone to possess a gun in or within 1,000 feet of a school. Since the statute did not regulate an economic activity or require the possession of the firearm to be connected to interstate commerce, it exceeded the power of Congress to regulate commerce among the states. This represented the type of police power exercise that is reserved to the states.

The plaintiff in *Morrison* was Cindy Brzonkala, a student at Virginia Tech who allegedly had been raped by two football players. When she could obtain no relief from the school, she became depressed, dropped out of the university, and filed a complaint in federal court under the Violence Against Women Act. This federal law made anyone who commits a crime of violence motivated by gender liable to the injured party for damages or for such other remedy the court deems appropriate. The Supreme Court dismissed the case, holding that the law was invalid as commerce clause legislation because it regulated "noneconomic, criminal activity that does not affect interstate commerce." Although Congress had held hearings and determined that gender-motivated violence affects interstate commerce, the Court dismissed this with the statement that "whether particular operations affect interstate commerce sufficiently to come under the power of Congress to regulate them is ultimately a judicial rather than a legislative question, and can be settled finally only by this Court." None of the four justices who dissented in *Lopez* and in *Morrison* sought to defend the laws as appropriate exercises of police power authority to protect life and liberty under section five of the Fourteenth Amendment. They strained instead to find that the ban on guns in school and the punishment for crimes of gender violence were statutes that fell within Congress' authority to "regulate Commerce with foreign Nations, among the several States, and with the Indian Tribes," not a very credible argument.[17]

CONGRESS CANNOT INDEPENDENTLY INTERPRET ITS SECTION FIVE AUTHORITY

In situations where the state action doctrine could not be a problem, Congress in the modern era occasionally has employed its section five power to prescribe due process or equal protection standards for the states to apply. In such cases, the Court has shown little deference, upholding the first of these statutes in 1966 with an important caveat, and overruling two later statutes in 1970 and 1997. In an outlier case, Justice William Brennan opined for the Court in *Katzenbach v. Morgan* (1966) that Congress could prescribe standards for state conduct that go beyond prior relevant holdings of the Supreme Court. The decision upheld a federal law ban on literacy tests in state elections, even though the Court had concluded in an earlier case that such tests did not violate the Fourteenth Amendment's equal protection clause, and therefore were constitutionally permissible. So long as Congress does not diminish protection for rights embodied in prior decisions of the Court, said Brennan, it can depart from case law. This "one-way ratchet" meant that Congress could not pass a statute to promote its own understanding of the public interest if this would limit a judicially established private right. The justices remained in control of constitutional interpretation because they retained final decision-making authority on the question of whether any given piece of legislation really does enhance appropriate protection for individual rights.[18]

The Court dropped even this conditional deference to Congress four years later, in the case of *Oregon v. Mitchell* (1970), when it held that Congress could not lower to eighteen the voting age in state and local elections. This extension of the franchise to a new class of citizens could not stand because it intruded upon the prerogatives of the states. *City of Boerne v. Flores* (1997) resolved the tension between *Katzenbach v. Morgan* (some interpretive authority for Congress provided that the legislation does not dilute any Fourteenth Amendment protection, as viewed by the Court), and *Oregon v. Mitchell* (no deference even though the statute expands the scope of the right to vote), by stating that Congress has no authority to interpret the amendment independently from the Court.

City of Boerne struck down the Religious Freedom Restoration Act of 1993 insofar as it applied to the states under the Fourteenth Amendment. This law was Congress' response to a 1990 Supreme Court case holding that neutral state laws of general applicability could apply to religious practices, even though they impose a burden on those practices and are not supported by a compelling governmental interest. The Religious Freedom law restored the strict scrutiny standard of judicial review which the Court had previously used in cases interpreting the First Amendment free exercise clause. This strict scrutiny standard had required the states to show that any burden they impose on the free exercise of religion is necessary to the achievement of a compelling governmental interest, and the least restrictive means to achieve that interest. When a Catholic bishop challenged a town's zoning ordinance under the Religious Freedom law, the Court held that the federal statute exceeded Congress' authority under section five of the Fourteenth Amendment. This enforcement power is "corrective or remedial, not definitional." The stringent test the Religious Freedom law demands of state laws "reflects a lack of proportionality or congruence between the injury to be prevented or remedied and the means adopted to achieve the legitimate end." The statute effects a substantive change in constitutional rights protection, and thereby undermines the "separation of powers [between Congress and the Court] and the federal balance [between federal and state authority]." The Court in the *City of Boerne* case insisted that interpreting the meaning of the Fourteenth Amendment is exclusively a judicial function. It therefore applied its recently adopted lower review standard instead of the one expressed in the federal statute, and upheld the state against the church's claim.[19]

The Supreme Court was not quite finished with section five interpretations due to a separate development under article I, section eight of the Constitution. Two cases in the 1990s established that Congress in article I legislation could not subject the states to private lawsuits as a means of enforcing federal laws because such suits would abrogate the sovereign immunity of the states. The 1988 Indian Gaming Regulatory Act required states to negotiate in good faith with Indian tribes to create compacts governing Indian gaming. If a state refused to engage in a good faith negotiation, the tribe could sue for relief in federal court. *Seminole Tribe of Florida v. Florida* (1996) struck down this law on the theory that the law abrogated Florida's sovereign immunity. In another case, when a group of state employees sued Maine to enforce their right to receive overtime pay under the provisions of the Fair Labor Standards Act, *Alden v. Maine* (1999) held Congress could not subject states to suit in state court either, for the same reason.[20]

These decisions shifted attention back to section five of the Fourteenth Amendment, since the Supreme Court had adopted the position that private litigants could sue their state government for an alleged infringement of their due process or equal protection rights. This meant that if a law which Congress enacted under its article I authority (or without citing an authority) could be characterized as a permissible Fourteenth Amendment statute, then private parties could sue to enforce their statutory rights in the courts.

But *City of Boerne v. Flores* (1997) stood as an obstacle to such a strategy. Its instruction that a federal statute could be considered an "appropriate" enforcement of the Fourteenth Amendment only if there existed "a congruence and proportionality between the injury to be prevented or remedied and the means adopted to that end," has proven to be a difficult test to satisfy.

For example, *Kimel v. Florida Board of Regents* (2000) involved the Age Discrimination in Employment Act. Congress passed the statute in 1967, extended its protections to cover state and local government employees seven years later, and in 1983 the Court held this extension was a valid exercise of Congress' power to regulate commerce. Following the decisions that article I laws could not be enforced against the states by means of private lawsuits, *Kimel* considered whether the Age Discrimination in Employment Act's judicial remedy could be saved under the Fourteenth Amendment. The Court decided that it could not be saved in this way. The act could not be treated as appropriate section five legislation because the nondiscrimination requirements were "disproportionate to any unconstitutional conduct that conceivably could have been targeted by the Act." Since age discrimination is "presumptively rational" under the equal protection case law, the statute "prohibited substantially more state employment decisions and practices than would likely be held unconstitutional by the Court."

Board of Trustees of the University of Alabama v. Garrett (2001) rejected an attempt of state employees to sue for money damages for the state's alleged failure to comply with the Americans with Disabilities Act. The legislative record of the act failed to show that Congress identified a pattern of irrational state discrimination in employment against the disabled, said the Court. Even if a pattern of unconstitutional discrimination could be squeezed out of the examples given, the rights and remedies created by the ADA would raise the same sort of concerns about congruence and proportionality as were found in *City of Boerne*. The Court used similar reasoning to prevent a private right of action under the Family and Medical Leave Act in *Coleman v. Court of Appeals of Md.* (2012).[21]

RETRIEVING CONGRESS' SECTION FIVE ENFORCEMENT POWER

In the early decades of the republic, Americans assumed that each of the branches in the federal government would apply their own understanding of the Constitution as they carried out their assigned duties and responsibilities. It was Congress' responsibility to make the laws, and its debates about the meaning of the Constitution were detailed and instructive. When Congress voted for the Fourteenth Amendment and the states ratified it, there was every reason to believe that the executive and judicial branches of the federal government would in good faith enforce the laws Congress might enact to support people's life, liberty, and property rights in the states, and for a while they did. Congress in 1870 established the Department of Justice, and from 1871 to the summer of 1873 the department's attorneys successfully prosecuted more than a thousand cases against members of the Ku Klux Klan and other white terrorist organizations in several southern states under the 1870 Enforcement Act and the 1871 Klan Act. The federal district courts and circuit courts of appeal enforced these laws against private actors and routinely confirmed their constitutionality if challenged.[22]

Encouraged by these successes and hopeful for a return to normalcy, President Ulysses S. Grant decided to cease active federal criminal investigations and return primary law enforcement responsibility to the states. The move had the support of many in Congress and a large portion of the American people, who wanted to promote a policy of national reconciliation and were growing weary of the government's efforts to achieve civil and political equality for Black people in the South.[23] In these changed circumstances of public opinion, the Supreme Court issued its series of landmark decisions that narrowly construed the Fourteenth Amendment section one clauses and eviscerated the section five authority of Congress. The Court joined the federal elective branches as a powerful third force in the nation's political affairs, assuming the role of supreme decider of constitutional meaning. It conferred legitimacy on state laws, and proscribed federal legislative protections, in some important cases impacting people's rights and personal safety.

Knowing what we do now about the original meaning of the Fourteenth Amendment could guide a fruitful revision of the early foundational decisions of the Supreme Court. For example, the section one interpretations in the *Slaughterhouse Cases* (1873), *Walker v. Sauvignet* (1875), and *Hurtado v. United States* (1884) and the section five state action decisions in *United States v. Harris* and the *Civil Rights Cases* (both 1883) could be "rewritten" to achieve compliance with the amendment's original meaning, as this was explained by its drafters and supporters. Such a reconsideration of history could pave the way for an improved regime of decision-making about our individual rights, and both state and federal government powers and responsibilities, under the Constitution.

Louisiana gave a state-created corporation the exclusive right for twenty-five years to establish and maintain slaughterhouses, landings for cattle and livestock, and yards for holding cattle and other animals intended for sale or slaughter in New Orleans, and prohibited others from having slaughterhouses and cattle yards within city limits. The corporation could charge only prescribed fees for the use of its wharves, and for each animal landed and slaughtered, and was required to give equal access to all owners of stock to land their animals, and to all butchers to slaughter, at those places. A state-appointed inspector would inspect all the animals intended for slaughter to ascertain their fitness for human consumption, and if satisfied on this score, to give a certificate to the owners of the animals. The Supreme Court in the *Slaughterhouse Cases* (1873) held that this was a reasonable police regulation for the health and comfort of the people of New Orleans, and dismissed the complaint of the butchers' trade association. This holding was a good one. But then the Court went on further to discuss the meaning of the Fourteenth Amendment.

An originalist revision of this discussion could be as follows: The butchers have claimed the state law abridges their citizen privileges and immunities and deprives them of due process for their property rights, under the Fourteenth Amendment, by forbidding them to operate their own slaughterhouses within the city limits of New Orleans. The privileges or immunities clause, and the due process of law clause, when read together with the equal protection clause, require the states to provide (not deny) equal protection for the life, liberty, and property rights of all persons subject to their jurisdiction, by the adoption and enforcement of reasonable and fair regulations. Louisiana has done so here. The butchers' right to practice their trade is not an absolute right, exempt from state regulation. Louisiana has imposed a reasonable health and environmental mandate that all livestock slaughtering and sale activities must be conducted on the premises of a single state-created corporation, when within the city limits of New Orleans. If Congress disagrees with this result, it can enact legislation under section five of the Fourteenth Amendment to ensure that the restraints being imposed on the butchers are reasonable and fair.

Walker v. Sauvignet (1875) correctly held that the Seventh Amendment right to a jury trial in civil cases, where the value in controversy exceeds twenty dollars, was not automatically extended to the states by the privileges or immunities clause or the due process clause in the Fourteenth Amendment. The jury trial requirement applies in federal courts, but is not a citizen privilege that must be honored in state courts. Moreover, said the Court, "Due process of law is process according to the law of the land. The process in the States is regulated by the law of the States." An original-meaning revision of the case opinion could add the observation that while due process in the states is regulated by state law, Congress under its section five authority could impose additional or different process requirements in defined circumstances to protect people's life, liberty, and property rights. This could include making juries available in civil cases.

Hurtado v. California (1884) persuasively explained why the Fifth Amendment grand jury requirement in capital cases does not apply to the states by virtue of the due process clause in section one of the Fourteenth Amendment. The Fifth Amendment contains both a grand jury clause and a due process clause, thereby showing that due process does not necessarily include a grand jury component. If the framers of the Fourteenth Amendment had intended to extend the grand jury provision to the states, for the courts to enforce, they would have included it in their text, as the framers of the Fifth Amendment had done. An original meaning addendum could include the point that if Congress believes a grand jury requirement in capital cases is an important process protection for the people in state cases, it could pass a law extending this safeguard under its section five authority. John Bingham said as much during the 1871 Klan Bill debate.

The revival and appropriate implementation of section five authority require the rejection of the state action doctrine, established in *United States v. Harris* and the *Civil Rights Cases* (both 1883), and the unreasonable insistence in *City of Boerne v. Flores* (1997) that Congress cannot independently interpret the meaning of the Fourteenth Amendment. The Republicans in the Klan Bill debate presented a persuasive analysis of why the state action doctrine, appropriate for the courts in section one cases, should not be extended to limit the section five police power of Congress to legislate protections for people's rights and safety. As for *City of Boerne* (1997), neither the quality of the Supreme Court's reviews of federal laws, nor the text of the founders' Constitution, nor the original meaning of the Fourteenth Amendment, can justify the claim of judicial supremacy or exclusivity in constitutional interpretation. The Court got it exactly wrong. Instead of Congress being confined to the enforcement of court-defined rights in the Fourteenth Amendment, the courts should enforce rights that Congress establishes through section five legislation.

NOTES

1. *Slaughterhouse Cases*, 83 U.S. 36, 74–81.
2. Justice Harlan Fiske Stone, in his dissenting opinion in *Colgate v. Harvey*, 296 U.S. 404, 445 (1935), listed fifty cases in which the Supreme Court had upheld a state law that had been challenged as a violation of the privileges or immunities clause. He supplemented the list with a few more cases in *Hague v. C.I.O.*, 302 U.S. 496 (1939). *Colgate* was the one case to overturn a state law as a violation of the privileges or immunities clause, and it was overturned four years later in *Hague*.
3. *Walker*, 92 U.S. 90.
4. *Munn*, 94 U.S. 113.
5. *Hurtado*, 110 U.S. 516.
6. *Pace*, 106 U.S. 583; *Plessy*, 163 U.S. 537.

7. *Slaughterhouse Cases*, 83 U.S. 36; *Cruikshank*, 92 U.S. 542; *Harris*, 106 U.S. 629; and *Civil Rights Cases*, 109 U.S. 26. For the Colfax massacre, see James Hamilton, "The Colfax Massacre a Forgotten Chapter of Violence," *Liberated Arts*, vol. 5, issue no. 1, article 2 (2018).

8. *Cruikshank*, 92 U.S. 542. The progeny of *Cruikshank* found the following rights to be national citizenship rights which could be protected by the federal government: *Ex parte Yarbrough*, 110 U.S. 651 (1884) (right to vote in federal election); *United States v. Waddell*, 112 U.S. 576 (1884) (right to enter upon unclaimed public lands and perfect title by occupancy under the federal homestead laws); *Logan v. United States*, 144 U.S. 263 (1892) (right to be protected against violence while in the custody of a federal marshal); *In re Quarles and Butler*, 158 U.S. 532 (1895) (right to inform a federal official about a federal law violation); *Motes v. United States*, 178 U.S. 458 (1900) (right to testify as a witness in federal court); and *United States v. Mosley*, 238 U.S. 383 (1915) (right to have votes counted by state election officials in an election for a member of Congress).

9. *Harris*, 106 U.S. 629, 630–32, and 637–40.

10. *Civil Rights Cases*, 109 U.S. 3, 4–5, 9–11, and 20–24.

11. *Civil Rights Cases*, 109 U.S. 3, 26–30, 33–35, and 44–52 (Justice Harlan dissenting opinion).

12. For the last-minute addition of the citizenship sentence to section one, see *Congressional Globe*, 39th Cong., 1st sess. (1866), 2869, May 29, 1866 (hereafter CG 39:1).

13. Justice Miller's misquotation of article IV and *Corfield* in the *Slaughterhouse Cases* is at 83 U.S. 36, 75–76.

14. Alfred Avins, *The Reconstruction Amendments' Debates: The Legislative History and Contemporary Debates in Congress on the 13th, 14th, and 15th Amendments* (Richmond: Virginia Commission on Constitutional Government, 1967), 38 (Bingham speech 1862); CG 39:1, 156–59 (Rep. Bingham, Jan. 9, 1866); CG 39:1, 2765–68 (Sen. Howard, May 23, 1866); and *Congressional Globe*, 42nd Cong., 1st sess. (1871) Appendix, 52 (Rep. Garfield, April 5, 1871).

15. The 1964 Civil Rights Act, Pub. L. No. 88–352, codified at 42 U.S.C. ch. 29. Title VI banned discrimination on the grounds of race, color, or national origin, and Title VII banned discrimination on the grounds of race, color, religion, sex, or national origin in the covered facilities and organizations. See *Heart of Atlanta Motel*, 379 U.S. 241, and *McClung*, 379 U.S. 294. The Douglas and Goldberg concurring opinions are at 379 U.S. 279 and 291.

16. See generally the United States Code of Popular Names, compiled by the Law Revision Council, United States House of Representatives.

17. *Lopez*, 514 U.S. 549; *Morrison*, 529 U.S. 598, 614.

18. *Morgan*, 384 U.S. 641.

19. *Oregon*, 400 U.S. 112; *City of Boerne*, 521 U.S. 507.

20. *Seminole Tribe*, 517 U.S. 44; *Alden*, 527 U.S. 706.

21. *Kimel*, 528 U.S. 56; *Garrett*, 531 U.S. 356; *Coleman*, 566 U.S. 30. The 1993 Family and Medical Leave Act (FMLA) entitled an employee to take up to twelve weeks of unpaid leave per year for, among other reasons, the employee's serious

health condition when the condition interfered with performance at work. The article I, section eight law created a private right of action, in cases of an alleged violation, to sue for equitable relief or damages against the employer (including a public agency) in any federal or state court. The Supreme Court in *Coleman* held that a state employee's suit must be dismissed because of the state's sovereign immunity. The statute could not be considered an appropriate enforcement of the Fourteenth Amendment because it was not tailored to prevent or remedy conduct transgressing the amendment's substantive provisions. When the FMLA was enacted, there was no evidence of sex discrimination or stereotyping in sick-leave policies. Accordingly, there was no "congruence or proportionality between . . . [a Fourteenth Amendment] injury to be prevented and the means adopted to that end," *City of Boerne*.

22. Robert J. Kaczorowski, *The Politics of Judicial Interpretation: The Federal Courts, the Justice Department, and Civil Rights, 1866–1876* (New York: Oceana Publishers, 1985), chs. 3–5.

23. Ibid.; Eric Foner, *Reconstruction: America's Unfinished Revolution, 1863–1877* (New York: Harper & Row, 1988).

Chapter 6

Fourteenth Amendment Due Process

The Court's enforcement of the due process clause in the Fourteenth Amendment divides into three eras. We have seen that in the early decades the justices' main interest in interpreting the amendment was to protect states' rights against what it feared would become undue interference and control from the federal government. It narrowly construed the three clauses in section one, and the section five enforcement power of Congress.

Having protected states' rights by these early interpretations, the still-conservative but now pro-business, free-market-economy Court, from the 1890s to 1937, overruled many state laws as substantive or procedural violations of the due process clause. In this period, labeled the "Lochner era" after a 1905 liberty of contract case, most of the overrides enforced the justices' views of peoples' and corporations' economic liberty and property rights. To its credit in this otherwise-discredited period, the Court required the states to use fair procedures in liberty and property deprivation cases, substantively upheld "family rights" in two cases (1923 and 1925), and in *Gitlow v. New York* (1925) began to absorb into the due process clause for application to the states the substantive freedoms embodied in the First Amendment. Under public pressure during the Great Depression and President Franklin Delano Roosevelt's New Deal programs of the 1930s, the Court ceased fashioning substantive protections for economic liberty and property.

In what commentators have called "the New Deal settlement of 1937," the Court changed its approach, allowing Congress, and the states within boundaries set by Congress, unfettered discretion to regulate the economy. Henceforth, legislators in the states and Congress, not judges, would determine the nature and scope—the substance—of economic liberty and property rights. Ever since 1937, in its overrides of state laws and enforcement actions under the due process clause, the Court has devoted attention to three categories of cases: It has continued to require fair procedures for state government deprivations of liberty or property; citing the two Lochner-era family rights cases with favor, it has granted substantive protection to some preferred, noneconomic liberties such as birth control and abortion; and it has utilized the due process clause as a vehicle to incorporate and apply to the states most of the guarantees and restraints in the Bill of Rights. This chapter focuses on the Supreme Court's enforcement of the due process clause standing alone, "on its own bottom." The next chapter will cover its extension of the Bill of Rights to the states.

PROTECTING ECONOMIC LIBERTY AND PROPERTY RIGHTS 1890S TO 1937

The commencement of the Court's economic due process jurisprudence logically can be traced to the case of *Chicago, M. and St. Paul Ry. v. Minnesota* (1890), which held that a state law which empowered a commission to establish rate schedules for railroads that were final and not subject to judicial review violated the due process clause. "The question of the reasonableness of a rate of charge for transportation by a railroad company . . . is eminently a question for judicial investigation, requiring due process for its determination." In dissent Justice Joseph Bradley (joined by Justices Horace Gray and Lucius Lamar) pointed out that the majority's decision "practically overrules" *Munn v. Illinois (*1877) and several railroad cases. He said that the decision of what is a reasonable charge by a corporation is "preeminently a legislative one, involving considerations of policy."[1]

Many economic due process decisions followed until 1937. The Court in *Missouri Pacific Ry. v. Nebraska* (1896) held that a Nebraska statute, which required a railroad to permit an association of farmers to erect and maintain a grain elevator on land within its right of way, deprived the railroad of property in violation of due process of law. The next year *Gulf C. and S.F. Ry. v. Ellis* decided that a Texas law, which made railroads pay court costs and attorney fees to litigants successfully prosecuting claims against them, deprived the railroads of due process and equal protection of the law. A number of cases ensued holding that states established rates too low to give the regulated company a reasonable return on its investment, or imposed a burden on business property without providing adequate compensation. Examples included *Smyth v. Ames* (1898) (A Nebraska statute setting freight rates so low as to be unreasonable amounted to a deprivation of the railroad's property without due process); *Wilcox v. Consolidated Gas Co.* (1909) (A New York law that required a public utility to perform its services in such a manner that its entire plant would have to be rebuilt at a cost on which no return could be obtained under the rates fixed by the law unconstitutionally deprived the utility of its property without due process); *Louisville and Nashville R.R.. v. Stock Yards Co.* (1909) (A Kentucky constitutional provision that required a carrier to deliver its cars to connecting carriers without providing adequate protection for their return or compensation for their use effected an invalid taking of property without due process); and *Northern Pacific Ry. v. North Dakota ex rel. McCue* (1915) (A North Dakota law compelling carriers to haul certain commodities at less than compensatory rates deprived them of property without due process).[2]

Some decisions struck down state taxes on out-of-state businesses and properties:

- *Union Transit Co. v. Kentucky* (1905): Because tangible personal property acquires a tax situs in the state where it is permanently located, an attempt by Kentucky to tax a Kentucky company's railway cars located in Indiana amounts to a deprivation of property without due process.
- *International Paper Co. v. Massachusetts* (1918): A license fee or excise of a given percent of the par value of the authorized capital stock of a foreign corporation doing both a local and interstate business, and owning property in several states, is a tax on the entire business and property of the corporation and therefore is an illegal burden on interstate commerce and a violation of due process by reason of affecting property beyond the borders of the taxing state.
- *Brooke v. City of Norfolk* (1928): State and city taxes in Virginia may not be levied on the corpus of a trust located in Maryland, the income from which accrues to a Virginia resident; the corpus is beyond the jurisdiction of Virginia and accordingly the assessments violate due process.[3]

Some decisions struck down state laws for not granting process that the Court considered was due, including:

- *Dewey v. City of Des Moines* (1899): An Iowa statute deprives a nonresident owner of property in Iowa of due process by subjecting him to personal liability to pay a special assessment when the state does not acquire personal jurisdiction via service of process.
- *Central of Georgia Ry. v. Wright* (1907): A Georgia statutory tax assessment procedure that allows the taxpayer to challenge a property valuation only for fraud and corruption does not afford due process.
- *Tumey v. Ohio* (1927): An Ohio law that compensates mayors serving as judges in minor prohibition offenses out of the fees and costs collected from defendants who are convicted violates due process.

- *Wuchter v. Pizzutti* (1928): A New Jersey statute which provides, in suits by residents against nonresidents for injuries resulting from the operation of motor vehicles by nonresidents, that service might be made on the secretary of state as the agent for the nonresidents, but which fails to provide any assurance that notice of such service will be communicated to the nonresidents, violates due process.[4]

The following representative sample of cases will show the nature and impact of the Court's economic due process jurisprudence to 1937. *International Harvester Co. v. Kentucky* (1914) held that Kentucky criminal antitrust provisions are void for vagueness and hence violate due process because a prohibition of combinations that establish prices that are greater or lower than the "real market value" of an article as established by "fair competition" and "under normal market conditions" affords no standard that is possible to know in advance and to obey. A Washington State law that proscribes private employment agencies by prohibiting them from collecting fees for their services deprives individuals of the liberty to pursue a lawful calling contrary to due process of law, said the Court in *Adams v. Tanner* (1917). *Pennsylvania Coal Co. v. Mahon* (1922) held that a law which forbids mining in such a way as to cause subsidence of any human habitation or public street or building, and which thereby makes commercially impracticable the removal of valuable coal deposits on the plaintiff's land, is arbitrary and amounts to a deprivation of property without due process. *Wolff Packing Co. v. Industrial Court* (1923) held that a Kansas law which compels a business engaged in the manufacturing and processing of food to continue operation in the event of a labor dispute, to submit the controversy to an arbitration board, and to abide by the latter's recommendation pertaining to the payment of minimum wages, subjects both employers and employees to a denial of liberty without due process of law. An Iowa law that imposes severe punishments upon contractors with the state who pay their workers less than "the current rate of per diem wages in the locality where the work is performed" is void for vagueness and violates due process, said the Court in *Connally v. General Const. Co.* (1926). *Weaver v. Palmer Bros.* (1926) held that a Pennsylvania law which prohibits the use of shoddy (used fabric pieces), even when sterilized, in the manufacture of bedding materials, is so arbitrary and unreasonable as to violate due process. *Frost Trucking Co. v. Railroad Carriers* (1926) decided that a California law which provides that private carriers by automobile for hire cannot operate in the state without obtaining a certificate of convenience and submitting to regulation as common carriers exacts an unconstitutional condition and denies due process. A New York law that prohibits ticket agencies from selling theater tickets at prices in excess of 50 cents over the price printed on the ticket is void because it regulates a business not affected with the public interest, and deprives such business of due process, according to *Tyson & Bro. v. Banton* (1927). *Ribnik v. McBride* (1928) held that a New Jersey law empowering the secretary of labor to fix the fees charged by employment agencies violates due process because the regulation is not imposed on a business affected with a public interest. *Louis K. Liggett Co. v. Baldridge* (1928) held that a Pennsylvania law which prohibits corporate ownership of a drugstore unless all the stockholders are licensed pharmacists has no reasonable relationship to public health and therefore violates due process. An Oklahoma law that prohibits anyone from engaging in the manufacture, sale, or distribution of ice without a state license, to be issued only on proof of public necessity and capacity to meet public demand, constitutes an invalid regulation of a business not affected with a public interest, and a denial of liberty to pursue a lawful calling contrary to due process, said the Court in *New State Ice Co. v. Liebmann* (1932).[5]

Notwithstanding the variety of economic due process case law sampled above, the period from the 1890s to 1937 has been called by many commentators, and by the post-1937 Supreme Court itself, the "Lochner era," after a 1905 liberty of contract case. The first liberty of contract case was *Allgeyer v. Louisiana* (1897), a unanimous decision that struck down a statute which subjected to a fine any person or business in Louisiana who entered into an insurance contract with a company not authorized to do business in the state. Allgeyer and Co. insured its cotton goods with a New York firm not authorized to do business in Louisiana. Writing for the Court, Justice Rufus Peckham said that Louisiana could prevent a foreign insurance company from doing business within its limits without a license and a local agent, but it could not penalize a resident for entering into a valid contract with that company. The "liberty" mentioned in the due process clause "means not only the right of the citizen to be free from the mere physical restraint of his person, as by incarceration," but the term also embraces the citizen's right "to be free in the enjoyment of all of his faculties, . . . to live and work where he will, to earn his livelihood by any lawful calling, . . . and for that purpose to enter into all contracts which may be proper, necessary, and essential to his carrying out to a successful conclusion the purpose above mentioned." As the contract was valid in the place where it was made and where it was to be performed—New York City—Louisiana could not prevent one of its citizens from entering into the contract, even though that citizen and the goods being insured were in Louisiana. In effect the Court was saying that the state could not police the insurance business within its borders by requiring companies to obtain a license in order to transact business with residents of the state.[6]

In a five-to-four decision for the Court in *Lochner v. New York* (1905), Justice Peckham held that New York's law providing that employees in the bakery industry could not work more than ten hours a day or sixty hours per week violates the due process liberty of employers and employees to enter into labor contracts of their own choosing. There is no reasonable ground on the score of public health or welfare for the state to limit the hours of work by bakers. Justice John Marshall Harlan (joined by Justices Edward White and William Day) dissented. Liberty of contract is subject to such regulations as the state may reasonably prescribe for the general health and welfare of society, and a statute should never be held invalid unless it is "beyond question, plainly and palpably in excess of legislative power." This cannot be said of the law limiting the work hours of bakers. In his own dissent Justice Oliver Wendell Holmes said the Constitution was not intended to embody a particular economic theory, "whether of paternalism . . . or of *laissez faire*." It was made "for people of fundamentally different views, and the accident of our finding certain opinions natural and familiar or novel and even shocking ought not to conclude our judgment whether statutes embodying them conflict with the Constitution."[7]

Coppage v. Kansas (1915) struck down as a violation of the freedom of contract a state law that made it a misdemeanor for an employer to require employees to agree to not join or remain a member of a labor union. The right of a person to sell his labor upon such terms as he deems proper is the same as the right of the purchaser of labor to prescribe the conditions upon which he will accept such labor. In *Burns Baking Co. v. Bryan* (1924) a Nebraska law that prescribed the minimum weights of loaves of bread to be made and sold and that, in order to prevent the palming off smaller for larger sizes, allowed a "tolerance" of only two ounces per pound in excess of the minimum, was found to be unreasonable, to be unnecessary to protect purchasers against the imposition of fraud by short weights, and therefore to deprive bakers and sellers of bread of their liberty without due process of law. The final in this series of liberty of contract decisions was *Morehead v. New York ex rel. Tipaldo* (1936), which, following the precedent of a federal law case, *Adkins v. Children's Hospital* (1923), held that a state law requiring employers to pay women minimum wages that would be equal to the fair and reasonable value of the services rendered and sufficient to meet the minimum cost of living necessary for their health, deprived employers and employees of their freedom of contract without due process of law.[8]

THE COURT'S REJECTION OF LOCHNER-ERA ECONOMIC DUE PROCESS

During the Great Depression of the 1930s the Court continued to carefully scrutinize state laws to uphold free-market principles, and also in 1935 and

1936 issued nine decisions that shredded major elements of the federal government's economic regulation and recovery efforts. President Franklin Delano Roosevelt presented his "Court-packing" plan to Congress in early 1937 in an effort to stop the Court from continuing to undercut the New Deal programs being enacted by Congress. The President proposed to add an additional justice for every sitting justice at least seventy years old who was not planning to retire. Although this legislation failed to pass the Senate, the Supreme Court abandoned its narrow constructions of Congress' article I powers and ceased issuing substantive due process decisions in review of federal and state business and labor laws. It thereafter allowed to Congress (and the states within boundaries set by Congress) virtually unlimited discretion to regulate the economy. While some commentators have attributed the Court's retreat to the Court-packing plan, a better explanation for the change in emphasis and approach is the fact that President Roosevelt needed to replace only one or two conservative justices to reshape the Court's ideology, and he was able to nominate and receive Senate confirmation for seven new Supreme Court justices from 1937 to 1941. And he chose well.[9]

While Roosevelt's Court-packing plan was pending in Congress, Chief Justice Charles Evans Hughes, in a five-to-four opinion for the Court in *West Coast Hotel v. Parrish* (1937), distinguished *Morehead* and overruled *Adkins* to uphold a state law that established minimum wages for women and children. The liberty safeguarded by the due process clause is "liberty in a social organization which requires the protection of laws regulating the evils which menace the health, safety, morals and welfare of the people," said Hughes. Regulation "which is reasonable in relation to its subject and is adopted in the interests of the community is due process." Quoting from an earlier case, he said that if laws "have a reasonable relation to a proper legislative purpose, and are neither arbitrary nor discriminatory, the requirements of due process are satisfied," and that "with the wisdom of the policy adopted, with the adequacy or practicality of the law enacted to forward it, the courts are both incompetent and unauthorized to deal."[10]

The Supreme Court has deferred to the states in their substantive regulations of economic liberty or property interests under the due process clause since 1937. *Day-Brite Lighting, Inc. v. Missouri* (1952), *Williamson v. Lee Optical of Oklahoma, Inc.* (1955), and *Ferguson v. Skrupa* (1963) mark the contours and rationale of the Court's policy in this area. Writing for the Court in *Day-Brite Lighting*, Justice William Douglas upheld Missouri's statute which provided that any employee entitled to vote could absent himself from work for four hours on election-day and prohibited employers from deducting wages for that absence. "The liberty of contract argument pressed on us is reminiscent of the philosophy of *Lochner v. New York*, . . . *Coppage v. Kansas*, . . . *Adkins v. Children's Hospital*, . . . and others of that vintage," said Douglas.

"Our recent decisions make plain that we do not sit as a super-legislature to weigh the wisdom of legislation nor to decide whether the policy which it expresses offends the public welfare." The state legislatures "have constitutional authority to experiment with new techniques; they are entitled to their own standard of the public welfare; they may within extremely broad limits control practices within the business-labor field. . . . That is the essence of *West Coast Hotel v. Parrish.*"[11]

In *Williamson v Lee Optical*, Douglas upheld an Oklahoma statute which made it unlawful for any person not a licensed optometrist or ophthalmologist to fit lenses to a face or to duplicate or replace into frames lenses or other optical appliances, except on a written prescription from a licensed ophthalmologist or optometrist. The law "may exact a needless, wasteful requirement in many cases," said Douglas, but it is "for the legislature, not the courts, to balance the advantage and disadvantage of the new requirement." Speculating as to possible motivations, he said the legislature "might have concluded that the frequency of occasions in which a prescription is necessary was sufficient to justify this regulation of the fitting of eyeglasses. Likewise, when it is necessary to duplicate a lens, a written prescription may or may not be necessary. But the legislature might have concluded that one was needed often enough to require one in every case." Concluded Douglas: "The day is gone when this Court uses the Due Process Clause of the Fourteenth Amendment to strike down state laws, regulatory of business and industrial conditions, because they may be unwise, improvident, or out of harmony with a particular school of thought." We emphasize again what Chief Justice Morrison Waite said for the Court in *Munn v. State of Illinois*, 94 U.S. 113, 134 (1877): "For protection against abuses by legislatures, the people must resort to the polls, not to the courts."[12]

Writing for a unanimous Court, Justice Hugo Black in *Ferguson v. Skrupa* (1963) upheld a Kansas statute making it a misdemeanor for any person to engage in the business of debt adjusting except as an incident to the practice of law in the state. There was a time, said Black, "when the Due Process Clause was used by this Court to strike down laws which were thought unreasonable, that is, unwise or incompatible with some particular economic or social philosophy," citing the examples of *Lochner v. New York* (1905), *Coppage v. Kansas* (1915), *Adams v. Tanner* (1917), *Adkins v. Children's Hospital* (1923), and *Jay Burns Baking Co. v. Bryan* (1924). This intrusion by the judiciary into the realm of legislative value judgments was strongly protested at the time by Justices Holmes and Brandeis. Unquestionably, concluded Black, "there are arguments that the business of debt adjusting has social utility, but such arguments are properly addressed to the legislature, not to us. . . . The Kansas debt adjusting statute may be wise or unwise. But relief, if any be needed, lies not with us but with the body constituted to pass laws for the State of Kansas."[13]

REQUIRING FAIR PROCEDURES FOR LIBERTY OR PROPERTY DEPRIVATIONS AFTER 1937

Notwithstanding these and other like cases since 1937, the Supreme Court never did abandon review of state policy decisions under the due process clause. It merely redirected the focus of interpretations. It continued to impose procedural safeguards on state deprivations of liberty and property interests. As we will see in the next section, it built upon two cases from the Lochner era to give substantive protection for a few noneconomic liberties. And as we will see in the next chapter, it used the due process clause as a vehicle to extend to the states most of the Bill of Rights.

A considerable number of procedural due process decisions in the Lochner era had required the states to grant appropriate notice and an opportunity to be heard before depriving persons of liberty or property, or to refrain from taxing or otherwise adversely affecting persons and property outside the state's own borders, or to not be so vague in criminal law definitions of prohibited conduct that the rules could not be easily understood and obeyed. These and similar lines of precedent were good decisions, recognized as such at the time, and they continued to have vitality for the post-1937 Court."[14]

A representative sample of the Court's post–New Deal fair procedure cases follows: *Connecticut Gen. Life Ins. Co. v. Johnson* (1938) held that a California privilege tax on foreign insurers admitted to the state, measured by gross premiums received, violated the due process rights of the plaintiff company insofar as it affected premiums received in Connecticut on contracts of reinsurance consummated there and covering policies of life insurance that had been issued by other insurers to California residents. California was without power to tax the reinsurance activities conducted beyond its borders. *Treichler v. Wisconsin* (1949) held that insofar as the Wisconsin emergency tax on inheritances is measured by intangible property located outside the state, the tax violates the due process clause. *Mullane v. Central Bank & Trust Co.* (1950) held that notice by publication, as authorized by the New York Banking Law for purposes of enabling banks managing common trust funds to obtain a judicial settlement of accounts binding on all having an interest in such funds, is not sufficient process for determining the property rights of persons whose whereabouts are known. *Eskridge v. Washington Prison Bd.* (1958) held that the denial of a free trial transcript to an indigent criminal defendant pursuant to a Washington statute which authorized a trial judge to furnish a transcript to an indigent defendant if in the judge's opinion "justice will thereby be promoted" denied equal protection and due process because the indigent defendant did not have the same opportunity that was available to those who could afford the transcript to have his case reviewed by an appellate court. *Giacco v. Pennsylvania* (1966) held that a state statute permitting jurors to determine whether an acquitted defendant should pay the costs of the trial is void for vagueness and the absence of any standard to prevent arbitrary impositions of costs. *Sniadach v. Family Finance Corp.* (1969) said that a Wisconsin prejudgment statute which authorizes freezing a defendant's wages from the time of garnishment until the culmination of the suit without affording the defendant a hearing violates the due process clause. *In re Winship* (1970) held that a New York statute which provides that proof of acts establishing the delinquency of a minor must be by a preponderance of the evidence violates the due process clause, which requires proof beyond a reasonable doubt. *Fuentes v. Shevin* (1972) held that Florida's statutes which permit installment sellers or other persons alleging an entitlement to property to cause the seizure of the property without any notice or opportunity to be heard on the issues violate the due process clause. An Oregon statute requiring a defendant to give pretrial notice of an alibi defense and the names of supporting witnesses but denying the defendant any reciprocal right of discovery of rebuttal evidence denies him due process of law, according to the Court's unanimous opinion in *Wardius v. Oregon* (1973). The Court's insistence upon procedural safeguards for consumers, civil litigants, and alleged or convicted criminals became much less common in the rulings of the Rehnquist and Roberts Courts after 1986.[15]

SUBSTANTIVE DUE PROCESS AFTER 1937: FROM FAMILY RIGHTS TO BIRTH CONTROL

In addition to its fair procedure rulings, the Supreme Court has given substantive protection to some preferred noneconomic "liberties." The story of this personal rights jurisprudence begins with two cases decided in the Lochner era, *Meyer v. Nebraska* (1923), and the unanimous opinion in *Pierce v. Society of Sisters* (1925). The state statutes reviewed in these two decisions were the products of anti-foreign and anti-Catholic sentiments, respectively, in the aftermath of World War I. *Meyer* considered a Nebraska law which forbade the teaching of any foreign language in any school up through the eighth grade. Although the legislature's desire to foster a homogenous people with American ideals prepared to understand current discussions of civil matters is easy to appreciate, said the Court, the individual has "certain fundamental rights" which must be respected. Here, the law impermissibly interferes materially with the calling of modern language teachers, with the opportunities of pupils to acquire knowledge, and with the power of parents to control the education of their children. *Pierce* struck down an Oregon law which forbade parents from sending their children to private school before the age of sixteen. The state cannot interfere with the liberty of parents to direct the upbringing and education of their children, said the Court, citing *Meyer*, nor can it seek to "standardize its children" by forcing them to accept instruction only from public school teachers.[16]

Meyer and *Pierce* would be cited favorably as family rights cases after 1937 as the Court gingerly approached the subject of substantive due process protection for liberty, selectively quoting from and building upon precedents. The legacy of *Lochner* hung as a shadow over the modern Court's opinions, with justices at pains to show that they were deciding the cases based upon the dictates of the Constitution, not merely inflicting upon society their own personal preferences or political ideology. The birth control cases of *Poe v. Ullman* (1961), *Griswold v. Connecticut* (1965), *Eisenstadt v. Baird* (1972), and *Carey v. Population Services Int'l* (1977), and the abortion decisions of *Roe v. Wade* (1973) and its progeny, illustrate the interpretative dynamics at work.

In *Poe v. Ullman* a married couple, a married woman, and their doctor sought a declaratory judgment that the Connecticut statutes which prohibit the use of contraceptive devices and the giving of medical advice on their use violate the Fourteenth Amendment "by depriving the plaintiffs of life and property without due process of law." Noting that the statutes had been enacted in 1879 and had not been enforced for a long time, and that counsel for the plaintiffs admitted that contraceptives are "commonly and notoriously sold in Connecticut drug stores," the Court dismissed the suit because it did not present a real case or controversy that needed to be resolved. Four of the justices dissented from the dismissal, and two of them said why the state law should be struck down. Douglas concluded crisply in his dissenting opinion, "Can there be any doubt that a Bill of Rights that, in time of peace, bars soldiers from being quartered in a home 'without the consent of the Owner' should also bar the police from investigating the intimacies of the marital relation? The idea of allowing the State that leeway is congenial only to a totalitarian regime."

In greater detail the second Justice John Marshall Harlan, a grandson of the first Justice John Marshall Harlan, explained why the statute, as applied to married couples wanting to use a contraceptive device, is an unconstitutional invasion of their personal privacy even though no specific privacy right is mentioned in the Constitution. It is a truism to say the due process clause in the Fourteenth Amendment "is not self-explanatory," observed Harlan. However, the Court has rejected two views advanced in the past in an attempt to curb the Court's abuse of its reviewing power. One view has sought to limit the due process clause to a "guarantee of procedural fairness," and the second has asserted the clause applies against the states only the restraints mentioned in the Bill of Rights. But "due process" in the consistent view of the Court has been a broader concept than the first and more flexible than the second. If due process were merely a "procedural safeguard" it would fail to reach situations where the deprivation of life, liberty or property is accomplished by legislation that operates in the future, and that, "given even the fairest possible procedure in application to individuals, nevertheless destroys the enjoyment" of these interests. Nor is the clause limited to being "a shorthand reference to what is explicitly set out elsewhere in the Bill of Rights." Due process liberty "is not a series of isolated points pricked out in terms of the taking of property; the freedom of speech, press, and religion; the right to keep and bear arms; the freedom from unreasonable searches and seizures; and so on. It is a rational continuum which, broadly speaking, includes a freedom from all substantial arbitrary impositions and purposeless restraints, . . . and which also recognizes . . . that certain interests require particularly careful scrutiny of the state needs asserted to justify their abridgment."[17]

Four years later, in *Griswold v. Connecticut*, the Court did hold that the law forbidding the use of contraceptives "violates the right of marital privacy which is within the penumbra of specific guarantees of the Bill of Rights." Writing for the Court, Justice Douglas referred to various guarantees that create "zones of privacy." The right of association contained in the penumbra of the First Amendment is one. The Third Amendment's prohibition against the quartering of soldiers in people's homes is another. The Fourth Amendment affirms the right of people to be secure in their persons, houses, papers and effects "against unreasonable searches and seizures." The Fifth Amendment's self-incrimination clause "enables the citizen to create a zone of privacy which government may not force him to surrender to his detriment." And the Ninth Amendment confirms that the enumeration of certain rights in the Constitution does not deny or disparage others retained by the people. Douglas added marital privacy in the conduct of intimate relations as one more privacy right protected from government invasion.

In his concurring opinion, Justice Arthur Goldberg (joined by Chief Justice Earl Warren and Justice William Brennan) said the concept of due process liberty protects those "personal rights that are fundamental and is not confined to the specific terms of the Bill of Rights." The Ninth Amendment evidences the latter point. In determining what rights are fundamental, judges are "not left at large to decide cases in light of their personal and private notions." Rather, they must look to the "traditions and collective conscience of our people" to determine if a principle is fundamental. Connecticut argues there is a rational relation between the statute and its admittedly legitimate state concern to discourage extramarital relations. However, as many cases have shown, where a fundamental right is implicated—marital privacy deserves to be considered a fundamental right—the state "may prevail only upon showing a subordinating interest which is compelling." That it cannot do here.

Justices Harlan and Byron White also issued concurring opinions, and Justices Black and Potter Stewart dissented, in *Griswold*. Harlan agreed with the Court's judgment but could not join its opinion because it evinced an approach to the case very much like that taken by the dissenters, namely, that the due process clause does not touch the statute unless it violates "some right assured by the letter or penumbra of the Bill of Rights." Harlan believed the due process clause "stands on its own bottom," and that the proper constitutional inquiry is whether the law violates basic values "implicit in the concept of ordered liberty," citing *Palko v. Connecticut* (1937). The Connecticut law here does violate such values. The "incorporation" theory of the dissenters Black and Stewart is based on the thesis that by limiting the content of the due process clause of the Fourteenth Amendment to the protection of explicit rights found elsewhere in the Constitution, in this instance in the Bill of Rights, judges will be confined to the interpretation of specific constitutional provisions, and will thereby be restrained from introducing their own notions of constitutional right and wrong into the "vague contours" of the due process clause. But specific provisions of the Constitution, no less than due process of law, lend themselves to "personal" interpretations by judges seeking to keep the Constitution current. Justice White in his concurrence said that the statute, as applied to married couples, deprives them of "liberty" without due process. The state argues that its statute serves its policy against "all forms of promiscuous or illicit sexual relationships, be they premarital or extramarital, concededly a permissible and legitimate legislative goal." But White said he failed to see how the ban on the use of contraceptives "by married couples in any way reinforces the State's ban on illicit sexual relationships."

In his dissent Justice Black said the law is "offensive" but not unconstitutional. There is no "right of privacy" in the Constitution, so the Court is wrong in its judgment to strike down the Connecticut law as applied to married couples. Nor does the Ninth Amendment add anything to support the decision. Contrary to the majority justices, Black rejected the idea that the Court is granted power "to measure constitutionality by our belief that legislation is arbitrary, capricious or unreasonable, or accomplishes no justifiable purpose." The due process clause, "with an 'arbitrary and capricious' or 'shocking the conscience' formula, was liberally used . . . to strike down economic legislation in the early decades of this century, threatening, many people thought, the tranquility and stability of the Nation. *See, e.g., Lochner v. New York*, 198 U.S. 45. That formula, based on substantive considerations of 'natural justice,' is no less dangerous when used to enforce the Court's views about personal rights than those about economic rights." In his own dissent Justice Stewart said he could find no right of privacy in the Bill of Rights or any other part of the Constitution, and so was unwilling to overrule the admittedly "unwise, or even asinine" law.[18]

Massachusetts law made it a felony for anyone to give a contraceptive drug or device to any person who is not married. *Eisenstadt v. Baird* (1972) extended *Griswold* by holding that the right of privacy in contraception use inheres in individuals as well as married couples, and that the Massachusetts statute accordingly violates the equal protection clause of the Fourteenth Amendment by providing dissimilar treatment for married and unmarried persons who are similarly situated.[19]

Carey v. Population Services Int'l (1977) concluded the series of birth control cases when it struck down a New York law which made it a crime for anyone to sell or distribute a contraceptive to a minor under the age of sixteen, for anyone other than a pharmacist to distribute contraceptives to persons sixteen or over, and for anyone, including pharmacists, to advertise or display contraceptives. Regulations imposing a burden on a decision as fundamental as whether to bear or beget a child may be justified only by compelling state interests, and must be narrowly drawn to express only those interests, said the Court. The law could not survive such strict scrutiny. The ban on advertising for contraceptives violates the First Amendment freedom of expression command. The requirement that only licensed pharmacists could distribute contraceptives to persons aged sixteen or over "clearly burdens the right of such individuals to use contraceptives if they so desire." And the ban on the sale or distribution to minors could not be justified as a permissible regulation of minors' morality "in furtherance of the State's policy against promiscuous sexual intercourse among the young" because the right to privacy in connection with decisions affecting procreation extends to minors as well as adults, and "the argument that sexual activity may be deterred by increasing the hazards attendant on it has been rejected by the Court as a justification for restrictions on the freedom to choose whether to bear or beget a child," citing *Eisenstadt v. Baird* (1972) and *Roe v. Wade* (1973).[20]

THE RIGHT TO ABORTION

Birth control was one thing, abortion quite another. In his review of the Texas statute which made it a crime to "procure or attempt an abortion" except when done on medical advice to save the life of the mother, Justice Harry Blackman in *Roe v. Wade* (1973) acknowledged at the outset the "sensitive and emotional nature of the abortion controversy, of the vigorous opposing views, . . . and of the deep and seemingly absolute convictions that the subject inspires," and said that the Court's task was to resolve the issue "by constitutional measurement, free of emotion and of predilection." The aspiration to achieve a constitutional answer "free of emotion and of predilection" was impossible to achieve then and remains so now. Blackmun cited a number of cases to show that, although the Constitution does not explicitly mention any right of privacy, the Court has recognized the right does exist, and cited other cases to show its extension to activities relating to marriage, procreation, contraception, family relationships, and childbearing and education. Then he decided, "The right of privacy, whether it be founded in the Fourteenth Amendment's concept of personal liberty and restrictions upon state action, as we feel it is, or, as the District Court determined, in the Ninth Amendment's reservation of rights to the people, is broad enough to encompass a woman's decision whether or not to terminate her pregnancy." This decision of course necessitated rejection of appellants' arguments that life begins at conception, or that the fetus is a "person" for purposes of the Fourteenth Amendment.

Even though abortion is a fundamental right, Blackmun continued, it is subject to some limitations, and at some point, the state's interests in protecting the health of the pregnant woman, and the potentiality of human life within her body, become dominant. Where fundamental rights are involved, past cases showed, regulation limiting these rights may be justified only by a "compelling state interest," and legislative enactments "must be narrowly drawn to express only the legitimate state interests at stake." Applying these Court-developed criteria for reviewing legislation, Blackman stipulated that in the first trimester of the woman's pregnancy the abortion decision and its effectuation must be left to the medical judgment of her doctor; thereafter the state in promoting its interest in the health of the mother may regulate the abortion procedure in ways reasonably related to maternal health; and subsequent to viability the state, in promoting its interest in the potentiality of human life, may if it chooses proscribe abortion "except where it is necessary, in appropriate medical judgment, for the preservation of the life or health of the mother."

In his concurring opinion Justice Stewart noted that in *Ferguson v. Skrupa* (1963) the Court "purported to sound the death knell for the doctrine of substantive due process." Barely two years later *Griswold v. Connecticut* held a birth control law unconstitutional. In view of what had been so recently said in *Skrupa*, the Court's opinion in *Griswold* "understandably did its best to avoid reliance on the Due Process Clause." Yet the law did not violate any guarantee in the Bill of Rights or any other specific provision in the Constitution. "It was clear to me then, and it is equally clear to me now, that the *Griswold* decision can be rationally understood only as a holding that the Connecticut statute substantively invaded the 'liberty' that is protected by the Due Process Clause." *Griswold* stands as "one in a long line of pre-*Skrupa* cases decided under the doctrine of substantive due process, and I now accept it as such." In a constitution for free people, the meaning of "liberty" must be broad indeed. Stewart concluded that the right of a woman to decide whether to bear a child is embraced within the personal liberty protected by the due process clause, and on the basis of that understanding he joined the Court's opinion.

Justices White and William Rehnquist dissented. White objected to the Court's decision that the Constitution values the "convenience, whim, or caprice of the putative mother more than the life or potential life of the fetus." Rehnquist had difficulty seeing how the case involved a right to privacy. An abortion operation is not "private" in the ordinary sense of the word. Moreover, if the Court had asked whether the Texas law bore a rational relationship to a legitimate state interest, the customary test applied in reviews of social and economic legislation, the obvious answer would have been that the abortion statute bears a rational relationship to the state's legitimate interest in protecting potential human life.[21]

Roe's progeny includes nineteen cases which struck down one or more aspects of state abortion laws, the most significant being *Planned Parenthood of Southeastern Pennsylvania v. Casey* (1992), which affirmed the essential holding of *Roe* that a woman has a right to terminate her pregnancy for any reason prior to the viability of the fetus. The plurality opinion by Justices Sandra Day O'Connor, Anthony Kennedy, and David Souter said these justices upheld *Roe* not because they believed the decision was correct, but on the basis of stare decisis, a doctrine which the Court applies when it believes the harm caused by overturning a judicial precedent would exceed the benefit. The opinion did reject *Roe*'s "rigid" trimester system, recognizing that the state's interest in protecting maternal health and the potential life within her are present from the beginning. The opinion also noted that in the cases since *Roe* the Court has decided that any regulation touching upon the abortion decision must survive strict scrutiny, to be sustained "only if drawn in narrow terms to further a compelling state interest." This approach ignored what *Roe* itself had recognized, that the state has an "important and legitimate interest in potential life." The plurality opinion therefore crafted a new review standard to strike a better balance between the woman's right and the state's legitimate interests: regulations should be permissible so long as they do not impose an "undue burden" on the woman's right to choose to have an abortion. Applying this test, *Casey* upheld most of the provisions in the Pennsylvania Abortion Control Act, striking down only the requirement that a married woman notify her husband of her intention to procure an abortion. In some cases this would pose a "significant obstacle" to the married woman's right to make her abortion decision.[22] The lowered review standard could still operate as an effective restraint on state policies on abortion regulation in cases like *Whole Woman's Health v. Hellerstedt* (2016). (The Texas statutes, which require that physicians performing abortions need admitting privileges at a hospital, and that abortion facilities must meet the minimum standards for ambulatory surgical centers, impose an "undue burden" on the liberty of the woman seeking to have an abortion.)[23]

Then the world changed for women. The Supreme Court in *Dobbs v. Jackson Women's Health Organization* (2022) overruled *Roe* and *Casey* and returned to the states control over abortion. The Mississippi law upheld in *Dobbs* provided that "except in medical emergencies and in the case of a severe fetal abnormality, a person shall not perform . . . or induce an abortion of an unborn human being" if the gestational age of the unborn human being is greater than fifteen weeks. The state argued in its brief that *Roe* and *Casey* were wrongly decided and that its gestational statute satisfies rational-basis review.

In his opinion for the Court in *Dobbs*, Justice Samuel Alito observed that abortion presents a profound moral issue on which Americans have sharply divergent views. Some believe a human person comes into being at conception and that abortion ends an innocent life. Others feel just as strongly that any regulation of abortion invades a woman's right to control her own body and prevents women from achieving full equality. Still others in a third group think abortion should be allowed in some but not all circumstances, and those within this group hold a variety of views about the restrictions that should be imposed. Although the Court in *Roe* acknowledged the states had a legitimate interest in protecting "potential life," it found this interest could not justify any restrictions on pre-viability abortions (i.e., abortions roughly within the first six months of pregnancy). At the time of *Roe*, thirty states still prohibited abortion at all stages. In the years prior to that decision, a third of the states had liberalized their laws, but *Roe* promptly ended that political process. Twenty-six states have now asked the Court to overrule *Roe* and *Casey* and allow states to regulate or prohibit pre-viability abortions. The due process clause has been held to guarantee some rights that are not mentioned in the Constitution, but any such right must be "deeply rooted in the Nation's history and tradition" and "implicit in the concept of ordered liberty," *Washington v. Glucksberg*, 521 U.S. 702, 721 (1997). The right to abortion does not fall within this category. *Roe*'s defenders characterize the right as similar to rights recognized in past decisions involving matters such as intimate sexual relations, contraception, and marriage, but abortion is fundamentally different, as *Roe* and *Casey* acknowledged, because it destroys what those decisions called "fetal life," and what the Mississippi law being reviewed in this present case describes as an "unborn human being." Alito concluded with the point that from now on laws regulating abortion, like other health and welfare laws, are "entitled to a strong presumption of validity."[24]

SUMMING UP THE COURT'S FOURTEENTH AMENDMENT DUE PROCESS JURISPRUDENCE

We have seen the Court go through three cycles in its interpretations of the Fourteenth Amendment due process clause, considered on its own, without regard to incorporations of the Bill of Rights. In the early decades the Court protected states' rights from what it feared could become undue interference from the federal government under all three clauses in section one of the amendment. It protected economic liberty and property rights in procedural due process and substantive due process decisions in the Lochner era, 1897–1937. Since 1937, under the due process clause, it has given process protection to liberty and property rights, and substantive protection to a few "fundamental," noneconomic rights, the most important of which it has recently disavowed.

Many of the procedural due process safeguards the Court enforced against the states on behalf of liberty and property rights in the Lochner era, and that it continued to develop and apply after 1937, were good outcomes for the parties being protected without producing undue negative side effects for the community. The decisions achieved fair results, and could be connected to constitutional text, which requires due "process" for government deprivations of life, liberty, or property. The only "stretch" was the treatment of corporations as "persons" under the protection of the Fourteenth Amendment's due process clause, a treatment that began in an 1886 case and has continued uninterrupted and unchallenged to this day.

The substantive due process cases are another matter. Many constitutional scholars past and present have read the due process clauses of the Fifth and Fourteenth Amendments to mean no more than this: in circumstances where the government is seeking to deprive a person of life, liberty, or property as punishment for a crime, or to deprive one of property in a civil case, the deprivation must be achieved by means of a fair procedure.[25] No holding of the Supreme Court in the many cases which it has decided under the due process clauses has ever articulated why the substance of a statute, rather than the process used to implement it, should be subjected to a due process review in the courts.

Many of the Court's substantive due process policy judgments during the Lochner era unreasonably interfered with the states' ability to regulate business and labor conditions, to ameliorate some of the harsh socioeconomic effects of laissez-faire capitalism, or otherwise to promote the public good. They were criticized at the time by progressives, and later condemned by most commentators and the Court itself. The post-1937 Court, haunted by the shadow of *Lochner*, strained to find a plausible basis to overturn state laws that it considered unsupportable infringements of personal liberty. This is clearly what happened in *Griswold v. Connecticut* (1965), for example, when Justice Douglas in his opinion for the Court based the right of a married couple to buy a contraceptive device and practice birth control upon the "penumbras and emanations" of several provisions in the Bill of Rights, rather than a substantive liberty per se, and Justice Goldberg in his concurring opinion joined by two others relied on the Ninth Amendment's reservation of rights to the people. The Court suffers a loss of credibility whenever it resorts to such subterfuges.

The Supreme Court acts as the nation's ultimate lawmaker when it engages in substantive due process reviews of legislation. It decides which public policies are reasonable and hence may be embodied in law, and which ones must be vetoed. Such a pinnacle position for the Court was not contemplated by the framers of the Constitution, or the drafters of the due process clause in the Fifth Amendment. As recounted in chapter 3, the best available historical and contextual evidence suggests that this clause meant the federal government should deprive a person of his or her life, liberty, or property only if it has a good reason to take such an adverse action. Perhaps the person has broken the law, or someone else has better title in a property case. Before the federal government deprives one of life, liberty, or property, it must provide notice and offer a hearing on the facts, in compliance with the standing law. This standing law would consist of relevant provisions in the Constitution as amended, a statute that serves as the predicate for the government's action, and the common law (i.e., judicial precedent). For example, assume the government searches a person's home with a valid search warrant and finds illegal drugs. It may prosecute the individual for the crime of possession of illegal drugs. The due process clause in the Fifth Amendment requires that the person be timely notified of the charges and be eligible for a prompt hearing on the facts, in accordance with the fair-trial procedures specified in the Fifth and Sixth Amendments, and with statutory and common law provisions that pertain to the case. Timely notice and hearing under the law is the process that is due.[26]

The Supreme Court ventured beyond this understanding in "substantive due process" cases such as *Dred Scott v. Sandford* (1857) (Congress cannot ban slavery in the territories); *Adair v. United States* (1908) (Congress cannot make it a crime for carriers engaged in interstate commerce to refuse to employ workers simply because they belong to a labor union); and *Adkins v. Children's Hosp.* (1923) (Congress cannot enact a minimum wage law for women and children in the District of Columbia).[27] Fifth Amendment substantive due process overturns of federal laws largely ended after 1937, and any new slippage into this territory would be flawed constitutional interpretation.

The Court has issued many substantive due process decisions under the Fourteenth Amendment's due process clause. In the Lochner era (1897 to 1937), it upheld persons' and corporations' economic liberty and property rights against state and local law "deprivations." The Court also protected family rights in two school cases (1923 and 1925), and beginning in 1925 it absorbed and applied to the states the substantive freedoms of religion, speech, press, and assembly in the First Amendment. After the New Deal settlement of 1937, the Court abandoned its concern for economic liberty and instead enforced substantive rights in the Bill of Rights, and a few other personal rights, such as birth control, and abortion (recently retracted), that it decided are important elements of Fourteenth Amendment substantive "liberty." Can any of the Supreme Court's substantive due process decisions under the Fourteenth Amendment be justified as legitimate constitutional interpretations?

Yes, the Court's inquiry into the substance of a state's legislative decision can be defended, with a caveat. The original meaning of the due process clause read together with the equal protection clause in the Fourteenth Amendment is different from the original meaning of the due process clause in the Fifth Amendment. The Republicans of 1866 who enacted the Fourteenth Amendment did not want merely to require each state to give notice and hearing to a person before it deprived him of life, liberty, or property under the state's laws and constitution, whatever those laws and constitution might provide. In reforming the Constitution of the United States and putting the union back together, their focus was on securing protection for the substance of each person's assumed natural life, liberty, and property rights, and equality under the law. They imposed a duty on the states to safeguard these rights of all persons subject to their jurisdiction by the enactment and enforcement of reasonable and just laws, and gave Congress the authority to support or change what the states were doing, or fill in gaps, by appropriate legislation. John Bingham drew from the article IV, section two privileges and immunities clause to describe the rights of citizens, and from the life, liberty, and property rights premise of the Fifth Amendment due process clause to describe the rights of all persons, that should receive the benefit of equal protection of the laws. The states have a duty and Congress has the police power to protect people's life, liberty, and property under fair and equal laws, substantively and not just procedurally.[28]

The Lochner-era Court was thus correct to say in *Allgeyer v. Louisiana* (1897) that the "liberty" mentioned in the Fourteenth Amendment due process clause "means not only the right of the citizen to be free from the mere physical restraint of his person, as by incarceration," but the term also embraces the citizen's right "to be free in the enjoyment of all of his faculties"; to hold in *Meyer v. Nebraska* (1923) that a state law which forbade the teaching of any foreign language in any school up through the eighth grade impermissibly interfered materially with the calling of modern language teachers, with the opportunities of pupils to acquire knowledge, and with the power of parents to direct the education of their children; and to assume in *Gitlow v. New York* (1925) that due process "liberty" in the Fourteenth Amendment includes the rights of freedom of speech and press.[29] If the Court in these and many other cases from the 1890s to 1937 had enforced its view of people's life, liberty, and property rights in the states by giving them substantive content, but with the caveat that Congress could respond to the Court's legislative-type policy call if it wanted to modify the result, a correct understanding of the Fourteenth Amendment could have been preserved.

This is equally true of the Court's substantive due process decisions since 1937. Such a caveat would have allowed it to impose its policy judgments on state laws under section one of the Fourteenth Amendment without negating a possible congressional response under section five. Preserving the role of Congress as the nation's ultimate lawmaker is consistent with the Constitution, the Fourteenth Amendment, and our status as a representative democracy.

NOTES

1. *Chicago, M. and St. P. Ry.*, 134 U.S. 418 (Court opinion), 461–62 (Justice Bradley dissenting). Although this opinion is a logical starting point to discuss the Court's substantive economic due process cases, there were four earlier ones which struck down state laws on substantive due process grounds. *State Tax on Foreign-Held Bonds*, 82 U.S. 300 (1873), held that a Pennsylvania law, insofar as it directed domestic corporations to withhold on behalf of the state a portion of interest due on bonds owned by nonresidents, impairs the obligation of contracts and denies due process by taxing property beyond its jurisdiction. Three cases, in 1875, 1882, and 1885, held that states could not issue bonds in order to raise funds for the support of private enterprises. See *Loan Ass'n v. Topeka*, 87 U.S. 655 (1875); *City of Parkersburg v. Brown*, 106 U.S. 487 (1882); and *Cole v. La Grange*, 113 U.S. 1 (1885).

2. *Missouri Pacific Ry.*, 164 U.S. 403; *Gulf, C. & S. F. Ry.*, 165 U.S. 150; *Smyth*, 169 U.S. 466; *Wilcox*, 212 U.S. 19; *Louisville & Nashville R.R.*, 212 U.S. 132; and *No. Pacif. Ry.*, 296 U.S. 585.

3. *Union Transit*, 199 U.S. 194; *Int'l. Paper*, 246 U.S. 135; and *Brooke*, 277 U.S. 27.

4. *Dewey*, 173 U.S. 193; *Central of Georgia Ry.*, 207 U.S. 127; *Tumey*, 273 U.S. 510; and *Wuchter*, 276 U.S. 13.

5. *Int'l. Harvester Co.*, 234 U.S. 216; *Adams*, 244 U.S. 590; *Pennsylvania Coal Co.*, 260 U.S. 393; *Wolff Packing Co.*, 262 U.S. 522; *Connally*, 269 U.S. 305; *Weaver*,

270 U.S. 402; *Frost Trucking Co.*, 271 U.S. 583; *Tyson and Bro.*, 273 U.S. 418; *Ribnik*, 277 U.S. 350; *Liggett Co.*, 278 U.S. 105; and *New State Ice Co.*, 285 U.S. 262.

6. *Allgeyer*, 165 U.S. 578. 584–89, 591–92.

7. *Lochner*, 198 U.S. 45, 52–54, 57, 60 (Court opinion), 65–68 (Justice Harlan dissenting), 70, 74 (Justice Holmes dissenting).

8. *Coppage*, 236 U.S. 1; *Burns Baking Co.*, 264 U.S. 504; and *Morehead*, 298 U.S. 587.

9. See generally G. Edward White, *The Constitution and the New Deal.* (Cambridge: Harvard University Press, 2000).

10. *West Coast Hotel*, 200 U.S. 379.

11. *Day-Brite Lighting*, 342 U.S. 421.

12. *Williamson*, 348 U.S. 483.

13. *Ferguson*, 372 U.S. 726.

14. For typical Lochner-era procedural due process overrides of state law, see some of the cases discussed in the text at ns. 4 and 5.

15. *Conn. Gen. Life Ins. Co.*, 303 U.S. 77; *Treichler*, 338 U.S. 251; *Mullane*, 334 U.S. 306; *Eskridge*, 357 U.S. 214; *Giacco*, 382 U.S. 399; *Sniadach*, 395 U.S. 337; *In re Winship*, 397 U.S. 358; *Fuentes*, 407 U.S. 67; and *Wardius*, 412 U.S. 470.

16. *Meyer*, 262 U.S. 380; *Pierce*, 268 U.S. 510.

17. *Poe*, 367 U.S. 497, 510–11, 515–19 (Justice Douglas dissenting), 522–23, 539–44 (Justice Harlan dissenting).

18. *Griswold*, 381 U.S. 479, 486–88, 493–95, 499 (Justice Goldberg concurring), 499–501 (Justice Harlan concurring), 502, 504–5 (Justice White concurring), 507–508, 511–22 (Justice Black dissenting), 528, 530 (Justice Stewart dissenting).

19. *Eisenstadt*, 405 U.S. 438.

20. *Carey*, 431 U.S. 678.

21. *Roe*, 410 U.S. 113, 116–18, 150–58, 164–65 (Justice Blackmun opinion for the Court), 167–71 (Justice Stewart concurring), 171–75 (Justice Rehnquist dissenting). Justice Blackmun also authored the Court's opinion in the companion case of *Doe v. Bolton*, 410 U.S. 179, which struck down provisions of the Georgia abortion law that required abortion patients to be a Georgia resident, that the abortion be performed in an accredited hospital, and that an abortion be approved by the hospital's abortion committee and two independent doctors. Justice White (joined by Justice Rehnquist) issued his dissent in both cases at 410 U.S. 421–23.

22. *Planned Parenthood v. Casey* plurality opinion, 505 U.S. 833. Justice John Paul Stevens concurred in part and dissented in part, 911–22, and Justice Blackmun concurred in part, concurred in the judgment, and dissented in part, 922–44. Four members of the Court, Chief Justice Rehnquist, and Justices White, Antonin Scalia, and Clarence Thomas said they would vote to overrule *Roe v. Wade*, 944–1002.

23. *Whole Women's Health*, 136 S. Ct. 2292.

24. *Dobbs*, 527 U.S. ___ (2022). Alito wrote for five justices. Chief Justice John Roberts in a concurring opinion agreed with the Court's judgment to uphold the Mississippi law but not its decision to overrule *Roe* and *Casey* entirely. The three dissenters were Elena Kagan, Sonia Sotomayor, and Stephen Breyer.

25. See, e.g., Christopher Wolfe, *How to Read the Constitution: Originalism, Constitutional Interpretation, and Judicial Power.* (Lanham, MD: Rowman & Littlefield, 1996), 41.

26. Some exceptions to notice and hearing have been tolerated in property cases. For example, *Murray's Lessee v. Hoboken Land and Improvement Co.*, 59 U.S. 272 (1856) upheld against a Fifth Amendment due process challenge the Treasury Department's use of a distress warrant to summarily seize and dispose of property for money allegedly owed the government by the New York collector of customs. The Court said that although due process generally implies regular allegations, an opportunity to be heard, and a trial, this was not "universally true." No provision in the Constitution or Bill of Rights prohibits the use of a distress warrant in these circumstances, and both England and America had used it against certain public debtors without any trial. The federal statute in this case authorized a lawsuit to be filed contesting the facts as alleged, and this may have given the Court comfort in supporting the executive's use of the warrant here.

27. *Dred Scott*, 60 U.S. 383; *Adair*, 208 U.S. 161; and *Adkins*, 261 U.S. 525.

28. Chapters 3 and 4 discuss the original meaning of the due process clauses in the Fifth and Fourteenth Amendments, respectively.

29. *Allgeyer*, 165 U.S. 578; *Meyer*, 262 U.S. 390; and *Gitlow,* 268 U.S. 652.

Chapter 7

The Fourteenth Amendment and the Bill of Rights in the States

The Supreme Court repeatedly held until 1925 that the Bill of Rights does not apply to the states. Then *Gitlow v. New York* decided to "assume" that the fundamental freedoms of speech and press embodied in the First Amendment should be applied to the states as aspects of due process "liberty" in the Fourteenth Amendment. The Court soon thereafter incorporated into the due process clause and applied to the states all the guarantees in the First Amendment. In the 1960s the Court issued a series of opinions that extended to the states most of the individual rights in the Fourth, Fifth, and Sixth Amendments, and the Eighth Amendment's cruel and unusual punishments clause. These decisions enforced protections for persons involved in criminal investigations and trials. Since the 1960s the Court has applied to the states two more provisions from the Bill, leaving a few still unincorporated.

THE BILL OF RIGHTS DOES NOT APPLY TO THE STATES PRIOR TO 1925

As previously discussed in chapter 5, the early cases of *Walker v. Sauvinet* (1875) and *Hurtado v. California* (1884) established that nothing in the Fourteenth Amendment applies any of the guarantees in the Bill of Rights to the states. This would remain consistently true until 1925. The main decisions holding that none of the Bill of Rights applies to the states included *Presser v. Illinois* (1886) (Second Amendment right to bear arms); *Spies v. Illinois* (1887) (Fourth, Fifth, and Sixth Amendments); *In re Kemmler* (1890), *McElvaine v. Brush* (1891), and *O'Neill v. Vermont* (1892) (Eighth Amendment cruel and unusual punishment); *Brown v. New Jersey* (1899) (Sixth Amendment fair trial requirements); *Maxwell v. Dow* (1900) (Fifth Amendment grand jury indictment and Sixth Amendment jury trial); *West v.*

Louisiana (1904) (Sixth Amendment right of the accused to be confronted by the witnesses against him); *Twining v. New Jersey* (1908) (Fifth Amendment privilege against self-incrimination); and *Prudential Insurance Co. of America v. Cheek* (1922) (First Amendment free speech).[1]

In refusing to apply one or more specific guarantees in these cases, the Court often stated broadly that the first eight (or ten) amendments operated only on the federal government and imposed no restrictions on the states, and that the Fourteenth Amendment did not change the result. This was true under the Fourteenth Amendment's privileges or immunities clause, following the dual citizenship analysis of the *Slaughterhouse Cases* (1873), wherein the fundamental rights of life, liberty, and property protection by government were rights of state citizenship which remained within the exclusive control of the states. And national citizenship rights, which *were* protected by the privileges or immunities clause, did not include any of the guarantees in the Bill of Rights, according to the progeny of the *Slaughterhouse Cases*. The Court achieved the same conclusion under the Fourteenth Amendment's due process clause, following the redundancy analysis in *Hurtado v. California* (1884), wherein the fact that the due process clause in the Fifth Amendment is accompanied by other separate and discrete provisions in the Bill of Rights demonstrated that those other provisions were not considered to be elements of due process.[2]

A few of the mainstream cases will convey the flavor of the Court's analysis that the Bill of Rights does not apply to the states, as well as the dissenting views of Justice Stephen Field in one case and of Justice John Marshall Harlan consistently. For example, *O'Neil v. Vermont* (1892) addressed a situation wherein Mr. O'Neil had been convicted in state court of "selling intoxicating liquor without authority," and was sentenced to fifty-four years in prison. When he complained that his sentence amounted to a "cruel and unusual punishment" in violation of the Constitution's Eighth Amendment, the Supreme Court said that "it has always been ruled that the Eighth Amendment . . . does not apply to the States," citing its 1866 decision in *Pervear v. Commonwealth*. In dissent, Justice Field observed that the punishment was "one exceeding in severity" given the nature of the offense. He agreed that prior to the Fourteenth Amendment, the Bill of Rights did not apply to the states, as held in *Barron v. Baltimore* (1833). However, Field had become convinced by the argument of counsel in *Spies v. Illinois* (1887) that the privileges and immunities of citizens of the United States as such have their recognition in or guaranty from the Constitution. While the first ten amendments, "as limitations on power, . . . are applicable only to the Federal Government, and not to the States, yet, so far as they declare or recognize the rights of persons, they are rights belonging to them as citizens of the United

States under the Constitution, and the Fourteenth Amendment, as to all such rights, places a limit upon state power by ordaining that no State shall make or enforce any law which shall abridge them." In his own dissent, Justice Harlan said he agreed with Field that "since the adoption of the Fourteenth Amendment, no one of the fundamental rights of life, liberty, and property recognized by the Constitution of the United States, can be denied or abridged by a State in respect to any person within its jurisdiction. These rights are principally enumerated in the earlier amendments of the Constitution."[3]

A man convicted of robbery in a Utah state court and sentenced to eighteen years in prison appealed his case on two constitutional grounds, that he was proceeded against by information rather than indictment, and that his jury trial consisted of only eight jurors rather than twelve, in violation of the Fifth and Sixth Amendments, respectively. Justice Rufus Peckham for the Court in *Maxwell v. Dow* (1900) rejected both claims, under the privileges or immunities clause and the due process clause. In order to limit the powers that it was feared might be claimed by the federal government under the Constitution as it was adopted, the First Congress proposed to the states the first ten amendments to that instrument in 1789. "They were intended as restraints and limitations upon the powers of the General Government, and were not intended to, and did not, have any effect upon the powers of the respective States." But the appellant in *Maxwell* now claims that all the provisions in the first ten amendments, "so far as they secure and recognize the fundamental rights of the individual" as against the exercise of federal power, are by virtue of the Fourteenth Amendment "to be regarded as privileges or immunities of a citizen of the United States," and hence cannot be abridged by a state.

The *Slaughterhouse Cases*, said Peckham, made such an argument untenable by pointing out that until the adoption of the Fourteenth Amendment the life, liberty, and property rights of the citizens of the states did not depend on the federal government "for their existence or protection" beyond the few express limitations the Constitution imposed on the states, "such, for instance, as the prohibition against *ex post facto* laws, bills of attainder, and laws impairing the obligation of contracts," in article I, section ten. Except for these and a few other limitations, "the entire domain" of the privileges and immunities of citizens of the states—their rights to government protection in their life, liberty, and property—lay within the power of the states and without that of the federal government. Justice Peckham could not believe that it was the purpose of the Fourteenth Amendment, by its simple declaration that no state shall make or enforce any law which shall abridge the privileges or immunities of citizens of the United States, "to transfer the security and protection of all the civil rights, which we have mentioned, from the States to the Federal Government." If such a dramatic consequence had been intended by Congress when it framed the amendment, it would have expressly said so in the text. It would have provided that no state shall abridge the privileges or immunities of citizens of the states, just as it did provide that no state shall abridge the privileges or immunities of citizens of the United States. As for the due process clause, besides his reliance upon *Hurtado,* Peckham quoted from a few other post–Civil War cases to show the Constitution's sweeping deference to the states in criminal law enforcements. Peckham concluded that under his construction of the amendment, "there can be no just fear that the liberties of the citizen will not be carefully protected by the States respectively. It is a case of self-protection, and the people can be trusted to look out and care for themselves."

In his dissenting opinion, Justice Harlan repeated his claim made in prior cases that the privileges and immunities enumerated in the first eight amendments belong to every citizen of the United States, guarded against federal power originally, and now against state power by the Fourteenth Amendment's command that "no state shall abridge the privileges or immunities of citizens of the United States." He also continued to insist that the Fourteenth Amendment's due process clause accomplishes the same result for all persons. When it forbade the deprivation by any state of life, liberty, or property without due process of law, "the intention was to prevent any State from infringing the guarantees for the protection of life and liberty that had already been guarded against infringement by the National Government." Harlan offered some examples to show the far-reaching consequences of the Court's reasoning in *Maxwell*. Suppose the state of Utah makes the Mormon religion the established religion of the state, to be supported by taxation on all the people of Utah. Or suppose the state prescribes as a punishment for crime burning at the stake or putting out the eyes of the accused. None of this could be gainsaid under the analysis in *Maxwell.* Under this decision, the Constitution "does not stand in the way of any State striking down guarantees of life and liberty that English-speaking people have for centuries regarded as vital to personal security, and which the men of the Revolutionary period universally claimed as the birthright of freemen."[4]

Writing for the Court in *Twining v. New Jersey* (1908), Justice William Moody gave the most comprehensive analysis of why the Fourteenth Amendment does not apply the Bill of Rights to the states. Two bank directors being tried for fraud refused to take the stand in their defense, and the prosecution argued to the jury that this tended to show they were guilty, as permitted by state law. Had this happened in federal court it would have violated the bankers' Fifth Amendment privilege against compelled self-incrimination. Did this action of the state violate the Fourteenth Amendment, either by abridging the privileges or immunities of citizens of the United States or by depriving persons of their life, liberty, or property without due process of law? Although admittedly the Bill of Rights amendments originally applied only to the federal government, the defendants argued that the personal rights therein specified are included among the fundamental rights of national citizenship now protected against state action by the privileges or immunities clause of the Fourteenth Amendment, that this was intended by its framers, and that otherwise this part of the amendment would have "little or no meaning and effect."

Justice Moody noted that the dual citizenship analysis of the *Slaughterhouse Cases*, which placed the rights of citizens mostly under the continued control of the states, had drawn the criticism of four dissenters (Justice Field in an opinion joined by three others), which "made clear the momentous consequence of the decision." The dissenters believed that the fundamental rights of citizenship, heretofore mostly within the control of the states, were brought into the national government's protection by the Fourteenth Amendment. They insisted that if the majority were correct in holding that the privileges or immunities clause only refers to rights which owe "their existence to the Federal Government, its national character, its Constitution, or its laws," to privileges and immunities "specially designated in the Constitution or necessarily implied as belonging to citizens of the United States, it was a vain and idle enactment, which accomplished nothing. . . . With privileges and immunities thus designated or implied, no State could ever have interfered by its laws, and no new constitutional provision was required to inhibit such interference." Moody observed that criticism of the case has "never entirely ceased," that it has not received "universal assent" by members of the Court, and undoubtedly "it gave much less effect to the Fourteenth Amendment than some of the men active in framing it intended, and disappointed many others." On the other hand, "if the views of the minority had prevailed it is easy to see how far the authority and independence of the States would have been diminished by subjecting all their legislative and judicial acts to correction by the legislative and review by the judicial branch of the National Government." In any event this part of the *Slaughterhouse Cases* has been often affirmed and is no longer in doubt.

The defendants in *Twining* also argued that their self-incrimination was a denial of the due process of law. The Court has always declined to give a comprehensive definition of due process and has preferred instead that its "full meaning should be gradually ascertained by the process of inclusion and exclusion in . . . cases as they arise." The key question is whether "the exemption from self-incrimination is of such a nature that it must be included in the conception of due process. Is it a fundamental principle of liberty and justice which inheres in the very idea of free government"? The history of the incorporation of the privilege in the Fifth Amendment is "full of significance in this connection." Five states ratified the Constitution without proposing amendments. Four others ratified with proposed amendments, none of which referred to the privilege. Only the final four states to ratify "insisted upon incorporating the privilege in the Constitution, and they separately and simultaneously with the requirement of due process of law." Two of these four states did not include the privilege against self-incrimination in their own constitutions, "where it would have had a much wider field of usefulness," until many years later. This survey shows the privilege was not "ranked among the fundamental and inalienable rights of mankind, and, what is more important here, it affirmatively shows that the privilege was not conceived to be inherent in due process of law, but, on the other hand, a right separate, independent, and outside of due process." Congress in submitting the amendments to the states treated the two rights as exclusive of each other, and such has been the view of the states in their own constitutions. Thus Moody, in his discussion of the fundamental rights of mankind in any free government, ends up with the redundancy point in *Hurtado.* Of course, Justice Harlan dissented, believing the entire Bill of Rights extend to the states.[5]

APPLYING THE FIRST AMENDMENT 1925 TO THE PRESENT

Prudential Insurance Co. v. Cheek (1922) opined that the Fourteenth Amendment does not impose upon the states "any restriction about 'freedom of speech.'"[6] Three years later, notwithstanding this specific precedent, and fifty years of case law insisting generally that the Bill of Rights does not apply to the states, the Court in *Gitlow v. New York* said, "For present purposes, we may and do assume that freedom of speech and of the press which are protected by the First Amendment from abridgment by Congress are among the fundamental personal rights and 'liberties' protected by the due process clause of the Fourteenth Amendment from impairment by the States." This decision then went on to uphold the state's criminal anarchy statute, which punished any person who advocates orally or in writing the propriety of overthrowing organized government by force or violence or by any unlawful means. The statute, said the Court, "imports a legislative determination that such utterances are so inimical to the general welfare and involve such danger of substantive evil that they may be penalized under the police power, and this determination must be given great weight, and every presumption be indulged in favor of the validity of the statute."

In dissent, Justice Oliver Wendell Holmes (joined by Justice Louis Brandeis) agreed with the majority that the "general principle of free speech" is included in the Fourteenth Amendment, in view of the scope that the Court in past cases had given to the word "liberty." Undoubtedly, Holmes's reference here was to the substantive economic due process cases so prominent in the Lochner era. The free-speech question in every case, he continued, is whether the words are used in such circumstances and are of such a nature as to "create a clear and present danger that they will bring about the substantive evils that the State has a right to prevent." There was "no present danger of an attempt to overthrow the government" by the defendant and the small minority who shared his views.[7]

The Supreme Court confirmed *Gitlow*'s assumption about the freedoms of speech and press being aspects of "liberty," protected against state action by the Fourteenth Amendment's due process clause, and vigorously applied all of the freedoms in the First Amendment in such cases as *Near v. Minnesota* (1931) (freedom of the press), *Hamilton v. Regents of the University of California* (1934) (free exercise of religion), *Grosjean v. American Press* (1936) (freedom of the press), and *DeJonge v. Oregon* (1937) and *Herndon v. Lowry* (1937) (freedoms of speech and peaceable assembly). Writing for the Court in *Near*, Chief Justice Charles Evans Hughes struck down a Minnesota law allowing anyone engaged in the business of publishing or circulating a "malicious, scandalous and defamatory" newspaper or magazine to be sued and enjoined from further publication, as a public nuisance, thereafter being subject to fine and imprisonment if the injunction is violated. A defense to the suit was possible but required evidence proved to the satisfaction of the court that the challenged material was true and published with good motives and for justifiable ends. Chief Justice Hughes said, "It is no longer in doubt that the liberty of the press and speech is safeguarded by the due process clause of the Fourteenth Amendment from invasion by state action," citing *Gitlow* and three subsequent cases. The requirement that a publisher of criticisms of public officials, whenever sued by those officials, must prove the truth of the allegations and also good motives and intent places an intolerable burden on the freedom of the press. This system is "the essence of censorship."[8]

A group of Methodist students at the University of California with religious and conscientious objections to war sought an exemption from the school's requirement that all students take a course in military training, and when this was denied, they appealed to the courts. *Hamilton v. Regents of University of California* (1934) presumed that the "liberty" protected by the Fourteenth Amendment due process clause includes religious freedom. However, this liberty does not mean the students must be allowed to remain in good standing even though they refuse to comply with the school's curriculum. In a concurring opinion, Justice Benjamin Cardozo (joined by Justices Brandeis and Harlan Fiske Stone) said, "I assume for present purposes that the religious liberty protected by the First Amendment against invasion by the nation is protected by the Fourteenth Amendment against invasion by the states." He agreed with the majority that there was no "obstruction by the state" to the "free exercise" of religion. Also, "instruction in military science is not instruction in the practice or tenets of a religion. Neither directly nor indirectly is government establishing a state religion when it insists upon such training."[9]

Grosjean v. American Press Co. (1936) struck down a Louisiana law that imposed, in addition to other taxes assessed by the state, a license tax of 2 percent of gross proceeds on all publishers of a newspaper, magazine, or periodical with a circulation of more than twenty thousand people. This tax restrained the freedom of the press in violation of the Fourteenth Amendment due process clause, said the Court. *DeJonge v. Oregon* (1937) and *Herndon v. Lowry* (1937) overturned convictions under state criminal syndicalism statutes in order to protect the freedoms of speech and peaceable assembly. In *DeJonge* the defendant had been convicted of a crime for assisting in the conduct of a meeting of the Portland, Oregon branch of the Communist Party. He "was not charged with teaching or advocating criminal syndicalism or sabotage or any unlawful acts, either at the meeting or elsewhere. . . . His sole offense . . . was that he had assisted in the conduct of a public meeting, albeit otherwise lawful, which was held under the auspices of the Communist Party." *Herndon* overturned a person's conviction for soliciting members and conducting a meeting for a political party whose doctrine may be said to approve an ultimate resort to violence in the indefinite future against organized government. The Georgia law, said the Court, with no requirement of proof that the accused advocated violence or engaged in any unlawful acts at the meeting, unduly interferes with the freedoms of speech and assembly.[10]

Although *Gitlow* had upheld New York's criminal anarchy law, saying the legislative determination about the potential harms of speech "must be given great weight, and every presumption be indulged in favor of the validity of the statute," the Supreme Court would soon embrace the idea that since the First Amendment freedoms protect important "fundamental rights" and are explicitly enumerated in the Constitution, they should be broadly interpreted and vigorously enforced in the states via the Fourteenth Amendment. For example, *Murdock v. Pennsylvania* (1943) construed a municipal ordinance which provided that all persons soliciting orders for goods or merchandise of any kind must procure a license and pay a fee of ascending amounts depending upon the length of time the selling of goods will occur. Justice William Douglas in his opinion for the Court said, in a phrase that would be repeated in future cases, the First Amendment freedoms of speech, press, and religion "are in a preferred position," and must be applied accordingly. The Court held that a group of Jehovah's Witnesses who were selling their religious literature on the public streets and in door-to-door canvassing of the neighborhood must be exempted from the license and tax. "A state may not impose a charge for the enjoyment of a right granted" by the Constitution.[11]

From 1925 to the present time, under the First Amendment as incorporated into the Fourteenth Amendment due process clause, the Supreme Court has struck down about forty-five city and town ordinances and 135 state laws.[12] Regardless of its prevailing political ideology over time, the Court majority has enforced a libertarian vision of society and government under the First Amendment. Based upon the proposition that the religion, speech, press, and assembly and petition clauses protect fundamentally important and fragile interests, the justices have strictly scrutinized state and local laws in many cases to avoid any possibility of a slippery slope whereby the full enjoyment of these rights might be compromised. Some of the decisions have been clearly good ones, some clearly bad, and many have been cases in which reasonable people could disagree on the merits. I will sample a few cases here.

In my opinion, clearly good outcomes include the following: *Thornhill v. Alabama* (1940) decided that a state law which forbids the publicizing of facts concerning a labor dispute, whether by sign, pamphlet, word of mouth or otherwise, infringes the freedoms of speech and press. *Taylor v. Mississippi* (1943) struck down a state law which made it a felony to teach or disseminate printed matter designed to encourage disloyalty or tending to "create an attitude" of disrespect for the flag or for the government of the United States or the state of Mississippi. *Virginia Board of Pharmacy v. Virginia Citizens Consumer Council* (1976) opined that a state statute declaring it unprofessional conduct for a pharmacist to advertise the price of prescription drugs violates the First Amendment right of people to receive such information.[13] The laws in these cases limited the freedom of expression without furthering any obvious state interest.

At the other end of the opinion scale, I believe clearly bad outcomes would include the following cases: Several teenagers burned a cross on a Black family's lawn, and the Court overturned their convictions in *R.A.V. v. City of St. Paul* (1992), holding that the city's Bias-Motivated Crime Ordinance, which proscribed the display of a symbol which one knows will arouse anger, alarm, or resentment in others based on race, color, creed or gender, is "facially invalid" under the First Amendment because it discriminates on the basis of speech content. *Brown v. Entertainment Merchants Association* (2011) held that California could not impose a fine for the sale or rental of "violent video games" to minors. *Packingham v. North Carolina* (2017) decided that a state law which makes it a crime for a registered sex offender "to access a commercial social networking Web site where the sex offender knows that the site permits minor children to become members or to create or maintain personal Web pages" impermissibly restricts lawful speech under the First Amendment.[14] In each of these cases the state was protecting its citizens against harms without unduly limiting the freedom of expression.

Many of the Court's First Amendment overrides fall into a broad middle range of opinions wherein reasonable people could disagree on the merits. This includes:

- *Jamison v. Texas* (1943): A Dallas ordinance making it unlawful to throw handbills, newspapers or advertising material on the streets and sidewalks of the city denies the freedom of the press by prohibiting the dissemination of information, and it denies the freedom of religion for those handbills containing an invitation to participate in a religious activity.
- *Saia v. New York* (1948): An ordinance that bans the use of sound amplification, but makes exceptions for the dissemination through loudspeakers of news, matters of public interest, and athletic events, with the permission of the police chief, is unconstitutional on its face as a prior restraint on speech.
- *Schwartz v. Vanasco* (1976): Summarily affirms a district court decision invalidating as overly broad a New York law prohibiting attacks against candidates for public office based upon their race, sex, religion or ethnic background, and prohibiting misrepresentations of a candidate's qualifications or positions.
- *Spence v. Washington* (1974): A state statute which prohibits the "improper use" of the flag or a display of the flag with an emblem superimposed on it was invalidly applied to a person who taped a peace symbol on his flag and displayed it upside down.[15]

These cases involve a balancing of legitimate state interests and rights of free expression.

A reader might disagree with my characterizations in these cases, or in any other representative sample of cases that might be offered. And that is the point of this exercise. The First Amendment freedoms are not self-defining. They often implicate complex calculations of public and private interests. This suggests that a degree of judicial deference to legislative judgments might be appropriate, to Congress if not to the states. This is an idea that will be explored further in the next chapter.

RESISTING INCORPORATION BEYOND THE FIRST AMENDMENT 1937–1960

In the years from 1925 to 1937, *Powell v. Alabama* (1932) was the one decision to move beyond the First Amendment, applying the Sixth Amendment right to assistance of counsel in a criminal case. This right should be made available in the circumstances of the case, said Justice George Sutherland in his opinion for the Court. Nine young, illiterate Black men, accused of raping two white women, were convicted and all but one was sentenced to death in a one-day trial in a courthouse surrounded by a hostile white mob. Justice Sutherland in *Powell* held that in a capital case, in these circumstances, the Fourteenth Amendment due process clause requires that the defendants should have the assistance of counsel for their defense. He reached this conclusion even though the right to counsel is guaranteed in the Sixth Amendment in a provision separate from the due process clause in the Fifth Amendment. He avoided *Hurtado v. California* (1884)'s redundancy rule by noting *Gitlow's* assumption in 1925 that the Fourteenth Amendment due process clause encompasses the freedoms of speech and press even though these rights are in First Amendment provisions separate from the due process clause in the Fifth Amendment.[16]

Then came *Palko v. Connecticut* (1937), wherein Justice Cardozo in a landmark decision presented an overview rationale of the Court's old and recent cases in order to demonstrate the principles at work in determining which provisions in the Bill of Rights should apply to the states, and which ones should not. In *Palko* the state had obtained a conviction of second-degree murder and a sentence of life imprisonment. Contending that errors of law had occurred in the trial, the state appealed, and in the second trial the defendant was convicted of first-degree murder and sentenced to death. He appealed his second trial and conviction as a violation of the Fifth Amendment's guarantee that "no person shall be subject for the same offense to be twice put in jeopardy of life or limb," taking the view that the first eight amendments apply to the states by virtue of the Fourteenth Amendment. "There is no such rule," said Justice Cardozo in his opinion for the Court.

The Supreme Court has held that a number of the restraints and guarantees in the Bill of Rights do not apply to the states: the Fourth Amendment ban on unreasonable searches and seizures, *Weeks v. United States* (1914); the Fifth Amendment requirement of a grand jury presentment or indictment in capital cases, *Hurtado v. California* (1884); the Fifth Amendment privilege against self-incrimination in criminal cases, *Twining v. New Jersey* (2008); the Sixth Amendment right to a jury trial in criminal cases, *Maxwell v. Dow* (1900); the fair trial requirements of the Sixth Amendment, *West v. Louisiana* (1904); and the Seventh Amendment right to a jury trial in civil cases where the value in controversy exceeds twenty dollars, *Walker v. Sauvinet* (1875). The rights to jury trial and grand jury indictment and the other Bill of Rights provisions cataloged here, which the Court has chosen not to extend to the states, may have value and importance, but to abolish them would not violate a "principle of justice so rooted in the traditions and conscience of our people as to be ranked as fundamental," *Snyder v. Massachusetts* (1934).

On the other hand, continued Cardozo, the due process clause of the Fourteenth Amendment may make it unlawful for a state to abridge the freedom of speech which the First Amendment safeguards against encroachment by Congress, *DeJong v. Oregon* (1937), *Herndon v. Lowry* (1937), or the like freedom of the press, *Grosjean v. American Press Co.* (1936), or the free exercise of religion, *Hamilton v. Regents* (1934), or the right of peaceable assembly, without which speech would be unduly trammeled, *DeJong* and *Herndon*, or the Sixth Amendment right of one accused of crime to have the benefit of counsel, *Powell v. Alabama* (1932). In these situations, the pledges in the original amendments, valid against the federal government, have been found to be "implicit in the concept of ordered liberty," and as such, valid against the states through the Fourteenth Amendment. "If the Fourteenth Amendment has absorbed [Bill of Rights provisions], the process of absorption has had its source in the belief that neither liberty nor justice would exist if they were sacrificed," *Twining v. New Jersey* (1908). Cardozo concluded that the double jeopardy clause does not embody a fundamental right that must be extended to the states.[17]

After *Palko* (1937), the Court majority proved reluctant to extend the strict scrutiny analytical approach it was taking under the First Amendment to embrace other Bill of Rights guarantees, in cases such as *Betts v. Brady* (1942), *Adamson v. California* (1947), *In re Oliver* (1948), and *Wolf v. Colorado* (1949). *Betts v. Brady* (1942) heard an appeal from a Maryland state trial in which an accused robber, unable to afford an attorney, asked that counsel be appointed to assist in his defense. The judge refused, and the man waived a jury trial, was convicted of the robbery based upon evidence presented to the judge, and was sentenced to eight years in prison. The *Betts* case considered whether the petitioner's conviction and sentence "was a deprivation of his liberty without due process of law, in violation of the Fourteenth Amendment, because of the court's refusal to appoint counsel at his request." Writing for the Supreme Court, Justice Owen Roberts decided that this did not violate due process, notwithstanding the Sixth Amendment's command that an accused in a criminal prosecution shall enjoy the right to "have the Assistance of Counsel for his defense."

Said Roberts, the due process clause of the Fourteenth Amendment "does not incorporate, as such, the specific guarantees found in the Sixth Amendment." The phrase "due process of law" formulates a concept "less rigid and more fluid" than other provisions of the Bill of Rights. An asserted denial of due process is to be tested by the totality of facts in each case. "That which may, in one setting, constitute a denial of fundamental fairness, shocking to the universal sense of justice, may, in other circumstances and in the light of other considerations, fall short of such denial." In *Powell v. Alabama* (1932), for example, "ignorant, friendless negro youths, strangers in the community, without friends or means to obtain counsel, were hurried to trial for a capital offense." The trial was conducted without benefit of effective defense counsel in a hostile environment, "in disregard of every principle of fairness," and this Court held the resulting convictions were without due process of law. But *Powell* added that whether the absence of counsel would violate due process "in other criminal prosecutions, or in other circumstances, . . . we need not determine." Here in *Betts*, Roberts concluded, a robbery was committed, the state's case consisted of evidence identifying the accused as the perpetrator, and the accused called and examined witnesses to prove that he was at another location when the crime was committed. The simple issue was the veracity of the witnesses for the state and the defense. As the state trial judge observed, "the accused was not helpless, but was a man forty-three years old, of ordinary intelligence and ability to take care of his own interests on the trial of that narrow issue."[18]

Adamson v. California (1947) considered a state law that permitted a criminal defendant's failure to take the stand at trial to be commented upon by the prosecution, and to be considered by court and jury. In his five-to-four decision for the Supreme Court, Justice Stanley Reed assumed that this permission would violate the Fifth Amendment's privilege against self-incrimination if done in a federal court trial, and then explained why it did not violate the Fourteenth Amendment for state cases. He cited precedents including the *Slaughterhouse Cases* (1873), *Twining v. New Jersey* (1908), and *Palko v. Connecticut* (1937) to show that neither the privileges or immunities clause nor the due process clause in the Fourteenth Amendment makes the privilege against self-incrimination applicable to the states. While the due process clause admittedly does require a fair trial, the privilege against self-incrimination is not a fundamental right which "inheres in the right to a fair trial."

In his concurring opinion in *Adamson*, intended as an answer to Justice Hugo Black's argument in dissent for a total incorporation of the Bill of Rights, Justice Felix Frankfurter observed that in the seventy years from the adoption of the Fourteenth Amendment to the seating of the present membership of the Court, only "one eccentric exception"—undoubtedly this referred to the first Justice Harlan—ever indicated the belief that the Fourteenth Amendment "was a shorthand summary of the first eight Amendments." To the notion that the Fourteenth Amendment's due process clause "was a way of saying that every State must thereafter initiate prosecutions through indictment by a grand jury, must have a trial by 12 in criminal cases, and must have trial by such a jury in common law suits where the amount in controversy exceeds $20," the short answer is that "it is a strange way of saying it. It would be extraordinarily strange for a Constitution to convey such specific commands in such a roundabout and inexplicit way." The due process clause of the Fourteenth Amendment "has an independent potency, precisely as does the Due Process Clause of the Fifth Amendment in relation to the Federal Government. It ought not to require argument to reject the notion that due process of law meant one thing in the Fifth Amendment and another in the Fourteenth."

Justice Black (joined by Justice Douglas) complained in his dissent that the decision in *Adamson* "reasserts a constitutional theory spelled out in *Twining v. New Jersey* that this Court is empowered by the Constitution with boundless power under 'natural law' periodically to expand and contract constitutional standards to conform to the Court's conception of what, at a particular time, constitutes 'civilized decency' and 'fundamental liberty and justice.'" Since *Marbury v. Madison* (1803) was decided, the practice has been firmly established, "for better or worse," that courts can strike down legislative enactments which violate the Constitution. "But to pass upon the constitutionality of statutes by looking to the particular standards enumerated in the Bill of Rights and other parts of the Constitution is one thing; to invalidate statutes because of the application of 'natural law,' deemed to be above and undefined by the Constitution, is quite another." Black's study of the legislative history of the Fourteenth Amendment persuaded him that one of the chief objects of the enactors in Congress was to make the Bill of Rights applicable to the states. In his own dissent, Justice Frank Murphy (joined by Justice Wiley Rutledge) said he agreed the specific guarantees in the Bill of Rights "should be carried over into the first section of the Fourteenth Amendment." But he was not prepared to say that the Fourteenth Amendment "is entirely and necessarily limited by the Bill of Rights." *Adamson* came within a single vote of applying the entire Bill of Rights to the states.[19]

In re Oliver (1948) addressed a petitioner's situation in Michigan wherein a judge had conducted a secret "one-man grand jury" investigation of crime. After the petitioner had given his testimony, the judge-grand jury, acting in the belief that the testimony was false and evasive (which belief was based partly on testimony given by at least one other witness in the petitioner's absence), summarily charged him with contempt, convicted him, and sentenced him to sixty days in jail. In his opinion for the Court, Justice Black held that these facts demonstrated a denial of procedural due process for two reasons. First, "In view of this nation's historic distrust of secret proceedings, . . . and the universal requirement of our federal and state governments that criminal trials be public," the Fourteenth Amendment guarantee that no one shall be deprived of liberty without due process of law meant that the petitioner could not be sentenced to prison without a public trial. Second, not affording the petitioner a reasonable opportunity to defend himself also violated due process. "A person's right to reasonable notice of a charge against him, and an opportunity to be heard in his defense . . . are basic in our system of jurisprudence, and these rights include, at a minimum, a right to examine the witnesses against him, to offer testimony, and to be represented by counsel." Black relied exclusively on a procedural due process analysis, without referencing or incorporating any of the fair trial requirements in the Sixth Amendment.[20]

Finally, Justice Frankfurter's opinion for the Court in *Wolf v. Colorado* (1949) applied to the states a prohibition on unreasonable searches and seizures because a right of privacy against unreasonable intrusions is an element of Fourteenth Amendment due process. "The security of one's privacy against arbitrary intrusion by the police—which is at the core of the Fourth Amendment—is basic to a free society. It is therefore implicit in 'the concept of ordered liberty,' and, as such, applicable to the States through the Due Process Clause." Frankfurter has done a variation on Justice Cardozo's analysis in *Palko*. Whereas Cardozo had absorbed the Bill of Rights provisions considered to be "implicit in the concept of ordered liberty," Frankfurter absorbed a right of privacy not expressed in the Bill. He then opined that although the Court had held since *Weeks v. United States* (1914) that evidence seized in an illegal search is inadmissible in federal courts, this evidence-exclusion rule should not be imposed on the states. A survey of the states revealed a variety of practices in the treatment of the fruits of illegal searches, and reasonable people could disagree about the need for the evidence-exclusion rule.

In a concurring opinion, Justice Black said he agreed with the Court's two conclusions: that the Fourth Amendment's prohibition on unreasonable searches and seizures is enforceable against the states, and that the federal exclusionary rule is "not a command of the Fourth Amendment, but is a judicially created rule of evidence which Congress might negate." It therefore need not be extended to the states. Black glossed over Frankfurter's careful distinction between the Fourth Amendment right (which remains limited to the federal government) and the Fourteenth Amendment's due process privacy right. Three justices dissented—Douglas, Murphy, and Rutledge—on their shared understanding that, in the absence of the evidence-exclusion rule, the protection against unreasonable searches and seizures has "no sanction," and "might as well be stricken from the Constitution."[21]

INCORPORATING CRIMINAL LAW PROTECTIONS IN THE 1960S

During this decade the Court incorporated into the Fourteenth Amendment due process clause and applied to the states most of the protections in the Fourth through the Eighth Amendments for persons under investigation, or being accused of, tried, or punished for a crime. In the first criminal procedure case, *Mapp v. Ohio* (1961) overruled *Wolf v. Colorado* (1949) to hold that the evidence-exclusion rule under the Fourth Amendment should be extended to the states after all. Writing for the Court, Justice Tom Clark noted the importance of the ban on unreasonable searches and seizures, and the recent trend in the states toward adoption of the rule. Some have said, as did Justice (then Judge) Cardozo in a state case, that under our exclusionary rule "the criminal is to go free because the constable has blundered." Undoubtedly this will happen, Clark admitted, but "there is another consideration—the imperative of judicial integrity." The second Justice John Marshall Harlan, a grandson of the first Harlan (joined by Justices Frankfurter and Whittaker) dissented. Since the desirability of the exclusionary rule is debatable and is not constitutionally required by the Fourth Amendment, the states should retain their discretion to follow it or not.[22]

Justice Black for the Court in *Gideon v. Wainwright* (1963) overruled *Betts v. Brady* (1942) and held that an indigent defendant, being tried for a felony in state criminal court, is constitutionally entitled to have defense counsel appointed to represent him for free. The Sixth Amendment right to the assistance of counsel in criminal prosecutions is a "fundamental right essential to a fair trial," and so applies to the states by virtue of the Fourteenth Amendment due process clause. Justice Arthur Goldberg in *Escobedo v. Illinois* (1964) extended the right to counsel in criminal prosecutions to include police interrogations of suspects. Concluded Goldberg, "the right to use counsel at the formal trial would be a very hollow thing if, for all practical purposes, the conviction is already assured by pretrial examination."[23]

Three cases enforced the Fifth Amendment's statement that no person "shall be compelled in any criminal case to be a witness against himself." *Malloy v. Hogan* (1964) held that the privilege against self-incrimination is available to a witness in a statutory inquiry as well as to a defendant in a criminal prosecution. even though the Fifth Amendment's protection literally speaks only of compelled self-incrimination in a "criminal case." *Griffin v. California* (1965) involved a criminal case but extended the protection in another way. It held that comment by a prosecutor or judge to the jury, to the effect that a defendant's failure to testify in his own defense could be considered in deciding the issue of guilt or innocence, runs afoul of the self-incrimination clause.[24] Chief Justice Earl Warren for the Court in *Miranda v. Arizona* (1966) extended the ban on self-incrimination to protect suspects in police interrogations, and he crafted an advisory warning that must be given. Prior to questioning, the suspect must be told that he has a right to remain silent, that anything he says can be used against him in court, that he has a right to the presence of an attorney, and that if he cannot afford an attorney, one will be provided if he desires. The suspect may waive these rights and agree to answer questions or make a statement, but unless and until such warnings and waiver are demonstrated by the prosecution at trial, no evidence obtained as a result of interrogation can be used against him. Four justices—Harlan, Byron White, Potter Stewart, and Clark—dissented in *Miranda*, as they had done in *Escobedo v. Illinois* two years earlier, for similar reasons. They did not believe the Fifth Amendment statement that no one shall be compelled to be a witness against himself in a criminal case and the Sixth Amendment right to assistance of counsel in a criminal prosecution logically apply to police interrogations prior to the commencement of any judicial proceeding. And as public policy, the decisions were too one-sided, crafting strenuous protections for criminal suspects at the expense of effective law enforcement.[25]

In addition to these cases, which embraced expansive interpretations of constitutional language, the Court applied the Eighth Amendment prohibition on the infliction of cruel and unusual punishments, *Robinson v. California* (1962); the Sixth Amendment criminal-trial rights of the defendant to confront witnesses against him, and to have compulsory process for obtaining witnesses in his favor, *Pointer v. Texas* (1965) and *Washington v. Texas* (1967), respectively; the Sixth Amendment right to a speedy trial, *Klopfer v. North Carolina* (1967); the Sixth Amendment right to a jury trial in criminal cases wherein the punishment can be two or more years imprisonment, *Duncan v. Louisiana* (1968); and the Fifth Amendment guarantee against double jeopardy, *Benton v. Maryland* (1969).

Robinson v. California (1962) overturned a state law which made it a misdemeanor for a person "either to use narcotics, or to be addicted to the use of narcotics." While the state could outlaw the use or sale of narcotics, said the Court, it would be a cruel and unusual punishment to make the mere "status" of being a narcotic addict a criminal offense. "Such addiction is a medical problem and should be treated accordingly."[26]

Pointer v. Texas (1965) involved the following situation: Pointer was arrested in Texas and taken before a state judge for a preliminary hearing on the charge of having robbed Kenneth Phillips of $375. Phillips identified Pointer as the man who had robbed him at gunpoint. Phillips moved to California prior to the trial; the state later used a transcript of his hearing testimony as evidence at trial, over the objections of Pointer's attorney that he must be allowed to confront the state's chief witness; and Pointer was found guilty and sentenced to prison. Writing for the Supreme Court, Justice Black overturned the conviction, holding that "the right granted to an accused by the Sixth Amendment to confront the witnesses against him . . . is a fundamental right essential to a fair trial."[27] In a concurring opinion, Justice Harlan thought the state judgment must be reversed because one's right to confront an adverse witness at trial is "implicit in the concept of ordered liberty," citing *Palko*, and is "reflected in the Due Process Clause of the Fourteenth

Amendment independently of the Sixth." Justice Stewart also concurred not on account of the Sixth Amendment, but because the state's refusal to permit the accused "to cross-examine, through counsel, the chief witness for the prosecution," deprived him of liberty without due process.[28]

Washington v. Texas (1967) addressed this factual situation: Jackie Washington was convicted of murder and sentenced to fifty years in prison. The prosecutor's evidence showed that either Washington or a man with him named Charles Fuller fired the shotgun that killed the deceased. At his trial Washington testified that Fuller, not he, fired the fatal shot, and the record showed that Fuller would have corroborated this version of events. However, Fuller had been convicted of the murder in an earlier trial and sentenced to fifty years in prison. Two Texas statutes provided that persons charged or convicted as co-participants in the same crime could not testify for one another, although there was no bar to their testifying for the state. In his opinion for the Court, Chief Justice Warren said we have not previously been called upon to decide whether the right of an accused to have compulsory process for obtaining witnesses in his favor, guaranteed in federal trials by the Sixth Amendment, "is so fundamental and essential to a fair trial that it is incorporated in the Due Process Clause of the Fourteenth Amendment." At one time it was thought the Sixth Amendment had no application to state criminal trials. That view no longer prevails, and "we have increasingly looked to the specific guarantees of the Sixth Amendment to determine whether a state criminal trial was conducted with due process of law." The right of an accused to have compulsory process for obtaining witnesses in his favor "stands on no lesser footing" than the other Sixth Amendment rights that have been found applicable to the states.[29]

Chief Justice Warren also wrote for the Court in *Klopfer v. North Carolina* (1967). Mr. Klopfer, a Duke University zoology professor, had been tried for criminal trespass in a case that ended in a mistrial when the jury failed to reach a verdict. The state's prosecutor obtained a "*nolle prosequi* with leave," an unusual North Carolina procedural device whereby the accused is discharged from custody but still remains subject to prosecution at any time in the future at the discretion of the prosecutor. After the passage of eighteen months from the original indictment, Klopfer moved to have his case tried or dismissed as soon as reasonably possible, since the pending indictment interfered with his professional activities and his travel plans. The appeal was denied and reached the Supreme Court. Warren held that the right to a speedy trial "is as fundamental as any of the rights secured by the Sixth Amendment," and he returned the case to the state for appropriate disposition.[30]

Under Louisiana law, simple battery was a misdemeanor punishable by up to two years in prison and a $300 fine. Young Gary Duncan sought a trial by jury in his case, but because the state constitution granted jury trials only in cases in which capital punishment or imprisonment at hard labor might be imposed, the trial judge denied the request, convicted Duncan of slapping a white boy in a skirmish, and sentenced him to serve sixty days in prison and pay a $10 fine. *Duncan v. Louisiana* (1968) on these facts overturned the decision and remanded the case. For the Court, Justice White said that in resolving conflicting claims concerning the "spacious meaning" of the due process clause, the Court has looked increasingly to the Bill of Rights for guidance, applying to the states many of the rights guaranteed in the first eight amendments. The test for determining whether a right protected by the Fifth and Sixth Amendments in federal criminal proceedings is also protected against state action by the Fourteenth Amendment has been phrased in a variety of ways in the Court's opinions. The question has been asked whether a right is among those "fundamental principles of liberty and justice which lie at the base of our civil and political institutions, *Powell v. Alabama* (1932), whether it is "basic in our system of jurisprudence," *In re Oliver* (1948), or whether it is a "fundamental right, essential to a fair trial," *Gideon v. Wainwright* (1963), *Malloy v. Hogan* (1964), and *Pointer v. Texas* (1965). "Because we believe that a trial by jury in criminal cases is fundamental to the American scheme of justice," concluded White, "we hold that the Fourteenth Amendment guarantees a right of jury trial in all criminal cases which—if they were to be tried in a federal court—would come within the Sixth Amendment guarantee." This includes any crime punishable by two years in prison.[31]

Justice Harlan (joined by Justice Stewart) issued a spirited dissent, and Justice Black (joined by Justice Douglas) issued a concurring opinion responding to Harlan's arguments. Louisiana, said Harlan, which provides trial by jury for all felonies, should not be prohibited from trying charges of simple battery to the judge alone. The Court has looked to rights in the Bill to find that some of them are "fundamental" under the *Palko v. Connecticut* (1937) test. The Court in *Duncan* says the jury trial right is "fundamental," but its use of the word would have astonished Justice Cardozo. The Court has done no analysis of jury trials as they relate to fair procedures. It turns out the word "fundamental" means "old," "much praised," and "found in the Bill of Rights." Such a definition is circular. The jury system has some "inherent defects." It is a cumbersome process, imposing great costs on both the state and the jurors, and contributing to delay in the machinery of justice. Seventy-five percent of criminal cases are settled by plea bargains, and 40 percent of the rest are tried by judges. Justice Brandeis was wise when he said in a 1922 case that "it is one of the happy incidents of the federal system that a single courageous State may, if its citizens choose, serve as a laboratory. . . . This Court, other courts, and the political process can correct any experiments in criminal procedure that prove to be unfair to defendants." That is not what is being done today. The Court is imposing upon every state one means of trying criminal cases; "it is a good means, but it is not the only fair means, and it is not demonstrably better than the alternatives States might devise."[32]

In his concurring opinion, Justice Black said that although the Congress which enacted the Fourteenth Amendment intended it to apply the entire Bill of Rights to the states, he was happy to accept the "selective process through which our Court has . . . held most of the specific Bill of Rights protections applicable to the States to the same extent they are applicable to the Federal Government." Although Justice Harlan objects to incorporating the Bill of Rights because the Fourteenth Amendment does not say, "The rights heretofore guarded against federal intrusion by the first eight Amendments are henceforth guaranteed against state intrusion as well," Black responded that the words, "No State shall make or enforce any law which shall abridge the privileges or immunities of citizens of the United States" seems to be "an eminently reasonable way of expressing the idea that, henceforth, the Bill of Rights shall apply to the States." Harlan leaves judges free to decide whether a particular rule "is implicit in the concept of ordered liberty," or "shocks the conscience," or runs counter to some other "undefined and undefinable standard." If due process means this, the Fourteenth Amendment might as well have been written that "no person shall be deprived of life, liberty or property except by laws that the judges of the United States Supreme Court shall find to be consistent with the immutable principles of free government." Black did not believe that our Constitution gives such unconfined power to judges. He also disagreed with Harlan's argument that applying the Bill of Rights to the states according to the same standards that protect these personal rights against federal encroachment "interferes with our concept of federalism in that it may prevent States from trying novel social and economic experiments." As Justice Goldberg wisely said in his concurring opinion in *Pointer v. Texas* (1965), "to deny to the States the power to impair a fundamental constitutional right is not to increase federal power, but, rather, to limit the power of both federal and state governments in favor of safeguarding the rights and liberties of the individual."[33]

In the final in this series of criminal law rights incorporations, *Benton v. Maryland* (1969) overruled *Palko v. Connecticut* (1937) and held that the "double jeopardy prohibition in the Fifth Amendment, a fundamental ideal in our constitutional heritage, is enforceable against the States through the Fourteenth Amendment." Mr. Benton had been tried in state court on charges of burglary and larceny. The jury found him not guilty of larceny but convicted him on the burglary count, and he was sentenced to ten years in prison. Shortly thereafter it was determined that the jury had been selected under an invalid constitutional provision, and Benton chose to have his conviction set aside. In the second trial, the state again charged Benton with both larceny and burglary, and this time the jury found him guilty of both crimes, and the judge sentenced him to fifteen years on the burglary count and five years for larceny. The Supreme Court decided to uphold the burglary conviction but reversed the larceny conviction as a violation of the double jeopardy clause.[34]

THE BILL OF RIGHTS IS MOSTLY INCORPORATED

Since the 1960s the Court has incorporated into the due process clause and applied to the states the Second Amendment right to bear arms in *McDonald v. Chicago* (2010) and the Eighth Amendment ban on excessive fines in *Timbs v. Indiana* (2019). In his decision for the Court in *McDonald*, Justice Samuel Alito noted that two years earlier, in *District of Columbia v. Heller* (2008), the Court held that the Second Amendment protects the right to keep and bear arms for self-defense, and struck down a law that banned the possession of handguns in the home. The city of Chicago and village of Oak Park have similar laws but argue that the Second Amendment does not apply to the states. Observing that the Court has previously held that most of the Bill of Rights provisions "apply with full force to both the Federal Government and the States," Alito ruled that the Second Amendment is fully applicable as well.

The petitioners in *McDonald* argued primarily that the right to bear arms is among their privileges and immunities as citizens of the United States, and that the narrow interpretation of the privileges or immunities clause in the *Slaughterhouse Cases* should now be rejected. As a secondary argument, they contended that the due process clause in the Fourteenth Amendment incorporates the Second Amendment. Although many legal scholars dispute the correctness of the narrow *Slaughterhouse Cases* interpretation, Alito saw no need to reconsider it now. Instead, he looked to determine if the right to keep and bear arms is "fundamental to our scheme of ordered liberty," *Duncan v. Louisiana* (1968), or "deeply rooted in the Nation's history and tradition," *Washington v. Glucksberg* (1997). He concluded that the right to bear arms in self-defense satisfies these criteria as a "fundamental right," in part based upon some of the original-meaning history of the Fourteenth Amendment. He noted, for example, that the Congress which passed the Fourteenth Amendment also passed the Freedmen's Bureau Act (1866), which had a section protecting "the constitutional right to bear arms"; that several members of Congress spoke of the need for Black people in the South to be able to arm themselves in self-defense in the aftermath of the Civil War; and that twenty-two of the thirty-seven states in the union in 1868 had constitutional provisions protecting the right to keep and bear arms.[35]

Timbs v. Indiana (2019), the excessive fines case, considered these facts: Tyson Timbs pleaded guilty in state court to dealing in a controlled substance and conspiracy to commit theft, and was sentenced to one year of home detention and five years of probation. The sentence also required Timbs to pay $1,203 in court costs and fees. At the time of Timbs's arrest, the police had seized his vehicle, a Land Rover SUV recently purchased for about $42,000. The state brought a civil suit for the forfeiture of the vehicle, charging that it had been used to transport heroin. The trial court in the civil suit held that the forfeiture of the car, worth more than four times the maximum fine assessable against Timbs for the drug violation, would be grossly disproportionate to the gravity of his offense, and hence in violation of the Eight Amendment's excessive fines clause. The state's highest court overturned this decision, holding that the Eight Amendment's excessive fines clause does not apply to the state. Hearing Timbs's appeal, the Supreme Court disagreed. This safeguard against excessive fines is "fundamental to our scheme of ordered liberty," with "deep roots in our history and tradition," *McDonald v. Chicago* (2010). The excessive fines clause is therefore incorporated into the due process clause of the Fourteenth Amendment. Incorporated guarantees under this amendment are enforceable against the states "according to the same standards" that these personal rights are protected against federal encroachment.[36]

What remains unincorporated? The Supreme Court has not yet applied to the states the Third Amendment's statement that no soldier in time of peace shall be quartered in any house without the consent of the owner, the Fifth Amendment grand jury indictment requirement, the Seventh Amendment right to a jury trial in civil cases where the value in controversy exceeds twenty dollars, and the Eighth Amendment ban on excessive bail. The Court has never issued a decision under the Third Amendment or the excessive bail clause, but there should be little doubt that if ever presented with an appropriate case it would incorporate these provisions into the Fourteenth Amendment and apply them to the states. Relevant to this point, the Second Circuit Court of Appeals in *Engblom v. Carey* (1983) has enforced the Third Amendment against the state of New York on these facts: Correctional officers in a prison, involved in an organized strike, were removed from their residences in the prison facility, which residences were then assigned to members of the national guard who had temporarily replaced them as prison guards. The correctional officers challenged the move as a peacetime quartering of troops in their homes in violation of the Third Amendment, and the Second Circuit agreed.[37] As for "excessive bail," it should be treated in the same way as excessive fines and cruel and unusual punishments, which have been incorporated as rights protected against the states.

The Court has refused to apply to the states the Fifth Amendment grand jury indictment requirement, *Hurtado v. California* (1884), and the Seventh Amendment right to a jury trial in civil cases involving more than twenty dollars, *Walker v. Sauvinct* (1875). It is unlikely these old cases will ever be overturned, and for good reason. While the grand jury has an ancient lineage in Anglo-American law, it has evolved to be prosecutor-friendly rather than a fair and effective screening mechanism for criminal proceedings. Grand juries are secret, and the jurors hear only the evidence the prosecutor wishes to present to them. According to a Justice Department study on plea bargaining, "Grand juries are notorious for being 'rubber stamps' for the prosecutor for virtually all routine criminal matters." The much more common practice today in the states is to hold preliminary hearings before a trial judge to assess the merits of a possible criminal prosecution. Such hearings are public and adversarial, the suspect can be present with counsel, and can present his evidence and cross-examine any witnesses for the state.[38]

The civil jury trial also has an ancient lineage in Anglo-American law but is today seldom used. The United States is almost alone in the world in the employment of civil jury trials. They are not part of the legal traditions of continental Europe, or of the legal systems derived from those traditions, including in Latin America and Asia. Even in England and its former colonies of Canada, Australia, and New Zealand, the civil jury trial has been virtually abolished. Although in our country most of the states provide for juries in certain civil cases, juries decide fewer than 1 percent of civil cases filed in court. The Seventh Amendment will probably remain undisturbed and unincorporated.[39]

JUSTICES FRANKFURTER, BLACK, AND THE SECOND JUSTICE HARLAN

The consistent opinions of these three justices, including some exchanges between Black and Frankfurter, and between Black and the second Justice Harlan, shed considerable light on the Supreme Court's approach to the Fourteenth Amendment and the Bill of Rights during the middle decades of the twentieth century, the height of the Court's incorporation discussions. Justice Frankfurter was deferential to the lawmakers in the states. He did not believe that any of the Bill's restraints on the federal government applied as such to the states, based on the express language in section one. Frankfurter was willing to overturn a state law or action under the due process clause, but only if the state's action invaded liberty or property rights without any plausible justification.

Justice Black expressed two main ideas during his long tenure on the Court. First, the Bill of Rights should be enforced against the states to the full extent that it is enforced against the federal government. Second, absent the presence in a case of a relevant provision in the Bill, the due process clause should not be used to second-guess the policy judgments of the states. Black was convinced that the people's liberty and property rights would be fully secure so long as the Bill of Rights were interpreted as a set of "absolutes" to restrain the actions of the legislative and executive branches of government. Aside from this Bill of Rights issue, Black, like Frankfurter, deferred to the decisions of the states' elected representatives. The second Justice Harlan agreed with Frankfurter that none of the Bill of Rights provisions, as such, should be incorporated into the Fourteenth Amendment and applied to the states. But unlike both Frankfurter and Black, he was willing to rely on the due process clause, which "stands on its own bottom," as he put it, to overrule substantive state policy decisions that violate basic values "implicit in the concept of ordered liberty," *Palko.*[40]

Justice Black was the only member of the Supreme Court who ever explored in any detail the history of the Fourteenth Amendment's adoption to determine if the Congress which enacted it in 1866 intended the Bill of Rights to be applied to the states. He concluded that the framers and supporters of the amendment did so intend, based primarily on a couple of statements made by Representative John Bingham of Ohio, who wrote the key provisions in sections one and five of the Fourteenth Amendment, and the speech of Senator Jacob Howard of Michigan, given in his presentation of the amendment for passage in the Senate. Black also quoted remarks of a few other congressmen as they discussed the amendment and the contemporaneous Civil Rights Act of 1866, and he cited the 1908 book of Horace Flack, who concluded that Congress enacted the Fourteenth Amendment for three reasons: to define citizenship, to give the Civil Rights Act constitutional validity, and to extend the Bill of Rights to the states.[41]

Based upon the original meaning of the Fourteenth Amendment, as covered in chapter 4, Justices Frankfurter, Black, and the second Justice Harlan were all partially correct in the opinions they expressed about the relationship between the Bill of Rights and the Fourteenth Amendment. Harlan was correct to say that the due process clause protects people's life, liberty, and property rights, that it is not confined to procedures or to applications of the Bill of Rights. Black was correct when he said John Bingham and Jacob Howard expected the Fourteenth Amendment to embrace the extension of Bill of Rights safeguards to the states. The Court's applications were consistent with the spirit of the amendment. And Frankfurter was correct to say that the express language of section one does not apply the Bill of Rights to the states. What these justices failed to appreciate, and to elucidate in their opinions, was that section five of the Fourteenth Amendment enables Congress to pass legislation to extend some or all of the Bill's guarantees to the states as ancillary protections for life, liberty, and property.

NOTES

1. *Walker*, 92 U.S. 90; *Hurtado*, 110 U.S. 516; *Presser*, 116 U.S. 252; *Spies v. Illinois*, 123 U.S. 131; *In re Kemmler*, 136 U.S. 436; *McElvaine*, 142 U.S. 55; *O'Neil*, 144 U.S. 323; *Brown*, 175 U.S. 172; *Maxwell*, 176 U.S. 581; *West*, 194 U.S. 258; *Twining*, 211 U.S. 78; and *Prudential Ins. Co.*, 259 U.S. 530.

2. *Slaughterhouse Cases*, 83 U.S. 16; *Hurtado*, 110 U.S. 516.

3. *O'Neil*, 144 U.S. 323, 326–27, 332 (Court opinion), 337–40, 360–61, 363 (Justice Field dissenting opinion), and 370 (Justice Harlan dissenting opinion).

4. *Maxwell,* 176 U.S. 581–82, 584–90, 593, 595, 601, 603, 605 (Court opinion), 606, 608, and 613–17 (Justice Harlan dissenting opinion).

5. *Twining*, 211 U.S. 78–79, 90–102, 106–13 (Court opinion), 117, 120–23, and 126 (Justice Harlan dissenting opinion).

6. *Prudential Ins. Co*., 259 U.S. 530, 543.

7. *Gitlow*, 268 U.S. 652–55, 664–69 (Court opinion), and 672–73 (Justice Holmes dissenting opinion).

8. *Near*, 283 U.S. 697, 701–7, and 711–13.

9. *Hamilton*, 293 U.S. 245–46, 262 (Court opinion), and 265–66 (Justice Cardozo concurring opinion).

10. *Grosjean*, 297 U.S. 233–34; *DeJonge*, 299 U.S. 353, 357–66; and *Herndon*, 301 U.S. 242, 244, and 259–63.

11. *Murdock*, 319, U.S. 105, 115.

12. See State Laws Held Unconstitutional, https://lawjustia.com; Ordinances Held Unconstitutional, https://lawjustia.com.

13. *Thornhill,* 310 U.S. 88; *Taylor*, 311 U.S. 583; and *Va. Bd. of Pharmacy*, 425 U.S. 748.

14. *R.A.V. v. City of St. Paul*, 505 U.S. 377; *Brown*, 564 U.S. 786; and *Packingham*, 137 S.Ct. 1730.

15. *Jamison*, 318 U.S. 413; *Saia*, 334 U.S. 558; *Schwartz*, 423 U.S. 1041; and *Spence*, 418 U.S. 405.

16. *Powell*, 287 U.S. 45–46, 49–51, 57–58, 65–69, and 71.

17. *Palko*, 302 U.S. 319–20, 322–29.

18. *Betts*, 316 U.S. 455–56, 461–465, and 472.

19. *Adamson*, 332 U.S. 46–53 (Court opinion), 59–66 (Justice Frankfurter concurring opinion), 68–69, 71–75, 80–83, 90 (Justice Black dissenting opinion), and 123–24 (Justice Murphy dissenting opinion).

20. *In re Oliver*, 333 U.S. 257–59, 267–73.

21. *Wolf*, 338 U.S. 25, 27 29, 33 (Court opinion), 39 40 (Justice Black concurring opinion), and 41 (Justice Murphy, joined by Justice Rutledge, dissenting opinion).

22. *Mapp*, 367 U.S. 643, 645–51, 655, 659 (Court opinion), and 679–80 (Justice Harlan dissenting opinion).

23. *Gideon*, 372 U.S. 335–44; *Escobedo*, 378 U.S. 478–79, 483, 487, and 490–91.

24. *Malloy*, 378 U.S. 1, 11; *Griffin*, 380 U.S. 609–13.

25. *Miranda*, 384 U.S. 436, 440–42, 444–45, 455, 458, 464–71, 478–79 (Court opinion); 499, 503 (Justice Clark dissenting opinion); 504–5, 510–12, 514–16, 524

(Justice Harlan dissenting opinion, joined by Justices Stewart and White); 526, 531, 535–37, and 539–44 (Justice White dissenting opinion, joined by Justices Harlan and Stewart). Compare these dissents in *Miranda* with the dissents in *Escobedo*, 378 U.S. 493–99.

26. *Robinson,* 370 U.S. 660, 662, 666–67.

27. *Pointer*, 380 U.S. 400–1, 403–6, and 408.

28. Ibid. 408–9 (Justice Harlan concurring), 409–10 (Justice Stewart concurring).

29. *Washington,* 388 U.S. 14–19, 23.

30. *Klopfer*, 388 U.S. 213–14, 216, and 218–23.

31. *Duncan*, 391 U.S. 145–49, 160–62.

32. Ibid., 391 U.S. 171–75, 179–80, 183–89, and 192–93 (Justice Harlan dissenting opinion, joined by Justice Stewart).

33. Ibid., 391 U.S. 162–71 (Justice Black concurring opinion, joined by Justice Douglas).

34. *Benton*, 395 U.S. 784–87, 793–95, and 797–98.

35. *McDonald*, 561 U.S. 742.

36. *Timbs,* 586 U.S. ___.

37. *Engblom,* 724 F.2d 28.

38. www.nolo.com/legal encyclopedia/why prosecutors choose grand juries instead of preliminary hearings.

39. www.constitutioncenter.org/interpretation:amendment vii.

40. See, e.g., the exchanges concerning the incorporation of the Bill of Rights between Frankfurter and Black in *Adamson v. California*, 332 U.S. 46 (1947), and between Black and the second Harlan in *Duncan v. Louisiana*, 391 U.S. 145 (1968). Frankfurter's deference to the states is reflected in his Court opinion in *Wolf v. Colorado*, 338 U.S. 25 (1949), and in his general unwillingness to apply Bill of Rights restraints to the states. Black's disparagement of the Court's "natural law-due process" Lochner-era decision-making process can be seen in his opinion for the Court in *Ferguson v. Skrupa*, 372 U.S. 726 (1963), and two years later in his dissenting opinion in *Griswold v. Connecticut*, 381 U.S. 479, 507–8, and 511–22. The second Harlan's stance on the Bill of Rights is further reflected in his concurring opinion in *Pointer v. Texas*, 380 U.S. 400, 408–9, and his willingness to second-guess the states' substantive policy judgments under the due process clause is evident in his dissenting opinion in *Poe v. Ullman*, 367 U.S. 497, 522–23, and 539–44 (1961), and in his concurring opinion in *Griswold v. Connecticut*, 381 U.S. 479, 499–501 (1965). The philosophies and work product of Justices Frankfurter, Black, and the second Harlan are reflected in greater detail in textbooks such as Jonathan D. Varat and Vikram D. Amar, *Constitutional Law: Cases and Materials* (St. Paul, MN: Foundation Press, 15th ed., 2017).

41. Black's history in his Appendix to the *Adamson* case extracts most of the relevant quotations concerning the Bill of Rights from the lead participants in the enactment of the Fourteenth Amendment. In fact, the Reconstruction Congress responsible for this amendment said little about the Bill and a lot about the Constitution as it should be understood, reformed and enforced to protect all of the people in all of the states in their rights to life, liberty, and property. That original-meaning history was explored in chapter 4.

Chapter 8

The Court's Enforcement of the Bill of Rights Against Congress

From the founding through the nineteenth century the Supreme Court applied provisions in the Bill of Rights to overrule a law of Congress only six times worthy of notice: the *Dred Scott* decision, already discussed; an 1870 opinion that was overturned by the Court itself the next year; an odd 1886 civil forfeiture case based on the "spirit" of the Fourth and Fifth Amendments rather than on what the amendments actually say; an 1893 just compensation clause ruling in favor of a corporation seeking to be paid not only the fair market value of its property but also for the anticipated loss of future profits; an 1896 decision enforcing the fair trial requirements of the Fifth and Sixth Amendments on behalf of Chinese aliens being held for deportation; and an 1899 case, holding that a prior conviction of three principals for theft of government property could not be conclusive evidence that the property was in fact stolen because such a rule of evidence would deny to the accused receiver of stolen property, at a later trial, his Sixth Amendment right to confront the witnesses against him (the three principals). This averages out to about one overturn every eighteen years, and only the Chinese alien case (1896) was a clearly good decision.[1]

The paucity of cases overruling Congress under the Bill of Rights continued in the twentieth century until the 1960s, consisting of the following: two isolated and odd cases, *Rasmussen v. United States* (1905) (Congress cannot authorize six-member juries to try misdemeanor cases in the Alaska territory even though the Sixth Amendment jury trial guarantee does not mention how many jurors are required), and *Lynch v. United States* (1934) (Congress' decision not to renew term life insurance contracts issued during World War I takes private property for public use without just compensation even though all of the existing insurance contracts would be honored); five Fifth Amendment due process cases, *Adair v. United States* (1908) (businesses can refuse to employ persons who belong to a labor union), *United States v. Cohen*

Grocery Co. (1921) (law penalizing companies that charge "unfair or unreasonable" prices for "necessaries" is void for vagueness), *Adkins v. Children's Hospital* (1923) (minimum wage law for women and children violates due process); *Tot v. United States* (1943) (statute cannot establish a rebuttable presumption that a person who illegally possesses a firearm acquired it in interstate commerce), and *Bolling v. Sharpe* (1954) (the due process clause should be interpreted to include an equal protection component); and three military cases, *Toth v. Quarles* (1955) (discharged serviceman cannot be tried by court-martial in South Korea for a murder he allegedly committed there while on active duty), *Reid v. Covert* (1957) (overturns the court-martial convictions of two women for the murder of their husbands who were on active duty in the military overseas at the time of their deaths), and *Trop v. Dulles* (1958) (loss of citizenship for one's military desertion in wartime is a cruel and unusual punishment in violation of the Eighth Amendment).[2] This averages out to about one overturn every six years. Moreover, canvassing all the cases from the founding of the republic until the 1960s, the Court's overturns of Congress based upon the Bill of Rights produced only one clearly good policy result with broad application, the due process incorporation of equal protection in *Bolling v. Sharpe* (1954).

Since the 1960s the Court has assumed a more active role in federal Bill of Rights cases, especially under the First Amendment free speech clause and the Fifth Amendment. While a few of these judicial vetoes of federal statutes can be defended as good results, most of the decisions were issued in cases where reasonable people could disagree on the merits of the policy choice made, or the decisions could be characterized as bad interpretations of the Constitution. The fact that the opinions were often by five-to-four or six-to-three votes demonstrates that close calls were being made. In these cases, the Court should have deferred to the policy judgments of Congress and enforced the statute.[3]

THE FIRST AMENDMENT

The only case under the First Amendment religion clauses that overturned a law of Congress, and this merely a small detail of the law, was decided in 1971, in *Tilton v. Richardson*. The Higher Education Facilities Act of 1965 made available federal construction grants for college and university buildings and facilities to be used exclusively for secular educational purposes. The statute excluded from support any building or facility "used . . . for sectarian instruction or as a place for religious worship." The United States retained a twenty-year interest in any building or facility constructed with funds under the act, and if during that time the recipient violated the statutory condition, the government could recover the money. Four church-related colleges and universities in Connecticut received grants under the program, and a taxpayer group sued on the theory that sectarian institutions should not be given public funds under any circumstances. The Court held that the law was constitutional except for the twenty-year limit on the government's ability to recover monies if a building or facility was used for a sectarian purpose. For the statute to avoid being an establishment of religion, the ban on the religious use of a building or facility constructed with grant money must be permanent.[4]

The First Amendment free speech reversals did not begin until 1965, about 175 years after the Bill of Rights was adopted. Then the overturns rapidly proliferated. In my opinion, three decisions were good results: *Lamont v. Postmaster General* (1965), holding that the Postmaster General could not screen the mails for communist propaganda sent from foreign countries; *Schacht v. United States* (1970), holding that permission for a nonmilitary person to wear a military uniform in a theatrical production could not be limited to portrayals that do not tend to discredit the armed forces; and *Legal Services Corporation v. Velazquez* (2001), holding that legal service providers who represent indigent clients and are recipients of government funding cannot, as a condition of accepting the funds, be banned from challenging or seeking a change in a welfare law.[5] These three cases were narrow in scope with no bad side effects for community values or the public good.

Most of the free speech cases fall into one of several categories, which will be discussed in turn: content regulation; obscenity and child pornography; time, place, and manner regulation; commercial speech; and campaign finance. The Court generally established these categories in state cases and then later applied them to Congress. The three outcomes that I have characterized as good ones, *Lamont*, *Schacht*, and *Legal Services Corp.*, were content regulation cases. The other decisions in this category were *Regan v. Time, Inc.* (1994), *United States v. Stevens* (2010), *United States v. Alvarez* (2012), and *Matal v. Tam* (2017). The law in *Time, Inc.* restricted the use of photographic reproductions of US currency to combat the crime of counterfeiting. Sensitive to freedom of expression concerns, Congress exempted from the ban the printing or publication of illustrations for "numismatic, educational, historical, or newsworthy purposes" so long as the illustration was done in black and white, and the plates were destroyed after their final authorized use. The Court held that the statute's purpose requirement was unconstitutional because it discriminated based on content. *United States v. Stevens* struck down a law that made it a crime to knowingly create, possess, or sell a depiction of animal cruelty if done for commercial gain. Animal cruelty was defined as an act in which a "living animal is intentionally maimed, mutilated, tortured, wounded, or killed." In striking down the law, Chief Justice John Roberts for the Supreme Court said that laws which regulate expression based on content are "presumptively invalid," with a few exceptions such as obscenity, defamation, fraud, incitement, and speech integral to criminal conduct. Roberts was unwilling to add animal cruelty to the list. *United States v. Alvarez* concluded that the 2005 Stolen Valor Act, making it a crime for one to falsely claim receipt of military decorations or medals, unconstitutionally abridges free speech. Content-based restrictions are presumptively invalid, and this includes lies where no economic harm was caused to anyone. *Matal v. Tam* struck down the Lanham Act's prohibition on the federal registration of trademarks that "disparage . . . or bring into contempt or disrepute" any persons. Tam's Asian rock band applied to register the name of their band, "The Slants," in their attempt to drain the term of its force as a derogatory name for Asians. The Patent and Trademark Office denied the trademark application under the act's disparagement clause, and upon Tam's appeal the Supreme Court held that the clause constitutes viewpoint discrimination banned by the First Amendment. Speech that demeans people based on race, ethnicity, gender, religion, age, disability or other similar ground is "hateful," said the Court, but the boast of our free speech jurisprudence is that we protect the freedom to express "the thought that we hate," quoting from a Justice Oliver Wendell Holmes dissent in a 1929 state case.[6]

Obscenity and child pornography are "expressive activities" that the Court has said are not protected by the First Amendment. The difficulties have been to manage the process of determining which material is obscene, and how to shield children from pornography without unduly infringing on the rights of adults. For example, a federal law allowed the Postmaster General to deny the use of the mails to commercial distributors of obscene literature whenever a judicial officer held a hearing and determined that the material was obscene. The Postmaster General could detain the distributor's mail pending the outcome of the hearing if he got a temporary restraining order from the district court in the distributor's district, based upon a showing of probable cause to believe the material was obscene. The Supreme Court in *Blount v. Rizzi* (1971) held that the program was fatally flawed because it did not require the Postmaster General to obtain a prompt and final judicial determination of the obscenity of the material before denying a distributor the use of the mails.[7]

Denver Area Educational Telecommunications Consortium, Inc. v. FCC (1996) struck down sections 10(b) and (c) of the 1992 Cable Television Consumer Protection and Competition Act, which sought to protect minors from broadcasts of "patently offensive" sex-related material on cable television. Section 10(b) required cable operators to segregate such programming, to place it on a single channel, and to block the channel from viewer access unless the viewer requested access in advance and in writing. Section 10(c) permitted cable system operators to prohibit the broadcasting of programming that the operator "reasonably believes describes or depicts sexual or excretory activities or organs in a patently offensive manner." The Supreme Court agreed with the government that the protection of children from patently offensive sex-related programming is a "compelling interest," but it concluded that section 10(b)'s "segregate and block" requirement was not "narrowly tailored" enough to meet its legitimate objective. Section 10(c)'s permission for cable operators to prevent certain sex-related transmissions also violated the First Amendment because such a "veto" was more likely to erroneously exclude borderline programs that should be broadcast than it was to protect children.[8]

Reno v. American Civil Liberties Union (1997) overturned two provisions of the Communications Decency Act of 1996 that sought to protect minors from harmful material on the Internet. Section 223(a) banned the "knowing" transmission of "obscene or indecent" messages to any recipient under eighteen years of age, and section 223(d) banned the "knowing" sending or displaying any message that "depicts or describes, in terms patently offensive as measured by contemporary community standards, sexual or excretory activities or organs." Despite the law's affirmative defenses for those who take "good faith, . . . effective . . . actions" to restrict minors' access to banned communications and those who restrict access by requiring certain designated forms of age proof, such as a credit card or adult ID, the Court held that the act's "indecent transmission" and "patently offensive display" provisions abridged free speech. The government had a legitimate interest in protecting children from harmful materials, but it did not demonstrate that less restrictive alternatives were unavailable to achieve this purpose.[9]

Section 505 of the Telecommunications Act of 1996 required cable television operators of channels "primarily dedicated to sexually-oriented programming" to limit their transmission to hours when children are unlikely to be viewing, set by administrative regulation as the time between 10 p.m. and 6 a.m. The Court in *United States v. Playboy Entertainment Group, Inc.* (2000) concluded that the government had failed to prove section 505 is the least restrictive means for addressing the problem, the viewing of sexually oriented programs by children. The Child Pornography Prevention Act of 1996 expanded the federal prohibition on child pornography to include not only pornographic images made using actual children, but also images, sometimes called "virtual child pornography," that appeared to depict minors but were produced by means other than using real children, such as using youthful-looking adults or computer-imaging technology. *Ashcroft v. Free Speech Coalition* (2002) held that the law's extension to virtual child pornography was overly broad and hence unconstitutional.[10]

The Supreme Court developed a test for time, place, and manner regulations, mostly in state and local law cases. The regulation must be content or viewpoint-neutral, narrowly drawn to promote a significant interest, and it must leave open alternative channels of communication. In three of the cases below, in my opinion, the federal laws could have been upheld as legitimate "place" regulations, and in the fourth one, the flag-burning case, the law could have been upheld as a legitimate "manner" regulation.

The first place-law banned, on the U.S. Capitol grounds surrounding Congress, any parade or assemblage or the display of any flag, banner or device designed to bring into public notice a party, organization, or movement without the prior permission of the President of the Senate or the Speaker of the House, or in their absence the Capitol Police Board. The second place-law banned, in the Supreme Court building or on its grounds, the display of any flag, banner or device designed to bring into public notice a party, organization, or movement. The third place-law made it unlawful, within five hundred feet of a foreign embassy in the District of Columbia, to display a sign that tends to bring the embassy's foreign government into public odium or disrepute (the display clause), or to congregate and refuse a police order to disperse (congregation clause). The decisions to overturn came in *Chief of Capitol Police v. Jeannette Rankin Brigade* (1972), *United States v. Grace* (1983), and *Boos v. Barry* (1988). The laws regulated small public spaces in and around particular buildings, were largely viewpoint-neutral, and left unlimited possibilities for public speech and assemblages elsewhere in the vicinity. The embassies case did implicate criticisms of a foreign government, and so was not viewpoint-neutral. But the government's interest in preserving the safety and dignity of foreign embassies under international law would seem to be sufficiently important to justify the narrowly drawn prohibition of protests within five hundred feet of an embassy building.[11]

After the Supreme Court in *Texas v. Johnson* (1989) held that a Texas statute, which made it a crime to desecrate the American flag in a way that the actor knew would offend onlookers, was unconstitutional as applied to an individual who had burned a flag during a political protest, Congress responded by passing the Flag Protection Act of 1989. The act punished anyone who "knowingly mutilates, defames, physically defiles, burns . . . or tramples upon" an American flag, except conduct related to the disposal of a worn or soiled flag. The Court in *United States v. Eichman* (1990) held that a prosecution for burning the flag was inconsistent with the First Amendment. The flag burning was "expressive conduct." While the federal law contained no content-based limitation, it was clear that the government's interest in protecting the flag against harm, as a symbol of the nation and certain national ideals, is related to the suppression of free expression. In dissent Justice John Paul Stevens, joined by three other justices, would have upheld the law because "certain methods of expression may be prohibited if (a) the prohibition is supported by a legitimate societal interest that is unrelated to suppression of the ideas the speaker desires to express; (b) the prohibition does not entail any interference with the speaker's freedom to express those ideas by other means; and (c) the interest in allowing the speaker complete freedom of choice among alternative methods of expression is less important than the societal interest supporting the prohibition." In the case of flag-burning, concluded Stevens, it is possible for people to have different opinions about whether the interest in allowing the speaker to choose his method of expression outweighs the societal interest in preserving the symbolic value of the flag.[12]

The Supreme Court has adopted a four-part test to determine whether a government regulation of commercial speech will survive the Court's scrutiny. Assuming the speech concerns a lawful activity and is not misleading, the regulation is permissible only if it directly addresses a substantial government interest, and is narrowly drawn to serve that interest. *Bolger v. Youngs Drug Products Corp.* (1983) struck down an ancient federal law that prohibited the mailing of unsolicited advertisements for contraceptives. The government's asserted interests in shielding households from materials they are likely to find offensive and aiding parents' efforts to control how their children learn about birth control were insufficient to overcome the individual and societal interests in the free flow of lawful and truthful commercial information. *Rubin v. Coors Brewing Co.* (1995) overturned a law that prohibited beer labels from displaying alcohol content, Congress' attempt to curb "strength wars" in beer advertising. In *Greater New Orleans Broadcasting Assoc., Inc. v. United States* (1999) the Court held that Congress and the FCC could not prohibit radio and television broadcasters from carrying advertising about privately operated casino gambling in states where the activity is legal. Although the government's interest in reducing the social costs associated with casino and other forms of gambling is "substantial," that interest is diminished by the law's exemptions for advertising about state-run, Indian tribe, and occasional nonprofit casinos.[13]

United States v. United Foods, Inc. (2001) struck down an assessment on the handlers of mushrooms where the proceeds were used to fund advertisements promoting mushroom sales. United Fruit successfully argued that it should not have to pay a subsidy for speech to which it objected (its preferred message was that its products, including mushrooms, are superior to others being offered in the marketplace). Just as the First Amendment prevents government from prohibiting speech, said the Court, it may prevent the government from compelling individuals to express certain views. The dissent pointed out that the assessment should properly be viewed as part of a program of economic regulation, and the advertisements as government speech.[14]

Drug compounding is a process by which a pharmacist or doctor combines, mixes, or alters ingredients to create a medication tailored to an individual patient's needs. The Food and Drug Modernization Act of 1997 exempted "compounded drugs" from standard FDA drug approval requirements so long as the producers abided by several restrictions, including that they refrain from advertising or promoting their compounded drugs. *Thompson v. Western States Medical Center* (2002) held that despite the government's three admittedly "substantial" interests in restricting commercial speech here—preserving the effectiveness and integrity of the law's new drug approval process and the protection of the public health it provides; preserving the availability of compounded drugs for patients who cannot use commercially available products approved by the FDA; and achieving the proper balance between these two competing interests—the law could not be upheld because the government failed to demonstrate that the restrictions are "not more extensive than is necessary to serve [those] interests."[15]

The first Supreme Court reversal of a campaign finance law on First Amendment grounds came in the landmark case of *Buckley v. Valeo* (1976), which equated spending money with "speech" in the sense that effective political communication in our mass society requires expenditures of money. *Buckley* set the framework for the debates among the justices in all subsequent Court decisions on the topic. While Justices Byron White and John Paul Stevens agreed that spending money is a necessary component of public speech in political campaigns, they have been willing to uphold the campaign finance laws of Congress as being reasonable regulations to serve important government interests. At the other end of the opinion spectrum, Justices Clarence Thomas and Antonin Scalia adopted the position that because political speech is a core First Amendment value, any attempt by Congress to limit the amount of money that can be infused into the political system is an unconstitutional abridgement of the freedom of speech.

Among other things, the Federal Election Campaign Act of 1971 limited the amount of permissible individual and group contributions to candidates for federal elective office, and the amount of individual and group expenditures on behalf of or by such candidates. *Buckley* upheld the caps on contributions because they served the basic government interest in safeguarding the integrity of the electoral process without impinging on the rights of persons and groups to engage in political debate. By contrast, it invalidated the expenditure caps because they did limit speech and were not necessary to avoid the real or apparent corrupting influence of money in politics.[16]

The Presidential Election Campaign Fund Act offered the presidential candidates of major political parties the option of receiving public funds for their general election campaign. If a candidate opted for public financing, the law made it a crime for an independent political action committee (PAC) to expend more than $1,000 to further that candidate's election. *FEC v. National Conservative Political Action Committee* (1985) struck down the spending cap because it limited the rights of free speech and association without any indication that such expenditures tend to corrupt or give the appearance of corruption. *FEC v. Massachusetts Citizens for Life* (1986) struck down a law that required corporations to make their political expenditures not from their own treasury funds, but rather from voluntary contributions by donors made to a separate PAC established by the corporation. *Colorado Republican Federal Campaign Committee v. FEC* (1996) struck down dollar limits the law imposed on political party expenditures in connection with the general election campaign of a congressional candidate. *McConnell v. FEC* (2003) invalidated a requirement that political parties must choose between independent and coordinated expenditures after nominating a candidate, and a ban on individuals aged seventeen or younger from making contributions to candidates or parties. Parties should be free to make unencumbered independent or coordinated expenditures during a campaign, said the Court, and there was "slim evidence" that the age prohibition was needed to prevent parents from using their children as conduits to circumvent the contribution limits. *FEC v. Wisconsin Right to Life, Inc.* (2007) crafted a major exception to the federal statutory limitations on broadcast ads by corporations and unions in periods close to primary and general elections by holding that a court should find an ad is the functional equivalent of express advocacy, and is hence banned, only if it is susceptible of no reasonable interpretation other than as an appeal to vote for or against a specific candidate. *Davis v. FEC* (2008) struck down the millionaire's amendment to the campaign finance reform law which provided that if a candidate spends more than $350,000 of his own money in seeking election to the House of Representatives, then the candidate's opponent is allowed to receive contributions beyond the normal federal law limits for House races. Intended to show that seats in Congress are not for sale to wealthy bidders, the law in effect diminished the effectiveness of the wealthy candidate's own speech, said the Court. *Citizens United v. FEC* (2010) struck down the prohibition on corporations and unions using their general treasury funds to make unlimited independent political contributions to candidates and causes. *McCutcheon v. FEC* (2014) ruled that Congress could not limit the aggregate amount of money which wealthy individuals can contribute in political campaigns.[17]

A few free speech overrides do not fit within the general categories discussed so far. The Public Broadcasting Act of 1967 established the corporation for public broadcasting ("CPB"), a nonprofit corporation, to distribute federal funds to noncommercial television and radio stations in support of educational programming. The law forbade any such station that received a grant from the CPB to "engage in editorializing." The Court in *FCC v. League of Women Voters of California* (1984) held that the ban on editorializing violates the First Amendment, rejecting the government's arguments that the ban was necessary, first, to protect stations from being coerced, as a result of federal financing, into becoming vehicles for government propagandizing or the objects of government influence, and, second, to keep these stations from becoming convenient targets for capture by private interest groups wishing to express their own partisan viewpoints. *United States v. Treasury Employees* (1996) struck down the Ethics in Government Act's ban on members of Congress and other federal government employees accepting an honorarium for making an appearance or speech or writing an article, as applied to executive branch employees below grade GS-16, because the prohibition was broader than it needed to be in order to address the government's legitimate concern that federal officials not misuse or appear to misuse their power by accepting money for their unofficial writing and speaking activities.[18]

Federal law prohibits the interception of wire, electronic, or oral communications, and the subsequent willful disclosure of their contents. During labor negotiations between a high school teachers' union and the local school board, an unidentified person intercepted and recorded a cell phone conversation between the chief union negotiator and the union president. After the parties agreed to a contract favorable to the teachers, a radio commentator played a tape of the recorded conversation on his public affairs talk show. Union officials sued for damages under the wiretapping law, alleging that their conversations had been illegally intercepted by an unknown person, that a local organization opposed to the union's demands obtained the tape and disclosed it to media representatives, and that these representatives repeatedly publicized the conversation even though they knew or had reason to know that it had been illegally intercepted. *Bartnicki v. Vopper* (2001) protected the disclosures under the First Amendment because "privacy concerns give way when balanced against the interest in publishing matters of public importance."[19]

A federal statute offering money to nongovernmental organizations engaged in the global fight against HIV/AIDS, tuberculosis, and malaria stipulated that the funds could be provided only to entities which have a policy against prostitution and sex trafficking. In *Agency for International Development v. Alliance for Open Society International, Inc.* (2013), the Alliance sued in order to become eligible to receive funds without having to compromise its position of neutrality on prostitution. The Court held that the statute's policy requirement must be stricken as a violation of the free speech principle which "prohibits the government from telling people what they must say." In his dissent Justice Scalia said the policy requirement was nothing more than a means of selecting suitable agents to implement the government's chosen strategy to eradicate HIV/AIDS. The First Amendment does not mandate a viewpoint-neutral government; it can choose among rival ideas and adopt some as its own.[20]

THE SECOND THROUGH THE FIFTH AMENDMENTS

In a five-to-four decision for the Supreme Court in *District of Columbia v. Heller* (2008), Justice Scalia held that the District of Columbia's law which prohibited the possession of handguns and required residents to keep their lawfully owned firearms "unloaded and disassembled or bound by a trigger lock or similar device," violated the Second Amendment right of individuals to keep and bear arms. Justices Stevens and Stephen Breyer wrote dissenting opinions, joined by each other and Justices David Souter and Ruth Bader Ginsburg. Stevens relied on the legislative history of the Second Amendment's adoption to show that the purpose of the amendment was to protect the people's right to keep and bear arms in the context of state militias, and did not address any nonmilitary-related right of individuals to own and use guns. Said Stevens:

> Guns are used to hunt, for self-defense, to commit crimes, for sporting activities, and to perform military duties. The Second Amendment plainly does not protect the right to use a gun to rob a bank; it is equally clear that it does encompass the right to use weapons for certain military purposes. Whether it also protects the right to possess and use guns for nonmilitary purposes like hunting and personal self-defense is the question presented by this case. The text of the Amendment, its history, and our decision in *United States v. Miller*, 307 U.S. 174 (1939) provide a clear answer to that question. The Second Amendment was adopted to protect the right of the people of each of the several States to maintain a well-regulated militia. . . . Neither the text of the Amendment nor the arguments advanced by its proponents evidenced the slightest interest in limiting any legislature's authority to regulate private civilian uses of firearms.

Justice Breyer agreed with Stevens's original meaning analysis and listed four propositions to which he believed the entire Court subscribed: The amendment protects an individual right; it was adopted to ensure the continuation and render possible the effectiveness of militia forces, citing *United States v. Miller*; it must be interpreted and applied with that goal in mind, *Miller*; and the right protected by the amendment is subject to government regulation. Breyer proposed an interest-balancing inquiry for gun-control regulation, with the Court "deferring to the legislature's empirical expertise and greater institutional fact-finding capacity." He could understand how "reasonable individuals can disagree about the merits of strict gun control as a crime-control measure" in an urban environment, but he could not understand how one can "take from the elected branches of government the right to decide whether to insist upon a handgun-free urban populace in a city now facing a serious crime problem."[21]

The Third Amendment mandate that no soldiers in peacetime be quartered in any home without the owner's consent has never been the subject of an act of Congress or a Supreme Court opinion. The homeowner's right is so specific that Congress has passed no law that remotely implicates it or that a court under a broad interpretation of the language might consider to be forbidden. This specificity is absent from many of the other Bill of Rights amendments, which has occasioned opportunities for the courts to second-guess the laws of Congress.

The Supreme Court has overturned two laws of Congress under the Fourth Amendment. The first override came in *Marshall v. Barlow, Inc.* (1978), which held that because the Occupational Safety and Health Act of 1970 (OSHA) authorized agents of the Labor Department to search work areas of covered employment facilities for safety hazards and violations of OSHA regulations without first obtaining a warrant, the law violated the Fourth Amendment. To the department's argument that warrantless searches were essential to the proper enforcement of OSHA because they allow inspections without prior notice and preserve the advantage of surprise, the Court said that warrants could be issued ex parte and executed without delay and prior notice, thereby preserving the element of surprise. The department need not show probable cause, but only that a specific business has been chosen for an OSHA search on the basis of a general administration plan.

Justice Stevens (joined by Justices William Rehnquist and Harry Blackmun) dissented from both elements of the Court's holding, based upon a literal reading of the Fourth Amendment's language. The amendment contains two separate clauses, each prohibiting a category of governmental conduct. The first clause states that the right to be free from unreasonable searches "shall not be violated," and the second one prohibits the issuance of warrants except "upon probable cause." The question in the case was whether the warrantless searches authorized by the statute were "unreasonable" within the meaning of the first clause. Stevens thought that such routine OSHA inspections were reasonable and hence constitutional. If the inspections had to comply with the warrant clause, on the other hand, they would have to be found unconstitutional because they would not be based on probable cause findings. The Court had unnecessarily weakened the warrants clause in order to preserve the viability of a federal regulatory inspection program that instead should have been enforced under a correct application of the reasonableness clause in the Fourth Amendment.[22]

Every time a person makes or receives a call on his cell phone, a time-stamped record of the cell phone's location is generated and kept in a data bank by a wireless service provider for its own business purposes. A robbery suspect confessed to the FBI that he and fifteen named accomplices had participated in armed robberies at nine different stores in Michigan and Ohio during the previous four months. The Stored Telecommunications Act permitted the government to search telecommunications records when it offers "specific . . . facts showing that there are reasonable grounds to believe" the records "are relevant and material to an ongoing criminal investigation." Acting under this law, prosecutors obtained court orders to search the time-recorded cell phone location records of Timothy Carpenter and several others among the named suspects for the prior four months. During the trial, seven of Carpenter's confederates claimed that he was the leader of the operation, and an FBI agent testified that Carpenter's phone records placed him near four of the charged robberies. Following his conviction, Carpenter appealed on the basis that the government had obtained his cell phone location records without a search warrant based on probable cause. In *Carpenter v. United States* (2018), Chief Justice Roberts ruled in a five-to-four decision that the government could not rely on court orders issued under the Stored Telecommunications Act. Warrantless searches are presumptively "unreasonable," and the act's criteria are not a suitable substitute for a showing of probable cause.[23]

Like the First Amendment free speech clause, the Fifth Amendment has generated many overturns of Congress. We will consider the self-incrimination, just compensation, and due process clauses in turn. No person shall be compelled "in any criminal case" to be a witness against himself. Eight times the Court has struck down a federal law based on this self-incrimination clause, and only the most recent decision involved the subject of testimony being compelled from a person in a criminal case. All the other statutes or proceedings involved civil law matters. The first decision, issued in 1886, arose in the context of a civil suit for property forfeiture, and the government was the defendant.[24] The next case, in 1965, invalidated a requirement that members of the Communist Party register with the government. Three companion cases were decided in 1968. One of them struck down requirements that gamblers pay an occupational tax and register with the Internal Revenue Service (IRS), another one held that persons who gamble could not be required to pay an excise tax on their winnings, and the third one held that possessors of certain firearms commonly used in criminal activities could not be required to file registration information with the government. Two cases in 1969 and 1971 applied these precedents to a marijuana tax and gambling taxes, respectively. None of these six decisions from 1965 to 1971 involved a person being compelled to be a witness against himself in a criminal case. The majority opinions speculated that the registrations and tax payments, harmless at the time being provided, posed a potential threat of someone being arrested and prosecuted in a future case, at which time the information could be used against him. The Court refused the government's offers in these cases to impose a use restriction on the information being sought by the government, as a means of preserving the statutes' constitutionality. The use restriction would have prevented any subsequent prosecution based upon any evidence obtained as a result of these registrations or tax payments.[25]

The one decision on the clause which grants a privilege against self-incrimination in criminal cases that involved a criminal case was *Dickerson v. United States* (2000). In 1966 the Court had decided in *Miranda v. Arizona*, a state law case, that certain warnings must be given to a criminal suspect during a custodial police interrogation as a prerequisite for his statement to be admitted as evidence at trial. Two years later, Congress enacted the Omnibus Crime Control and Safe Streets Act, which made the admissibility of a statement made by a suspect while in police custody turn on whether it was given voluntarily, as determined by the trial judge in the totality of the circumstances, including the time elapsing between the arrest and arraignment of the defendant making the confession; whether the defendant knew the nature of the offense with which he was charged or of which he was suspected; whether he was advised or knew that he was not required to make any statement, and that any such statement could be used against him; and whether he was without assistance of counsel when questioned and giving his confession. These factors tracked the *Miranda* warnings but allowed trial courts more discretion to admit confessions into evidence. The petitioner in *Dickerson* (2000), under indictment for bank robbery and related federal crimes, moved to suppress a statement he made to the FBI on the ground that he had not received *Miranda* warnings before being interrogated. The Supreme Court held that since *Miranda* was a "constitutional decision" that governs the admissibility of statements made during custodial interrogation in both state and federal courts, it could not be overruled by an act of Congress. The Court therefore suppressed the alleged bank robber's statement. In his dissenting opinion Justice Scalia (joined by Justice Thomas) said one would search the majority opinion in vain for a statement that what the federal statute allows—use at trial of a voluntary confession—violates the Constitution. This is because such a statement would be "absurd." The statute excludes from trial precisely what the Constitution excludes from trial—compelled confessions.[26]

The first just compensation clause case was *Monongahela Navigation Co. v. United States* (1893), which involved proceedings by the federal government to acquire the company's lock and dam to complete a water transportation project. Congress said that the company's right to collect future tolls did not have to be considered in the calculation of "just compensation," which the government must pay whenever it takes private property for public use. The Court decided that future tolls must be included to satisfy the just compensation requirement. The annual tolls were $2,800 at the time of the suit but were expected to increase significantly with the development of some new coal mines that would send ships through the lock and dam. Even though there were no dissents in the case, reasonable people might believe that paying what the private property was currently worth should be sufficient compensation, without having to factor in plans of other companies to locate along the riverbank and generate additional river traffic in the future.[27]

The three other cases overturning federal laws under the just compensation clause did not in fact involve government takings of private property for public use, the precise and literal subject matter of the clause. *Lynch v. United States* (1934), in its review of yearly renewable term insurance policies issued during World War I, held that the Congress could not cease making available annual renewals of such policies to save money, even though the 1933 law putting the government out of the term life insurance business honored all current contracts and said that it would not affect any judgments in suits then pending. *Hodel v. Irving* (1987) and *Babbitt v. Youpee* (1997) overturned attempts of Congress to prevent the further fractionalization of the ownership of Indian lands by stipulating that any interests amounting to less than 2 percent of the acreage would escheat to the tribe rather than pass to heirs. Indian landowners could always sell or give away any portion of their property while they were alive, no matter how small, but upon their death only interests comprising more than 2 percent of the acreage could be transferred by devise or descent. Reasonable people could believe that Congress had provided sufficient protection for de minimis property interests.[28]

The Supreme Court has relied on the due process clause to review the substance of laws of Congress regulating property or exercises of liberty. Many critics have challenged the Court's "substantive due process" doctrine. John Hart Ely for one has famously said the idea that due "process" encompasses the "substance" of a law—as opposed to merely requiring a fair procedure—is an oxymoron.[29] The legislative history of the due process clause's creation, discussed in chapter 3, belies the notion that the framers and supporters of the clause at the time contemplated that courts would use the clause to second-guess the policy judgments and preferences of the political branches. Any such idea certainly would have generated a lot of discussion at the time, and none surfaced. All available evidence suggests that the concept and purpose of the due process clause was simply a guarantee of appropriate process—for example, notice and a fair opportunity to defend oneself in a hearing or trial—in circumstances where the government for some reason is taking action to deprive a person of his life, liberty, or property.

I will briefly survey the substantive due process overrides of Congress with a view to assess the merits of the Court's policy judgments, without regard to whether they were justified by the language of the Constitution. The infamous *Dred Scott* (1857) decision has already been discussed. In a four-to-three opinion, *Hepburn v. Griswold* (1870) held that Congress could not make paper money legal tender for the payment of all public and private debts, including debts that had been contracted to be repaid in gold or silver prior to the enactment of the law. The majority opined that such a retroactive application of the statute to previously contracted debts violated the "spirit" of the Fifth Amendment, which stipulates that no property shall be taken for public use without just compensation and no person shall be deprived of property without due process of law. The next year, after President Ulysses S. Grant with Senate concurrence appointed two new justices, *Knox v. Lee* (1871) in a five-to-four vote overturned *Hepburn* and upheld the law for the payment of all debts, including previously contracted ones. If Congress cannot make Treasury notes legal tender for the payment of all debts, said the Court, "a power possessed by every independent sovereign other than the United States," the country's business could not be properly conducted. The Fifth Amendment's protection of property refers only to a "direct appropriation, and not to consequential injuries resulting from the exercise of lawful power." A new tariff, an embargo, or a war may bring losses upon individuals, but nobody ever supposed that because of this "a tariff could not be changed, . . . or an embargo be enacted, or a war declared."[30]

The next three cases were economic due process decisions: *Adair v. United States* (1908) struck down a law that forbade carriers engaged in interstate commerce from firing employees for joining a labor union. *United States v. Cohen Grocery Co*. (1921) held that a federal law making it a crime to charge an "unjust or unreasonable rate" for "necessities" must be considered void for vagueness, rejecting the government's argument that it is impossible to fix rules of conduct to cover every fact or circumstance, and that juries could decide what is unreasonable in doubtful cases. *Adkins v. Children's Hospital* (1923) struck down a minimum wage law for women and children which the Congress had enacted for the District of Columbia.[31] The *Adair* and *Adkins* decisions on business and labor relations were criticized at the time by labor leaders and progressives, and in later decades would be generally decried by academic and legal critics, political leaders, and the Supreme Court itself.

Three cases invalidated statutory presumptions in criminal laws: The Firearms Control Act of 1938 made it unlawful for anyone who has committed a crime of violence or is a fugitive from justice to receive a firearm that has been transported in interstate commerce, and presumed that a firearm in the possession of such a person had been so transported, a presumption that *Tot v. United States* (1943) said could not stand. A liquor law made it a crime to own an illegal still, and said that one's presence at the still is sufficient to convict unless he explains his presence to the jury's satisfaction, a presumption that *United States v. Romano* (1965) did not accept. Federal law made it a crime to conceal and transport cocaine known to be illegally imported into the country, and presumed a defendant's possession of the drug is sufficient to convict unless he explains his possession to the satisfaction of the jury. *Turner v. United States* (1970) said Congress could not establish the presumption of illegal importation because a lot of cocaine is produced in the United States. In these cases, the person found in possession of a firearm, an illegal still, or cocaine, could present evidence to a court showing why his behavior was lawful, thereby shifting the burden of proof back to the government. Reasonable people could believe this was sufficient for liberty when balanced against the needs for public health and safety.[32]

Aptheker v. Secretary of State (1964) held that Congress could not ban Communist Party members from obtaining and using a passport, and *United States v. Robel* (1967) struck down a law that prevented registered Communists from working in designated critical defense facilities. Dissenting opinions in the cases thought that the government should be able to protect itself and the general community against international travelers and workers in certain specified defense facilities who belonged to an organization committed to the violent overthrow of the United States. *U.S. Dept, of Agriculture v. Murry* and *U.S. Dept. of Agriculture v. Moreno* (companion 1973 cases) held that the food stamp program could not deny benefits to a household which included a member who has reached his eighteenth birthday and is claimed as a dependent child for federal income tax purposes by a taxpayer who is not a member of an eligible household, or any household consisting of unrelated members, respectively. Congress was attempting to save money by excluding from food stamp benefits "college students" and "children of wealthy parents" in *Murry*, and hippie communes in *Moreno*.[33]

The Supreme Court added an equal protection component to the due process clause in *Bolling v. Sharpe* (1954), a companion case to the famous *Brown v. Board of Education* (1954). *Brown* held that the equal protection clause of the Fourteenth Amendment prohibits the states from maintaining racially segregated public schools. While there is no equal protection clause applicable to the laws of Congress, *Bolling* held that the racial segregation school laws that Congress long ago had enacted in the District of Columbia denied to Black children the due process of law guaranteed by the Fifth Amendment. Chief Justice Earl Warren for a unanimous Court reasoned that the concepts of equal protection and due process, "both stemming from our American ideal of fairness, are not mutually exclusive."[34] While the legal analysis was weak—the idea that due process and equal protection are not mutually exclusive does not explain how, when, or why due process acquired an equal protection component—this rewrite accomplished a good policy result.

Bolling's "due process equality" progeny includes *Richardson v. Davis* (1972) (Social Security Act cannot reduce the benefits coming to illegitimate children upon the death of a parent in order to satisfy the maximum payment due to the surviving spouse and legitimate children), and *Frontiero v. Richardson* (1973) (military statutes cannot assume spouses of male members of the uniformed services are dependents for purposes of obtaining increased quarters allowances and medical and dental benefits, but require the spouses of female members to demonstrate they are in fact dependent for over half of their support).[35] Several more Court cases in the 1970s followed these precedents to invalidate various Social Security benefit provisions as violations of the equal protection component of the Fifth Amendment due process clause on the basis that the laws' gender classifications reflected outdated views about the roles of men and women in modern society.[36] These decisions bringing the laws up to date undoubtedly would have had the majority support of Congress if members had chosen to devote their time and energies to effectuate these specific reforms. The Court, operating with just nine justices and a cohesive liberal majority, could tweak the Social Security and military service benefits statutes to achieve just results in targeted cases more easily and quickly than could the diverse members of Congress, focusing on other legislative priorities

THE SIXTH THROUGH THE TENTH AMENDMENTS

Under the Chinese exclusion acts the government could deport Chinese aliens, both legal and illegal entrants into the country, and prior Supreme Court decisions had upheld these laws. However, when Congress added a provision that allowed such aliens to be imprisoned for up to one year pending their deportation, solely upon the judgment of a judge or commissioner of the United States, *Wong Wing v. United States* (1896) held that while temporary detention was permissible, imprisonment for up to one year could only be imposed in conformity with the fair trial requirements of the Fifth and Sixth Amendments. This was a good though narrow decision, narrow because it did not question the federal government's right under existing laws to deport Chinese aliens at any time for any reason, including those aliens who were legal residents.[37]

Three years later, *Kirby v. United States* (1899) nullified a provision in the federal criminal code relating to persons accused of receiving stolen property of the United States. Under the code, the separate conviction of those charged with the theft could be considered conclusive evidence that the goods were in fact stolen. The Court found that such a rule denied Joe Kirby, an accused receiver of stolen goods, his Sixth Amendment right to be confronted with the witnesses against him at his own trial—in this case the three men who had been convicted of robbery and were serving time in prison for stealing government property, including the goods found in Kirby's possession. Reasonable people could believe that a prior conviction of the three principals was sufficient evidence to establish that the goods had been stolen. The prosecutor still had to prove to the jury's satisfaction that Kirby knew the property he received was stolen, and that he intended to appropriate it for his own benefit. The federal law governing the territory of Alaska provided for six-person jury trials in misdemeanor cases, in recognition of the fact that Alaska was a vast landmass, sparsely populated. *Rasmussen v. United States* (1905) held that this violated the Sixth Amendment right to a jury trial, even though the amendment merely states an accused has the right to a speedy and public trial, by an impartial jury of the district where the crime was committed, and does not say how many jurors are required.[38]

Military trials are subject to a different set of constitutional rules than are civilian trials. The Supreme Court's overturns of Congress in several Uniform Code of Military Justice cases were problematic both as constitutional interpretations and as policy decisions. Congress has the authority under article I of the Constitution to make rules "for the Government and Regulation of the land and naval Forces." Article III, section two says that criminal trials shall be held in the state where the crimes have been committed, "but when not committed within any State, the Trial shall be at such Place or Places as the Congress may by Law have directed." And the Fifth Amendment grand jury requirement does not extend to "cases arising in the land or naval forces, or in the Militia, when in actual service in time of War or public danger."

A majority of the Supreme Court justices in the 1950s and 1960s did not trust the military to do justice as effectively as civilian courts, so they placed several classes of cases and defendants beyond the reach of the Uniform Code. Article 3(a) of the code said that any person charged with having committed, while in military service, a crime punishable by more than five years in prison, and for which he cannot be tried in any court in the United States, may be tried by court-martial even after leaving the service. *Toth v. Quarles* (1955) addressed the case of a man who had served in the U.S. Air Force in Korea and was honorably discharged. Five months later Toth was arrested by the military authorities on a charge of having murdered a Korean national while serving at an air base there. He was taken to Korea to be tried by court-martial. Justice Black for the Supreme Court held that the article I constitutional power of Congress to make rules for the armed forces could not be extended to include persons no longer in the military, rejecting the government's argument that unless the law was sustained, discharged soldiers would escape punishment altogether for crimes they committed while in the service overseas. The dissenting justices in the case complained that the Court's judgment turned loose a man accused of murder, and said they hoped to avoid any further interpretive limitations on the power granted to Congress by the Constitution to make rules for the government and regulation of the armed forces without the jury and venue requirements of the Fifth and Sixth Amendments. "The advantages and disadvantages of indictment, venue and jury trial for the military have been weighed and determined adversely to the Court's conclusion by the Constitution and the Congress."[39]

Article 2(11) of the Uniform Code authorized court-martial trials of "all persons . . . accompanying the armed forces of the United States in foreign countries." Justice Black in his opinion for the Court in *Reid v. Covert* (1957) overturned the court-martial convictions of two women for the murder of their husbands, who were serving in the military overseas at the time of the deaths. Said Black, the constitutional power of Congress to make rules for the military does not extend to civilians, even if they are dependents living with servicemen on an overseas military base. The dissenters said Congress had no feasible alternative to its choice of subjecting civilians associated with the armed forces abroad to the Uniform Code. The establishment of article III federal courts in the sixty-three countries where American forces are stationed would be "manifestly impossible"—the problem of jury selection alone shows this—and the trial of offenders by an article III court in this country would not be a solution either. The "hundreds of petty cases involving black market operations, narcotics, immorality and the like, could hardly be brought here for prosecution even if the Congress and the foreign nation involved authorized such a procedure." The Court has created a problem for which there is no solution.[40]

Four companion cases in 1960 held that a provision of the Uniform Code which authorized the court-martial of "all persons serving with, employed by, or accompanying the armed forces" in foreign countries could not be applied to the following classes of persons for their alleged crimes: A civilian employee of the army could not be tried by court-martial for the capital offense of premeditated murder committed while serving in France, *Grisham v. Hogan*. The dependent wife of a soldier on service in Germany could not be prosecuted for a noncapital offense, *Kinsella v. Singleton*. Nor could civilian employees of the military forces serving overseas in peacetime be tried by court-martial for noncapital crimes, *McElvoy v. Guagliardo* and *Wilson v. Bohlender*. The dissenting justices insisted that these types of cases fell within a reasonable interpretation of the constitutional power of Congress to provide rules and regulations for the armed forces overseas, and posed practical difficulties as well. The final decision in this series of cases, *O'Callahan v. Parker* (1969), ruled that a crime must be "service connected" in order to be subject to court-martial, even though there is no such requirement expressed in the Constitution. This decision was overruled eighteen years later.[41]

In what seems like a good outcome, *United States v. Jackson* (1968) reviewed a 1934 federal kidnapping statute that allowed the death penalty if the jury so recommended, but limited the penalty to a term of years up to life imprisonment for anyone who pleaded guilty or waived a jury trial. Presumably Congress wanted to ensure that a kidnapper could not be sentenced to death without the benefit of a trial and decision by an impartial jury of his peers. But the Supreme Court identified a constitutional infirmity. The law discouraged defendants from choosing to have a jury trial because by doing so they would expose themselves to the death penalty. The Court severed the death penalty to protect the Sixth Amendment right to a jury trial and left the rest of the law intact.[42]

A 1990 law allowed a court to freeze, before trial, assets belonging to a defendant accused of violations of federal health care or banking laws, including property acquired as a result of the alleged crime, or traceable to it, or other "property of equivalent value." Sala Luis was charged with fraudulently obtaining nearly $45 million through crimes related to health care. To preserve $2 million remaining in Luis's possession for the payment of restitution and criminal penalties, the government secured a pretrial order prohibiting her from dissipating assets, including assets unrelated to her alleged crimes. The Supreme Court vacated the restraint order in *Luis v. United States* (2016), holding that Luis must be able to use her untainted assets to retain counsel of her choice. The Sixth Amendment right of an accused to have the assistance of counsel in a criminal trial outweighs the government's interest in having funds available later for payment of statutory penalties and restitution to victims.[43]

The one Seventh Amendment decision relating to Congress struck down a portion of federal copyright law. Columbia Pictures Television, Inc. terminated agreements licensing several television series to stations owned by E. Elvin Feltner after royalty payments became delinquent. When Feltner's stations continued to broadcast the programs without permission, Columbia sued for copyright infringement. Columbia won on its claims, and then exercised the option afforded by section 504(c) of the Copyright Act of 1976 to recover statutory damages in lieu of actual damages. The federal district court denied Feltner's request for a jury trial and awarded Columbia statutory damages following a bench trial. Justice Thomas for the Supreme Court in *Feltner v. Columbia Pictures Television, Inc.* (1998) reversed the lower court's decision, holding that the Seventh Amendment provides a right to a jury trial in these circumstances. Section 504(c) of the Copyright Act said damages should be assessed in an amount "the court deems just." This reference to a "court" appears to mean a judge, not a judge and jury, reasoned Thomas, and therefore it violates the Seventh Amendment. In a concurring opinion in *Feltner*, Justice Scalia agreed to send the case back for a jury trial to assess damages but was unwilling to say Congress had acted unconstitutionally. The statute's reference to a "court" could mean a judge, or it could mean a judge and jury. Scalia preferred to read the section 504(c) language in a way that preserved its constitutionality.[44]

The Eighth Amendment also generated only one overturn of Congress. *Trop v. Dulles* (1958) struck down section 401(g) of the 1940 Nationality Act, as amended in 1944 during World War II, which stipulated that a citizen "shall lose his nationality" by deserting the military or naval forces of the United States in time of war, provided he is convicted by court-martial and is dismissed or dishonorably discharged from service. Robert Trop, an American citizen, while serving in the army in French Morocco in 1944, was convicted of desertion and sentenced to a dishonorable discharge and imprisonment for three years. He returned to the United States and in 1952 applied for a passport. The State Department denied his application on the grounds that he had lost his citizenship. In a strange opinion, Chief Justice Warren in *Trop* held that the loss of citizenship for wartime desertion is a "cruel and unusual" punishment in violation of the Eighth Amendment. He reached this result even though wartime desertion is punishable by death, so there could be no argument that the penalty of denationalization "is excessive in relation to the crime."

In his opinion for the four dissenting justices in *Trop*, Felix Frankfurter said that when an act of Congress is challenged, the function of the Court is to determine whether legislative action lies "clearly outside the constitutional grant of power" being relied upon. It is not the business of the Court to "pronounce policy." Congress may well have thought that making loss of citizenship a consequence of wartime desertion "would affect the ability of the military authorities to control the forces with which they were expected to fight and win a major world conflict." Assuming section 401(g) imposes a "punishment," concluded Frankfurter, the majority's decision that denationalization would be a cruel and unusual punishment "stretched that concept beyond the breaking point. . . . Is constitutional dialectic so empty of reason that it can be seriously urged that loss of citizenship is a fate worse than death?"[45]

United Public Workers v. Mitchell (1947) upheld the Hatch Act's prohibitions on federal government employees taking an "active part in political management or in political campaigns." In the course of finding that the employees' First and Fifth Amendment rights were not violated by the act's provisions to protect the integrity of the civil service, the Court presented a succinct and persuasive summary of how the Ninth and Tenth Amendments should be viewed in any case where an exercise of power by Congress is being challenged as unconstitutional. Said the Court:

> The powers granted by the Constitution to the Federal Government are subtracted from the totality of the sovereignty originally in the states and the people. Therefore, when objection is made that the exercise of a federal power infringes upon rights reserved by the Ninth and Tenth Amendments, the inquiry must be directed toward the granted power, under which the action of the Union was taken. If granted power is found, necessarily the objection of invasion of those rights, reserved by the Ninth and Tenth Amendments, must fall.[46]

Notwithstanding this sage analysis, the modern Supreme Court in three decisions has put a gloss on the Tenth Amendment's statement that powers not delegated to the United States are reserved to the states or the people. It did so to protect states' rights. The first decision came in response to Congress' amendment of the Fair Labor Standards Act in 1974 to extend the act's minimum wage and maximum hour provisions to virtually all state and local government employees. For the Court in *National League of Cities v. Usery* (1976), Justice Rehnquist opined that insofar as the act operated to displace the states' ability to structure employer-employee relationships in areas of traditional governmental functions, such as fire prevention, police protection, sanitation, public health, and parks and recreation, it did not fall within the authority granted to Congress to regulate commerce. In attempting to exercise its commerce clause power to prescribe minimum wages and maximum hours to be paid by the states in their sovereign capacities, Congress had sought to wield its power in a fashion that would impair the states' "ability to function effectively in a federal system."

In dissent Justice Brennan (joined by Justices White and Marshall) insisted the Court's decision "manufactured an abstraction without substance, founded neither in the words of the Constitution nor on precedent." There is no "state sovereignty" preserved in the Constitution to override national government decisions. So long as Congress is acting within its sphere of delegated authority, its judgment prevails over any contrary state or local policy. "Judicial restraint in this area merely recognizes that the political branches of our Government are structured to protect the interest of the States, as well as the Nation as a whole, and that the States are fully able to protect their own interest in the premises." Members of Congress are elected from the states, for example, and have a motivation to look out for their welfare. In a separate dissenting opinion Justice Stevens added that the federal government can impose and has imposed many obligations and restrictions on the states and their employees:

> The Court holds that the Federal Government may not interfere with a sovereign State's inherent right to pay a substandard wage to the janitor at the state capitol. The principle on which the holding rests is difficult to perceive. The Federal Government may, I believe, require the State to act impartially when it hires or fires the janitor, to withhold taxes from his paycheck, to observe safety regulations when he is performing his job, to forbid him from burning too much soft coal in the capitol furnace, . . . from overloading a state-owned garbage truck, or from driving either the truck or the Governor's limousine over 55 miles an hour. Even though these and many other activities of the capitol janitor are activities of the State *qua* State, I have no doubt that they are subject to federal regulation.[47]

Nine years later, Justice Blackmun in *Garcia v. San Antonio Metropolitan Transit Authority* (1985) changed his mind, and in a five-to-four decision for the Court he overruled *Usery*. Blackmun said the task of defining "traditional governmental functions" that deserve to be protected from federal regulation had proven to be a difficult standard for the courts to apply. Instead, the extent to which Congress can impose requirements and restrictions on the states should be determined by the normal operations of the political branches. Within the federal structure of the government the states are well positioned to protect themselves against any unreasonable or oppressive interference from Congress, whose members are elected in the states and are motivated to look out for their interests. Blackmun might have added to these practical considerations the obvious point which the Court had made in *United Public Workers* (1947)—if Congress is properly acting within one of its delegated powers in article I, that conclusion is sufficient to dispose of any claim being made under the Tenth Amendment.[48]

The Court pursued a different states' rights rationale in *New York v. United States* (1992) when it preserved the "core sovereignty" of the states, embodied in the Tenth Amendment, by protecting them from the "choice" presented in the Low-Level Radioactive Waste Policy Act of either regulating the radioactive waste hazards being generated by private companies within their borders according to the instructions set forth in the law or, alternatively, taking title to the waste products and assuming liability for all damages associated therewith. Writing for the Court, Chief Justice Rehnquist decided this take-title provision unconstitutionally "commandeers the lawmaking processes of the states by directly compelling them to enact and enforce a federal regulatory program." Although Congress under its commerce clause authority could compel generators of waste hazards to comply with federal standards, it could not achieve this compliance with federal standards by pressuring the state legislatures to act. "In providing for a stronger central government, . . .

the Framers explicitly chose a Constitution that confers upon Congress the power to regulate individuals, not States."

In his dissenting opinion Justice White (joined by Justices Blackmun and Stevens) noted that the law was primarily a state-sponsored initiative "to achieve a state-based set of remedies to the waste problem." The states "sought not federal pre-emption or intervention, but rather congressional sanction of interstate compromises they had reached." Given the scanty textual support for the majority's anti-commandeering theory of federalism, it would be more sensible to "defer to a coordinate branch of government in its decision to devise a solution to a national problem of this kind." In a separate dissent Stevens responded to Rehnquist's claim that the Constitution allows Congress to regulate individuals, not states. He pointed out that the Articles of Confederation government could issue directives to the states, but it could not deal directly with individuals. The framers drafted the Constitution to strengthen the federal government. One element of the strengthened federal government was its ability to regulate individual conduct, but this did not mean Congress could no longer issue directives to the states.[49]

Printz v. United States (1997) extended the Court's anti-commandeering rule to include state executive officials. They too could not be required to enforce federal law. As an interim gun control measure, Congress in the 1993 Brady Handgun Violence Prevention Act relied on local law enforcement to conduct background checks on prospective firearms purchasers to make sure they were not underage, a convicted felon, a substance abuser, an unlawful alien, a person who had committed domestic violence, or a person ineligible to purchase a firearm under state or local law, until the U.S. attorney general could establish a national instant-check system. The majority in *Printz* held that this use of local officials to administer a federal program violated the sovereignty of the states. The Court repeated the point made in *New York* (1992) that the framers explicitly chose a Constitution that confers upon Congress the power to regulate individuals, not states. "The innovation of this design was that our citizens would have two political capacities, one state and one federal, each protected from incursion by the other."

Justice Stevens (joined by Justices Souter, Ginsburg, and Breyer) dissented. When Congress exercises powers delegated to it by the Constitution, "it may impose affirmative obligations on executive and judicial officers of state and local governments as well as ordinary citizens. This conclusion is firmly supported by the text of the Constitution, the early history of the Nation, decisions of this Court, and a correct understanding of the basic structure of the Federal Government." The Brady Act was passed in response to what Congress described as an "epidemic of gun violence." The act's legislative history noted that 15,377 Americans were murdered with firearms in 1992 and that 12,489 of these deaths were caused by handguns.

The Tenth Amendment merely provides that the "powers not delegated to the United States by the Constitution, nor prohibited by it to the States, are reserved to the States respectively or to the people. . . . It does not purport to limit the scope or effectiveness of the exercise of powers that *are* delegated to Congress" (Stevens's emphasis). Alexander Hamilton in *Federalist Paper No. 27* made clear that the new Constitution, "by extending the authority of the federal head to the individual citizens of the several States, will enable the government to employ the ordinary magistracy of each in the execution of its laws." Stevens concluded, "There is not a clause, sentence, or paragraph in the entire text of the Constitution of the United States that supports the proposition that a local police officer can ignore a command contained in a statute enacted by Congress pursuant to an express delegation of power enumerated in Article I."[50]

SUMMING UP THE COURT'S POLICY JUDGMENTS IN BILL OF RIGHTS CASES

A majority of the provisions in the Bill of Rights never became the basis for a Supreme Court decision striking down a law of Congress. This includes the First Amendment's mandates that Congress shall pass no law prohibiting the free exercise of religion, or abridging the freedom of the press, or the right of the people to peaceably assemble and petition the government for a redress of grievances; the Third Amendment's stipulation that no soldier shall in time of peace be quartered in any home without the owner's consent; the Fifth Amendment's grand jury and double jeopardy clauses in criminal cases; a couple of specific requirements for a fair criminal trial in the Sixth Amendment; the Eighth Amendment's prohibitions on excessive bail and fines; and the Ninth Amendment's statement that the enumeration of certain rights in the Constitution shall not be construed to deny or disparage others retained by the people.

In the Bill of Rights decisions which did result in an overruling of Congress, the Court generated its best public policy result in *Bolling v. Sharpe* (1954), reading an equal protection component into the Fifth Amendment due process clause.[51] Other clearly good outcomes, mostly narrow in scope, were two jury trial cases, *Wong Wing v. United States* (1896) (Chinese aliens awaiting deportation cannot be imprisoned for up to a year without a jury trial), and *United States v. Jackson* (1968) (kidnapping law cannot allow a more severe penalty in jury trial than in nonjury trial); an establishment of religion case, *Tilton v. Richardson* (1971) (higher education projects at both secular and religious schools can be funded so long as completed buildings are placed permanently off-limits for religious use); and three freedom of expression cases involving content restrictions:

- *Lamont v. Postmaster General* (1965): People can receive foreign mail designated by the government as "communist political propaganda" without having to affirmatively ask the postal service to send it through).
- *Schacht v. United States* (1970): Law allowing a nonmilitary person to wear a military uniform in a theatrical production cannot condition permission on the portrayal not tending to "discredit that armed force").
- *Legal Services Corporation v. Velasquez* (2001): Government cannot require, as a condition of its grants to free legal service providers, that such providers agree to not represent clients attempting to amend or otherwise challenge existing welfare laws.[52]

These cases upheld rights without negatively impacting any legitimate public policy interest.

All the other overturns of Congress were either bad results or cases where reasonable people could disagree on the merits. Let us first consider the amendments which have generated few decisions striking down a law of Congress. The one Second Amendment case, *District of Columbia v. Heller* (2008), ignored the original meaning of the people's Second Amendment right to keep and bear arms, which was tied to militia duty, and struck down the city's handgun prohibition, thereby endangering public safety. *Marshall v. Barlow, Inc.* (1978) and *Carpenter v. United States* (2018) should have held that the warrantless searches were "reasonable" in the circumstances, and thus permissible under the Fourth Amendment. In the trial of an alleged receiver of stolen goods, *Kirby v. United States* (1899) should have allowed the prior robbery conviction of three principals to be conclusive evidence that the goods in question were in fact stolen, rather than insisting that the Sixth Amendment right of an accused to confront witnesses meant that the convicted robbers must be available for cross-examination at Kirby's trial. Even though the Sixth Amendment does not stipulate how many jurors must be used in jury trials, *Rasmussen v. United States* (1905) struck down Alaska's territorial law which permitted six-person jury trials in misdemeanor cases. *Luis v. United States* (2016) held that the Sixth Amendment embodies the right of an accused in a criminal trial to have the assistance of high-priced counsel of his or her choice, which outweighs the government's interest in preserving funds for payment of penalties and restitution to victims in the event of a guilty verdict at trial. *Feltner v. Columbia Pictures Television, Inc.* (1998) read a federal copyright law's statement that damages could be assessed in an amount "the court deems just" to preclude a jury trial, as is guaranteed by the Seventh Amendment in civil cases, whereas Justice

Scalia's concurring opinion persuasively read this language to include the possibility of a jury trial if the defendant wanted one. *Trop v. Dulles* (1958), in an odd opinion, decided that a person's loss of citizenship as a penalty for desertion from the military in wartime would be a "cruel and unusual punishment" in violation of the Eighth Amendment, even though the Court admitted that wartime desertion is punishable by death in appropriate circumstances.[53]

Now consider the amendments which have generated most of the overturns. Aside from the three narrow decisions mentioned above, the vetoes of Congress in free speech cases can be classified as reasonable-people-can-disagree cases. However, on a range of acceptability, I find myself substantially more in agreement with the legislative and policy judgments of Congress than with the opinions of the judges who overturned them. Freedom of speech is obviously to be treasured and protected as one of our most valuable constitutional rights. But was it really necessary to conclude that the Congress could not place some restrictions on the photographic reproduction of US currency as a protective measure against counterfeiting; could not make it a crime to commercially produce and sell videos of animal cruelty; could not outlaw dial-a-porn phone messages; could not effectively regulate the broadcasting of "patently offensive" sex-related material on cable television; could not ban the "knowing" transmission of obscene or indecent messages to minors on the Internet; could not outlaw the commercial production and distribution of "virtual" child pornography; could not regulate or proscribe picketing and demonstrations on the grounds surrounding the Capitol building or the Supreme Court building; could not make it unlawful within five hundred feet of a foreign embassy in the District of Columbia to display a sign that tends to bring the foreign government into public odium or disrepute; could not outlaw the burning of the American flag; could not proscribe the mailing of unsolicited advertisements for contraceptives to people's homes; could not exempt "compounded" drugs from the FDA's standard approval requirements, on the condition that the providers of such drugs refrain from advertising or promoting their use; could not restrain casino gambling advertising in states where casino gambling is legal; could not tax the handlers of mushrooms in order to finance the promotion of mushroom sales; could not include a section in the Ethics in Government Act making it illegal for federal employees to accept honoraria in payment for their writings and speeches; and could not penalize the disclosure of confidential communications illegally intercepted and recorded?[54]

We have not come close to achieving a consensus on the proper balance between free speech and the need to protect political campaigns against corruption or the appearance of corruption resulting from large contributions and expenditures of money by corporations and wealthy individuals on behalf of incumbents and candidates seeking to replace them. All the campaign finance cases from *Buckley v. Valeo* (1976) through *McCutcheon v. FEC* (2014) have been contested among the justices on the Supreme Court and have generated controversy among members of Congress, constitutional scholars, public policy advocacy organizations, and interested citizens. No consensus resolution is in sight. It is not clear in these circumstances why the policy judgments of Congress should continue to be second-guessed by the Court on those rare occasions when both houses of Congress and the President are able to agree on a particular reform.[55]

The Fifth Amendment provides that no person may be compelled to be a witness against himself in any "criminal case." Seven of the eight cases in which the Court overturned a law of Congress based on this self-incrimination clause involved civil law settings, not criminal laws or prosecutions. *Dickerson v. United States* (2000) did involve a criminal prosecution, and overturned a statute designed to give a court discretion to judge whether a suspect's confession while in police custody was truly "voluntary," and therefore admissible evidence, based upon the totality of circumstances surrounding the confession. The statute spelled out several factors for the court to consider in making its determination that tracked the set of *Miranda* warnings the Supreme Court had "legislated" decades earlier in a state-law criminal case.[56]

The Fifth Amendment also provides that private property shall not be taken for public use without just compensation. Three of the four cases overturning laws of Congress under this clause did not actually involve takings of private property for public use. The one case that did—*Monongahela Navigation Co. v. United States* (1893)—held that the payment of the fair current value of the company's property being taken, a lock and dam on a river, was not sufficient. The Court decided that a stream of expected higher future tolls at the lock and dam must be added to the cost, based upon the anticipated development of new coal mines along the riverbank.[57]

The Fifth Amendment due process clause overturns of substantive policy decisions of Congress generally entailed negative consequences for society that outstripped any benefit that might have been gained for individual rights. For example, consider:

- *Hepburn v. Griswold* (1870): (Treasury notes cannot be made legal tender for previously contracted debts that were payable in gold or silver.)
- *Adair v. United States* (1908): (Businesses can refuse to hire and can fire employees because they wish to belong to a labor union.)
- *United States v. Cohen Grocery Store Co.* (1921): (The Food Control Act could not outlaw "unreasonable or unfair" prices for "necessaries,"

letting courts determine at trial what is unreasonable or unfair in the circumstances.)
- *Adkins v. Children's Hospital* (1923): (Congress cannot enact a minimum wage law for women and children.)

The Court deleted presumptions in three criminal statutes:

- *Tot v. United States* (1943): (Person barred from receiving a firearm transported in interstate commerce who is found in possession of the firearm cannot be presumed to have acquired it in interstate commerce.)
- *United States v. Romano* (1965): (Person who is present at an illegal still cannot be presumed to be the owner.)
- *Turner v. United States* (1970): (Person secretly transporting cocaine cannot be presumed to have acquired it through illegal importation.)

In each case, the person in possession of the firearm or cocaine or present at an illegal still could present evidence in court to rebut the presumption and shift the burden of proof back to the prosecution. The Court struck down laws preventing Communist Party members from having a U.S. passport or from working in certain designated critical defense facilities, in *Aptheker v. Secretary of State* (1964) and *United States v. Robel* (1967), respectively, rejecting dissenting opinions which thought that the government should be able to protect itself and the general public against international travelers and workers in defense facilities who belonged to an organization committed to the violent overthrow of the United States. Companion 1973 cases overturned the efforts of Congress to preserve funds in the food stamp program through denials of benefits to households occupied by college students, adult children whose parents claimed them as dependents in tax returns, or unrelated individuals.[58]

The Uniform Code of Military Justice cases (one in 1955, one in 1957, and four companion cases in 1960) exempted dismissed service members, civilian dependents, and civilian employees from being tried in military courts for crimes allegedly committed while they were with the armed forces overseas. This preference for regular civilian courts, while perhaps understandable as an abstract speculation, was not based on any presentation of aggregate data which showed that innocent defendants were more likely to be found guilty in military trials than in civilian ones. Moreover, these decisions created a problem with no good solution because it was impracticable to bring all such defendants home to the United States to stand trial or to establish article III federal courts around the world wherever the armed forces were located.[59]

The Tenth Amendment states a truism when it says that powers not delegated to the United States by the Constitution, nor prohibited by it to the states, are reserved to the states or the people. Three times in five-to-four decisions the modern Supreme Court relied on the "spirit" of this amendment to uphold states' rights at the expense of Congress:

- *National League of Cities v. Usery* (1976): (The wage and hour provisions of the nation's Fair Labor Standards Act could not be applied to state and local government employees.)
- *New York v. United States* (1992): (Congress could not pressure state legislatures to adopt a federal regulatory program for the disposal of radioactive waste generated within their borders.)
- *Printz v. United States* (1997): (Congress could not require the executive branch of the state governments to enforce compliance with an interim federal handgun regulation.)[60]

Neither the Tenth Amendment nor any other provision in the Constitution places the state governments off-limits to the laws of Congress enacted pursuant to its delegated powers. As has been often true in our history, the Court's majority in these three cases was implementing its own policy preference (here, states' rights) rather than applying any clear constitutional limitation.

NOTES

1. *Hepburn v. Griswold*, 75 U.S. 603 (1870), a due process of law ruling on paper money, overturned in *Knox v. Lee*, 79 U.S. 457 (1871); *Boyd v. United States*, 116 U.S. 616 (1886) (civil forfeiture case); *Monongahela Navigation Co. v. United States*, 116 U.S. 616 (1893) (just compensation clause case); *Wong Wing v. United States*, 163 U.S. 228 (1896) (trial rights for Chinese aliens awaiting deportation); and *Kirby v. United States*, 174 U.S. 47 (1899) (a criminal defendant's trial right to confront witnesses against him). The first four of these nineteenth century decisions are included in my discussion of the Fifth Amendment, and the final two are included in my discussion of the Sixth Amendment.

2. *Rasmussen*, 197–516; *Lynch*, 292 U.S. 571; *Adair*, 208 U.S. 161; *Cohen Grocery*, 255 U.S. 281; *Adkins*, 261 U.S. 525; *Tot*, 319 U.S. 463; *Bolling*, 347 U.S. 497–500; *Toth*, 350 U.S. 11; *Reid*, 354 U.S. 1; and *Trop*, 356 U.S. 86.

3. I have taken my cases from two sources: Congressional Research Service, comp., *Acts of Congress Held Unconstitutional in Whole or in Part by the Supreme Court of the United States* (Washington, DC: Government Printing Office, 2002, with supplements through 2016), and "Judicial Review of Congress" data set at www.princeton.edu/-kewhitt.

4. *Tilton*, 403 U.S. 672–75, 680, 682–84.

5. *Lamont*, 381 U.S. 301–6; *Schacht*, 398 U.S. 58–63; *Legal Services Corp.*, 531 U.S. 533–43, 545–54, 556–60. The first two cases involved expansive readings of the free speech clause. *Lamont* was not protecting the free speech rights of anyone, certainly not the rights of foreign communist publishers. Instead, it protected a right of readers to receive publications of their choice without interruption or intimidation. *Schacht* expanded "speech" to include the wearing of military uniforms in theater productions.

6. *Time, Inc.*, 468 U.S. 641–50, 652, 659; *Stevens*, 559 U.S. 460–72, 478–79; *Alvarez*, 567 U.S. 709; and *Tam*, 582 U.S. ___.

7. *Rizzi*, 410 U.S. 422.

8. *Denver Educational Telecomm.*, 518 U.S. 727–33, 736, 740, 747, 753–60, 762, and 767.

9. *Reno*, 521 U.S. 844–49, 853, 855, 857–61, 866–67, 872–75, 882, and 885.

10. *Playboy*, 529 U.S. 803–7, 811–16, 821, 825–27; *Ashcroft*, 535 U.S. 234–36, 240–41, 243, 247. 251, and 253–54.

11. *Jeanette Rankin Brigade*, 342 F. Supp. 575, 585 (D.C.C. 1972), affirmed 409 U.S. 972 (1972); *Grace*, 461 U.S. 171–72, 176–78, and 180–82; *Boos*, 485 U.S. 312–15, 317–19, 321–23, and 331–32.

12. *Eichman*, 496 U.S. 300–15, 319 (Court opinion), 319, and 322 (Justice Stevens dissenting opinion).

13. *Youngs Drug Products*, 463 U.S. 60–73; *Coors Brewing Co.*, 514 U.S. 476–78, 480–86, 489, 491; *Greater New Orleans Broadcasting Assn.*, 527 U.S. 173–76, 180–81, 183, 186–90, and 192.

14. *United Foods, Inc.*, 533 U.S. 405–13, 416–17 (Court opinion), and 419–29 (Justice Breyer dissenting opinion).

15. *Western States Med. Center*, 535 U.S. 357–60, 364–67, 369, and 371.

16. *Buckley*, 424 U.S. 1–8, 10–11, 13–14, 51–64, 66–68, 71, 74–86, 90, 92–93, 109–10, 118–20, 124–27, 137–38, 140–41, and 143 (per curiam).

17. *Nat. Conserv. Pol. Action Cmte.*, 470 U.S. 480; *Mass. Citizens for Life, Inc.*, 479 U.S. 238; *Colo. Repub. Campaign Cmte.*, 518 U.S. 604; *McConnell*, 540 U.S. 93; *Wisconsin Right to Life, Inc.*, 551 U.S. 449; *Davis*, 524 U.S.724; *Citizens United*, 558 U.S. 310; and *McCutcheon*, 572 U.S. 815.

18. *League of Women Voters*, 468 U.S. 364–66, 375–78, 380–81, 383–89, 395–401; *Treasury Employees*, 513 U.S. 454–58, 462, 464, 466, 470–72, 474–77, and 479–80.

19. *Bartnicki*, 532 U.S. 514–18, 523, 527, and 534–35.

20. *Alliance for Open Society*, 570 U.S. 205.

21. *Heller*, 554 U.S. 570.

22. *Barlow, Inc.*, 436 U.S. 307–13, 315–17, 320–22 (Court opinion), 325–30, 332–35 (Justice Stevens dissenting opinion).

23. *Carpenter*, 585 U.S. ___ (2018). The four dissenters did not argue that the act's criteria could be the predicate for a "reasonable," though warrantless, search of Carpenter's telecommunication records, thereby satisfying the Fourth Amendment's first clause. They claimed instead that there was no need for a search warrant in any event under the Supreme Court's precedents because Carpenter could have no expectation of privacy in his cell phone location records kept by third-party wireless carriers.

24. *Boyd v. United States*, 116 U.S. 616, 621, 630–35, and 638 (1886). This case reviewed a forfeiture case under the 1874 revenue law. The collector of customs in the port of New York seized thirty-five cases of plate glass being imported from England by E.A. Boyd and Sons under what the collector believed was a fraudulent invoice to avoid customs duties. The company sued the government to regain possession of the goods. At the trial it became important to show the value of the glass previously imported by the claimant. The judge required the company to produce its invoice or have the government's allegation accepted as proven, as the revenue act authorized him to do. The company produced the invoice, and the jury found in favor of the government, condemning the glass that had been seized and giving a judgment of foreclosure. Boyd and Sons appealed. The Supreme Court overruled the forfeiture, saying that although the Fourth Amendment search and seizure clause and the Fifth Amendment privilege against self-incrimination did not "technically" or "literally" apply to the law as worded, the law and proceeding were within their "spirit. Suits for forfeiture are "quasi-criminal" proceedings.

25. *Albertson v. Subversive Activities Control Board*, 382 U.S. 70–73, 77–80 (1965) (Communist Party registration); *Marchetti v. United States*, 390 U.S. 39 (1968) (gamblers' occupational tax); *Grosso v. United States*, 390 U.S. 62 (1968) (excise tax on wagering); *Haynes v. United States*, 390 U.S. 85 (1968) (firearm registration); *Leary v. United States*, 395 U.S. 6 (1969) (marijuana tax); and *United States v. U.S. Coin and Currency*, 407 U.S. 715 (1971) (retroactive application to the gambler occupation tax).

26. *Dickerson*, 530 U.S. 428, 431–32, 434–37, 443 (Court opinion), 444–46, and 465 (Justice Scalia dissenting opinion).

27. *Monongahela Navig. Co.*, 148 U.S. 312.

28. *Lynch*, 292 U.S. 571; *Irving*, 481 U.S. 704; and *Youpee*, 519 U.S. 534.

29. John Hart Ely, *Democracy and Distrust: A Theory of Judicial Review* (Cambridge: Harvard University Press, 1980), 18.

30. *Hepburn*, 75 U.S. 603; *Knox*, 79 U.S. 457.

31. *Adair*, 208 U.S. 161; *Cohen Grocery*, 255 U.S. 281; and *Adkins*, 261 U.S. 525. The Court in the modern era has continued to employ the due process void-for-vagueness doctrine applied in *Cohen Grocery*. For example, *Johnson v. United States*, 576 U.S. ___ (2015) addressed the following situation: After Johnson pleaded guilty to being a felon illegally in possession of a firearm, the prosecution sought an enhanced sentence for his offense under the 1984 Armed Career Criminal Act (ACCA), which allowed the imposition of an increased prison term upon a defendant with three or more prior convictions for a "violent felony," defined to include any felony involving "conduct that presents a serious potential risk of physical injury to another." The government argued that Johnson's prior conviction for illegal possession of a sawed-off shotgun could be considered a violent felony to help satisfy the test for an enhanced sentence. The federal district court agreed, sentenced him to fifteen years, and the federal appellate court affirmed. The Supreme Court reversed, concluding the ACCA's enhanced sentencing option for prior "violent felony" convictions was "unconstitutionally vague" in violation of the due process clause.

Applying the same analysis as in *Johnson*, the Court in *Sessions v. Dimaya*, 518 U.S. ___ (2018) held that the Immigration and Naturalization Act's authorization to deport aliens who are convicted of a "crime of violence," defined to include an offense that "by its nature, involves a substantial risk that physical force against the person or property of another may be used in the course of committing the offense," must be stricken as unconstitutionally vague.

32. *Tot,* 319 U.S. 463; *Romano,* 382 U.S. 136; and *Turner*, 396 U.S. 398.

33. *Aptheker*, 378 U.S. 500; *Robel*, 389 U.S. 858; *Murry*, 413 U.S. 508; and *Moreno*, 413 U.S. 528.

34. *Bolling*, 347 U.S. 497–500.

35. *Davis*, 409 U.S. 1069, and *Frontiero*, 411 U.S. 677.

36. *Weinberger v. Wiesenfeld*, 420 U.S. 636 (1974) (Social Security granted survivors' benefits based on the earnings of a deceased husband and father both to the widow and to the couple's minor children in her care, but granted benefits based on the earnings of a deceased wife and mother only to the minor children and not to the widower—this discriminates against female wage earners by affording them less protection for their survivors than is provided for male wage earners); *Califano v. Goldfarb*, 430 U.S. 199 (1977) (Social Security survivors' benefits based on the earnings of a deceased husband were payable to his widow regardless of dependency, but such benefits on the basis of the earnings of a deceased wife were payable to her widower only if he was receiving at least half of his support from her—this discriminates against female wage earners by affording them less protection for their surviving spouses than is provided to male employees); *Califano v. Silbowitz*, 430 U.S. 924 (1977) (Social Security Act entitled a husband to insurance benefits through his wife's benefits provided he received at least half of his support from her at the time she became entitled, but required no such showing of support for the wife to qualify for benefits through her husband); and *Califano v. Westcott*, 443 U.S. 909 (1979) (Social Security Act's Aid to Families with Dependent Children provided benefits to families whose dependent children are deprived of parental support because of the unemployment of the father, but no such benefits when the mother becomes unemployed).

The modern Court has continued to apply this due process equality concept to federal statutes. For example, *Sessions v. Morales-Santana*, 528 U.S. ___ (2017), concluded that the Immigration and Naturalization Act's provision granting citizenship to a child born abroad to an unwed U.S. citizen-mother who has lived continuously for one year in the United States at any time in her adult life prior to the child's birth but not affording the same privilege of citizenship to a child born abroad to an unwed U.S. citizen-father violated the equal protection component of the Fifth Amendment due process clause, citing the 1970s cases of *Frontiero*, *Wiesenfeld*, and *Goldfarb* to show that the Court applies heightened scrutiny to gender classifications, and also citing *United States v. Virginia*, 518 U.S. 515 (1996), a state law case decided under the equal protection clause of the Fourteenth Amendment, for the proposition that gender discrimination requires an "exceedingly persuasive justification" to survive scrutiny.

37. *Wong Wing*, 163 U.S. 228–31, 233–36, 238

38. *Kirby*, 174 U.S. 47; *Rasmussen*, 197 U.S. 516–19, 525–26.

39. *Toth*, 350 U.S. 11, 13–17, 19–22 (Court opinion), 23–29, 31–32, 34–37, and 43 (Justice Reed dissenting opinion).

40. *Covert*, 354 U.S. 1–5, 7, 10–13, 19–21, 32, 37, 39 (Court opinion), 78–80, 83–89 (Justice Clark dissenting opinion).

41. *Grisham*, 361 U.S. 278; *Singleton*, 361 U.S. 234; *Guagliardo*, 361 U.S. 281; *Wilson*, 361 U.S. 287; and *O'Callahan*, 395. U.S. 258. *O'Callahan* was overruled by *Solorio v. United States*, 483 U.S. 435 (1987).

42. *Jackson*, 390 U.S. 570–72, 578, 581–83, and 585–86.

43. *Luis*, 578 U.S. ___ (2016).

44. *Feltner*, 523 U.S. 340–43, 345–47, 353–55 (Court opinion), 355–56, and 358 (Justice Scalia concurring opinion).

45. *Trop*, 356 U.S. 86–94, 97, 99, 101 (Court opinion), 114–17, 119–22, 125, and 127–28 (Justice Frankfurter dissenting opinion).

46. *United Public Workers*, 330 U.S. 75, 94–97.

47. *Usery*, 426 U.S. 833–34, 842, 845, 849–82 (Court opinion), 856–60, 875–81 (Justice Brennan dissenting opinion), and 880–81 (Justice Stevens dissenting opinion).

48. *Garcia*, 469 U.S. 528, 530–47.

49. *New York*, 505 U.S. 144–50, 154, 156–66, 177–80, 184–85 (Court opinion), 188–90, 202, 207 (Justice White dissenting opinion), and 210–11 (Justice Stevens dissenting opinion).

50. *Printz*, 521 U.S. 898–903, 910–14, 918–22, 925–33 (Court opinion), 939–42, and 944–45 (Justice Stevens dissenting opinion).

51. *Bolling* and its progeny are discussed in the text at ns. 34–36, supra.

52. *Wong Wing*, 163 U.S. 128; *Jackson*, 390 U.S. 570; *Tilton*, 403 U.S. 672; *Lamont*, 381 U.S. 301; *Schacht*, 398 U.S. 58; and *Legal Services Corp.*, 531 U.S. 533.

53. *Heller*, 554 U.S. 570; *Barlow, Inc.*, 436 U.S. 307; *Carpenter*, 585 U.S. ___; *Kirby*, 174 U.S. 47; *Rasmussen*, 197 U.S. 516; *Luis*, 578 U.S. ___; *Feltner*, 523 U.S. 340; and *Trop*, 356 U.S. 86.

54. See the cases discussed in the text at ns. 6–15, supra.

55. See the cases discussed in the text at ns. 16–17, supra.

56. See the cases discussed in the text at ns. 24–26, supra.

57. *Monongahela Navig. Co.*, 148 U.S. 312. The three cases that did not involve actual takings of private property for public use are discussed in the text at n.29, supra.

58. *Hepburn*, 75 U.S. 603; *Adair*, 208 U.S. 161; *Cohen Grocery*, 255 U.S. 281; *Adkins*, 261 U.S. 525; *Tot*, 319 U.S. 463; *Romano*, 382 U.S. 136; *Turner*, 346 U.S. 398; *Aptheker*, 378 U.S. 500; and *Robel*, 389 U.S. 858. The two food stamp cases were *U.S. Dept. of Agriculture v. Murry*, 413 U.S. 508 (1973), and *U.S. Dept. of Agriculture v. Moreno*, 413 U.S. 528 (1973).

59. The six Uniform Military Code cases are discussed in the text at ns. 39–41, supra.

60. *Usery*, 426 U.S. 833; *New York*, 505 U.S. 144; and *Printz*, 521 U.S. 898.

Chapter 9

Choosing Policies for Abortion, Religious Liberty, and Free Speech

This chapter builds on the constitutional law history discussed so far to consider in greater detail three currently important, controversial subjects: abortion, the freedom of religion, and the freedom of speech. We have seen that the Republicans of 1866 gave the states a duty and Congress the police power to protect people's life, liberty, property, and safety under fair, equal laws, substantively and not just procedurally. During Reconstruction, the New Deal 1930s, and the Great Society 1960s, in bursts of progressive energy, Congress enacted laws to protect civil rights, to offer baseline economic security for the lower and middle classes, and to promote civil rights and economic welfare, in the respective periods. It is time for Congress to assert its long-dormant constitutional role under section five of the Fourteenth Amendment. Possibilities for legislative solutions in three currently important, controversial areas of rights definition and enforcement are discussed: abortion, religious liberty, and free speech.

ABORTION

Roe v. Wade (1973) held that the right of privacy, included within the concept of liberty in the Fourteenth Amendment, is broad enough to encompass a woman's decision of whether to terminate her pregnancy. Because this privacy right is "fundamental," any regulation of abortion must be narrowly drawn to serve a compelling government interest. Although the fetus is not a "person" within the meaning and protection of the Constitution, the state has an interest in the "potential life" which it represents, so after fetal viability (about twenty-four weeks into the pregnancy), the state may prohibit abortion except where necessary to preserve the woman's life or health. The plurality decision in *Planned Parenthood of Southeastern Pennsylvania v. Casey*

(1992) preserved the right to abortion as an element of the woman's liberty, but lowered the standard of judicial review to permit regulations of abortion so long as they do not impose an "undue burden" on the woman's decision of whether to terminate her pregnancy. *Dobbs v. Jackson Women's Health Organization* (2022) overruled *Roe* and *Casey*, holding that a woman's liberty does not include a constitutional right to abortion. The subject of abortion can and should be resolved by the people's elected representatives. Any restriction or prohibition of abortion, if it is challenged in court, "is entitled to a strong presumption of validity. It must be sustained if there is a rational basis on which the legislature could have thought that it would serve some legitimate state interest." The Court is signaling here that state prohibitions and restrictions on the woman's liberty to choose to have an abortion are likely to be upheld in the courts, since the legislature will be presumed to have a legitimate interest in preserving fetal life.[1]

In the years leading up to *Roe*, four states had decriminalized abortions performed by a licensed physician in the early months of pregnancy. Fourteen other states enacted a version of the American Law Institute's Model Penal Code (1959), which authorized abortions to protect the physical or mental health of the woman, or if the pregnancy resulted from rape or incest, or the child would be born with a serious physical or mental defect.[2] In *United States v. Vuitch* (1971), the Supreme Court reviewed a 1901 federal law enacted by Congress for the District of Columbia, which as slightly revised in 1953 allowed physicians to perform abortions necessary to preserve the life or health of the woman. The Court upheld the law against a challenge that it should be considered void for vagueness under the Fifth Amendment's due process clause because of the difficulty of knowing when an abortion operation should be considered "necessary" to preserve the "health" of the woman. The Court said the term "health" could be interpreted to include the psychological as well as the physical well-being of the patient, and this was a type of judgment doctors routinely make when considering surgery. This statement in *Vuitch* presumably would offer grounds for the physician to decide in virtually every case that a patient's psychological well-being would be negatively impacted if she had to carry an unwanted pregnancy to term. Construed in this way, the law resembled the outcome in *Roe* two years later.[3]

Every year since 1976, Congress, in an appropriation bill or joint resolution, has limited the use of federal funds to reimburse the cost of an abortion under the Medicaid program. The 1977 version barred the use of Medicaid funds for an abortion except to save the woman's life. The 1978 and 1979 versions also made an exception if two physicians certified that "severe and long-lasting physical damage to the woman would result if the pregnancy were carried to term." The 1980 law allowed funding to preserve the woman's life, or when the pregnancy resulted from rape or incest. The Supreme Court in *Harris v.*

McRae (1980) upheld all versions of the Medicaid funding ban, including the most-narrow life preservation exception. The Court reasoned that the government had not done anything to prevent a woman from exercising her right to have an abortion; it merely was choosing not to financially support the decision in most cases. From 1981 to 1993 Congress funded Medicaid abortions only to save the pregnant woman's life, and since 1994 has also covered cases of rape or incest. Congress has applied similar abortion-funding limitations for military personnel, federal employees, Native Americans, prisoners, and persons covered by the Affordable Care Act.[4]

The Supreme Court in *Stenberg v. Carh*art (2000) struck down Nebraska's ban on "partial-birth abortions," unless done to save the life of the woman, because it did not also include an exception for her health. Justice Potter Stewart in his opinion for the Court said that under *Roe*, as modified by *Casey*, before fetal viability a woman has a right to terminate her pregnancy, and a state law is unconstitutional if it imposes an "undue burden" on the woman's decision. Post-viability, the state may proscribe abortion except where "necessary in appropriate medical judgment, for the preservation of the [woman's] life or health." The Court rejected Nebraska's contention that there was no need for a health exception in its law because safe alternatives remain available and a ban on partial-birth abortions would create no risk to women's health. Congress responded to the *Stenberg* decision in 2003 by enacting a federal ban on partial-birth abortions, based upon its findings that a "moral, medical, and ethical consensus exists that the practice of performing a partial-birth abortion . . . is a gruesome and inhumane procedure that is never medically necessary." The statute provided that the ban does not apply to any partial-birth abortion necessary to preserve the life of the woman. Justice Anthony Kennedy for the Court in *Gonzalez v. Carhart* (2007) upheld the federal ban, not because of the congressional findings, but rather in reliance on his own conclusion that there was medical disagreement about whether the act's prohibition would ever impose a significant health risk. In her dissent Justice Ruth Bader Ginsburg complained that for the first time since *Roe* the Court was blessing an abortion prohibition with no exception for the woman's health.[5]

There is a lingering question about the basis and extent of federal legislative authority to deal with abortion in the states. In its 2003 partial-birth abortion ban, Congress said that any "physician who, in or affecting interstate or foreign commerce, knowingly performs" such an abortion, unless it is necessary to save the mother's life, is subject to fine and imprisonment. In *Gonzalez* the Court assumed, without any discussion, congressional authority to enact the law. In a one-paragraph concurring opinion, Justice Clarence Thomas (joined by Justice Antonin Scalia) agreed with the judgment to uphold the ban, but in a possible signal to future litigants he noted that "whether the Act constitutes a permissible exercise of Congress' power under the Commerce Clause is not before the Court." The parties did not raise or brief the issue, and the lower courts did not address it. Justice Samuel Alito's opinion for the Court in *Dobbs* was notably silent on whether the people's elected representatives now being placed in charge of the abortion issue would include members of Congress. In his concurring opinion, Justice Brett Kavanaugh filled in this space by saying that the Constitution leaves the abortion issue for the people and their elected representatives to resolve "through the democratic process in the States or Congress."[6]

In 2021 the House Democrats passed a bill and placed it on the Senate calendar, "H.R. 3755—Women's Health Protection Act of 2021," styled an "Act To protect a person's ability to determine whether to continue or end a pregnancy, and to protect a health care provider's ability to provide abortion services." This responded to state initiatives to curtail access to abortion, and anticipated that the six conservative Republican justices now in control of the Supreme Court might overturn *Roe v. Wade.* The bill's statement of findings made many points, including these: Abortion services are essential to health care and access to those services is central to people's ability to participate equally in the economic and social life of the United States. Notwithstanding the Supreme Court's numerous decisions since 1973 that recognize the constitutional right to terminate a pregnancy before fetal viability, and after viability when necessary to preserve the life or health of the pregnant woman, access to abortion services has been obstructed across the United States in various ways, by blockades of health care facilities, restrictions on or prohibitions of insurance coverage, parental involvement laws (notification and consent), restrictions that shame and stigmatize people seeking abortion services, and medically unnecessary regulations that complicate and delay access to abortion services. Reproductive justice requires that every individual possess the right to make their own decision about having children without interference from the state. Human rights treaties ratified by the United States protect access to abortion.

The findings statement justified Congress' authority to pass the bill: Abortion-specific restrictions affect the cost and availability of abortion services. People travel across state lines and otherwise engage in interstate commerce to access this essential medical care. Health care providers engage in a form of economic and commercial activity when they provide abortion services, and there is an interstate market for abortion services. Abortion restrictions affect interstate commerce in numerous ways. For example, to provide abortion services health care providers engage in interstate commerce to purchase medicine, medical equipment, and other necessary goods and services. In sum, Congress has authority to enact this law to protect abortion services pursuant to its powers under the commerce clause and the necessary and proper clause in article I, section eight, and its powers under section five of the Fourteenth Amendment. The bill went on to describe its purpose—to permit health care providers to provide abortion services without requirements more burdensome than those imposed on medically comparable procedures—defined some terms, and concluded with a general rule to preempt state law limitations and requirements designed to impede or prohibit abortion.[7]

Following the *Dobbs* decision, House Democrats reenacted their 2021 bill to protect abortion rights, still citing the powers delegated to Congress in the commerce clause and the necessary and proper clause in article I of the Constitution (and section five of the Fourteenth Amendment) because commerce-clause support for civil liberty and civil rights laws has been relied upon by Congress and generally accepted by the Court since the 1960s.[8] However, the original meaning of section five of the Fourteenth Amendment should give direction to any future discussion and attempted regulation of abortion in Congress. This is not an interstate commerce issue. It involves a policy matter under the Fourteenth Amendment, weighing a pregnant woman's liberty to decide her own fate against the state's interest in protecting fetal life. Currently the states range from permitting abortion in all circumstances to prohibiting all abortions except to save the life of the mother.

Opinion polls show that a majority of Americans favor permitting abortion in some but not all cases.[9] If this attitude solidifies around a common middle ground, Congress might be prompted to enact some version of the American Law Institute's model law, which legalized abortion to preserve the pregnant woman's life or health, or in cases of rape or incest, or if the child would be born with a serious physical or mental disability. States which allow abortions more freely than this would not be affected by such a federal minimum baseline law. If the Congress manages to pass a statute, in any constitutional challenge that is taken up in the Supreme Court the Solicitor General could remind the Court that its most recent decision on abortion declared that resolution of the sensitive and divisive policy matter must rest with the people's elected representatives, which logically includes members of Congress acting under their Fourteenth Amendment section five authority.

RELIGIOUS LIBERTY

The First Amendment's command that Congress shall "make no law respecting an establishment of religion" carries a double meaning, as was made plain in the First Congress' drafting of the clause. Congress cannot establish a national religion, nor can it interfere with any state's establishment of religion. Congress under a separate clause cannot prohibit the free exercise of religion. What an "establishment" of religion or the "free exercise" of religion might entail are open-ended questions. For example, does government financial aid to religion amount to an establishment of religion? Does a neutral, nondiscriminatory law that incidentally burdens or hinders religious practice prohibit the free exercise of religion? Such issues have been primarily worked through by the Court in relation to the states under the Fourteenth Amendment, even though this amendment imposes a different regime for religion.

The Fourteenth Amendment does not mention religion or the religion clauses. Its most relevant part says that the state shall not "deny to any person within its jurisdiction the equal protection of the laws." Equal protection for what? Protection for the privileges and immunities of citizens, which cannot be abridged by state law, and for the life, *liberty*, and property of all persons, which cannot be deprived without due process (my emphasis). Equal protection of the laws for liberty—which logically includes religious liberty—is a state obligation. The Supreme Court has never used this straightforward textual analysis to decide a case involving religion in the states.

Instead, *Cantwell v. Connecticut* (1940), in a unanimous opinion, laid the foundation for all the Court's subsequent applications of the religion clauses to the states. It said the concept of liberty in the Fourteenth Amendment embraces the liberties guaranteed by the First Amendment. Accordingly, the First Amendment's declaration that Congress shall make no law respecting an establishment of religion, or prohibiting the free exercise thereof, applies to the legislatures in the states under the Fourteenth Amendment. Two other early cases, *Murdock v. Pennsylvania* (1943) and *Everson v. Board of Education* (1947), set a framework for analysis that would influence many decisions on the religion clauses.[10]

Murdock reviewed a city ordinance which required that persons soliciting orders for goods, paintings, pictures, wares, or merchandise of any kind, or delivering articles under orders so obtained, must procure a license and pay a tax to the city treasurer based upon the length of time the business would be conducted. Jehovah's Witnesses went from door to door distributing literature and soliciting people to purchase religious books and pamphlets, and sold some books, without obtaining a license and paying the tax. They were arrested and fined for violating the ordinance. Declaring that the First Amendment freedoms of speech, press, and religion are in a "preferred position," the Court struck down the law as construed and applied to the Jehovah's Witnesses. The four dissenting justices objected that the city should be able to raise revenue by means of a reasonable and nondiscriminatory license tax on solicitations of orders for and sales of goods and merchandise, including religious literature.

Under a state law which authorized it, Ewing, New Jersey, reimbursed parents for the costs of their children's bus transportation to and from school. The program included the public schools and some private (mostly Catholic) schools. *Everson* considered whether paying money to parents of children who attend Catholic school constitutes an impermissible establishment of religion. In his opinion for the Court, Justice Hugo Black quoted Thomas Jefferson for the proposition that the establishment clause in the First Amendment "erects a wall of separation between church and State." Accordingly, New Jersey cannot, consistent with this clause, contribute tax funds to the support of any religious institution. On the other hand, New Jersey also cannot hamper persons in the free exercise of their religion. "The First Amendment requires the state to be neutral in its relations with groups of religious believers and nonbelievers; it does not require the state to be their adversary." Measured by these standards, we cannot say the First Amendment prohibits New Jersey from expending tax-raised funds to pay the bus fares of parochial school pupils as part of a general program under which it pays the fares of pupils attending public and other private schools. The four dissenting justices said the inclusion of parents of Catholic school students breaches the high wall of separation between church and state.

Several views emerged in these two cases. All nine justices in *Everson* agreed that the establishment clause imposes a wall of separation between church and state. The minority said this means the state cannot aid religious schools in any way, even if the no-aid rule imposes a special disability on people because of their religion. The majority opinion in *Everson* held that a neutral law of general application complies with the establishment clause even though some aid is indirectly provided to religious schools. Similarly, the minority opinion in *Murdock* said that a neutral law of general application complies with the free exercise clause even though it imposes a burden on religious practice. The majority opinion in *Murdock* held that under the free exercise clause the state cannot burden religious practice even in a neutral law of general application.

The separation ideal in *Everson* played out in four types of establishment-clause cases: government aid to religious schools; access of student and community religious organizations to public school facilities or resources; prayer in public schools and in other government contexts; and religious displays or memorials. With one early exception,[11] the Court has allowed indirect state aid to religious schools when done (as it always is) as part of a program to assist all private schools. *Board of Education v. Allen* (1968) decided New York could provide books to students in all private (including religious) schools because they were given to the students, not to the schools, and therefore "the financial benefit is to parents and children, not to schools." *Mueller v. Allen* (1983) upheld a Minnesota law that allowed taxpayers to deduct from state income taxes, their expenses incurred for elementary and secondary education, and *Zelman v. Simmons-Harris* (2002) upheld Cleveland, Ohio's tuition vouchers for students to attend participating public and private (mostly religious) schools, in each case because funds would reach secular or religious schools by the choices of parents. The dissenting justices generally did not want to compromise on the separation of church and state.[12]

The Court tended to veto direct aid to religious schools until the Rehnquist and Roberts Courts adopted a more permissive view of accommodations for religion under the establishment clause. The leading case of *Lemon v. Kurtzman* (1971) established a three-part test for evaluating direct aid to religious schools: the statute's purpose and effect must be secular, and it must not foster excessive state entanglement with religion. Justice Byron White, the sole dissenter in *Lemon*, pointed out that the test created an impenetrable barrier to direct aid for religious schools. The state must ensure its aid is used only for secular purposes, but the need to monitor for compliance entangles the government with religion. The Court struck down a variety of aid programs, culminating in *Aguilar v. Felton* (1985), which held that the establishment clause barred New York City from sending public school teachers into religious schools to teach remedial classes to educationally disadvantaged children because this necessitated an excessive entanglement of church and state in the administration of the benefits. The city had to move the remedial instruction program to neutral sites away from the religious school-premises, at additional cost to the city and inconvenience to parents. Twelve years later, sensing a change in the Court's establishment-clause jurisprudence, the city and a new group of parents sued for relief, and *Agostini v. Felton* (1997) overturned *Aguilar*, noting that the city's remedial education services are available to all eligible children, no matter their religious belief or where they go to school.[13]

Three recent decisions authored by Chief Justice John Roberts nicely summarize the Court's current approach on state aid to religious schools: *Trinity Lutheran Church of Columbia, Inc. v. Comer* (2017), *Espinoza v. Montana Department of Revenue* (2020), and *Carson v. Makin* (2022). In each case the state, to comply with its understanding of the need to separate church and state under the establishment clause, excluded religious schools or persons from receiving public benefits available to all other qualifying recipients. And in each case, the Court pivoted away from the establishment clause concern to support the free exercise of religion. The church in *Trinity Lutheran* operated a preschool and daycare center, which would have qualified for a grant to improve its playground except for the state constitution's mandate that no aid shall be given to any religious organization. Roberts held that the church school's exclusion from a neutral aid program violates the free exercise clause. Drawing a wide berth around religious establishment concerns is not a sufficiently compelling reason for the discrimination. *Espinoza* addressed this situation: Montana granted tax credits to those who donate to organizations that award scholarships for private school education. Because the state's constitution barred government aid to any religious school, the program prohibited families from using the scholarships at religious schools. The Court held that the no-aid provision violates the free exercise clause. This clause "protects religious observers against unequal treatment." *Carson* addressed a similar situation: Maine offered tuition assistance to parents in school districts that neither operate a secondary school nor contract with a school in another district. The state limited its tuition assistance to public schools and private schools which are "nonsectarian in accord with the First Amendment." Citing *Trinity Lutheran* and *Espinoza*, the Court held that Maine's nonsectarian requirement violates the free exercise clause.[14]

The Court decided in cases such as *Lamb's Chapel v. Center Morides Union Free School District* (1993), *Rosenberger v. University of Virginia* (1995), and *Good News Club v. Milford Central School* (2001), that student or community religious organizations must have equal access with others to public school facilities or resources. The Court's concern to protect free speech trumped the separation of church and state concept in these cases. New York authorized local school districts to permit outside groups to use public-school facilities when the school was not in session, but the use could not be for religious purposes. When Lamb's Chapel, an evangelical church, was denied permission to show a religious-based film series on family values, it sued for relief. The Court in *Lamb's Chapel* ruled this denial violated the church's freedom of speech and expression. A student asked the University of Virginia for $5,800 from a student activity fund to subsidize the publishing costs of a Christian magazine, and was denied because the magazine promotes "a particular belief in or about a deity," and therefore was prohibited by university funding guidelines. *Rosenberger* held that the denial of funding to the student due to the content of his message violated his freedom of speech. The establishment clause does not justify a refusal to extend free speech rights to religious speakers. Milford Central School allowed community groups to utilize its facilities outside school hours, but denied access to the Good News Club, a Christian organization, because its proposed activity of conducting Bible lessons and praying was a use "for a religious purpose," prohibited by the school's community-use policy. *Good News Club* held such viewpoint discrimination violates the group's free speech rights and no establishment-clause concern justifies that violation.[15]

Establishment-clause cases have also dealt with a perceived need for cultural separation of church and state. *Engel v. Vitale* (1962), the first school prayer case, decided that New York could not require a state-composed prayer—"Almighty God, we acknowledge our dependence upon Thee, and we beg Thy blessings upon us, our parents, our teachers, and our country"—to be recited in the public schools at the beginning of each school day, even though the prayer is denominationally neutral and pupils who wish to do so may remain silent or leave the room while the prayer is recited. *Abbington School District v. Schempp* (1963) held that the public schools in Pennsylvania could not sponsor Bible readings and the recitation of the Lord's Prayer, even if individual students may be excused from participation upon the request of their parents. *Wallace v. Jaffree* (1985) struck down Alabama's authorization for a moment of silence in the public schools "for meditation or voluntary prayer." The Court found establishment clause violations outside the classroom as well, in *Lee v. Weisman* (1992) (inclusion of clergy to offer prayers at public school graduation ceremonies), and in *Santa Fe Independent School District v. Doe* (2000) (student-initiated-and-led prayers at high school football games). The final in this series of school prayer cases, *Kennedy v. Bremerton School District* (2022), concluded that the school's firing of its football coach because of his practice of kneeling and praying on the field after games was based on a misunderstanding of the establishment clause. The free speech and free exercise of religion clauses protect persons engaged in prayer from government reprisal.[16]

Outside the context of elementary and secondary schools, the Court has allowed prayer offerings in other government settings. *Marsh v. Chambers* (1983) said the Nebraska legislature could have a state chaplain lead prayers at the start of its sessions, noting that the practice of opening sessions of Congress with a prayer has been continued for two hundred years, ever since the First Congress drafted the First Amendment, and a similar practice has been followed for more than a century in Nebraska and many of the states. *Town of Greece v. Galloway* (2014) held that Greece, New York, could continue to open its monthly town meetings with a prayer, reciting the same history and tradition as *Marsh*, and noting that the town does not discriminate against minority faiths in determining who may offer a prayer, and nobody is required to participate.[17]

Religious displays and memorials have generated conflicting opinions under the establishment clause. For example, *Lynch v. Donnelly* (1984) and *Allegheny County v. ACLU* (1989) reached different conclusions about the Nativity scene (crèche). Pawtucket, Rhode Island annually erected a Christmas display in the city's shopping district, which included a Santa Claus, a Christmas tree, a banner that says "Seasons Greetings," and a crèche. The Court in *Lynch* found no establishment clause violation, notwithstanding the religious significance of the crèche. The Constitution does not require the complete separation of church and state. "In God We Trust" is on our currency, and "one nation under God" is in our Pledge of Allegiance to the

American flag. There are countless examples of government's acknowledgment of our religious heritage. The city's crèche display is part of a holiday celebration, and its primary purpose and effect are secular. Justice O'Connor concurred because the crèche in these circumstances did not amount to an "endorsement" of religion.

Allegheny County involved two holiday displays in downtown Pittsburgh. a creche placed on the steps of the county courthouse, and an eighteen-foot-high Chanukah menorah placed outside a city building next to a forty-five-foot-high Christmas tree. Four justices voted to accept both displays, and three justices voted to strike down both displays. Justice Harry Blackmun (with O'Connor's concurrence) announced the Court's judgment, which was to condemn the crèche and accept the menorah. Blackmun said the crèche angel's words, "Glory to God for the birth of Jesus Christ," endorses a Christian message in violation of the establishment clause. The menorah does not have the effect of endorsing religion given its setting, next to a Christmas tree and the mayor's sign saluting liberty. Chief Justice William Rehnquist and Justices Kennedy, White, and Scalia accepted both displays. The establishment clause does not require "neutrality" toward religion; it permits some latitude in accommodating the central role religion plays in our society. Justices William Brennan, Thurgood Marshall, and John Paul Stevens said the Court should establish a "strong presumption" against the public use of religious symbols. They opposed both the crèche and menorah displays because they conveyed messages of government support for Christianity, or for Christianity and Judaism, not pluralism.[18]

McCreary County v. ACLU of Kentucky and *Van Orden v. Perry* (five-to-four decisions in 2005) reached different conclusions on the Ten Commandments. Justice David Souter for the Court in *McCreary County* opted for the removal of the Commandments from county courthouse walls because the government must be neutral on religion. Chief Justice Rehnquist held for the Court in *Van Orden* that the establishment clause allows the display of a monument inscribed with the Ten Commandments on the Texas state capitol grounds. He followed the line of cases that have. recognized the strong role of religion and religious tradition in our nation's history. Justice Stephen Breyer voted with the majority in both cases.[19]

The free exercise clause has posed a central question for the Court: to what extent (if any) should religious persons or organizations be exempted from a neutral law of general application because the law burdens or hinders their religious practice? The logic of *Murdock* (1943) (the freedoms of speech, press, and religion are in a "preferred position," so the sellers of religious literature should be exempted from the license tax that applies to everyone else marketing and selling their wares) led in a natural progression to *Sherbert v. Verner* (1963)'s test in free exercise cases, i.e., is there a "compelling government interest" which justifies the law's "burden" on religious practice? Adelle Sherbert, a member of the Seventh-day Adventist Church, lost her job because of her refusal to work on Saturday, the Sabbath Day of her faith. When she applied for unemployment benefits, South Carolina's Employment Commission denied her claim on the ground that she was unwilling to accept Saturday employment, and hence was unavailable for suitable work when offered, as required by state law. The Supreme Court said the state forces the applicant to choose between following her religious belief and forfeiting benefits, or else abandoning one of the precepts of her religion in order to accept work. Enforcement of the state eligibility provision is not a compelling government interest that justifies this burden on the free exercise of religion.[20]

The burden on religion/compelling government interest test led to only four overturns of state law under the free exercise clause in the next twenty-seven years, three clones of *Sherbert* (cases in which claimants were denied unemployment benefits because they refused work on religious grounds), and *Wisconsin v. Yoder* (1972) (Amish children need not comply with the state's compulsory education law beyond the eighth grade). In all other cases, the Court stretched to find no burden on religion (when there really was one) or the presence of a compelling government interest (when there really was none).[21] The Court changed course in *Employment Division v. Smith* (1990). Oregon's controlled substances law banned the use of peyote, a hallucinogenic drug. Messrs. Smith and Black were fired by their employer because they ingested peyote for a sacramental purpose at a ceremony of their Native American Church. Their applications for unemployment compensation were denied under a state law disqualifying persons discharged for work-related "misconduct." The Court considered if the free exercise clause required the state to provide an exception for the religious use of peyote in its controlled substances law, and concluded there was no such requirement. *Smith* adopted a new benchmark for deciding challenges to government action in free exercise cases: an otherwise valid, neutral law is constitutional even though it burdens a religious practice. The Court said it is appropriate to use the compelling government interest requirement to challenge government discriminations based on race, or regulations of speech content. But this is not comparable to the free exercise claim being asserted in this case. What it produces in those other fields—equality of treatment, and an unrestricted flow of contending speech—are constitutional norms. What it would produce if accepted here—a private right to ignore generally applicable laws—is a "constitutional anomaly."[22]

Congress and Oregon responded by legalizing the use of peyote in Native American religious ceremonies.[23] Congress also passed the Religious Freedom Restoration Act, which mandates that no federal or state government action shall substantially burden a person's exercise of religion, even if the burden results from a rule of general applicability, unless this furthers a compelling government interest, and is the least restrictive means of furthering that interest. When the Court in *City of Boerne v. Flores* (1997) refused to apply RFRA to the states under the Fourteenth Amendment, Congress followed up with a narrowed version of RFRA, the Religious Land Use and Institutionalized Persons Act. Let us break down the elements. RLUIPA applies to both the federal and state governments, and operates on rules of general applicability that do not discriminate against anyone, on religious grounds or for any other reason. The law covers implementations of land use regulations that impose a substantial burden on the religious exercise of a person or organization, such as a church, and regulations that impose a substantial burden on the religious exercise of a person confined in an institution, such as a prison. Congress relied on its commerce clause and spending clause powers to enact the law, so its application is limited to a program or activity that receives financial assistance, or to a burden that affects commerce with foreign nations, among the states, or with Indian tribes. In situations where RLUIPA is triggered, the burden must be removed unless it furthers a compelling government interest, by the least restrictive means available.[24]

Cutter v. Wilkinson (2005) upheld the constitutionality of section three of RLUIPA against a facial challenge that its accommodation for prisoners' religious practices violated the establishment clause. Years later, Gregory Holt, an inmate in the Arkansas prison system and a practicing Muslim, sought relief from enforcement of the prison system's grooming policy, which banned facial hair absent a medical condition. In *Holt v. Hobbs* (2015), the state did not dispute that Holt's desire to grow a beard was religiously motivated, but it argued that the no-beard policy prevented the hiding of contraband and facilitated prisoner identification. The Court concluded that these concerns could be addressed by other available means and did not justify the burden on Holt's religious practice.[25]

Although the Court does not apply the Religious Freedom Restoration Act to the states, it uses the act to review federal-law burdens on religious practices.[26] For example, in *Gonzales v. O'Centro Espirita Beneficento Uniao do Vegetal* (2006), a small religious sect sued for an injunction to block enforcement of the Federal Controlled Substances Act so that its 130 members would not be prevented from drinking a sacramental tea that contains a hallucinogen banned by the act. The Court issued a preliminary injunction because the government had not satisfied its obligation under RFRA to demonstrate a compelling interest to apply the ban to the sect's use of the tea in their religious ceremonies. *Burwell v. Hobby Lobby Stores, Inc* (2014) addressed a dramatically different situation. Federal regulations implementing the Affordable Care Act required employers with over fifty workers to provide health care plans for their employees that include insurance coverage for contraceptive services. "Religious nonprofit organizations" were eligible for an exemption from this coverage for contraception. Hobby Lobby is a closely held, for-profit corporation which operates more than five hundred arts-and-crafts stores and has more than thirteen thousand employees. The family owners of the corporation, Christians who were opposed to certain forms of contraception on religious grounds, sued to obtain the same type of exemptive relief that religious organizations enjoy under the regulations. In his five-to-four opinion for the Court, Justice Alito expanded the scope of the exemption option to include closely held, for-profit corporations like Hobby Lobby. He called them "religious corporations."[27]

An appreciation for the limited nature of the establishment and free exercise clauses in the First Amendment, and a focus on the literal text of the Fourteenth Amendment, could guide Congress and the Court to a more appropriate treatment of religion in our social and political life. Getting realistic about the establishment and free exercise clauses in our ruminations about the meaning of the Constitution would be a good start. The Congress has never come close to establishing a national church in violation of the First Amendment, and given the religious diversity of the country, it never will. Over 80 percent of Americans express a belief in God, making it extremely unlikely that Congress will be motivated to pass a law to prohibit the free exercise of religion. Religious persons and institutions, like everyone else, have a duty to comply with generally applicable laws, including the many that impose burdens or constraints. Absent a measure which discriminates against practitioners of a particular faith, the First Amendment free exercise clause will not justify a lawsuit against the federal government.

As for the states, the Court's decision to "incorporate" the establishment and free exercise clauses into the due process clause of the Fourteenth Amendment was a mistake because it diverted attention from the relevant constitutional text. The Fourteenth Amendment commands that the states shall not deny equal protection of the laws for people's "liberty," which obviously includes religious liberty. The principle of no direct aid to religious schools expressed in *Everson* (1947) and *Lemon* (1971) and their establishment clause-progeny sowed the seeds for unequal treatment of religious interests. *Agostini v. Felton* (1997) focused on an establishment clause concern because that has been the focus of the Court in school aid cases, but the decision correctly applied the equal protection principle when it permitted public school teachers to go into public and private schools and provide remedial educational services to disadvantaged children, noting that the services were available to all eligible children no matter their religious belief or where they went to school. *Trinity Lutheran Church of Columbia, Inc. v. Comer* (2017) spoke in terms of the free exercise of religion, but the decision correctly applied the Fourteenth Amendment's equal protection principle when it held that the church's preschool and daycare center could not be disqualified from a public aid program solely because it is a religious institution.[28]

With the separation of church and state ideal removed from the scene, along with the establishment clause, the school prayer and religious display cases presented no constitutional issue. The following examples of government cultural support for religion did not deny equal protection of the laws to anyone in their exercise of religious liberty: the nondenominational prayer to God in *Engle*, and the Bible reading and Lord's Prayer in *Schempp*, both based on voluntary student participation; the "moment of silence for meditation or voluntary prayer" in *Jaffree*; and the prayers delivered at graduation ceremonies in *Weisman* and at high school football games in *Santa Fe School District*. The same is true of the permanent displays of the Ten Commandments on public property, and the seasonal displays of the creche and menorah.[29] Instead of a constitutional issue, the school prayers and religious displays really implicated a social and political consideration. Aside from the moment of silence in *Jaffree*, which involved no religious or cultural message of any kind, the prayers and displays could have had negative side effects on some members of the community. School prayers could expose some students to peer pressure, and religious displays might cause religious minorities or nonbelievers to think of themselves as "outsiders" in a country with a Christian or Judeo-Christian heritage. Legislative bodies should be sensitive to people's feelings when they contemplate the adoption of a new school exercise or religious display on public property.

State government discriminations against religion or religious practices have appeared in three different contexts. First, and most commonly, states have intentionally discriminated against religion, under a misguided establishment-clause concern to separate church and state to the fullest extent possible. The cases involving financial aid to religious schools or organizations illustrate this problem. Other examples include Tennessee's disqualification of members of the clergy to serve in the state legislature, struck down in *McDaniel v. Paley* (1978), and Washington State's college scholarship program for high school seniors that excluded students who wanted to pursue a degree in theology, upheld in *Locke v. Davey* (2004).[30] Rejection of the separation ideal as a valid constitutional objective, and a focus on equal protection for religious liberty, should eliminate such intentional discriminations. Second, some discriminations have been inadvertent or due to oversight. For example, *Sherbert* (1963) involved two South Carolina statutes relevant to Adelle Sherbert's situation. One law required applicants for unemployment benefits to be available for work on Saturdays. Another law stated generally that persons did not have to work on Sunday, their day of worship. Since Sherbert's day of worship was Saturday, she should have qualified for benefits without having to be available for work on Saturday. Third, occasionally a facially neutral law has targeted an unpopular religious group, as in *Church of the Lukumi Babalu Aye, Inc. v. Hialeah* (1993). The church members in this case practiced the Santeria religion, which employs animal sacrifice as one of its principal forms of devotion. Pigs, goats, and other animals are slaughtered, cooked, and eaten. When the church leased land in Hialeah, Florida, the city council promptly passed ordinances to prohibit the slaughter of animals "in any type of ritual," with broad exemptions available for food establishments and others. The Court struck down the ordinances because they "gerrymandered" all sorts of animal killings except the one performed in the Santeria religious ritual. All such state discriminations against religious liberty violate the equal protection clause.[31]

The main issue that looms today is not government discrimination against religion, but rather the potential for religious persons and organizations to gain government permissions that can do harm to the rights and interests of third parties. For example, the Obama administration's regulations implementing the Affordable Care Act made nonprofit religious employers eligible for an exemption from the general requirement to provide employees insurance coverage for contraception, and in *Hobby Lobby* the Court said it was applying RFRA to expand the exemption option to include closely held, for-profit corporations whose owners have a religious objection to contraception. Justice Ginsburg for four dissenting justices complained that, "In a decision of startling breadth the Court holds that commercial enterprises can opt out of any law (saving only tax laws) they judge to be incompatible with their sincerely held religious beliefs . . . In the Court's view, RFRA demands accommodation of a for-profit corporation's religious beliefs no matter the impact that accommodation may have on third parties," in this case thousands of women employed by Hobby Lobby.[32]

Or consider *Makepiece Cakeshop, Ltd. v. Colorado Civil Rights Commission* (2018), which should have been an easy civil rights decision. A baker refused to bake a wedding cake for a same-sex couple because of his religious opposition to same-sex marriage. The couple filed a charge under the state's antidiscrimination law, which prohibits discrimination based on sexual orientation in a "place of business engaged in any sales to the public." The Colorado civil rights commission ruled in favor of the couple, the state courts upheld its ruling and enforcement order, and in a seven-to-two opinion for the Supreme Court Justice Kennedy reversed the decision. He said the case presents difficult issues as to the proper reconciliation of two principles: the authority of the state to protect the rights and dignity of gay persons who face discrimination, and the right of all persons to exercise fundamental freedoms under the First Amendment. The "delicate question" of when a person's free exercise of religion must yield to an otherwise valid exercise of state power needs to be determined in an unbiased forum. Whatever the outcome of some future controversy involving facts resembling these, some of the Colorado commission's statements evidenced a hostility toward religion, so its actions violated the free exercise clause and must be set aside.[33]

Congress could perform a service for the rule of law by repealing RFRA and RLUIPA, and giving guidance for acceptable accommodations of religious practice. We have seen some examples of exemptions from neutral laws or regulations that seem justified, and a couple that probably were not good decisions. After *Goldman v. Weinberger* (1986) upheld a U.S. Air Force regulation that incidentally forbade an Orthodox Jew from wearing a yarmulke while in uniform and on duty, rejecting a First Amendment free exercise of religion challenge, Congress passed a statute permitting members of the armed forces to wear an item of religious apparel while in uniform unless the Secretary of Defense determined that the wearing of the item would interfere with the member's military duties. Permission for a Muslim in prison to practice his religion by growing a beard, as an exemption from the prison's no-beard policy, in *Holt* (2015); Congress' legalization of the use of peyote in Native American religious ceremonies, as an exemption from state controlled substances laws; and the Court's decision in *Gonzalez v. O'Centro Espirita* (2006) to allow members of a small religious sect to drink a sacramental, hallucinogenic tea, as an exemption from the federal controlled substances law, seem like reasonable accommodations to protect religious liberty without doing harm to third parties. By contrast, the ability of religious employers to be exempted from the Affordable Care Act's imposed obligation to provide insurance coverage for contraception does harm innocent third parties—their female employees who are being deprived of cost-free health care access to contraception. Justice Kennedy's observation in *Makepiece Cakeshop* (2018) concerning the delicate balance that must be drawn between protection for the equal status and dignity of gay people and the general right of all people to exercise their First Amendment right of religious freedom might be taken as an invitation to Congress to work out some general guidelines. Any federal legislation that is produced on this subject should have as a centerpiece the concept that accommodations for religious liberty should be a shield for members of the faith, not a sword for use against the interests and rights of third parties.[34]

FREE SPEECH

The "freedom of speech" clause has been broadly interpreted to include not only the spoken word but also, for example, writings, artistic expression, literature, movies, and conduct that conveys a message. The Supreme Court normally subjects laws that regulate the content of speech to strict scrutiny. It has said such laws are presumptively unconstitutional, or that they must be narrowly drawn to achieve a compelling government interest.[35] Because the judicial review standards for speech content regulation are so difficult to satisfy, the courts under the direction of the Supreme Court have exempted many categories from First Amendment protection, including speech that libels or defames someone, perjury, fraudulent speech, "fighting words," speech incident to a crime, speech that creates a hostile workplace environment, speech that violates a trademark or plagiarizes another's words, "patently offensive" speech that is directed at a captive audience or broadcast on the airwaves, obscene speech, and child pornography.[36] Of course, in these categories the existence in any particular case of libelous speech, perjury, fraudulent speech, obscenity and so on must be established to the satisfaction of the court before it can be penalized.

Congress would perform a good service for free speech analysis if it legislated one quick fix and convened a study group to consider three topics where the current state of the law seems unsatisfactory. The quick fix involves hate speech as treated in *R.A.V. v. City of St. Paul* (1992). The city's Bias-Motivated Crime Ordinance punished as a misdemeanor the display of a symbol which "arouses anger, alarm, or resentment in others on the basis of race, color, creed, religion or gender." Several teenagers burned a cross on a neighboring Black family's lawn. The Court held the ordinance was "facially unconstitutional in that it prohibits otherwise permitted speech solely on the basis of the subjects the speech addresses."[37] This (and like decisions) should receive a legislative response. Hate speech can be precisely identified so it is easily recognized; it has no value; it coarsens social discourse; and it can be harmful and hurtful to targeted individuals and groups. Congress could add this to libel, obscenity, etc., as another category of speech exempt from First Amendment protection, and our free speech rights would not be diminished one iota. There is no slippery slope to be concerned about here.

The three First Amendment topics that deserve special attention are lies, speech that instigates or sets in motion terrorism or violence, and the regulation of money in politics. For lies, consider *United States v. Alvarez* (2012), which concluded that the 2005 Stolen Valor Act, making it a crime for a person to falsely claim receipt of a military decoration or medal, unconstitutionally abridges free speech. This federal law was a narrow one, and when Alvarez claimed he had received the Congressional Medal of Honor, he obviously knew his statement was false. The Court nevertheless struck down the statute because content-based restrictions are presumptively invalid, and this falsehood did not cause material harm to anyone.[38] This case is insignificant on its own, but the notion that lies should receive strict-scrutiny First Amendment protection absent material harm caused to a person or company is flawed.

The proliferation of "fake news" on social media, and the big political lie that President Joseph Biden won the 2020 election because of widespread voter fraud, are two examples among others that have caused no individualized harm but have done damage to the community and undermined the truth-seeking function of our representative democracy. The challenge is to figure out how "intentional" lies can be distinguished from opinions and honest mistakes (presumably many people believe there was or may have been widespread 2020 voter fraud), and to create a framework for penalizing such filtered-out lies without unduly compromising free speech rights.

The closest analog to terrorism speech that we have available for study is the history of the statutory and case law treatment of speech advocating the violent overthrow of government. *Gitlow v New York* (1925) upheld Benjamin Gitlow's conviction under the state's criminal anarchy law, which penalized anyone who advocates orally or in writing the necessity and duty of overthrowing organized government by force or violence or by unlawful means. The statute, said the Court, "imports a legislative determination that such utterances are so inimical to the general welfare and involve such danger of substantive evil that they may be punished under the police power, and this determination must be given great weight, and every presumption be indulged in favor of the validity of the statute." In his dissenting opinion, Justice Oliver Wendell Holmes (joined by Justice Louis Brandeis) said the free-speech question in every case is whether the words are used in such circumstances and are of such a nature as to "create a clear and present danger that they will bring about the substantive evils that the State has a right to prevent. The Socialist Gitlow and his few associates posed no such threat to the state."[39] Holmes's view would ultimately prevail in later cases.

Congress copied from the New York law in its enactment of the 1940 Smith Act, making it a crime for a person to advocate, advise or teach the duty of overthrowing any government in the United States by force or violence, or to organize or be a member of a group that advocates or teaches such a duty. During the "Red Scare" following World War II, the federal government was successful for a time in prosecuting Communists and Communist sympathizers under the Smith Act. In the leading case of *Dennis v. United States* (1951), the Supreme Court upheld the convictions of eleven leaders of the Communist Party. The Court said whether an attempt to overthrow the government of the United States poses a clear and present danger should not be determined according to the likelihood of success. The appropriate standard to apply in review of the statute is whether the gravity of the evil, discounted by its improbability, warrants a restriction on free speech. A clear and present danger existed in this case, taking into account the strength and sophistication of the organization, as well as the unstable nature of governments around the world, tension between the United States and Communist countries, and recent revolutions abroad in similar situations. As the popular fear of disloyalty abated, *Yates v. United States* (1957) overturned the convictions of fourteen members of the California Communist Party and narrowed the scope of the Smith Act. The Court said this statute does not prohibit the advocacy and teaching of the forcible overthrow of government as an abstract principle divorced from any concrete action to instigate action toward that end. The Smith Act remains on the books today at 18 U.S.C. 2385.[40]

The Court established its current standard of review for statutes that penalize speech which advocates violence or law violation in *Brandenburg v. Ohio* (1969), a state law case. Ohio's 1919 statute (one of many similar laws adopted during the first "Red Scare") made it illegal to advocate the necessity or propriety of "crime, sabotage, violence, or unlawful methods of terrorism as a means of accomplishing industrial or political reform," or assembling in a group that advocates such actions. Brandenburg invited a local television reporter to attend a meeting of organizers of the Ku Klux Klan at a farm outside Cincinnati. The reporter with a cameraman filmed the proceedings. The assembly included speeches denouncing Negros and Jews, some hooded members of the Klan wielding firearms, the burning of a wooden cross, and Brandenburg's announcement that we are marching on Congress 400,000 strong on July 4. Portions of the filmed meeting were shown on local and national television stations. The Court overturned Brandenburg's conviction on these facts, saying that its decisions have fashioned the principle that government can forbid advocacy of the use of force or of law violation only if the advocacy is "directed to inciting or producing imminent lawless action and is likely to produce such action."[41]

As Mark Tushnet has noted, this test "appears to be conjunctive: an intent element ('directed to'); a focus on words ('inciting or producing'); a temporal element (imminence); and a requirement of a close causal connection between the words and the evil to be averted ('likely to incite or produce')."[42] Such a stringent test may be inadequate to deal effectively with today's conditions. In recent years our cities have experienced violent demonstrations and protests with resulting deaths, injuries and property damage, the most high-profile case being the January 6, 2021, assault on the Capitol. What a study committee would need to consider is how to frame precise statutory language that penalizes words which instigate or set in motion terrorism or violence, without unduly intruding upon free speech.

Congress since the early 1970s has passed quite a few laws regulating the use of money in politics, for the purpose of avoiding corruption or the appearance of corruption in the political system. The Court has carefully scrutinized these laws, even though they have all been content-neutral concerning speech, for a couple of reasons. Republican government is nourished by a free exchange of ideas, so political speech has always been considered high-value speech. Also, it is logical to look for institutional bias, to be skeptical that legislators will adopt fair limitations that do not advantage themselves as incumbents in office or make life more difficult for their political opponents. However, this skepticism is not supported by the empirical evidence, which shows that Congress generally has legislated reasonable rules to govern campaign finance, and that the Court's policy choices have not been improvements.[43] Under the current complex web of federal regulations that have survived constitutional challenge, corporations, political action committees, and wealthy individuals are able to contribute and spend a lot of money to support their favored officeholders or candidates, often anonymously. Any committee that might be established should try to produce a set of recommendations that will increase the transparency of money flows in the system and impose reasonable, enforceable caps on political contributions and expenditures.

This chapter has covered three constitutional rights currently in a state of flux. Gaining some control over the use of money in politics is particularly important because that can affect everything else government does. Our treasured rights are not absolutes, and not abstractions. They must be regulated as the community develops policies to deal with issues that confront us in an ever-changing, complex world. All things considered, it is best that the regulators and keepers of the nation's ideals be our elected and accountable political leaders rather than a small body of appointed, life-tenured judges poised to decide what government cannot do.

NOTES

1. *Roe*, 410 U.S. 113; *Planned Parenthood v. Casey*, 505 U.S. 833; and *Dobbs*, 517 U.S. ___.

2. For abortion laws to 1973, see *Roe*, 410 U.S. at 118–19, 139–40, and for the ALI's Model Penal Code for abortion and early state adoptions of a version of the code, see Appendix B to the companion case of *Doe v. Bolton*, 410 U.S. 179, 205–07 (1973).

3. *Vuitch*, 402 U.S. 62.

4. *McRae*, 448 U.S. 297; Mary Ziegler, *Abortion and the Law in America: Roe v. Wade to the Present* (Cambridge, UK: Cambridge University Press, 2020), ch. 2. For the federal laws restricting funding for abortion under Medicaid and other federal programs, see Hyde Amendment and Coverage for Abortion Services kkf.org// women's-health-policy.

5. *Stenberg*, 530 U.S. 914; *Gonzalez v. Carhart*, 550 U.S. 124; Partial Birth Abortion Ban Act of 2003, 18 U.S.C. sec. 1531.

6. 18 U.S.C. sec. 1531; *Gonzalez v. Carhart,* 550 U.S. 124; and *Dobbs,* 517 U.S. ___.

7. Congress.gov/bill/117th-congress-house-bill/3755/text.

8. Women's Health Protection Act of 2022 congress.gov/bill/117th-congress/senate-bill/4132.

9. E.g., pewresearch.org/fact-tank/2022/06/13/abortion 61% say abortion should be legal in all or most cases; Abortion/Gallup Historical Trends, https://news.gallup.com>poll>abortion—Chart on responses to question: Do you think abortion should be legal under any circumstances, legal only under certain circumstances, or illegal in all circumstances?

10. *Cantwell*, 310 U.S. 296; *Murdock*, 319 U.S. 105; and *Everson*, 330 U.S. 1.

11. *Committee for Public Education and Religious Liberty v. Nyquist*, 413 U.S. 756 (1973), struck down a New York law which featured one direct and two indirect forms of aid for private elementary and secondary schools (including religious schools) that served low-income students. The program provided direct grants for maintenance and repair at schools, tuition reimbursement for low-income parents, and tax relief for middle-income parents. Citing *Board of Education v. Allen* (1968), three dissenting justices would have upheld the tuition reimbursements and tax relief provisions.

12. *Bd. Edn. v. Allen*, 392 U.S. 236; *Mueller*, 466 U.S. 388; and *Zelman*, 536 U.S. 639.

13. *Lemon*, 403 U.S. 602; *Aguilar*, 473 U.S. 402; and *Agostini*, 521 U.S. 203.

14. *Trinity Lutheran*, 582 U.S. ___; *Espinoza*, 591 U.S. ___; and *Carson*, Slip Op. 20–1088.

15. *Lamb's Chapel*, 508 U.S. 384; *Rosenberger*, 515 U.S. 819; and *Good News Club*, 533 U.S. 98. The four dissenting justices in *Rosenberger* said it was an establishment clause case, not a free speech case.

16. *Engel*, 370 U.S. 421; *Schempp*, 329 U.S. 403; *Weisman*, 505 U.S. 577; *Santa Fe Sch. Dist.*, 530 U.S. 290; and *Kennedy*, 517 U.S. ___.

17. *Wallace*, 463 U.S. 783, and *Town of Greece*, 572 U.S. 565.

18. *Lynch*, 465 U.S. 668, and *Allegheny County*, 492 U.S. 573.

19. *McCreary County*, 545 U.S. 844, and *Van Orden*, 545 U.S. 677.

20. *Sherbert*, 374 U.S. 398.

21. Christopher L. Eisgruber and Lawrence G. Sager, *Religious Freedom and the Constitution* (Cambridge: Harvard University Press, 2007), 39–44.

22. *Smith*, 494 U.S. 872.

23. Eisgruber and Sager, *Religious Freedom*, 78–79.

24. *City of Boerne*, 521 U.S. 507; RLUIPA, 42 U.S.C. ch. 21C, sec. 2000cc.

25. *Cutter*, 544 U.S. 709; *Holt*, 574 U.S. 352.

26. The Court has never explained its bifurcated approach. Probably it was protecting states' rights in the *City of Boerne*, as well as its supremacy in constitutional interpretation. Apparently, it is willing to let Congress impose limitations upon itself and the federal agencies if that is what the legislators want.to do.

27. *Gonzalez v. O'Centro Espirita*, 546 U.S. 418; *Hobby Lobby*, 573 U.S. 682.

28. *Agostini*, 521 U.S. 203, and *Trinity Lutheran*, 582 U.S. ___.

29. For the school prayer cases, see text at n. 16; for the religious display cases, see text at ns. 18 and 19.

30. *McDaniel*, 435 U.S. 618, and *Locke*, 540 U.S. 712.

31. *Sherbert*, 374 U.S. 398, and *Church of Lukumi*, 508 U.S. 520.

32. *Hobby Lobby*, 573 U.S. 682.

33. *Makepiece Cakeshop*, 584 U.S. ___.

34. *Goldman*, 476 U.S. 547; Religious Apparel: Wearing While in Uniform, 10 U.S.C. sec. 774; *Holz*, 574 U.S. 352; *Gonzalez v. O'Centro Espirita*, 546 U.S. 418; and *Makepiece Cakeshop*, 584 U.S. ___.

35. However, the regulation of commercial speech content is subject to a lowered level of scrutiny—assuming the commercial speech concerns a lawful activity and is not misleading, the regulation must be narrowly drawn to serve a substantial government interest. See the text in chapter 8 at ns.13–15.

36. This summary is compiled from a list presented by Richard Delgado and Jean Stefancic, *Must We Defend Nazis? Why the First Amendment Should Not Protect Hate Speech and White Supremacy* (New York: New York University Press, 1997), 63, where the authors state that "over the past century the courts have carved out or tolerated dozens of 'exceptions' to free speech."

37. *R.A.V.*, 505 U.S. 377, 381.

38. *Alvarez*, 567 U.S. 709.

39. *Gitlow*, 268 U.S. 652–55, 664–69 (Court opinion), and 672–73 (Holmes dissent).

40. *Dennis*, 341 U.S. 494, and *Yates*, 354 U.S. 298. The 1940 law was called the Alien Registration Act, and titles II and III dealt with aliens. Congress copied title I, section one from the 1917 Espionage Act, which had been repealed in 1921. This section punished any person who advises, counsels, urges, or in any manner causes insubordination, disloyalty, mutiny, or refusal of duty by any member of the military forces of the United States, and punished the distribution of written materials which carry such advice, etc. It is the government overthrow provisions in sections two and three of title I that have been referred to as the Smith Act, after their sponsor, Rep. Howard Smith of Virginia, and it is these provisions which are now codified in 18 U.S.C. 2385.

41. *Brandenburg*, 395 U.S. 444.

42. Mark Tushnet, *Advanced Introduction to Freedom of Expression* (Northampton, MA: Edward Elgar Publishing, 2018), 33.

43. For the campaign finance statutes and cases, see chapter 8 text at ns. 16–17, 55.

Chapter 10

The Court Should Veto Only Clear Mistakes of Congress

In theory the legislature should be predominant in a representative democracy. It expresses the will of the people and is accountable to them. The history of the Supreme Court's overrides of acts of Congress under the Fourteenth Amendment and the Bill of Rights does not suggest that this principle of majority rule should be discarded when the federal government regulates and implements our constitutional rights. In its discussion of the Court's role in our constitutional system, the report of the Presidential Commission on the Supreme Court (December 2021) observed:

> Proposals to disempower the Court generally rest on two interrelated assumptions. First, Court rulings that statutes violate the Constitution typically require exercising judgment about the meaning of the Constitution, over which reasonable people might disagree, as is often illustrated by divisions among the Justices themselves in constitutional cases. Second, in cases of reasonable disagreement over whether a law comports with the Constitution, principles of democracy necessitate that Congress and the executive branch have opportunities to check the judgments of an unelected judiciary and to advance their own views about what the Constitution requires.[1]

The commission considered a number of reform options to change the role and operation of the judiciary: Set term limits for Supreme Court judges—eighteen years, for example—long enough to ensure their independence and short enough to keep them reasonably responsive to the outcomes of democratic elections. Increase the size of the Court. Strip the Supreme Court and other federal courts of jurisdiction to hear certain kinds of cases. Impose supermajority voting requirements on courts or otherwise require them to defer to legislative judgments about constitutionality. Authorize congressional overrides of judicial decisions striking down legislation.[2] This chapter discusses these reform options, and then closes with a proposed constitutional amendment to correct some mistakes of the past concerning Congress' authority to enforce the Fourteenth Amendment, and to stipulate going forward that a federal law may be refused enforcement only by a unanimous vote of the Supreme Court.

TERM LIMITS, EXPANDED COURT SIZE, OR DENIALS OF FEDERAL COURT JURISDICTION

The Court's size could be expanded by statute, but term limits presumably would require a constitutional amendment. Article III says federal judges shall hold their office "during good Behavior." If this equates to life tenure, as historical practice and some commentators suggest, term limits could only be imposed by a constitutional amendment. By contrast the Constitution does not say anything about the size of the Supreme Court, and Congress has changed the Court's size seven times, most recently in 1869 when it increased the Court's membership to nine justices.[3] Neither of these two reform options—term limits or an expanded Court—would change the relationship between the Court and Congress in constitutional interpretations. Neither would really change the role or operation of the Court. The justices (however many they may be, and however long their tenure) by majority vote could still overturn federal laws that they decide are incompatible with the Constitution for some reason.

Congress has considerable authority over the jurisdiction of the lower federal courts and the appellate jurisdiction of the Supreme Court. Article III vests the nation's judicial power in "one supreme Court," and in such lower courts as the Congress may from time to time "ordain and establish." Article III, section two, grants to the Court original jurisdiction in a few specific categories of cases, affecting ambassadors, ministers and consuls, and those in which a state is a party.[4] Erwin Chemerinsky has observed that to date the Supreme Court's original jurisdiction has been exercised mostly to resolve conflicts between two or more states.[5] In the other cases to which the judicial power of the United States extends, article III confers "appellate Jurisdiction" on the Supreme Court, "with such Exceptions, and under such Regulations as the Congress shall make." Most of the Supreme Court's reviews of federal and state laws for compliance with the Constitution, as amended—including all the cases discussed in this book—have been exercises of appellate jurisdiction, subject to the exceptions and regulations authority of Congress. Michael Perry and Charles Black have observed that Congress could use its article III powers to preserve and protect majoritarian decision-making under the Constitution.[6]

The Supreme Court consistently has held that the power of Congress to create lower federal courts includes the power to define and regulate their jurisdiction. In an early example, *Sheldon v. Sill* (1850) enforced the statutory restrictions on the lower federal courts' diversity jurisdiction, observing, "Courts created by statute can have no jurisdiction but such as the statute confers."[7] Supreme Court decisions in 1938 and 1943 upheld the withdrawals of federal court jurisdiction to issue injunctions in labor disputes, or to hear civil actions under the Emergency Price Control Act of 1942, respectively. For a unanimous Court, Chief Justice Harlan Fiske Stone succinctly stated the constitutional rule on lower federal court jurisdiction in the 1943 case, *Lockerty v. Phillips*: All federal courts other than the Supreme Court derive their jurisdiction "wholly from the exercise of the authority to 'ordain and establish' inferior courts, conferred on Congress." This power to ordain and establish lower federal courts includes the power of "investing them with jurisdiction either limited, concurrent, or exclusive, and of withholding jurisdiction from them in the exact degrees and character which to Congress may seem proper for the public good."[8]

The power of Congress to regulate and control the appellate jurisdiction of the Supreme Court is equally clear. Chief Justice Oliver Ellsworth, one of the framers of the Constitution, had been a member of the convention's committee on detail that drafted the article III text giving Congress the power to regulate and to make exceptions to the Supreme Court's appellate jurisdiction. He announced the rule for the Court's appellate jurisdiction in *Wiscart v. Dauchy* (1796): "Here, then, is the ground, and the only ground, on which we can sustain an appeal. If Congress has provided no rule to regulate our proceedings, we cannot exercise our jurisdiction, and if the rule is provided, we cannot depart from it." Justice Samuel Chase said in a 1799 Court decision that "the political truth is that the disposal of the judicial power (except in a few specified instances) belongs to congress." Chief Justice John Marshall held in *United States v. More* (1805) that the Supreme Court possessed no criminal appellate jurisdiction because the Congress had not granted it. In *Durousseau v. United States* (1810), he emphasized again that the Court could exercise appellate jurisdiction only when and to the extent Congress confers it in explicit terms. Chief Justice Roger Taney avowed in *Barry v. Mercein* (1847): "By the constitution of the United States, the Supreme Court possesses no appellate power in any case, unless conferred upon it by act of Congress; nor can it when conferred be exercised in any other form or by any other mode of proceeding than that which the law prescribes."[9]

In a dramatic and high-profile case, when a Mississippi newspaper editor in military custody filed a habeas corpus petition to obtain his release, as authorized by the 1867 Habeas Corpus Act, the Congress, worried that the Supreme Court might interfere with its reconstruction program in the South, repealed the law to prevent the Court from considering the appeal. Chief

Justice Salmon Chase in *Ex parte McCardle* (1869), in a unanimous opinion, upheld Congress' withdrawal of jurisdiction and dismissed the case. He said that the Court could not inquire into the motives of the legislature. "We can only examine its power under the Constitution; and the power to make exceptions to the appellate jurisdiction of this court is given. Without jurisdiction the court cannot proceed in any case. Jurisdiction is power to declare the law, and when it ceases to exist, the only function remaining to the court is that of announcing the fact and dismissing the case."[10] In *The Francis Wright* (1881), upholding Congress' power to confine the Supreme Court's reviews in admiralty cases to questions of law, the Court said, "While the appellate power of this court extends to all cases within the judicial power of the United States, actual jurisdiction under the power is confined within such limits as Congress sees fit to prescribe. . . . What those powers shall be, and to what extent they shall be exercised, are, and always have been, subjects of legislative control."[11]

Constitutional scholars have produced many studies of jurisdiction-stripping.[12] According to Henry Monaghan, the "traditional" or "conventional" opinion expressed in the literature is that there are no limitations on the ability of Congress to withhold or withdraw jurisdiction from the federal court system (except for the narrow original jurisdiction of the Supreme Court). For this position, "impressive academic support exists, including not only Herbert Wechsler, Charles Black, and Gerald Gunther but also William Van Alstyne, Paul Bator and Martin Redish." However, other commentators have claimed that in the exercise of its article III powers the Congress has a duty to comply with the other provisions in the Constitution and Bill of Rights. It cannot deny a federal judicial forum to adjudicate a case or controversy, the theory goes, if to do so would violate someone's rights.[13] This line of argument assumes Congress cannot be the authoritative decision-maker on the question of whether its lawmaking complies with the Constitution, that its interpretations must always be subject to a challenge in court if anyone's right might be implicated. This assumption is compatible with the doctrine of judicial supremacy but not with the republican principle of majority rule by the people's elected and accountable representatives.

After more than two hundred years of precedent holding that article III places within the unfettered control of Congress the jurisdiction of the lower federal courts and the appellate jurisdiction of the Supreme Court, *Boumediene v. Bush* (2008) refused to abide by a congressional denial of jurisdiction. Congress had passed a law that said the aliens who had been captured abroad in the war on terror and were being held in confinement at Guantanamo Bay, Cuba, as alleged enemy combatants, could not file for habeas corpus relief in the federal courts. The Court in *Boumediene* noted article I, section nine of the Constitution provides that the writ of habeas corpus "shall not be suspended" unless the public safety requires it in cases of invasion or rebellion. Congress had not complied with the requirements for habeas corpus suspension—there had been no invasion or rebellion—and the Court held that the law's procedures for deciding cases in the military tribunals at Guantanamo Bay were not an adequate substitute for potential habeas relief in the courts.[14]

Following *Boumediene*, Congress arguably has no article III authority to deny federal court jurisdiction whenever a federal law implicates someone's rights. Even prior to this case, the jurisdiction-denial authority of Congress would not have enabled it to insulate its laws from judicial overturn. Article III only allows Congress to control the jurisdiction of the lower federal courts and the appellate jurisdiction of the Supreme Court. It does not provide authority to control the jurisdiction of state courts or the original jurisdiction of the Supreme Court. A state court might refuse to enforce a federal law that in its opinion violates the Constitution. Or a state government that believes a federal statute is unconstitutional could ask the Supreme Court to exercise its original jurisdiction and overturn the statute. For example, the landmark case of *South Carolina v. Katzenbach* (1966), upholding the Voting Rights Act of 1965 against the state's challenge, was a decision issued under the Court's original jurisdiction.[15]

While a constitutional amendment that denies jurisdiction to any court in the United States to review federal laws in all cases or in a meaningful range of cases—for example, congressional interpretations/enforcements of the Fourteenth Amendment and the Bill of Rights—would overcome these limitations, it is unlikely that such a dramatic removal of judicial review authority to second-guess Congress could gain the approval of two-thirds of the members in both houses of Congress and three-fourths of the states. Nor is it clear that such an experiment would be a good idea. A constitutional amendment to strip the courts of jurisdiction to review federal law on a single issue (the Presidential Commission mentions abortion or a hypothetical wealth tax) or on a narrow set of issues might be more likely to be adopted, but it would not change much and is hardly worth the effort.

CONGRESSIONAL OVERRIDES OF JUDICIAL OPINIONS

The Presidential Commission considered a reform to empower Congress to override judicial opinions striking down legislation. I discuss a broader proposal, to allow Congress to override judicial decisions with which it disagrees, including opinions upholding a state law challenged on constitutional grounds. Some of the Supreme Court's worst decisions have been ones that gave its national stamp of approval to contested state laws. For example, *Plessy v. Ferguson* (1896) decided that Louisiana's racial segregation law was "reasonable," and *Buck v. Bell* (1927) upheld Virginia's eugenics law that authorized the sterilization of allegedly feeble-minded persons.[16]

Congressional overrides of decisions by the Supreme Court (or any court) would necessitate a constitutional amendment in order to effectuate reform. The amendment might say that any law of Congress which overturns a judicial opinion is exempt from judicial veto in any court. Absent such an amendment, override laws, like any other laws, would be vulnerable to a challenge in court. The modern history of Congress-Supreme Court interactions demonstrates this point.

Congress has sometimes responded to Supreme Court decisions by legislating a new rule to apply in future cases, with mixed results. Successful congressional overriding statutes either drew no litigation challenge or succeeded in court, as in the following examples: The Pregnancy Discrimination Act of 1978 requires public and private employers to include pregnancy as a covered benefit in their health insurance plans. This overruled Supreme Court decisions holding that exclusions for pregnancy do not constitute unlawful gender discrimination under the equal protection clause. After *Zurcher v. Stanford Daily* (1978) approved the issuance of a warrant to search for and seize evidence in the possession of a newspaper, pertaining to criminal activity by third parties, Congress in the Privacy Protection Act of 1980 generally prohibited such searches and required officers to proceed by a subpoena instead. The Equal Access Act of 1984 says public secondary schools that receive federal funds must permit student groups to conduct meetings in open public forums, on school premises, without regard to the "religious, political, philosophical or other content of the speech" at such meetings. The law was a response to decisions by school boards and courts which had excluded religious clubs and prayer groups from open public forum opportunities that were made available to other student groups. The restrictions had been prompted by Supreme Court opinions in cases like *Engel v. Vitale* (1962) (no prayer in public school) and *School District of Abington Township v. Schempp* (1963) (no Bible reading in public school). Notwithstanding its earlier decisions, the Supreme Court in *Board of Education of the Westside Community Schools* v. *Mergens* (1990) accepted the government's contention that the new federal law does not violate the First Amendment ban on the establishment of religion. After *Goldman v. Weinberger* (1986) upheld a U.S. Air Force regulation that incidentally did not allow an Orthodox Jew to wear a yarmulke while in uniform and on duty, rejecting a First Amendment free exercise of religion challenge, Congress passed a statute to change the regulation. The 1987 Civil Rights Restoration Act—based upon findings that Court decisions had narrowed or cast doubt upon the proper enforcement of Titles VII and IX of the 1964 Civil Rights Act, a section in the 1973 Rehabilitation Act, and the 1975 Age Discrimination Act—clarifies that the "program or activity" addressed in these federal laws refers to all the operations of the affected government agencies, educational institutions, and private employers. The 1991 Civil Rights Act responded to a series of Supreme Court decisions in 1988 and 1989 that narrowed the scope of the nation's equal employment laws. The act supports affirmative action for minorities and women, counteracting the Court's concern about "quotas"; reaffirms the disparate impact rule in racial discrimination cases, established in *Griggs v. Duke Power Co.* (1971) and then weakened in *Wards Cove Packing Co. v. Antonio* (1989); authorizes monetary damages for intentional unlawful discrimination; and finally, makes it easier to challenge discriminations in seniority systems.[17]

Congress in other circumstances has failed to change public policy following Supreme Court decisions because the Court rejected the new rule, as happened in the following three examples delivered by the Rehnquist Court (1986–2005) under the Bill of Rights: The Warren Court, in *Miranda v. Arizona* (1966), extended the Fifth Amendment ban on compelled self-incrimination in a criminal case to include protection for suspects in police interrogations. Until Congress and the states could establish effective rules to protect people's constitutional rights to silence and to counsel in these situations, the justices crafted an advisory warning that the police had to give to any person being held in custody or otherwise detained. The suspect could waive his rights and agree to answer questions or make a statement, but unless the prosecution could demonstrate that such warnings and waiver had been given and received, no evidence obtained from the interrogation could be used at the trial.[18] Two years after *Miranda*, Congress enacted a provision in the Omnibus Crime Control and Safe Streets Act of 1968 to allow a suspect's statement made while in police custody to be admitted if it was given voluntarily, as determined by the trial judge in the totality of the circumstances, including the time elapsing between the arrest and arraignment of the defendant making the confession; whether the defendant knew the nature of the offense with which he was charged or of which he was suspected; whether he was advised or knew that he was not required to make any statement, and that any such statement could be used against him; and whether he was without assistance of counsel when questioned and giving his confession. This evidence-admissibility rule generally tracked the *Miranda* warnings but allowed trial courts more discretion to admit confessions into evidence.[19]

Ignored for several decades, the legislative rule finally came up to the Rehnquist Court for consideration in *Dickerson v. United States* (2000). The petitioner in *Dickerson*, indicted for bank robbery and related federal crimes, moved to suppress a statement he made to the FBI on the ground that he had not received *Miranda* warnings before being interrogated. The Supreme Court held that since *Miranda* is a "constitutional decision" that governs the admissibility of statements made during custodial interrogation in both state and federal courts, it could not be overruled by an act of Congress. The Court suppressed the alleged bank robber's statement.[20]

After the Supreme Court in *Texas v. Johnson* (1989) held that a Texas statute, which made it a crime to desecrate the American flag in a way that the actor knew would offend onlookers, is an unconstitutional violation of free speech as applied to an individual who had burned a flag during a political protest, Congress responded by passing the Flag Protection Act of 1989. The act punishes anyone who "knowingly mutilates, defames, physically defiles, burns . . . or tramples upon" an American flag. The Court in *United States v. Eichman* (1990) held that a prosecution for burning the flag would be inconsistent with the First Amendment. Flag burning is "expressive conduct." While the federal law admittedly contains no content-based limitation, the government's interest in protecting the flag as a symbol of the nation and certain national ideals is related to the suppression of free expression. Reasonable people could agree with the four dissenters in this case that the freedom of speech would not be harmed if a "speaker" has to choose some means other than an act of flag destruction to express his ideas.[21]

City of Boerne v. Flores (1997) rebuffed Congress' request in a 1993 law that the Court restore the strict scrutiny standard of review it had used in free-exercise-of-religion cases prior to 1990. This law was Congress' response to a 1990 Supreme Court decision holding that neutral state laws of general applicability could apply to religious practices, even though they impose a burden on those practices and are not supported by a compelling governmental interest. Although I personally favor the Court's 1990 test rather than the strict scrutiny review standard Congress sought to reinstate—in my opinion, so long as a law is neutral to all persons affected, special exceptions should not have to be carved out for religious adherents—the decision in *City of Boerne* is typical of the Supreme Court's longstanding refusal to defer to Congress, the federal agency named in the Fourteenth Amendment to enforce its provisions.[22]

A constitutional amendment might provide that any law of Congress which overrides a judicial opinion is exempt from veto in any court. This reform option would give Congress the final voice on constitutional issues that have been taken up in the courts. It invites comparison with section thirty-three of the Canadian Charter of Rights and Freedoms (1982), known as the "notwithstanding clause," which says that "Parliament or the legislature of any province may expressly declare in an Act of Parliament or of the legislature, as the case may be, that the Act . . . shall operate notwithstanding a provision included in section two or in sections seven to fifteen of this Charter." These sections in the aggregate closely resemble the American Bill of Rights and Fourteenth Amendment. Section two, titled "Fundamental Freedoms," guarantees to everyone the freedoms of religion, opinion and expression, press, peaceable assembly, and association, obviously tracking our own First Amendment. Sections seven through fourteen are titled "Legal Rights." Section seven, like our due process clause, says everyone has the right to life, liberty and security of the person, and the right not to be deprived thereof except in accordance with principles of fundamental justice. Like the criminal law provisions embodied in our Fourth through Eighth Amendments, sections eight to fourteen of the Canadian Charter guaranty to everyone the following rights, among others: to be secure against an unreasonable search and seizure, to enjoy *Miranda*-type rights if arrested or detained, to be given prompt notice of any alleged offense, to receive a prompt and public trial, which may be by jury in serious cases, to hire counsel to assist in one's defense, to not be a witness against oneself, to not be exposed to double jeopardy, to not be denied bail without just cause, and to not suffer a cruel and unusual punishment. Finally, section fifteen, titled "Equality Rights," resembles our own equal protection clause in the Fourteenth Amendment. Subsection one says every individual is equal before and under the law, and has the right to the equal protection and equal benefit of the law, without discrimination based on race, national or ethnic origin, color, religion, sex, age, or mental or physical disability. Subsection two says subsection one does not preclude an affirmative action program to ameliorate the conditions of people disadvantaged because of their race or other mentioned criteria.[23]

The congressional override reform option differs from the Canadian notwithstanding clause in several key respects. The override is limited to court decisions; the notwithstanding clause allows the legislature to insulate an act either prospectively or in response to a court decision. The override is available only to Congress; the notwithstanding clause is available to Parliament or a provincial legislature. The override has no sunset provision; a law enacted under the authority of the notwithstanding clause expires after five years unless it is expressly renewed by the legislature. The override applies to all constitutional issues; the notwithstanding clause applies to sections two and seven through fifteen of the Canadian Charter.

The Canadian Parliament has never used the notwithstanding clause, and only a few of the provinces have used it, a few times.[24] One of the reasons for this might be the wording of the clause, which allows the federal or provincial legislature to insulate an act from one or more of the fundamental freedoms and rights protected by the Charter. By contrast, the congressional override focuses on judicial opinions. It authorizes the legislature to override a court's opinion about a constitutional right, i.e., to resolve an institutional disagreement about a right, not to nullify the right itself. This probably means the congressional override authority would be used more often than the notwithstanding clause has been used in Canada. The likely repercussions on our government operations in the states and nation are difficult to predict, and for this reason the congressional override authority is not a desirable reform.

DEFERENTIAL STANDARD OR SUPERMAJORITY VOTE REQUIREMENT FOR REVIEWS OF FEDERAL LAWS

Judicial deference to laws of Congress would be consistent with much constitutional history and commentary. The framers' remarks at the constitutional convention, Alexander Hamilton's and Chief Justice Marshall's expressed rationales for judicial review, the cases decided in the first eighty years of the republic, and the opinions of prominent constitutional scholars and judges since then, all offer support for the idea that federal laws should be enforced absent a clear constitutional violation. The framers at the constitutional convention who participated in the debate on the council of revision plan conceived of the judicial review function in narrow terms. James Madison and John Mercer advocated an executive-judicial veto power over congressional bills but they did not believe that enacted laws should be controllable in the courts. Their allies in the debate, James Wilson and George Mason, favored up front judicial participation in vetoes of bills because of their expectation or understanding that once laws are passed, they would never be struck down in the courts, even if they are unwise, unjust, or pernicious, unless they are also "plainly unconstitutional." Elbridge Gerry and Luther Martin, successful opponents of the council of revision, said that judges would have a legitimate role to play in striking down laws which clearly violate the Constitution, but judges should never be treated as statesmen, involve themselves in public policy, or act as guardians of the rights and interests of the people, which are the responsibility of the legislature.[25]

Hamilton in *Federalist Paper No. 78* said the federal judiciary could refuse to enforce a federal law if it is contrary to the "manifest tenor" of the Constitution, or there happens to be an "irreconcilable variance" between the law and the Constitution. Chief Justice Marshall in *Marbury v. Madison* (1803) gave three examples of when the Court should not enforce a law because it conflicts with the Constitution. In his illustrations, the Constitution spoke in precise terms—no tax on any state's exports, no bill of attainder or ex post facto law, and no treason except on the testimony of two witnesses or a confession in open court—and the hypothetical statutes of Congress he proffered clearly violated these specific prohibitions, by imposing a tax on exports of cotton, tobacco, or flour; by passing a bill of attainder or an ex post facto law; or by changing the Constitution's evidentiary rule on treason with a declaration that one witness, or a confession out of court, is sufficient to convict a person of treason. Hamilton and Marshall thus implicitly assumed in these observations that ordinarily the federal courts should be expected to enforce the federal statutes brought to them in cases and controversies. Only in the event of an incontrovertible conflict between the Constitution and the statute should the judgment of the legislature be overturned.[26]

As discussed in chapter 1, from the founding until 1870 the Court upheld federal statutes in all important cases except for one.[27] As the Supreme Court began to override some federal laws regulating the economy and protecting civil rights during the last third of the nineteenth century, some commentators and judges argued that judicial review should be cabined by deference to the nation's legislature in all doubtful cases. For example, Harvard law professor James Bradley Thayer, in a classic 1893 article, said the Supreme Court should declare an act of Congress unconstitutional "only when those who have the right to make laws have not merely made a mistake, but have made a very clear one—so clear that it is not open to rational question." In a subsequent book on Chief Justice Marshall, he pointed out the negative consequences that flow from a regular reliance on judicial review of legislation: It should be remembered that the exercise of the power of judicial review "is always attended with a serious evil, namely, that the correction of legislative mistakes comes from the outside." The tendency of a common and easy resort to judicial review is to "dwarf the political capacity of the people, and to deaden its sense of moral responsibility."[28]

Thayer influenced Justices Oliver Wendell Holmes, Louis Brandeis, Felix Frankfurter, and Judge Learned Hand, among others. Concerning Supreme Court reviews of Congress, Holmes said, "I do not think the United States would come to an end if we lost our power to declare an act of Congress void." Judge Hand observed in an often-quoted statement from his essay on the Bill of Rights, "For myself it would be most unwelcome to be ruled by a bevy of Platonic Guardians, even if I knew how to choose them, which I most assuredly do not. If they were in charge, I would miss the stimulus of living in a society where I have, at least theoretically, some part in the direction of public affairs. Of course I know how illusory would be the belief that my vote determined anything, but nevertheless when I go to the polls I have a satisfaction in the sense that we are all engaged in a common venture."[29] Hand also said: "A society so riven that the spirit of moderation is gone, no court *can* save; a society where that spirit flourishes, no court *need* save; and in a society which evades its responsibility by thrusting upon courts the nurture of that spirit, that spirit in the end will perish."[30]

Jeremy Waldron, in his book *Law and Disagreement* (1999), has criticized the Supreme Court's dominant role in defining and regulating our rights:

> Issues such as the following have had to be dealt with in the United States, as matters of constitutional right: abortion, affirmative action, campaign finance reform, criminal procedure in capital cases, drug use in religious ceremonies, defamation in relation to free speech, gun control, hate speech, homelessness, immigrants' rights, land use restrictions, panhandling, pornography, reapportionment, school prayer, voter registration, welfare, and zoning. We all know that these are matters fraught with difficulty and moral complexity, matters on which reasonable people disagree—including reasonable citizens, reasonable legislators, and reasonable judges.

In view of the inevitability of disagreement about rights among reasonable people, said Waldron, in a functioning democratic society there is no reason to believe that an unelected body of nine people in robes should have the power to strike down legislative judgments with which they disagree, sometimes on a vote of five to four. The practice of rights-based judicial review of legislation often is defended by "pointing to the possibility that democratic majoritarian procedures may yield unjust or tyrannical outcomes. And so they *may*. But so may any procedure that purports to solve the problem of social choice in the face of disagreements about what counts as injustice or what counts as tyranny," including the majority votes of Supreme Court judges. In a follow-up article, Waldron noted that in democratic countries around the world, which do not allow legislation to be invalidated by judicial review, such as Britain, Canada, Australia, and New Zealand, the people have regularly decided by ordinary legislative procedures their contested fundamental rights issues. "The quality of these debates . . . make nonsense of the claim that legislators are incapable of addressing such issues responsibly—just as the outcomes of those proceedings cast doubt on the familiar proposition that popular majorities will not uphold the rights of minorities."[31]

The Constitution provides apparent authority for Congress to impose by statute a rational basis review standard (or a similar deferential review standard) on the federal courts. Article I, section eight authorizes it to make all laws necessary and proper for carrying into execution its own powers, and "all other Powers vested by this Constitution in the Government of the United States, or in any Department or Officer thereof." This necessary and proper clause, sometimes called the "sweeping clause," thus empowers Congress to enact laws for carrying into execution the executive and judicial powers of the United States, an authority which it has used regularly and often for the executive branch. There are now fifteen executive departments and many more department units and independent agencies (collectively, the "agencies"), all of them created by Congress and subject to its direction. Congress establishes general policies for agencies to pursue, details their jurisdiction and powers, dictates priorities, prescribes rules for agency decision making, overturns decisions with which it disagrees, uses oversight hearings to maintain effective supervision, and exercises a systemic influence over executive operations.[32]

Congress has done nothing comparable to control the operations of the federal judiciary, probably out of respect for judicial independence. Although the sweeping clause would seem to authorize legislation that requires the federal courts to use a deferential rational basis review standard for federal laws, two reasons counsel against the attempt. State courts would not be covered. More importantly, the Supreme Court would probably reject such a statute. When Congress passed a law to require the Court to resurrect its strict-scrutiny standard of review for state laws that impose a burden on the free exercise of religion, *City of Boerne v. Flores* (1997) overturned the law as a violation of the separation of powers principle and an invasion of the judges' exclusive interpretive power under the Fourteenth Amendment. The Court applied its own review standard in the case.[33]

A constitutional amendment that says no court may overturn a federal law unless there is no rational basis for the legislative judgment probably would not effectively transfer interpretive power and responsibility from the judiciary to Congress. As the Presidential Commission notes, this reform option's success would depend upon "the extent to which judges were willing to internalize an externally imposed deference standard."[34] It is contrary to human nature to expect that judges will perpetually submerge their own strongly-held opinions and enforce laws that they believe are unconstitutional. While the Court from 1937 to 1995 applied a rational basis review standard to uphold Congress' broad-ranging regulations of the economy, since then it has voided several laws enacted under the article I commerce clause or spending clause authority. In doing so, the justices applied their own constitutional understanding without mentioning the rational basis review standard. For example, *Lopez v. United States* (1995) and *United States v. Morrison* (2000) refused to allow Congress to prohibit guns in schools, or to provide a civil remedy for female victims of violent crime, respectively. The Court in both cases included a statement that "whether particular operations affect interstate commerce sufficiently to come under the constitutional power of Congress to regulate them is ultimately a judicial rather than a legislative question, and can be settled finally only by this Court."[35]

National Federation of Independent Business v. Sebelius (2012) represented another silent abandonment of the rational basis review standard for economic regulations. The 2010 Affordable Care Act, designed to increase the number of Americans who are covered by health insurance and to decrease the cost of medical care, was the signature legislative achievement of President Barack Obama's first term in office. The law's individual mandate required most persons to acquire and maintain a minimum level of health insurance. Persons who fail to comply with this obligation had to make a "shared responsibility payment" to the federal government, collected by the IRS with their tax return. The law also expanded the scope of Medicaid coverage for poor people by loosening the eligibility requirements. Federal funding would cover the states' increased costs, but if a state refused to implement the new eligibility rules, it could lose its federal Medicaid funds. The Eleventh Circuit Court of Appeals struck down the individual mandate under the commerce clause but upheld the Medicaid expansion as an exercise of Congress' power to spend money with conditions.

In his five-to-four opinion for the Supreme Court in *Independent Business v. Sibelius*, Chief Justice John Roberts overturned the lower court's decision on both points. He agreed the individual mandate was not a regulation of commerce, but he saved it by characterizing it as a permissible tax. He then held that the Medicaid expansion exceeded Congress' authority under the spending clause. Four dissenting justices would have struck down the entire law because the individual mandate and the Medicaid expansion were both unconstitutional, and without these provisions Congress would not have passed the law. Even though health care represents 18 percent of the nation's economy, and Congress had spent nearly two years in a detailed drafting effort to improve insurance coverage and lower medical costs in the economy, only Justices Ruth Bader Ginsburg and Sonia Sotomayor were willing to uphold the law in its entirety.[36]

A supermajority vote requirement for judicial reviews of federal law may be briefly discussed. This is largely relevant for state courts and the Supreme Court. Federal district judges preside alone or on three-judge panels, so district court decisions are unanimous or two to one. Three-judge panels typically preside in federal courts of appeal cases, with opinions being unanimous or two to one. Although the Supreme Court operates by majority vote, article III is silent on the subject, and Congress under its article I sweeping clause authority would seem to have the power to impose a supermajority vote rule by statute. Yet the same two reasons that counseled against enactment of a statutory deferential standard for judicial reviews of federal law apply here. State courts would be unaffected, and the Court would likely reject a supermajority vote requirement as an unconstitutional interference with its independent decision-making authority. A constitutional amendment to impose the rule on all courts would probably prevent some federal laws from being overridden. However, as the Presidential Commission points out, "court majorities may be able to achieve their preferred outcomes despite a super-majority requirement by narrowly interpreting laws rather than finding them unconstitutional."[37]

A PROPOSED CONSTITUTIONAL AMENDMENT

None of the options discussed by the commission would effectively transfer appropriate policy-making authority from the Supreme Court to Congress, a change that is especially needed in cases involving the Bill of Rights and the Fourteenth Amendment. Here is a constitutional amendment worth considering:

> The Fourteenth Amendment requires that the states provide equal protection of the laws for the life, liberty, and property of people subject to their jurisdiction. Congress may enforce this state duty by appropriate legislation directed at private actors or public officials. Congress in making laws has an obligation to interpret the Constitution as amended, including the Bill of Rights and the Fourteenth Amendment. If any court overturns a federal law on constitutional grounds, the opinion is automatically stayed until it is appealed to the Supreme Court and is affirmed by a unanimous vote. The law remains enforceable unless overturned in this manner. The unanimous vote rule also applies to any federal law reviewed by the Supreme Court in an exercise of its original jurisdiction.

Although the Presidential Commission discussed a supermajority vote rule, a unanimous vote rule is required to minimize the possibility of federal laws being overruled in cases where reasonable people disagree on the merits. Among the many doubtful cases which have been decided by a supermajority vote are, for example, *Dred Scott v. Sandford* (1857) (seven to two) and the *Civil Rights Cases* (1883) (eight to one), and more recently, *Dickerson v. United States* (2000) (seven to two), *United States v. Stevens* (2010) (eight to one), and *Independent Business v. Sibelius* (2012) (seven to two, just discussed). Two justices in *Dred Scott* persuasively argued that the article IV, section three authority granted to Congress to "make all needful Rules and Regulations" in the federal territories empowered it to ban slavery in those territories. Justice John Marshall Harlan insisted in the *Civil Rights Cases* that the state action doctrine should not be applied to limit Congress' enforcement power in section five of the Fourteenth Amendment. Justice Antonin Scalia (joined by Justice Clarence Thomas) in his *Dickerson* dissent voted to uphold the Omnibus Crime Control Act because although it departed from the *Miranda* warnings template fashioned in an earlier Supreme Court decision, it permitted only voluntary confessions to be used at a trial, which is the objective of the Fifth Amendment's self-incrimination clause. Justice Samuel Alito in *United States v. Stevens* voted to enforce a law which penalized acts of horrific animal cruelty because he did not consider these actions to be deserving of "free speech" protection.[38]

This proposed constitutional amendment preserves the basic elements and functioning of the government and the Constitution, and yet also embraces potentially fundamental change. The conservative features are the following: All the existing case law would remain in place unless and until modified by new federal laws. All the courts under the direction of the Supreme Court would continue to engage in judicial reviews of state laws and executive actions, and federal laws and executive actions. The unanimous vote requirement would not apply to cases involving state law. Unlike the jurisdiction-stripping and congressional-override reform options considered by the commission, which remove from the judiciary any authority to override Congress on a specified issue or set of issues, under the unanimous vote proposal the Supreme Court retains its status as the ultimate interpreter of the Constitution. It may uphold a challenged federal law by majority vote, or else override the law by consensus.

This reform proposal is responsive to history and republican political theory. The three clarifications—that the states have an affirmative obligation under the Fourteenth Amendment to protect the life, liberty, and property of people subject to their jurisdiction, that Congress can enforce this duty by appropriate legislation which reaches private or public actors, and that Congress can independently interpret the Bill of Rights and the Fourteenth Amendment—are admittedly big changes to how our government has long operated, but they are justified by the original meanings of the Constitution as amended. They correct mistakes of the past rooted in congressional passivity and judicial hubris. The unanimous vote requirement going forward also entails a fundamental change in the relationship between the judiciary and Congress. This too is justified by the history of interactions between the Supreme Court and Congress. The Court seldom has exposed Congress to have made a clear constitutional mistake in its legislation, and in some important rulings has seriously diminished the ability of Congress to protect private rights and promote good public policies. We deserve better.

NOTES

1. Presidential Commission on the Supreme Court of the United States, *Draft Final Report* December 7, 2021, 152.

2. Ibid., ch. 2 (membership and size of the Court), ch. 3 (term limits), and ch. 4 at 153.

3. Ibid., 67–69, 73–74 (size), and ch. 3 (term limits).

4. The Presidential Commission's *Report* discusses "Proposals to Restrict the Supreme Court's Jurisdiction," 154–69.

5. Erwin Chemerinsky, *Federal Jurisdiction* (New York: Wolters Klewer, 8th ed., 2021), 738.

6. Ibid., 215–16.

7. *Sheldon*, 49 U.S. 441.

8. *Lockerty*, 319 U.S. 182. The 1938 case upholding congressional limitations on court jurisdiction to issue injunctions in labor disputes was *Lauf v. E.G., Shinner and Co.*, 303 U.S. 323.

9. *Wiscart*, 3 U.S. 321; *More*, 7 U.S. 159; *Durousseau*, 10 U.S. 307; and *Mercein*, 46 U.S. 103.

10. *McCardle*, 74 U.S. 506.

11. *The Francis Wright*, 105 U.S. 381.

12. See, e.g., Michael C. Dorf, "Congressional Power to Strip State Courts of Jurisdiction," 97 *Texas Law Review* 1, 4 (2018); Gerald Gunther, "Congressional Power to Curtail Federal Court Jurisdiction: An Opinionated Guide to the Ongoing Debate," 36 *Stanford Law Review* 895, 896–97 (1984); Mark Tushnet and Jennifer Jaff, "Why the Debate Over Congress' Power to Restrict the Jurisdiction of the Federal Courts Is Unending," 72 *Georgetown Law Journal* 1311, 1319–20 (1984); Martin H. Redish, "Constitutional Limitations on Congressional Power to Control Federal Jurisdiction: A Reaction to Professor Sager," 77 *Northwestern Law Review* 143 (1982); Lawrence Gene Sager, "Forward: Constitutional Limits on Congress's Authority to Regulate the Jurisdiction of the Federal Courts," 95 *Harvard Law Review* 17 (1981); and Henry M. Hart, Jr., "The Power of Congress to Limit the Jurisdiction of Federal Courts, An Exercise in Dialectic," 66 *Harvard Law Review* 1362 (1953).

13. Henry Monaghan, "Jurisdiction Stripping Circa 2020: What the Dialogue (Still) Has to Teach Us," 69 *Duke Law Journal* 1, 15 (2019).

14. *Boumediene*, 553 U.S. 723. Heather P. Scribner, "A Fundamental Misconception of Separation of Powers: *Boumediene v. Bush*," 14 *Texas Review of Law and Policy* 90 (2009–2010) has a good discussion of this decision and the statutes and cases leading up to it.

15. *South Carolina*, 338 U.S. 301.

16. *Plessy*, 163 U.S. 561; *Buck*, 274 U.S. 200.

17. Pregnancy Discrimination Act of 1978, 42 U.S.C. sec. 2000 (c)(k); Privacy Protection Act of 1980, 42 U.S.C. sec. 2000aa; Equal Access Act of 1984, 20 U.S.C. secs. 4071–74; Religious Apparel: Wearing While in Uniform, 10 U.S.C. sec. 774; Civil Rights Restoration Act of 1987, Pub. L. No. 100–259, codified at various places in the United States Code; Civil Rights Act of 1991, Pub. L. No. 102–166, codified at various places in the United. States Code; *Zurcher v. Stanford Daily*, 436 U.S. 574 (1978); *Goldman v. Weinberger*, 476 U.S. 547 (1986); and *Westside Community Schools v. Mergens*, 496 U.S. 226 (1990). See generally Abner J. Mikva and Jeff Bleich, "When Congress Overrules the Court," 79 *California Law Review* 729 (1991); Ira C. Lupu, "Statutes Revolving in Constitutional Law Orbits," 79 *Virginia Law Review* 1 (1993); and Daniel J. Meltzer, "Congress, Courts, and Constitutional Remedies," 86 *Georgetown Law Journal* 2537 (1998).

18. *Miranda*, 384 U.S. 436, 467 (1966).

19. Omnibus Crime Control and Safe Streets Act of 1968, Pub. L. 90–351, 82 Stat. 197, title II, sec. 701, amending 18 U.S.C. ch.223, by adding a new sec. 3501, "Admissibility of Confessions."

20. *Dickerson*, 530 U.S. 428.

21. *Johnson*, 491 U.S. 397; *Eichman*, 496 U.S. 310.

22. *City of Boerne*, 521 U.S. 507.

23. Constitution Act, 1982, Canadian Charter of Rights and Freedoms; Presidential Commission *Report*, 183; Section 33-Notwithstanding Clause-Department of Justice https://www.justice.gc.ca>eng>ccrf-ccdl>art; Nicholas Stephanopoulos, "The Case for the Legislative Override," 10 *UCLA Journal of International and Foreign Affairs* 250 (2005); Robert Leakey and Eric Mendelsohn, "Notwithstanding Clause: Legislatures and the Electorate," 72 *University of Toronto Law Journal* 189 (Spring 2022).

24. Constitution Act, 1982, Canadian Charter of Rights and Freedoms sec. 33; Leakey and Mendelson, "Notwithstanding Clause," 72 Univ. Toronto L J 189 (Spring 2022).

25. Madison pressed his council of revision plan, but expressed his view that enacted federal laws should not be subject to judicial override only privately, in letters of 1788 and 1817. See Walter F. Murphy, James E. Fleming, and Sotirios A. Barber, *American Constitutional Interpretation* (Westbury, NY: Foundation Press, 2nd ed., 1995), 279 (1788 letter), and Max Farrand, ed., *Records of the Federal Convention of 1787* (New Haven: Yale University Press, vol. 4, Appendix A, 1966), 424 (1817 letter). Adrienne Koch, ed., *Notes on Debates in the Federal Convention of 1787 Reported by James Madison* (New York: W.W. Norton & Co., 1987), 336–38, 340, 461–62 (Madison), 462 (Mercer), 336–37 (Wilson), 341 (Mason), 61, 66, 338 (Gerry), and 339 (Martin).

26. Hamilton, *Federalist Paper No. 78*, in Garry Wills, ed., *The Federalist Papers by Alexander Hamilton, James Madison and John Jay* (New York: Bantam Books, 1982), 394–95; *Marbury* 5 U.S. 179–80. Marshall made the assumption of judicial deference to the legislature explicit in such later landmark cases as *Fletcher v. Peck*, 10 U.S. 87, 128 (1810) (In order for the Court to declare an act of the legislature unconstitutional, "the opposition between the law and the constitution should be such that the judge feels a clear and strong conviction of their clear incompatibility with each other"), and *Trustees of Dartmouth College v. Woodward*, 17 U.S. 518, 625 (1819) ("in no doubtful case, would [the Court] pronounce a legislative act to be contrary to the constitution").

27. See the text in ch. 1 at n. 2.

28. James Bradley Thayer, "The Origin and Scope of the American Doctrine of Constitutional Law," 7 *Harvard Law Review* 129, 144 (1893). Archibald Cox, "The Role of Congress in Constitutional Determinations," 40 *University of Cincinnati Law Review* 199, 260 (1971) has the quote from Thayer's book on Marshall.

29. Akhil Reed Amar, *The Bill of Rights: Creation and Reconstruction* (New Haven: Yale University Press, 1998), 4 has the Holmes quote. Learned Hand, *The Bill of Rights* (Cambridge: Harvard University Press, 1958), 73–74.

30. Cox, "Role of Congress," 40 *U. Cin. L.R.* 199, 260 has the Hand quote

31. Jeremy Waldron, *Law and Disagreement* (Oxford, UK: Clarendon Press, 1999), 227–28; Jeremy Waldron, "The Core of the Case Against Judicial Review," 115 *Yale Law Journal* 1346, 1349–50 (2006).

32. For the history of congressional exercises of control of the executive department, see, e.g., Congressional Research Service, "Congress's Authority to Influence and Control Executive Branch Agencies," updated May 12, 2021, 2–15, pdf. The CRS sums up: The "four pillars of statutory control" over the administrative agencies are structural design, delegations of authority, procedural controls on agency decision-making, and agency funding.

33. *City of Boerne*, 521 U.S. 507.

34. Presidential Commission *Report*, 178.

35. *Lopez*, 514 U.S. 549, 557; *Morrison*, 529 U.S. 598, 614.

36. *Natl. Fed. Ind. Bus. v. Sebelius*, 567 U.S 519.

37. Presidential Commission *Report*, 170–77.

38. *Dred Scott*, 60 U.S. 393; *Civil Rights Cases*, 109 U.S. 26; *Dickerson*, 530 U.S. 428; and *Stevens*, 559 U.S. 460.

Appendix

TABLE OF CASES

Abbington School District v. Schempp, 329 U.S. 403 (1963)
Adamson v. California, 332 U.S. 46 (1947)
Adair v. United States, 208 U.S. 161 (1908)
Adams v. Tanner, 244 U.S. 290 (1917)
Adkins v. Children's Hospital, 261 U.S. 525 (1923)
Agency for International Development v. Alliance for Open Society International, Inc., 570 U.S. 205 (2013)
Agostini v. Felton, 521 U.S. 203 (1997)
Aguilar v. Felton, 473 U.S. 402 (1985)
Albertson v. Subversive Activities Control Board, 382 U.S. 70 (1965)
Alden v. Maine, 527 U.S. 706 (1999)
Allegheny County v. ACLU, 492 U.S. 573 (1989)
Allgeyer v. Louisiana, 165 U.S. 578 (1897)
Apthecker v. Secretary of State, 378 U.S. 500 (1964)
Ashcroft v. Free Speech Coalition, 535 U.S. 234 (2002)
Babbitt v. Youpee, 519 U.S. 534 (1997)
Barron v. Mayor and City Council of Baltimore, 32 U.S. 243 (1883)
Barry v. Mercein, 46 U.S. 103 (1847)
Bartnicki v. Volpe, 532 U.S. 514 (2001)
Benton v. Maryland, 395 U.S. 784 (1969)
Betts v. Brady, 316 U.S. 455 (1942)
Bigelow v. Virginia, 421 U.S. 809 (1975)
Blount v. Rizzi, 410 U.S. 410 (1971)
Board of Education v. Allen, 392 U.S. 236 (1968)
Board of Trustees of the University of Alabama v. Garrett, 531 U.S. 356 (2000)
Bolger v. Youngs Drug Products, 463 U.S. 460 (1983)
Bolling v. Sharpe, 347 U.S. 497 (1954)

Boos v. Barry, 485 U.S. 310 (1988)
Boumediene v. Bush, 553 U.S. 723 (2008)
Boyd v. United States, 116 U.S. 616 (1886)
Bradwell v. Illinois, 83 U.S. 130 (1873)
Brandenburg v. Ohio, 395 U.S. 444 (1969)
Brnovich v. Democratic National Committee, 594 U.S. ___ (2019)
Brooke v. City of Norfolk, 277 U.S. 27 (1928)
Brown v. Board of Education, 347 U.S. 483 (1954)
Brown v. Entertainment Merchants Association, 175 U.S. 172 (2011)
Brown v. New Jersey, 175 U.S. 172 (1899)
Buck v. Bell, 274 U.S. 200 (1927)
Buckley v. Valeo, 424 U.S. 1 (1976)
Burns Baking Co. v. Bryan, 264 U.S. 504 (1924)
Burwell v. Hobby Lobby Stores, Inc., 573 U.S. 682 (2014)
Califano v. Goldfarb, 430 U.S. 199 (1977)
Califano v. Silbowitz, 430 U.S. 924 (1977)
Califano v. Westcott, 443 U.S. 909 (1979)
Cantwell v. Connecticut, 310 U.S. 296 (1940)
Carey v. Population Services. Int'l., 431 U.S. 678 (1977)
Carlson v. California, 310 U.S. 106 (1940)
Carpenter v. United States, 585 U.S. ___ (2018)
Carson v. Makin, Slip Opinion No. 20-1088 (2022)
Central of Georgia Ry. v. Wright, 207 U.S. 127 (1907)
Chicago, B. & Q. R. Co. v. Chicago, 166 U.S. 226 (1897)
Chicago, M. & St. Paul Ry. v. Minnesota, 134 U.S. 418 (1890)
Chief of Capitol Police v. Jeanette Rankin Brigade, 342 F.Supp. 575 (D.D.C.), affirmed 409 U.S. 972 (1972)
Church of the Lukimi Babalu Aye, Inc. v. Hialeah, 508 U.S. 520 (1993)
Citizens United v. FEC, 558 U.S. 310 (2010)
City of Boerne v. Flores, 527 U.S. 507 (1997)
Civil Rights Cases, 109 U.S. 3 (1883)
Coleman v. Court of Appeals of Maryland, 566 U.S. 30 (2012)
Colgate v. Harvey, 296 U.S. 404 (1935)
Colorado Republican Federal Campaign Committee v. FEC, 518 U.S. 604 1996)
Committee for Public Education and Religious Liberty v. Nyquist, 413 U.S. 756 (1973)
Connally v. General Const. Co., 269 U.S. 305 (1926)
Connecticut Gen. Life Ins. Co. v. Johnson, 303 U.S. 77 (1938)
Coppage v. Kansas, 236 U.S. 1 (1915)
Corfield v. Coryell, 6 Fed. Cas. 546 (1823) (No. 3,230) (C.C.E.D. Pa.)
Cutter v. Wilkinson, 544 U.S. 709 (2005)

Dartmouth College v. Woodward, 17 U.S. 518 (1819)
Davidson v. New Orleans, 96 U.S. 97 (1878)
Davis v. FEC, 524 U.S. 724 (2008)
Day Brite Lighting, Inc. v. Missouri, 342 U.S. 421 (1952)
Denver Area Educational Telecommunication Consortium v. FCC, 518 U.S. 727 (1996)
DeJonge v. Oregon, 299 U.S. 353 (1937)
Dennis v. United States, 341 U.S. 494 (1951)
Dewey v. City of Des Moines, 173 U.S. 193 (1899)
Dickerson v. United States, 530 U.S. 428 (2000)
District of Columbia v. Heller, 559 U.S. 570 (2008)
Dobbs v. Jackson Women's Health Organization, 527 U.S. ___ (2022)
Doe v. Bolton, 410 U.S. 179 (1973)
Dred Scott v. Sandford, 60 U.S. 393 (1957)
Duncan v. Louisiana, 391 U.S. 145 (1968)
Durousseau v. United States, 10 U.S. 307 (1810)
Eisenstadt v. Baird, 405 U.S. 438 (1972)
Employment Division v. Smith, 494 U.S. 872 (1990)
Engblom v. Carey, 724 F.2d 28 (2nd Cir., 1983)
Engel v. Vitale, 370 U.S. 421 (1962)
Epperson v. Arkansas, 393 U.S. 97 (1968)
Escobedo v. Illinois, 378 U.S. 476 (1964)
Eskridge v. Washington Prison Bd., 357 U.S. 214 (1958)
Espinoza v. Montana Department of Revenue, 591 U.S. ___ (2020)
Eu v. San Francisco County Democratic Central Comm., 489 U.S. 214 (1989)
Everson v. Board of Education, 330 U.S. 1 (1947)
Ex parte McCardle, 74 U.S. 506 (1869)
Ex parte Yarborough, 110 U.S. 651 (1884)
FEC v. League of Women Voters of California, 486 U.S. 364 (1984)
FEC v. Massachusetts Citizens for Life, Inc., 479 U.S. 238 (1986)
FEC v. National Conservative Political Action Committee, 470 U.S. 480 (1985)
FEC v. Wisconsin Right to Life, Inc., 551 U.S. 449 (2007)
Feltner v. Columbia Pictures Television, Inc., 523 U.S. 340 (1998)
Ferguson v. Skrupa, 372 U.S. 726 (1963)
Fletcher v. Peck, 10 U.S. 87 (1810)
Frontiero v. Richardson, 411 U.S. 677 (1973)
Frost Trucking Co. v. Railroad Carriers, 271 U.S. 583 (1926)
Fuentes v. Shevin, 407 U.S. 67 (1972)
Garcia v. San Antonio Transit Authority, 469 U.S. 528 (1985)
Giacco v. Pennsylvania, 382 U.S. 399 (1966)

Gibbons v. Ogden, 22 U.S. 1 (1824)
Gideon v. Wainwright, 372 U.S. 335 (1963)
Gitlow v. New York, 268 U.S. 652 (1925)
Goldman v. Weinberger, 476 U.S. 547 (1986)
Gonzalez v. Carhart, 550 U.S. 424 (2007)
Gonzalez v. O'Centro Espirita (2006)
Good News Club v. Milford Central School, 533 U.S. 98 (2001)
Graham v. Richardson, 403 U.S. 365 (1971)
Greater New Orleans Broadcasting Assn., Inc. v. United States, 527 U.S. 173 (1999)
Griffin v. California, 380 U.S.604 (1965)
Grisham v. Hogan, 361 U.S. 278 (1968)
Griswold v. Connecticut, 381 U.S. 479 (1965)
Grosjean v. American Press, 297 U.S. 233 (1936)
Grosso v. United States, 390 U.S. 62 (1968)
Gulf C. and S.F. Ry. v. Ellis 165 U.S. 150 (1897)
Hague v. C.I.O., 302 U.S. 496 (1939)
Hamilton v. Regents of the University of California, 293 U.S. 245 (1934)
Hammer v. Dagenhart, 247 U.S. 251 (1918)
Harper v. Virginia Board of Elections, 383 U.S. 663 (1966)
Harris v. McRae, 448 U.S. 297 (1980)
Haynes v. United States, 390 U.S. 85 (1968)
Hepburn v. Griswold, 75 U.S. 603 (1870)
Herndon v. Lowry, 301 U.S. 242 (1937)
Hodel v. Irving, 481 U.S. 704 (1987)
Holt v. Hobbs, 574 U.S. 352 (2015)
Hurtado v. California, 110 U.S. 516 (1884)
Hylton v. United States, 3 U.S. 171 (1796)
In re Heff, 197 U.S. 488 (1905)
In re Kemmler, 136 U.S. 436 (1886)
In re Oliver, 333 U.S. 257 (1948)
In re Quarles and Butler, 158 U.S. 532 (1895)
In re Winship, 397 U.S. 358 (1970)
International Harvester Co. v. Kennedy, 234 U.A. 216 (1914)
International Paper Co. v. Massachusetts, 246 U.S. 135 (1918)
Jamison v. Texas, 318 U.S. 413 (1943)
Johnson v. United States, 576 U.S. ___ (2015)
Katzenbach v. McClung, 379 U.S. 294 (1964)
Katzenbach v. Morgan, 384 U.S. 641 (1966)
Kennedy v. Bremerton School District, 517 U.S. ___ (2022)
Kimel v. Florida Board of Regents, 528 U.S. 56 (1999)
Kinsella v Singleton, 361 U.S. 254 (1968)

Klopfer v. North Carolina, 386 U.S. 213 (1967)
Knox v. Lee, 79 U.S. 457 (1871)
Lamb's Chapel v. Center Morideo Union Free School District, 508 U.S. 384 (1993)
Lamont v. Postmaster General, 381 U.S. 301 (1965)
Lauf v. E.G., Shinner, 303 U.S. 323 (1938)
Lawrence v. Texas, 519 U.S. 558 (2003)
Leary v. United States, 395 U.S. 6 (1969)
Legal Services Corporation v. Velasquez, 531 U.S. 533 (2001)
Lee v. Weisman, 505 U.S. 577 (1992)
Lemon v. Kurtzman, 403 U.S. 602 (1971)
License Tax Cases, 72 U.S. 462 (1867)
Lochner v. New York, 198 U.S. 45 (1905)
Locke v. Davey, 540 U.S. 712 (2004)
Lockerty v. Phillips, 319 U.S. 182 (1943)
Logan v. United States, 144 U.S. 263 (1892)
Louis K. Liggett Co. v. Baldridge, 278 U.S. 105 (1928)
Louisville and Nashville R.R. v. Stockyards Co., 212 U.S. 32 (1909)
Loving v. Virginia, 388 U.S. 1 (1967)
Luis v. United States, 578 U.S. ___ (2016)
Lynch v. Donnelly, 465 U.S. 668 (1984)
Lynch v. United States, 292 U.S. 571 (1934)
Makepiece Cakeshop, Ltd. v. Colorado Civil Rights Commission, 584 U.S. ___ (2018)
Malloy v. Hogan, 378 U.S. 1 (1964)
Mapp v. Ohio, 367 U.S. 643 (1961)
Marchetti v. United States, 390 U.S. 39 (1968)
Marsh v. Chambers, 463 U.S. 783 (1983)
Marshall v. Barlow, Inc., 436 U.S. 307 (1978)
Martin v. Hunter's Lessee, 14 U.S. 304 (1816)
Matal v. Tam, 582 U.S. ___ (2018)
Maxwell v. Dow, 176 U.S. 581 (1900)
McConnell v. FEC, 540 U.S. 247 (2002)
McCreary County v. ACLU of Kentucky, 545 U.S. 844 (2005)
McCulloch v. Maryland, 17 U.S. 316 (1819)
McCutcheon v. FEC, 572 U.S. 815 (2014)
McDaniel v. Paley, 435 U.S. 618 (1978)
McDonald v. Chicago, 561 U.S. 742 (2010)
McElvaine v. Brush, 142 U.S. 155 (1891)
McElvoy v. Guadliardo, 361 U.S. 281 (1968)
Meyer v. Nebraska, 262 U.S. 380 (1923)
Miama Herald Publ. Co. v. Tornillo, 418 U.S. 241 (1974)

Miranda v. Arizona, 384 U.S. 436 (1966)
Missouri Pacific Ry. v. Nebraska, 164 U.S. 403 (1896)
Monongahela Nav. Co. v. United States, 148 U.S. 312 (1893)
Morehead v. New York ex rel. Tipaldo, 298 U.S. 587 (1936)
Motes v. United States, 178 U.S. 458 (1900)
Mueller v. Allen, 466 U.S. 388 (1983)
Munn v. Illinois, 94 U.S. 113 (1877)
Murdoch v. Pennsylvania, 319 U.S. 105 (1943)
Mullane v. Central Bank & Trust Co., 334 U.S. 306 (1950)
Murray's Lessee v. Hoboken Land and Improvement Co., 59 U.S. 272 (1856)
National Federation of Independent Business v. Sebelius, 567 U.S. 519 (2012)
National League of Cities v. Usery, 426 U.S. 833 (1976)
Near v. Minnesota, 283 U.S. 697 (1931)
New State Ice Co. v. Liebmann, 285 U.S. 262 (1932)
New York v. United States, 505 U.S. 144 (1992)
New York Times Co. v. Sullivan, 376 U.S. 254 (1964)
Northern Pacific Ry. v. North Dakota ex rel. McCue, 296 U.S. 585 (1915)
Norwood v. Baker, 172 U.S. 269 (1898)
Obergefeld v. Hodges, 576 U.S. ___ (2015)
O'Callahan v. Parker, 395 U.S. 258 (1969)
O'Neil v. Vermont, 144 U.S. 323 (1892)
Oregon v. Mitchell, 400 U.S. 112 (1970)
Pace v. Alabama, 106 U.S. 583 (1883)
Packingham v. North Carolina, 137 S.Ct. 1730 (2017)
Palko v. Connecticut, 302 U.S. 319 (1937)
Pennsylvania Coal Co. v. Mahon, 260 U.S. 393 (1922)
Pierce v. Society of Sisters, 268 U.S. 510 (1925)
Planned Parenthood of Southeastern Pennsylvania v. Casey, 505 U.S. 833 (1992)
Plessy v. Ferguson, 163 U.S. 537 (1896)
Poe v. Ullman, 367 U.S. 497 (1961)
Pointer v. Texas, 380 U.S. 400 (1965)
Pollock v. Farmers' Loan and Trust Co., 157 U.S. 429 (1895), affirmed and expanded 158 U.S. 1 (1895)
Powell v. Alabama, 287 U.S. 45 (1932)
Presser v. Illinois, 116 U.S. 252 (1886)
Prigg v. Pennsylvania, 41 U.S. 534 (1842)
Printz v. United States, 521 U.S. 899 (1997)
Prudential Ins. Co. v. Cheek, 259 U.S. 530 (1922)
Rasmussen v. United States, 197 U.S. 516 (1905)

R.A.V. v. City of St. Paul, 505 U.S. 377 (1992)
Reed v. Reed, 404 U.S. 71 (1971)
Regan v. Time, Inc., 468 U.S. 641 (1984)
Reid v. Covert, 354 U.S. 1 (1957)
Reno v. American Civil Liberties Union, 521 U.S. 844 (1997)
Reynolds v. Sims, 377 U.S. 533 (1964)
Ribnik v. McBride, 277 U.S. 350 (1928)
Richardson v. Davis, 409 U.S. 1069 (1972)
Robinson v. California, 370 U.S. 660 (1962)
Roe v. Wade, 410 U.S. 113 (1973)
Rosenberger v. University of Virginia, 515 U.S. 819 (1995)
Rubin v. Coors Brewing Co., 514 U.S. 476 (1995)
Rucho v. Common Cause, 588 U.S. ___ (2019)
Sable Communications of California, Inc. v. FCC, 492 U.S. 115 (1992)
Saia v. New York, 334 U.S. 558 (1948)
Santa Clara County v. Southern Pacific Railroad, 118 U.S. 394 (1886)
Santa Fe Independent School District v. Doe, 530 U.S. 290 (2000)
Schacht v. United States, 398 U.S. 58 (1970)
Schwartz v. Vanasco, 423 U.S. 1041 (1976)
Seminole Tribe of Florida v. Florida, 517 U.S. 44 (1996)
Sessions v. Dimaya, 518 U.S. ___ (2018)
Sessions v. Morales-Santana, 528 U.S. ___ (2017)
Shapiro v. Thompson, 394 U.S. 618 (1969)
Shelby County, Alabama v. Holder, 570 U.S. 524 (2013)
Sheldon v. Sill, 49 U.S. 441 (1850)
Shelton v. Tucker, 364 U.S. 479 (1960)
Sherbert v. Verner, 374 U.S. 398 (1963)
Slaughterhouse Cases, 83 U.S. (16 Wall.) 36 (1873)
Smythe v. Ames, 169 U.S. 466 (1898)
Sniadach v. Family Finance Corp., 395 U.S. 337 (1969)
Solorio v. United States, 483 U.S. 485 (1987)
South Carolina v. Katzenbach, 338 U.S. 301 (1966)
Spence v. Washington, 418 U.S. 405 (1974)
Spies v. Illinois, 123 U.S. 131 (1887)
Stanley v. Georgia, 394 U.S. 557 (1986)
Stenberg v. Carhart, 530 U.S. 914 (2000)
Stuart v. Laird, 5 U.S. 299 (1803)
Terrace v. Thompson, 263 U.S. 197 (1923)
Texas v. Johnson, 491 U.S. 397 (1991)
The Francis Wright, 105 U.S. 381 (1881)
Thompson v. Western States Medical Center, 535 U.S. 357 (2002)
Thornhill v. Alabama, 310 U.S. 88 (1940)

Tilton v. Richardson, 403 U.S. 672 (1971)
Timbs v. Indiana, No. 17-109 (2019)-
Torasco v. Watkins, 367 U.S. 483 (1961)
Tot v. United States, 319 U.S. 463 (1943)
Toth v. Quarles, 350 U.S. 11 (1955)
Town of Greece v. Galloway, 572 U.S. 565 (2014)
Treichler v. Wisconsin, 338 U.S. 251 (1949)
Trinity Lutheran Church of Columbia, Inc. v. Comer, 582 U.S. ___ (2017)
Trop v. Dulles, 356 U.S. 86 (1958)
Tumey v. Ohio, 273 U.S. 510 (1927)
Turner v. United States, 396 U.S. 398 (1970)
Twining v. New Jersey, 211 U.S. 78 (1908)
Tyson & Bro. v. Benton, 273 U.S. 418 (1927)
Union Transit Co. v. Kentucky, 199 U.S. 194 (1905)
United Public Workers v. Mitchell, 330 U.S. 75 (1947)
United States v. Alvarez, 567 U.S. 709 (2012)
United States v. Carolene Products Co., 304 U.S. 144 (1938)
United States v. Cohen Grocery Co., 255 U.S. 281 (1921)
United States v. Cruikshank, 92 U.S. 542 (1876)
United States v. Dewitt, 46 U.S. 41 (1870)
United States v. E.C. Knight and Co., 156 U.S. 1 (1895)
United States v. Eichman, 496 U.S. 310 (1990)
United States v. Grace, 461 U.S. 171 (1983)
United States v. Harris, 106 U.S. 629 (1883)
United States v. Heart of Atlanta Motel, 379 U.S. 241 (1964)
United States v. Jackson, 390 U.S. 570 (1968)
United States v. Lopez, 514 U.S. 549 (1995)
United States v. More, 7 U.S. 159 (1805)
United States v. Morrison, 529 U.S. 598 (2000)
United Sates v. Mosley, 238 U.S. 383 (1915)
United States v. Playboy Entertainment Group, Inc., 529 U.S. 803 (2000)
United States v. Robel, 389 U.S. 258 (1967)
United States v. Romano, 382 U.S. 186 (1965)
United States v. Stevens, 569 U.S. 460 (2010)
United States v. Treasury Employees, 513 U.S. 454 (1996)
United States v. Virginia, 518 U.S. 515 (1996)
United States v. Wardell, 112 U.S. 576 (1884)
United States v. United Foods, Inc., 533 U.S. 405 (2001)
U.S. Dept. of Agriculture v. Moreno, 413 U.S. 528 (1973)
U.S. Dept. of Agriculture v. Murry, 413 U.S. 508 (1973)
United States v. U.S. Coin and Currency, 401 U.S. 715 (1971)
United States v. Vuitch, 402 U.S. 62 (1971)

VanOrden v. Perry, 545 U.S. 677 (2005)
Virginia Board of Pharmacy v. Virginia Citizens Consumer Council, 425 U.S. 728 (1976)
Wachter v. Pizzuti, 276 U.S. 13 (1928)
Walker v. Sauvinet, 92 U.S. 90 (1875)
Wallace v. Jaffree, 463 U.S. 783 (1985)
Wardius v. Oregon, 412 U.S. 470 (1973)
Washington v. Texas, 388 U.S. 14 (1967)
Weaver v. Palmer Bros. 270 U.S. 402 (1926)
Weinberger v. Westerfeld, 420 U.S. 636 (1974)
West v. Louisiana, 194 U.S. 258 (1904)
West Coast Hotel v. Parrish, 200 U.S. 379 (1937)
West Virginia State Board of Education v. Barnette, 319 U.S. 624 (1943)
Westside Community Schools v. Mergens, 496 U.S. 226 (1990)
Whole Women's Health v. Hellerstedt, 136 S.Ct. 2292 (2016)
Wilcox v. Consolidated Gas Co., 212 U.S. 19 (1909)
Wilkinson v. Jones, 480 U.S. 926 (1987)
Williamson v. Lee Optical of Oklahoma, Inc., 348 U.S. 483 (1955)
Wilson v. Bohlender, 361 U.S. 287 (1968)
Wiscart v. Dauchy, 3 U.S. 321 (1796)
Wisconsin v. Yoder, 406 U.S. 205 (1972)
Wolf v. Colorado, 338 U.S. 25 (1949)
Wolff Packing Co. v. Industrial Court, 262 U.S. 522 (1923)
Wong Wing v. United States, 163 U.S. 228 (1896)
Yates v. United States, 354 U.S. 298 (1957)
Zelman v. Simmons-Harris, 536 U.S. 639 (2002)
Zurcher v. Stanford Daily, 436 U.S. 574 (1978)

Bibliography

Abortion/Gallup Historical Trends, https://news.gallup.com>poll>abortion—Chart on responses to question: Do you think abortion should be legal under any circumstances, legal under certain circumstances, or illegal in all circumstances?

Amar, Akil Reed. *The Bill of Rights: Creation and Reconstruction.* New Haven: Yale University Press, 1998.

Anastaplo, George. "The Declaration of Independence," 9 *Saint Louis University Law Journal* 390 (1965).

Annals of Congress, 1st Cong, 1st sess. 1789

Avins, Alfred. *The Reconstruction Amendments' Debates: The Legislative History and Contemporary Debates in Congress on the 13th, 14th, and 15th Amendments.* Richmond: Virginia Commission on Constitutional Government, 1967.

Bailyn, Bernard, ed. *The Debate on the Constitution: Federalist and Antifederalist Speeches, Articles, and Letters During the Struggle over Ratification.* New York: The Library of America, Parts One and Two, 1993.

Belz, Herman. *Emancipation and Equal Rights: Politics and Constitutionalism in the Civil War Era.* New York: W.W. Norton & Co., 1978.

Berkin, Carol. *The Bill of Rights: The Fight to Secure America's Liberties.* New York: Simon & Schuster, 2015.

Bickel, Alexander M., *The Least Dangerous Branch: The Supreme Court at the Bar of Politics* c. 1962, 2nd ed., with a foreword by Harry H. Wellington. New Haven: Yale University Press, 1982.

Bodenhamer, David J., and James W. Ely, Jr., eds. *The Bill of Rights in Modern America.* Bloomington, Indiana: Indiana University Press, 2008.

Brownstein, Alan, ed. *The First Amendment: The Establishment of Religion Clause—Its Constitutional History and the Contemporary Debate.* Amherst, NY: Prometheus Books, 2008.

Chemerinsky, Erwin. *Federal Jurisdiction.* New York: Wolters Klewer, 8th ed., 2021.

Choper, Jesse H. *Judicial Review and the National Political Process: A Functional Reconsideration of the Role of the Supreme Court.* Chicago: University of Chicago Press, 1980.

Choper, Jesse H., Richard H. Fallon, Jr., Yale Kamisar, Steven H. Shiffrin, Michael C. Dorf, and Frederick Schauer. *Constitutional Law: Cases, Comments, and Questions*. St. Paul, MN: West Academic Publishing, 12th ed., 2019.

Civil Rights Act of 1964, codified at 42 U.S.C. sec. 2000 et seq.

Civil Rights Act of 1968, Title VIII (Fair Housing Act), codified at 42 U.S.C. sec. 3601 et seq.

Cogan, Neil H., ed. *The Complete Bill of Rights: The Drafts, Debates, Sources and Origins*. New York: Oxford University Press, 2nd ed., 2015.

Congress.gov/bill/117th-congress-house-bill/3755/text. Abortion Rights Bill, 2021.

Congressional Globe, 39th Cong., 1st sess. 1866.

Congressional Globe, 41st Cong., 2nd sess. 1870.

Congressional Globe, 42nd Cong., 1st sess. 1871.

Congressional Research Service, comp., *Acts of Congress Held Unconstitutional in Whole or in Part by the Supreme Court of the United States*. Washington, DC: Government Printing Office, 2002, with supplements through 2016,

———. "Congress's Authority to Influence and Control Executive Branch Agencies," updated May 12, 2021, pdf.

Constitution Act, 1982 laws-lois.justice.gc.ca/const/page-13.html.

Cox, Archibald. "The Role of Congress in Constitutional Determinations," 40 *University of Cincinnati Law Review* 199 (1971).

Curtis, Michael Kent. *No State Shall Abridge: The Fourteenth Amendment and the Bill of Rights*. Durham: Duke University Press, 1986.

Delgado, Richard, and Jean Stefanic. *Must We Defend Nazis? Why the First Amendment Should Not Protect Hate Speech and White Supremacy*. New York: New York University Press, 2018.

DePauw, Linda Grant, ed. *Documentary History of the First Federal Congress, 1789–1791, Volume 1, Senate Legislative Journal*. Baltimore: Johns Hopkins University Press, 1972.

Dorf, Michael C. "Congressional Power to Strip State Courts of Jurisdiction," 97 *Texas Law Review* 1 (2018).

Eisgruber, Christopher L., and Lawrence G. Sager. *Religious Freedom and the Constitution*. Cambridge: Harvard University Press, 2007.

Elazar, Daniel J. "Our Thoroughly Federal Constitution," 38–66, in Goldwin, Robert A., and William A. Schambra, eds., *How Federal Is the Constitution?* Washington, DC: American Enterprise Institute, 1987.

Ely, James W., Jr. "The Oxymoron Reconsidered: Myth and Reality in the Origins of Substantive Due Process, 16 *Constitutional Commentary* 315 (1999).

Ely, John Hart. *Democracy and Distrust: A Theory of Judicial Review*. Cambridge: Harvard University Press, 1980.

Fairman, Charles. "Does the Fourteenth Amendment Incorporate the Bill of Rights? The Original Understanding," 2 *Stanford Law Review* 5 (1949).

Fannie Lou Hamer, Rosa Parks, and Coretta Scott King Voting Rights Act Reauthorization and Amendment of 2006, Pub. L. No. 109–246.

Farrand, Max, ed. *The Records of the Federal Convention of 1787*. New Haven: Yale University Press, 4 vols., 1966.

.Fehrenbacher, Don E. *The Dred Scott Case: Its Significance in American Law*. New York: Oxford University Press, 1978.

fjc.gov/history/judges/impeachments - federal—judges.

Flack, Horace E. *The Adoption of the Fourteenth Amendment*. Baltimore: Johns Hopkins University Press, 1908.

Foner, Eric. *Reconstruction: America's Unfinished Revolution, 1863–1877*. New York: Harper & Row, 1988.

Gallup Poll on Race and Education 50 Years after *Brown v. Board of Education*, 8 (Approval Ratings on U.S. Supreme Court decision in *Brown v. Board of Education*, May 21–26, 1954).

Garvey, Todd. "The Take Care Clause and Executive Discretion in the Enforcement of the Law," Congressional Research Service Report R43708, September 4, 2014. www.crs.gov.

Gillman, Howard, and Erwin Chemerinsky. *The Religion Clauses: The Case for Separating Church and State*. New York: Oxford University Press, 2020.

Glidden, William B. *Congress and the Fourteenth Amendment: Enforcing Liberty and Equality in the States*. Lanham, MD: Lexington Books, 2013.

———. *The Supreme Court versus Congress: Disrupting the Balance of Power, 1789–2014*. Santa Barbara: Praeger, 2015.

Greenawalt, Kent. *Religion and the Constitution Volume 1: Free Exercise and Fairness*. Princeton, NJ: Princeton University Press, 2006.

Gunther, Gerald. "Congressional Power to Curtail Federal Court Jurisdiction: An Opinionated Guide to the Ongoing Debate," 36 *Stanford Law Review* 895 (1984).

Hamilton, James. "The Colfax Massacre: A Forgotten Chapter of Violence," *Liberated Arts*, vol. 5, issue no. 1, article 2 (2018).

Hand, Learned. *The Bill of Rights*. Cambridge: Harvard University Press, 1958.

Hart, Henry M. Jr., "The Power of Congress to Limit the Jurisdiction of Federal Courts, An Exercise in Dialectic," 66 *Harvard Law Review* 1362 (1953).

House Report No. 22, Victoria Woodhull Hearing, January 30, 1871

Hyde Amendment and Coverage for Abortion Services, kkf.org// women's-health-policy..

Hyneman, Charles S., and George W. Carey. *A Second Federalist: Congress Creates a Government*. Columbia, SC: University of South Carolina Press, 1970.

James, Joseph B. *The Framing of the Fourteenth Amendment*. Champaign: University of Illinois Press, 1965.

———. *The Ratification of the Fourteenth Amendment*. Macon, GA: Mercer University Press, 1984.

Jensen, Merrill. *The New Nation: A History of the United States during the Confederation, 1781–1788*. New York: Alfred A. Knopf, 1950.

"Judicial Review of Congress" data set at www.princeton.edu/-kewhitt.

Kaczorowski, Robert. *The Politics of Judicial Interpretation: The Federal Courts, Department of Justice, and Civil Rights*, 1866–1876. New York: Oceana Publications, 1985.

Kammen, Michael G, ed. *The Origins of the American Constitution: A Documentary History*. New York: Penguin Press, 1986.

Kelly, Alfred H., Winifred A. Harbison, and Herman Belz. *The American Constitution Its Origins and Development*, vol. 1, 7th ed. New York: W.W. Norton & Co., 1991.

Kendrick, Benjamin R. *The Joint Committee of Fifteen on Reconstruction: 39th Congress, 1865–1867*. New York: Columbia University Press, 1914. Reprint by Negro Universities Press, 1969.

Ketchum, Ralph. *James Madison: A Biography*. Charlottesville: University of Virginia, 1990.

Keynes, Edward. *Liberty, Property, and Privacy: Toward a Jurisprudence of Substantive Due Process.* University Park, PA: Pennsylvania State University Press, 1996.

Koch, Adrienne. ed. *Notes on Debates in the Federal Convention of 1787 Reported by James Madison*. New York: W.W. Norton & Co., 1987.

Leakey, Robert, and Eric Mendelsohn. "Notwithstanding Clause: Legislatures and the Electorate," 72 *University of Toronto Law Journal* 189 (Spring 2022).

Levy, Leonard W. *Seasoned Judgments: The American Constitution, Rights, and History.* New Brunswick, NJ: Transaction Publishers, 1995.

———. *Origins of the Bill of Rights*. New Haven: Yale University Press, 1999.

Long-Term Gallup Poll Trends: A Portrait of American Public Opinion Through the Century, 2. Willingness to Support a Woman for President.

Lupu, Ira C. "Statutes Revolving in Constitutional Law Orbits," 79 *Virginia Law Review* 1 (1993).

Lutz, Donald S. *The Origins of American Constitutionalism*. Baton Rouge: Louisiana State University Press, 1988.

Magliocca, Gerard N. *The Heart of the Constitution: How the Bill of Rights Became the Bill of Rights.* New York: Oxford University Press, 2017.

May, Gary. *Bending Toward Justice: The Voting Rights Act and the Transformation of American Democracy.* New York: Basic Books, 2013.

McCarthy, Justin. Record High 70% in U.S. Support Same-Sex Marriage, 1–3 (Gallup Poll Data 1996–2021).

Meltzer, Daniel J. "Congress, Courts, and Constitutional Remedies," 86 *Georgetown Law Journal* 2537 (1998).

Mikva, Abner J., and Jeff Bleich. "When Congress Overrules the Court," 79 *California Law Review* 729 (1991).

Monaghan, Henry. "Jurisdiction Stripping Circa 2020: What the Dialogue (Still) Has to Teach Us," 69 *Duke Law Journal* 1 (2019).

Monk, Linda R. *The Bill of Rights A User's Guide*. New York: Hachette Books, 5th ed., 2018.

Murphy, Paul L, ed. *Pre-1960 Developments in the Bill of Rights Area*. New York: Garland Publishing, Inc., 2 vols., 1990.

Murphy, Walter F., James E. Fleming, and Sotirios A. Barber. *American Constitutional Interpretation*. Westbury, N.Y.: Foundation Press, 2nd ed., 1995.

National Voter Registration Act, 107 Stat. 77, Pub. L. No. 103–31, May 20, 1993.

Omnibus Crime Control and Safe Streets Act of 1968, Pub. L. 90–351, 82 Stat. 197, Title II, sec. 701, amending 18 U.S.C. ch. 223, by adding a new sec. 3501, "Admissibility of Confessions."

Partial Birth Abortion Ban Act of 2003, 18 U.S.C. sec. 1531.

pewresearch.org/fact-tank/2022/06/13/abortion 61% say abortion should be legal in all or most cases.

Perry, Richard L, ed. *Sources of Our Liberties: Documentary Origins of Individual Liberties in the United States Constitution and Bill of Rights*. New York: American Bar Association, 1959.

Prakash, Sarkrishna B., and John C. Yoo. "The Origins of Judicial Review," 70 *University of Chicago Law Review* 887 (2003).

Presidential Commission on the Supreme Court of the United States. *Draft Final Report*, December 7, 2021.

Rakove, Jack N. *Original Meanings: Politics and Ideas in the Making of the Constitution*. New York: Penguin Books, 1997.

——, comp. *James Madison Writings*. New York: The Library of America, Inc.,1999.

Redish, Martin H. "Constitutional Limitations on Congressional Power to Control Federal Jurisdiction: A Reaction to Professor Sager," 77 *Northwestern Law Review* 143 (1982).

Religious Apparel: Wearing While in Uniform, 10 U.S.C. sec. 774.

Religious Land Use and Institutionalized Persons Act, 42 U.S.C., ch. 21C, sec. 2000cc.

Saad, Lydia. Gallup Vault: A History of Resistance to See Women Working, 1–2.

Sager, Lawrence Gene. "Forward: Constitutional Limits on Congress's Authority to Regulate the Jurisdiction of the Federal Courts," 95 *Harvard Law Review* 17 (1981).

Schwartz, Bernard. *The Bill of Rights: A Documentary History*. New York: Chelsea House Publishers in association with McGraw Hill, vol. 2, 1971.

Scribner, Heather P. "A Fundamental Misconception of Separation of Powers: *Boumediene v. Bush*," 14 *Texas Review of Law and Policy* 90 (2009–2010).

Senate Report No. 112, "Report of the Joint Committee on Reconstruction," June 8, 1866.

State Laws Held Unconstitutional, https://lawjustia.com; Ordinances Held Unconstitutional, https://lawjustia.com.

Stephanopoulos, Nicholas. "The Case for the Legislative Override," 10 *UCLA Journal of International and Foreign Affairs* 250 (2005).

Ten Broek, Jacobus. *Equal Under Law*. New York: Collier Books, enlarged edition, 1965.

Thayer, James Bradley. "The Origin and Scope of the American Doctrine of Constitutional Law," 7 *Harvard Law Review* 129 (1893).

Thorpe, Francis N., ed. *The Federal and State Constitutions, Colonial Charters, and Other Organic Laws of the United States*, 7 vols. Washington, DC: Government Printing Office, 1909.

Tushnet, Mark. "Alternative Forms of Judicial Review," 101 *Michigan Law Review* 2781 (2008).

———. *Advanced Introduction to Freedom of Expression*. Northampton, MA: Edward Elgar, 2018.

Tushnet, Mark, and Jennifer Jaff. "Why the Debate Over Congress' Power to Restrict the Jurisdiction of the Federal Courts Is Unending," 72 *Georgetown Law Journal* 1311 (1984).

Tushnet, Mark, Mark A. Graber, and Sanford Levinson, eds. *The Oxford Handbook of the U.S. Constitution*. New York: Oxford University Press, 2016.

Urofsky, Melvin I. *Money and Free Speech: Campaign Finance Reform and the Courts*. Lawrence: University Press of Kansas, 2005.

Varat, Jonathan D., and Vikram D. Amar, *Constitutional Law: Cases and Materials*. St. Paul, MN: Foundation Press, 15th ed., 2017.

Vorenberg, Michael. *Final Freedom: The Civil War, the Abolition of Slavery, and the Thirteenth Amendment*. New York: Cambridge University Press, 2001.

Voting Rights Act of 1965, 79 Stat. 437, Pub. L. No. 89–110

Waldron, Jeremy. *Law and Disagreement.* Oxford, UK: Clarendon Press, 1999.

———. "The Core of the Case Against Judicial Review," 115 *Yale Law Journal* 1346 (2006).

Wechsler, Herbert. *The Nationalization of Civil Liberties and Civil Rights*. Published as a Supplement to the *Texas Quarterly*, vol. 12, no. 2, 1969 Appendix: "Survival and Repeal of Civil Rights Laws Enacted During the Period 1866 to 1875."

White, G. Edward. *The Constitution and the New Deal*. Cambridge: Harvard University Press, 2000.

Whittington, Keith E. *Repugnant Laws: Judicial Review of Acts of Congress From the Founding to the Present*. Lawrence: University Press of Kansas, 2019.

Wiecek, William. *The Sources of Antislavery Constitutionalism in America, 1760–1848*. Ithaca: Cornell University Press, 1977.

Wills, Garry, ed. *The Federalist Papers by Alexander Hamilton, James Madison, and John Jay*. New York: Bantam Books, 1982.

Wolfe, Christopher. *How to Read the Constitution: Originalism, Constitutional Interpretation, and Judicial Power*. Lanham, MD: Rowman & Littlefield, 1996.

Women's Health Protection Act of 2022, congress.gov/bill/117th-congress/senate-bill/4132.

Wood, Gordon S. *The Creation of the American Republic, 1776–1787* Durham: University of North Carolina Press, 1969.

www.constitutioncenter.org/interpretation:amendment vii.

www.nolo.com/legal encyclopedia/why prosecutors choose grand juries instead of preliminary hearings.

Ziegler, Mary. *Abortion and the Law in America: Roe v. Wade to the Present.* Cambridge, UK: Cambridge University Press, 2020.

Index

About the Author

William B. Glidden earned a PhD in American history at the University of Illinois and taught history and political science at Clarkson College of Technology in Potsdam, New York, for three years. Then he obtained a law degree at New York University Law School and spent his career as a lawyer in the Law Department of the Comptroller of the Currency, a bureau in the Treasury Department which regulates national banks. Mr. Glidden has previously published ten articles and a book chapter on banking law subjects and two books on constitutional law history: *Congress and the Fourteenth Amendment: Enforcing Liberty and Equality in the States* (Lexington Books, 2013), and *The Supreme Court versus Congress: Disrupting the Balance of Power, 1789–2014* (Praeger ABC- CLIO, 2015).

www.ingramcontent.com/pod-product-compliance
Lightning Source LLC
LaVergne TN
LVHW091527200926
848483LV00002B/325